Using Aldus FreeHand® 3.0

Using Aldus Freehand® 3.0

THE PROFESSIONAL HANDBOOK
FOR ILLUSTRATORS AND DESIGNERS

Sharyn Venit
Bruce Fraser

BANTAM BOOKS
NEW YORK • TORONTO • LONDON • SYDNEY • AUCKLAND

USING ALDUS FREEHAND 3.0
A Bantam Book
August 1991

Aldus, the Aldus logo, Aldus PageMaker, and Aldus FreeHand are registered trademarks of Aldus Corporation. Apple, Macintosh, LaserWriter, MultiFinder, AppleShare, A/UX, and AppleTalk are registered trademarks of Apple Computer, Inc. and Finder, QuickDraw, and TrueType are trademarks of Apple Computer, Inc. ITC Zapf Dingbats is a registered trademark of International TypeFace Corporation. PostScript, Adobe Illustrator, and Adobe are registered trademarks of Adobe Systems, Incorporated. Compugraphic is a registered trademark of Compugraphic Corporation. MacPaint and MacDraw are registered trademarks of Claris Corporation. Helvetica and Times are registered trademarks and Linotronic is a trademark of Linotype AG. PANTONE® and PANTONE MATCHING SYSTEM are registered trademarks of Pantone, Inc. Microsoft and MS-DOS are registered trademarks of Microsoft Corporation. IBM is a registered trademark of International Business Machines Corporation. Suitcase is a trademark of Fifth Generation Software. Quark XPress is a registered trademark of Quark, Inc. Throughout the book, the trade names and trademarks of some companies and products have been used, and no such uses are intended to convey endorsement of or other affiliations with the book or software.

All rights reserved.
Copyright © 1991 by Sharyn Venit and Bruce Fraser
Cover design copyright © by Bantam Books
Produced by TechArt San Francisco
No part of this book may be reproduced or transmitted in any form or by any means, electronic or mechanical, including photocopying, recording, or by any information storage and retrieval system, without permission in writing from the publisher.
For information address: Bantam Books

ISBN 0-553-35444-2

Published in the United States

Bantam Books are published by Bantam Books, a division of Bantam Doubleday Dell Publishing Group, Inc. Its trademark, consisting of the words "Bantam Books" and the portrayal of a rooster, is registered in U.S. Patent and Trademark Office and in other countries. Marca Registrada, Bantam Books, 666 Fifth Avenue, New York, New York 10103

PRINTED IN THE UNITED STATES OF AMERICA

0 9 8 7 6 5 4 3 2 1

Preface

Using Aldus Freehand 3.0 is a complete reference designed to answer your questions about all FreeHand commands, tools, and techniques. The book is an invaluable tool for professionals who use the program every day, and will be useful to anyone seeking professional results. It can also be used as a training manual for beginning FreeHand users, or as a reference for professional designers who need to know the capabilities of FreeHand.

The book includes expert advice about all FreeHand features, tips about increasing speed and productivity, and specific techniques used to create special effects or to solve particular problems. The beginning user will quickly learn how to use FreeHand tools and commands. The intermediate user will learn new and valuable techniques for producing complicated illustrations. The advanced user will receive expert tips on how to use FreeHand more effectively, and gain insight into how experienced illustrators solve complex problems with FreeHand.

How This Book Is Organized

We have organized this book into four parts:

Part I: Introduction

The first chapter—"Introducing Aldus Freehand 3.0"—briefly describes FreeHand and its context—desktop publishing. This chapter also identifies the features that were introduced with version 3.0, and the equipment requirements for installing and running FreeHand 3.0. The second chapter—"Basic Concepts"—is a simple tutorial for absolute beginners. Here you will find an overview of the screen display in FreeHand including the document window, the Toolbox, the information bar, the menus, and the Colors palette.

Part II: Advanced Techniques

The next seven chapters describe some of the techniques and procedures experts use to save time or solve difficult problems. These chapters are not intended to be read or followed sequentially. We recommend that you simply skim through these chapters, quickly looking at the illustrations for each technique, so you become familiar with the information available here. Then, look up techniques as needed while you are developing your own artwork.

Chapter 3 offers tips specific to creating lines and curves—whether they are open or closed paths. The next three chapters relate specifically to closed paths: Chapter 4 offers tips on creating specific shapes, Chapter 5 describes three-dimensional effects, and Chapter 6 offers techniques for creating colors, styles, and fills. Chapter 7 covers special methods of handling text. Chapter 8 describes how to set up a grid system and other ways to align objects. Chapter 9 describes methods and reasons for working in layers.

If you are using FreeHand for the first time, we recommend that you read and try the procedures described in Chapter 12 for using the tools, especially the Pen tool, before going through these chapters.

Part III: Case Studies

The impact of desktop publishing on professional publishers, corporate publications departments, and self-publishing associations and individuals is best seen through the experiences of those who have made the transition from traditional methods to electronic publishing over the past few years. Chapters 10 and 11 of this book offer case studies of professional illustrations that were once produced using traditional methods and are now produced using FreeHand. For each example you will find descriptions of how the illustrator organized the artwork and/or handled tricky elements.

Part IV: Reference

The last three chapters of this book compose a reference section that describes each tool, palette, and command in detail: Chapter 12 describes each tool in the order in which it appears in the Toolbox. Chapter 13 describes the three palettes: the Colors palette, the Layers palette, and the

Styles palette. Chapter 14 describes each command in the order of appearance in the menus.

Appendices

Appendix A is an introduction to basic Macintosh operations and defines some of the terms that are particular to the Macintosh and FreeHand. Appendix B explains how fonts are installed and managed on your system. Appendix C offers a list of tips on what you can do to save disk space, reduce screen redraw time, and reduce printing time when working with FreeHand files.

Appendix D is a glossary of special terms used in graphic design, illustration, and printing. (Terms more specific to FreeHand are defined as they are introduced throughout this book.)

Conventions Used in This Book

We have included icons or symbols throughout this book to make it easy for you to interpret references to icons you will see on the screen while working in FreeHand. Most of the symbols embedded in the text are self-explanatory in that they look like the element they are intended to represent, such as the ⌘ symbol for the Command key.

We have used a special arrow symbol (➤) as a shorthand method of referencing commands on submenus. Instead of saying "…choose the Fit in window command from the Magnification submenu in the View menu…" we say simply "…choose View ➤ Magnification ➤ Fit in window …."

TIP

Paragraphs marked as "Tip" will make the most interesting reading for users who want to rapidly increase their expertise with Aldus FreeHand. Hints, tricks, and insights included in this section will enhance your productivity.

CAUTION

The Caution heading appears above paragraphs that mention things you should not or cannot do in FreeHand, or things that might happen if you change something on a page. In most cases, these are simply things you need to be aware of in making decisions. It is unlikely that any decision you make will have a disastrous effect on a document, so you need not be worried about trying new commands.

These sections might also offer guidelines on when not to use a particular tool, command, or technique, or might discuss some of the trade-offs that might be required (such as slower speed and larger file size in exchange for complex artwork).

The best way to learn FreeHand is to use it. If you have never used FreeHand before, go through the tutorial provided with the program to get a quick overview of the program's features.

No matter what your level of experience, you will find many useful tips throughout this book for using FreeHand efficiently. Beyond descriptions and examples of tools and commands, you will find a wealth of information gleaned from using and teaching Aldus FreeHand since it was first released. We hope you will find it a useful information source that serves you long and well.

Acknowledgements

We want to thank a number of people for the content and quality of this book.

First, all of the examples of artwork shown in Part III: Case Studies (Chapters 10 and 11) were all contributed by professional artists and art departments. In Chapter 10 (Commercial Art): the Alberto Vineyards Wine Label was designed by artist Susan Equitz of TechArt (San Francisco); the High-Technology War informational graphic was contributed by Jeff Glick, Graphics Director, *U.S. News & World Report* (Washington, D.C.); the artwork for K2 Skis was contributed by Rich Greene, Graphic Arts Manager, and created by Mike Johnson, K2 Corporation (Vashon Is., WA); the comic strip was created by John Laney, Interactive Design (Seattle); an assortment of artwork was created by Henk Dawson (Seattle); and the realistic representations of industrial tools were contributed by Brian Bartness, Mate Punch and Die Co., (Anoka, MN).

In Chapter 11 (Cartography): the San Francisco Bay Area Regional Transit Map was originally designed by Reineck & Reineck (San Francisco) in 1981 using traditional techniques, then recreated by the in-house graphics department (special thanks to Marilyn Reynolds, Barbara Wilkie, and Peter Beeler) at Metropolitan Transportation Commission (MTC, Oakland, CA). The Seattle Street Map was contributed by the art department (Carol Mockridge, Leah Clark, and Rheta Deal) of METRO (Municipality of Seattle, Washington). The San Francisco Bay Area Road Map and the Oakland Downtown Business Development Map were contributed by Neil Dinoff, Eureka Cartography (Berkeley, CA) and *San Francisco Business Times.*

Special thanks are due to Pete Mason (Altsys) and Wendi Dunlap (Aldus) for their invaluable advice and insight into the inner workings of FreeHand.

Finally, we want to thank all the editors, proofreaders, and production assistants who helped bring this book to its best conclusion, including: Michael Roney, Maureen Drexel, and Tom Szalkiewicz at Bantam; Sandy Horwich, editor (Berkeley, CA); Lisa Pletka (Pleasanton, CA); and Grace Moore, Kim Nogay, and Susan Equitz at TechArt (San Francsico).

Contents

Preface   v
Acknowledgements   ix
Contents   xi

Part I Introduction   *1*

1   Introducing Aldus FreeHand 3.0   3
   FreeHand Capabilities   4
      Paths and Bezier Curves   4
      Fill Patterns   6
      Typographic Controls   7
      Imported TIFF Images   8
      Spot and Process Color   8
      High Resolution Output   8
   FreeHand Interface   9
      Alignment Aids   9
      Palettes   9
   New Features in FreeHand 3.0   11
   FreeHand and Your Desktop Publishing System   12
      Equipment Requirements   12
      FreeHand and Fonts   13
      FreeHand and Scanned Images   14
      Opening PostScript Artwork from Other Sources   15
      FreeHand and Page Layout Applications   15
      Transferring FreeHand Artwork to IBM PC
         Documents   15
   Summary   16

2 Basic Concepts 17

Installing FreeHand 17
Starting FreeHand from the Desktop 18
    Starting FreeHand 19
    Opening a New File 19
The Document Window 22
    Tools 24
    The Information Bar 24
    Using the Rulers 25
    Displaying Palettes 26
Examining the Menus 28
    Using the Help Function 28
    The File Menu 29
    The Edit Menu 29
    The View Menu 30
    The Element Menu 30
    The Type Menu 32
    The Attributes Menu 32
Using Tools and Commands 33
    Using the Rectangle Tool 34
    Using the Pointer Tool 37
    Using the Duplicate Command 38
    Using the Rotating Tool 39
    Temporarily Selecting the Pointer Tool 40
    Using the Align Command 41
    Shading Objects 43
    Preview 45
    Save—Often 46
    Using the Text Tool 47
    Selecting and Editing Text 49
    Save 52
    Print 53
    Quit 53
Summary 54

Part II Techniques 55

3 Lines and Curves (Paths) 57
Drawing Curves and Lines 59
    The Number 1: Straight Lines 59
    The Number 2: Mixed Curves and Straight Lines 61
    The Number 3: Two Curves with a Corner Point 63
    The Number 4: 45-Degree Angles 65
    The Numbers 5 and 6: Review the Principle 66
    The Number 7: Drawn and Traced 69
    The Number 8: Traced Composite Paths 70
Dashed and Dotted Lines 72
Compound Lines 75
Compound Dashed Lines 78
Compound Arrows 82
Using Dashed Lines as Rectangles or Ellipses 84
Ribbons 86
Parallel Curves 88
Hand-drawn Look: Method 1 90
Hand-drawn Look: Method 2 92
Hand-drawn Look: Method 3 94
Quadrille Rules 96

4 Shapes (Closed Paths) 99
Creating Arrows and Symmetrical Objects 101
Tracing Imported Graphics 104
Importing Charts 106
Drawing Bar Charts 108
Drawing Pie Charts 110
Organization Charts 114
Holes in Solid Objects 118
Composite Paths as Masks 120
Polygons 122
Stars: Method 1 124
Stars: Method 2 128

Symmetrical Objects   132
Radial Symmetry: Method 1   134
Radial Symmetry: Method 2   136
Shared Borders   138

5   Three-Dimensional Effects   141

Coils and Springs   142
Cubes: Method 1   144
Cubes: Method 2   146
Cubes: Method 3   148
Interlocking Objects   151
Cylinders   154
Drop Shadows: Method 1   156
Drop Shadows: Method 2   157
Flower Petals   159
Highlights   161

6   Fills and Patterns   165

Applying Fills   167
  Using the Colors Palette to Fill an Object   167
  Filling an Element through the Fill and Line Dialog Box   168
  Filling an Element through the Styles Palette   169
Using Custom Fills   170
Using the Styles Palette   171
Creating Color Templates   172
Copying Colors from One Document to Another   174
Creating a Color Library   176
Creating Optimal Blends   182
Blending for Spot Color Separation   188
Blending to Create New Colors or Grays   190
Clipping Paths as Masks   194
Masking to Change Fills   196
Masking to Create Highlights   197
Off-center Radial Fills   198

Contents   xv

    Patterns #1—Discrete Objects   200
    Patterns #2—Continuous Symmetry   204
    Patterns #3—Continuous Asymmetry   208

7 Working with Text   211
    Typing, Editing, and Formatting Text   212
    Aligning Text Blocks: Method 1   215
    Aligning Text: Method 2   217
    Tabular Text   218
    Joining Text to a Curved Path   220
    Importing Text   225
    Overprinting Text in Color Separations   227
        Black Text with Stroke Overprinting Gray Field   227
        Black Text with Background Knocked Out   227
    "Hidden" Notes   228
    Converting Text to Paths   230

8 Spacing and Alignment   233
    Using Rulers and Guides   235
    Using the Grid System   238
    Measuring with a Point   241
    Custom Grid # 1—Perspective   242
    Custom Grid # 2—Page Layout   246
    Aligning Objects   248
    Dividing Equally   250
    Creating Spacing Guides   252

9 Working in Layers   255
    Benefits of Working in Layers   257
        Simplify Complex Artwork   257
        Save Screen Redraw Time   258
        Save Printing Time   258
        Use the Background Layer for Non-printing Elements   258
        Create Different Versions of Artwork   259
    Rearranging Overlapping Objects Within a Layer   260

        Method 1: Using the Bring Forward (or Send Backward)
           Command   260
        Method 2: Using the Send to Back Command   260
     Managing Overlapping, Identical Objects   262
        When There Are Only Two Objects   262
        When There Are Three or More Objects   263
     Layering Overlapping, Identical Objects   265
     Layering Spot Color Separations   267
     Layering Different Type Specifications   269
     Layering to Produce Overhead Transparencies   271

Part III Case Studies   273

   10   Commercial Art   275
        Alberto Vineyards Wine Label   276
           Overview   276
           Details   276
           Credits   278
        The High-Technology War   279
           Overview   279
           Details   279
           Credits   282
        K2 Skis   283
           Overview   283
           Details   283
           Credits   283
        Comic Strip   286
           Description   286
           Details   286
           Credits   288
        Highlights from Henk Dawson   289
           Description   289
           Details   289
           Credits   293
        Technical Illustrations from Mate Punch and Die
        Company   294

Description   294
Details   294
Credits   294

11 Cartography   297

San Francisco Bay Area Regional Transit Maps   298
Overview   298
Details   298
Credits   301
Seattle Street Map   302
Description   302
Details   302
Credits   302
San Francisco Bay Area Road Map   304
Description   304
Details   304
Credits   304
Oakland Downtown Business Development Map   306
Description   306
Details   306
Credits   306

Part IV Reference   *309*

12 The Information Bar and the Toolbox   311

The Information Bar   313
Introduction to the Toolbox   317
Selecting a Tool   317
Grabber Hand Tool   319
Pointer Tool   319
Selecting One Object   320
Selecting One Object that is Part of a Group   321
Selecting an Anchor Point   322
Selecting Multiple Objects   322
Selecting Objects on Different Layers   324
Deselecting All Objects   324

Moving Objects   324
Scaling Objects   325
Double-clicking Objects for Element Information   327
Text Tool   328
Selecting and Formatting a Text Block   330
Dragging Text Block Handles to Change Size
   or Spacing   331
Selecting and Editing Portions of Text   331
Basic Shape Tools   333
Rectangle, Rounded-rectangle, and Ellipse Tools   334
Line Tool   336
Freeform Drawing Tools   336
About Paths, or Bezier Curves   337
Freehand Tool   338
Pen Tool   340
Knife Tool   352
Curve Tool   353
Corner Tool   354
Connector Tool   355
Transformation Tools   355
Rotating Tool   356
Reflecting Tool   358
Scaling Tool   360
Skewing Tool   362
Tracing Tool   364
Magnifying Tool   367

13   The Colors, Layers, and Styles Palettes   371

Colors Palette   373
Applying Colors   375
Changing the Default Color   376
Adding, Editing, Moving, and Removing Colors   376
Layers Palette   379
The Default Palette   380
Selecting the Active Layer   381
Moving Elements from One Layer to Another   382
Moving Layers   382

Making Layers Visible or Invisible   382
Adding and Editing Layers   383
Removing Layers   384
Styles Palette   384
Advantages of Using Styles   385
Applying Styles   387
Creating Styles   388
Copying a Style in the Palette   390
Copying Styles from One Illustration to Another   390
Editing Styles   391
Removing Styles from the Palette   391

14   Menu Commands   393

Choosing a Command   393
Dialog Box Entries   394
The Apple Menu   398
About FreeHand...   399
Help...   400
Chooser   401
Control Panel   402
The File Menu   404
New...   404
Open...   407
Close   409
Save   409
Save as...   409
Revert   411
Document setup...   411
Preferences...   414
Page Setup...   418
Print...   419
Place...   425
Export...   426
Quit   428
The Edit Menu   428
Undo   429
Redo   430

Cut   431
Copy   431
Paste   432
Clear   433
Cut contents   433
Paste inside   434
Select all   436
Duplicate   436
Clone   438
Move...   438
Transform again   439
The View Menu   440
Windows   440
Magnification   442
Preview   443
Rulers   444
Grid   445
Guides   446
Lock guides   446
Snap to point   447
Snap to guides   447
Snap to grid   448
The Element Menu   448
Bring to front   449
Bring forward   449
Send backward   450
Send to back   450
Element info...   451
Points   461
Lock   462
Unlock   463
Group   463
Ungroup   464
Alignment...   465
Blend...   468
Constrain...   470
Join elements   471
Split element   475

The Type Menu   476
  Font   477
  Size   478
  Leading   479
  Type style   480
  Effect   481
  Type specs...   486
  Spacing...   487
  Horizontal scaling...   488
  Baseline shift...   488
  Convert to paths   489
  Alignment   490
The Attributes Menu   492
  Fill and line...   493
  Halftone screen...   503
  Set note...   505
  Remove fill   505
  Remove line   506
  Colors...   506
  Styles...   510
  Hairline, .5pt, 1 pt, 1.5 pt, 2 pt, 4 pt, 6 pt, 8 pt, and
    12 pt   512

Appendixes   513

Appendix A. Macintosh Basics   515
Summary of Basic Macintosh Operations   515
  The Desktop   517
  Opening, Closing, Moving, and Sizing Windows on the
    Desktop   518
  Choosing a Command from a Menu   520
  Making Entries in Dialog Boxes   521
Managing Files from the Desktop   522
  Copying   523
  Moving   523
  Renaming   523
  Deleting   523

Appendix B. Using Fonts with Aldus FreeHand   525
What Are Fonts?   525
Bitmap and Outline Fonts   525
PostScript Fonts   526
TrueType Fonts   528
Printing Issues   529

Appendix C. Time and Space: The New Frontier   531
To Decrease Screen Redraw Time   531
To Decrease Printing Time   532
To Minimize Memory Requirements   534
To Minimize File Size   534

Appendix D. Glossary   537

Index   549

■ Part I ■

Introduction

The first two chapters are intended to introduce Aldus FreeHand to those who have never used the program.

CHAPTER	DESCRIPTION
1. Introducing Aldus FreeHand 3.0	Describes FreeHand and its context—desktop publishing. This chapter also indemnifies the features that were introduced with version 3.0, and the equipment requirements for installing and running FreeHand 3.0..
2. Basic Concepts	A simple tutorial for absolute beginners. Here you will find an overview of the screen display in FreeHand including the Document window, the Toolbox, the information bar, the menus, and the Colors palette.

1

Introducing Aldus FreeHand 3.0

Aldus FreeHand 3.0 is a powerful illustration tool with strong built-in typographic and color capabilities.

Most computer graphics programs fall into one of two categories. Bitmap programs like MacPaint render images pixel-by-pixel on the screen, and mimic artist's tools like paintbrushes and airbrushes. Object-oriented programs like MacDraw render images as mathematical descriptions of lines, curves, and primitive shapes, and simulate drafting tools like Rapidograph pens, t-squares, and compasses. The drawback of the first type is that the results are limited by the resolution of your computer's screen, so the printed results often look coarse and jagged. The second type is good for pure drafting and technical illustration, but usually lacks fine control over line weights, curves, and color specifications.

Unlike these kinds of computer graphics programs, FreeHand is built around the PostScript page description language, which has become an industry standard in computer-assisted publishing and prepress. FreeHand and other PostScript graphics programs use an underlying metaphor that differs from other paint and draw programs. Instead of mimicking traditional artists' tools, with FreeHand you build artwork by layering opaque shapes called *paths* one on top of the other. The closest analogy to traditional, non-computer-assisted graphic arts is paper collage, where you cut out and layer different shapes made of colored or patterned paper. But FreeHand offers much more flexibility than traditional collage, and lets you produce results that would be either impossible or enormously time-consuming to produce traditionally.

Working with paths is much easier and more flexible than working with paper cutouts. Unlike a paper cutout, you can go back and change the shape of the path at any time, change the line and fill specifications, and make exact copies of the path to use elsewhere in your artwork. You can use FreeHand's transformation tools to scale, rotate, skew, and reflect paths to precise percentages and angles. You can even have FreeHand create a series of intermediate shapes and colors by blending one path to another.

FreeHand is a production tool as well as a design tool. Once your paper collage was completed, if you wanted to reproduce it in print you would need to have it photographed, then have color separations made from the photograph. With FreeHand, you can print composite proofs in shades of gray on monochrome printers, or in color on color printers, and print final color separations directly to film on a PostScript imagesetter. All the color pages in this book were produced using FreeHand and a PostScript imagesetter.

FreeHand Capabilities

The wine label shown on the next page is used here to illustrate some of FreeHand's features, and is described in more detail in Chapter 10.

Paths and Bezier Curves

You will learn more about drawing with FreeHand in the tutorial in Chapter 2, but here are some basic concepts. A path can be a single point, a series of points that define a curved or straight line, or a complex closed shape. To define a straight line, you simply click the mouse button and drag to place the endpoints, called *anchor points*. Curved lines have anchor points too, but they also have two additional points called *direction handles*. To draw a curve, you click to place an anchor point, then drag a direction handle out of the anchor point.

Each curve segment is defined by two anchor points and two direction handles, one associated with each anchor point. The resulting curves, called *Bezier curves*, are very accurate, yet easy to control. You create paths by clicking anchor points and dragging direction handles. You

Chapter 1. Introducing Aldus FreeHand 3.0   5

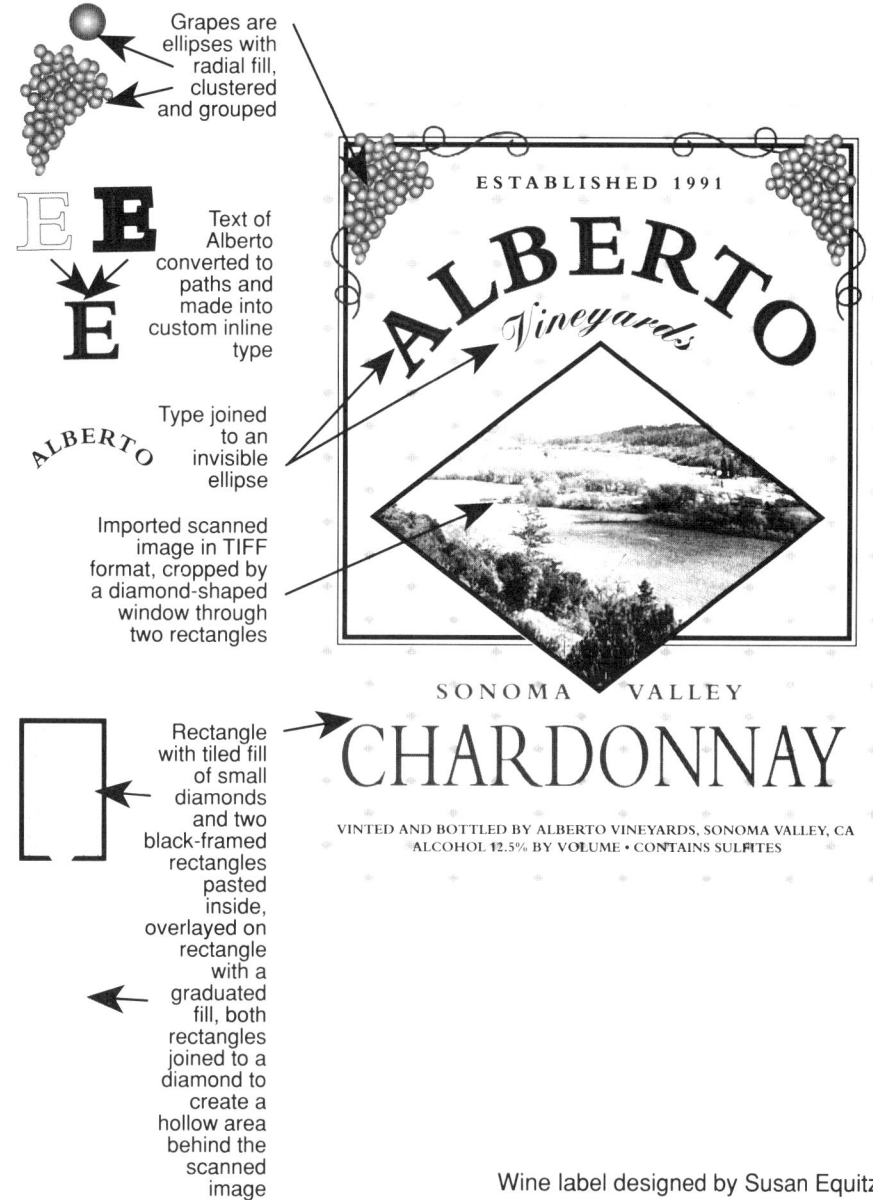

Figure 1.1 Wine label demonstrates FreeHand's capabilities

can mix straight lines and curve segments, and make paths open or closed. An open path has two endpoints. A closed path forms one continuous line.

Figure 1.2 A curved path with an anchor point and direction handles

You can give different line weights to paths, from the finest line your printer can print up to a 288-point line, and you can make the line any color you want. With closed paths, you can specify a fill as well as a line. A fill can be a solid color, a pattern, or a smooth gradation from one color to another. You can also specify no line, and no fill. An open path with no line will be invisible in the final artwork, as will a closed path with no fill and no line.

You can make two or more paths into a composite path to create see-through "windows." In the wine label, the diamond shape in the center of the label was joined with the outer rectangle of the label to form a composite path, thus opening a diamond-shaped "window" through to the scanned image. You can also paste artwork (including scanned images) inside a path, so that only the part of the artwork surrounded by the path shows through. This cookie-cutter effect is called a *clipping path*.

Fill Patterns

In addition to filling paths with solid color, FreeHand lets you specify graduated fills, which blend smoothly from one color to another. You can choose the starting color, the ending color, and the direction in which the colors blend. The wine label contains a graduated fill blending from a dark shade at the top of the label to a light shade at the bottom.

When you need more precise control over color transitions, or when you want to blend shapes as well as colors, you can create blends, which are a series of intermediate shapes with intermediate colors between the two paths being blended.

You can create pattern fills composed of repeating or "tiled" designs. You create the pattern elements as you would any other FreeHand artwork. Once you have defined a tile design, you can apply it as a pattern fill to any closed path. The small diamonds in the wine label are an example of a tiled pattern.

Composite paths are paths that have been joined into a single object. One use of these is to create transparent holes in a path, such as the diamond-shaped hole in the wine label, showing a scanned image that is actually positioned behind the rectangle of the label. Composite paths can also be used when you want to apply a single graduated or patterned fill to several paths.

Typographic Controls

FreeHand also offers strong typographic controls. You can adjust the font size and leading in increments of 1/100th of a point, and control word spacing, letter spacing, baseline shifting (superscripting and subscripting), and kerning. You can apply color to type, and use the transformation tools to rotate, reflect, scale, and skew type just as you would any other path.

You can join text to a path. The baseline of the type then follows the direction of the path. You can use this feature for effects like the circular text commonly found on buttons, or for names of roads or rivers on maps, or any other place where you want to run text along a curve or an arbitrary line.

You can convert type set in PostScript Type 1 or Type 3 fonts into editable paths whose anchor points and direction handles you can move to change the actual letter shapes. You can modify the shapes of the letterforms, use the converted type as a clipping path, or join the converted type to another path to make a composite path, so that the letters appear as holes in the path to which they are joined. Chapter 10 explains how and why the word "Alberto" in the wine label was converted to paths.

Imported TIFF Images

You can import scanned images such as line art, black-and-white photographs, and color photographs, and make them part of your artwork, as was done with the Sonoma Valley view in the wine label. You can even paste a photorealistic image inside a path. This is like cutting a shape out of a photograph and pasting it into your collage. Imported color images print in color on color printers, and separate correctly when you print color separations from FreeHand.

Spot and Process Color

FreeHand allows you to work with spot color, process color, or a mixture of both. Spot color is color that will be reproduced in the final printed artwork by printing with a specially-mixed ink that exactly matches the desired color. Process color is color that will be reproduced in the final printed artwork by overprinting percentages of four separate inks: cyan, magenta, yellow, and black.

The four-color process provides an economical means of reproducing the whole spectrum of color using only four inks, and is necessary for printing color continuous-tone images such as photographs. Each spot color uses a separate ink, so illustrations that contain more than three colors usually use process color instead of spot color, as each ink used drives up the cost of the print job. Sometimes it is necessary to use a spot color in addition to process color. For example, many corporate logos use a custom color that cannot be exactly reproduced with process color, and the corporation or its advertising agency will often insist that the color be exact. FreeHand lets you mix spot and process color, and will generate as many color separations as are necessary.

You can define custom colors using any of three different color models, RGB (red, green, blue), HLS (hue, lightness, saturation), or CMY (cyan, magenta, yellow), or you can choose from a built-in library of over 700 colors from the PANTONE® Color Matching System, an industry standard for spot color. You can also have FreeHand convert Pantone colors to their closest process color equivalent.

High Resolution Output

Finally, FreeHand benefits from a property of the PostScript page description language: device independence. This simply means that a

PostScript printer will always reproduce the artwork as accurately as it can, limited only by the resolution of the printer. You can use PostScript laser printers to proof your artwork, and use PostScript color printers to print color comps, before printing final artwork on a high-resolution imagesetter. In this way, you will be sure that the results from the imagesetter will be the same as they were from the laser printer, only better.

FreeHand Interface

Many of FreeHand's features cannot be seen in the final artwork, but they help in its creation. The figure on the next page shows the wine label seen earlier in this chapter, as it appears in the FreeHand window.

Alignment Aids

FreeHand has features that help you position your artwork accurately. You can display rulers along the top and left sides of the drawing window, and specify the unit of measurement they use. Dotted lines in the ruler track the horizontal and vertical position of the mouse cursor as you move it.

You can drag non-printing guides from the ruler, and make them a distinctive color, so you don't mistake them for part of the artwork. If you turn on the Snap to guides feature, the guides exert a "magnetic" pull on elements in the drawing: if you drag an object within a specified distance of a guide, it snaps precisely into alignment with the guide.

As a further alignment aid, FreeHand also has a repeating invisible grid, which also exerts a "magnetic" pull. You can set the distance between grid points, and turn the grid on and off.

Immediately below the menu bar, the information bar displays the vertical and horizontal coordinates of the mouse cursor, or the position of the currently selected element. As you drag an element, the information bar displays the original position, the current position, and the angle and distance between the original and current positions.

Palettes

FreeHand's palettes are windows that float above the drawing window. As with other windows, you can move them around the screen by dragging their title bars, resize them by dragging the size box, or close

10 *Using Aldus FreeHand 3.0*

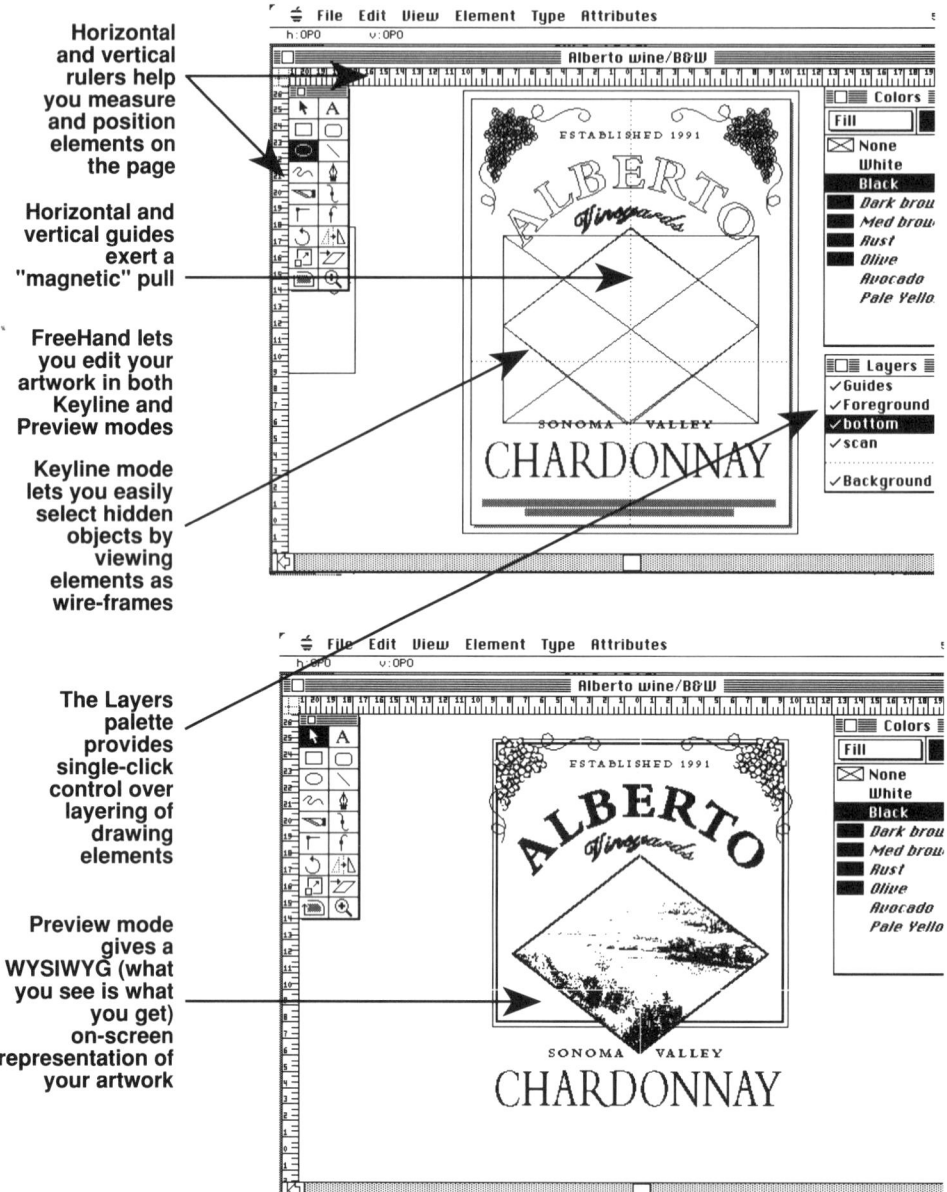

Figure 1.3 The FreeHand drawing window, showing the wine label illustration as it appears in FreeHand

them by clicking their close box. You open palettes by choosing them from the Windows menu. The Colors, Layers, and Styles palettes all contain scrolling lists of available items that you can choose with a single mouse click, and each has a pop-up menu that lets you create, edit, copy, and remove items from the palette.

The Layers palette lets you put different elements of your artwork on different layers. You can give each layer a name, change the stacking order of layers, move elements from one layer to another, make layers temporarily invisible, and choose which layers to print. You can choose to make only the current drawing layer active, in which case you effectively lock all the other layers against accidental changes, or you can make all the visible layers active.

When you work with complex illustrations, FreeHand's layers save time and confusion by letting you turn off all layers except the ones on which you are currently working. This makes the screen redraw faster and prevents you from selecting other elements of the artwork by accident.

The Colors palette provides an easy way to define colors and apply them to lines and fills in your artwork with one or two mouse clicks.

The Styles palette lets you save a collection of attributes (color, fill, line, and halftone screen) as a single style, and apply that style to multiple elements in your artwork with a single mouse click.

New Features in FreeHand 3.0

FreeHand 3.0 builds upon the strengths of its predecessor, FreeHand 2.0, and adds improvements in performance, a more streamlined user interface, and new functionality. For FreeHand 2.0 users, we have listed some of the important new features you will encounter in FreeHand 3.0.

- Context-sensitive online help. Press Command-?, then move the ?-shaped pointer to the menu item or window element you want to know more about.
- Layers palette, Colors palette, and Styles palette provide fast, easy control.
- Faster screen redrawing in both Preview and keyline modes.
- Convert type set in PostScript Type 1 and Type 3 fonts to editable paths.
- Import and color-separate color TIFF images.
- Composite paths allow objects with transparent holes.

- Greater precision (to 1/10000th of a point).
- Auto path-splitting at print time greatly reduces limitcheck errors without damaging the document.
- Select and edit grouped objects without ungrouping them.
- Select "hidden" objects that lie behind other objects.
- Paste behind a selected element with Shift-Paste.
- Show text effects on-screen.
- View graduated and radial fills at high resolution on 24-bit monitors.
- Snap to point makes aligning points and joining paths easier.
- Runs under System 7.0 and A/UX. FreeHand 3.0 can take advantage of System 7.0's 32-bit addressing and virtual memory features.

FreeHand and Your Desktop Publishing System

FreeHand is only one component of a full publishing system that includes a computer and a printer, and might also include:

- A scanner
- Added printer fonts
- Other graphics software
- Page layout software

FreeHand can interact with all of these elements by importing and exporting graphics and type.

Equipment Requirements

FreeHand 3.0 requires at least a Macintosh Plus with a hard disk, System 6.0.3 or later, and a minimum of 2 MB of RAM, of which 1.5 MB must be available for FreeHand. More memory is definitely preferable. The default RAM allocation for running under MultiFinder or System 7.0 is 2.5 MB. You can change the amount of RAM allocated to FreeHand through the Get Info command in the Finder's File menu, but if you allocate less than 1.5 MB, FreeHand will run very slowly if at all.

The complete FreeHand package, including tutorial files and examples, takes up 5.6 MB of hard disk space. If you install only the program files, you can reduce the space required to 3.8 MB.

The recommended configuration is a Macintosh II family computer with a color monitor and 4 MB or more of RAM. For accurate display of on-screen color, a 24-bit video card is desirable, but FreeHand will attempt to display color as accurately as possible using an 8-bit video card. You can increase the amount of memory available to FreeHand by disabling any Startup documents (INIT files) you are currently using by dragging them out of the System Folder, and by reducing the size of the RAM cache in the General control panel (under System 6.0.x) or the Memory control panel (under System 7.0).

A PostScript printer is highly recommended. FreeHand will print the screen representation of your artwork to non-PostScript printers, but these printers cannot reproduce hairlines or many of FreeHand's special PostScript effects. FreeHand can also print to PostScript imagesetters for high-quality final output, and can print slides on PostScript-compatible film recorders such as the LaserGraphics LFR and the Agfa Matrix with the Chromascript RIP.

A scanner is a useful tool, but not an essential one. Flatbed scanners allow you to create image files of line art and grayscale or color continuous-tone images like photographs. You can import these image files into FreeHand and incorporate them in your artwork as is, use them as templates, or use FreeHand's Tracing tool to trace them. If you want to scan photographic images, you should use a scanner that captures 8 bits per pixel for black-and-white photographs, or 24 bits per pixel for color photographs.

FreeHand and Fonts

Try to use PostScript fonts when you work with type in FreeHand. PostScript fonts are available from many vendors, including Adobe Systems, BitStream, and Monotype. Most of FreeHand's special type effects work only with PostScript fonts, and you can scale PostScript fonts to any size. To use a PostScript font, you must have both the screen (bitmap) font and the printer (outline) font on your computer.

You can also use bitmapped fonts, but you cannot apply any of FreeHand's special type effects to them, and unless you use an installed size, they will appear jagged on the final output.

Apple Computer, Inc., recently introduced a new font type called TrueType. You can scale TrueType fonts to any size, or carry out transformations like rotating, reflecting, and skewing. TrueType fonts will print smoothly at any size or after any transformation, but you cannot convert them to editable outlines, or apply any of FreeHand's special type effects to them.

Utility programs like Fifth Generation Software's Suitcase II and Alsoft's Master Juggler let you keep your fonts anywhere on your hard disk, and load and unload them at any time.

For more information on fonts, see Appendix B, "Using Fonts with Aldus FreeHand."

FreeHand and Scanned Images

FreeHand allows you to import scanned images in TIFF (Tag Image File Format), EPS (Encapsulated PostScript), PICT, or MacPaint formats. MacPaint format is limited to 72-dots-per-inch black-and-white images; it is generally only suitable to use for templates for tracing unless you are deliberately seeking a jagged appearance for a special effect. The other three formats are suitable for line art, continuous-tone grayscale images, and continuous-tone color images. However, importing scanned images in PICT format requires much more memory than importing the same image in TIFF or EPS format. If at all possible, you should always convert scanned PICT-format images to either TIFF or EPS before you import them into FreeHand.

Once you have imported a scanned image, you can do different things with it. You can use it as a template that you trace manually using any of FreeHand's drawing tools. If you place it on a non-printing background layer, it will be available any time you need to refer to it, but it will not interfere with your printed artwork.

You can also incorporate a scanned image directly into your artwork. Additionally, you can paste a scanned image inside a clipping path, or scale or rotate it. If it is a grayscale image, you can adjust the contrast and brightness, choose a halftone screen, and apply a spot color to it. You cannot alter the contrast and brightness of imported color images, but you can scale and rotate them, choose halftone screens, and print process color separations so that the color image is reproduced properly in the final printed piece.

When you incorporate scanned images into your artwork, you should be sure to scan them at a resolution suitable for your final output. For grayscale images, Aldus recommends scanning at a resolution of approximately 120% of the line screen setting you will use in the printed piece.

For example, if you will be printing with a 133 lines per inch (lpi) screen, an image scanned at 150 dots per inch will yield good results. Scanning at a higher resolution will increase the size and complexity of the file without providing any significant improvement in image quality.

Opening PostScript Artwork from Other Sources

You can use PostScript artwork created in other programs. You can open files saved in Adobe Illustrator 1.1 format by using the Open command. FreeHand converts the files to new untitled FreeHand documents, leaving the original files unchanged. You can then use FreeHand's tools to edit the artwork.

Alternatively, you can import PostScript art with the Place command. When you do so, you will see either a screen representation of the imported art, or a gray box with the same dimensions as the imported art, depending on whether the original application included a preview image in the file. When you import art instead of opening it, you cannot edit the components of the artwork. You can, however, use any of FreeHand's transformation tools on it, and you can paste it inside a clipping path.

FreeHand and Page Layout Applications

You can use FreeHand artwork in Macintosh page layout applications such as Quark XPress and Aldus PageMaker. You can export FreeHand artwork as an EPS file, a format accepted by most Macintosh page layout applications.

If you include a preview image in the EPS file, the image will display in the page layout program. If you do not include a preview image, the page layout application will display a gray box with the same dimensions as the image, but the image will print correctly on PostScript printers. EPS files without preview images are usually significantly smaller than those that include a preview image.

Transferring FreeHand Artwork to IBM PC Documents

You can also export FreeHand documents in an EPS format that can be read by most page layout programs that run under DOS or Windows on PC-compatibles. You can include a preview image of the artwork in the EPS file if you wish.

Summary

The best way to learn FreeHand's features and capabilities is to try using it! See the rest of the book...

2

Basic Concepts

This chapter offers a quick self-demo that takes you through basic Macintosh and FreeHand operations without attempting to comprehensively explain every tool and command (as is done in Part IV of this book).

If you are already familiar with FreeHand 3.0 or earlier versions, you can skip this chapter entirely. If you are familiar with the Macintosh computer and with other drawing applications on the Macintosh (such as MacDraw or Adobe Illustrator), we suggest you read quickly through this chapter to get an idea of how FreeHand compares to the other applications you know. If you have never used a drawing application, you should go through the steps in this chapter using FreeHand on the computer.

If you have never used a Macintosh, some of the basic operations are explained in Appendix A, "Macintosh Basics." You may also need to refer to Apple Computer's manuals for the Macintosh operating environment to find information not presented in this book.

Installing FreeHand

Because Aldus FreeHand offers a vast array of features and capabilities, it is a large program that is shipped on three floppy disks. During the installation process, the pieces on these disks are assembled into one large program file on your hard disk (along with other files that support Aldus FreeHand). The manuals that come with Aldus FreeHand contain complete instructions for installing the program.

18   Using Aldus FreeHand 3.0

The installation process is simple—you insert the installation disk in the floppy disk drive and double-click the Install icon, and then follow the prompts to insert the other disks that come with the package. The installation program also lets you choose where to install the program (on which hard disk, in which folder), and whether to install the full package or to save space on your hard disk by not installing all of the printer drivers, sample files, and tutorial files that come with Aldus FreeHand 3.0.

If you accept the installation defaults, a folder named Aldus FreeHand 3.0 is created on your hard disk that contains all the elements you have chosen to install.

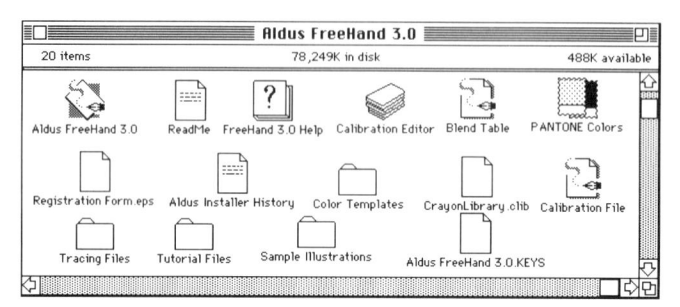

Figure 2.1 The Aldus FreeHand 3.0 folder is automatically created on your hard disk

Starting FreeHand from the Desktop

The most common method of starting a program is to double-click the program icon. This is the usual shortcut to the alternative of clicking the application icon once to select it and then choosing Open from the File menu. You can also use a desk accessory such as On Cue (by ICON Simulations, Inc., Wheeling, IL) to list FreeHand on a menu so you do not have to bother finding and opening folders.

You can also start Aldus FreeHand by double-clicking a FreeHand document icon. This method simultaneously opens the document and starts the program—but if you are following the steps of this tutorial, it is better to start with a blank page.

The next section begins a series of steps that you can simply read, but it would be better to follow the steps on your own computer if you are learning FreeHand for the first time.

Starting FreeHand

Step 1
Double-click the Aldus FreeHand 3.0 folder to open it, and then double-click the Aldus FreeHand 3.0 application icon.

Aldus FreeHand 3.0   Aldus FreeHand 3.0

Figure 2.2 Aldus FreeHand 3.0 folder (left) and application icon (right) when viewed by Icon on the desktop

When you first start FreeHand, the screen displays information about the version you are using. The screen then shows pull-down menu titles on the menu bar listing Aldus FreeHand's command categories. Some of the menu titles are gray and cannot be selected because no document is open. The screen might also display an information bar, a Toolbox, a Colors palette, a Layers palette, and/or a Styles palette—depending on how your defaults are set up. (The descriptions of the Toolbox and the palettes in Chapters 12 and 13 explain how to change the defaults for displaying these windows.)

You can choose New from the File menu to open a new file (as you will do in this tutorial), choose Open from the File menu to open an existing FreeHand document, choose Preferences to change the defaults for new FreeHand documents, or choose Quit to exit FreeHand (see the descriptions of the FreeHand commands in Chapter 14 of this book).

Opening a New File

Step 2
Choose New from the File menu (⌘N) to start a new document.

20   *Using Aldus FreeHand 3.0*

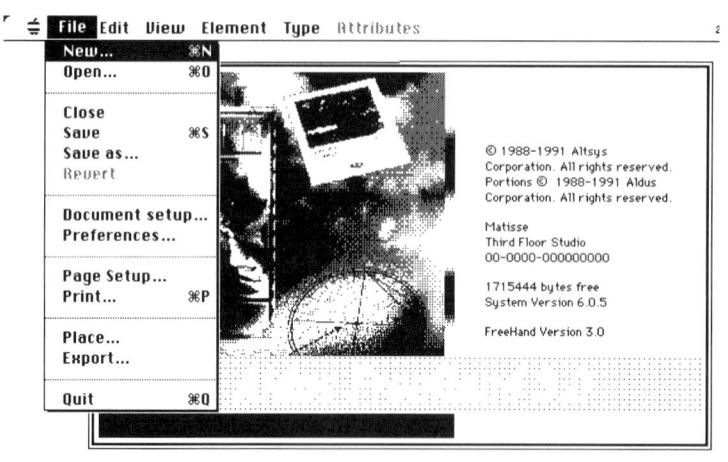

Figure 2.3 The New command in the File menu

The New command displays the Document setup dialog box, where you specify the page size for the artwork.

Figure 2.4 Document setup dialog box

Methods of making entries in dialog boxes are summarized in Appendix A; you use several of those methods in this dialog box, as demonstrated in the next steps.

Step 3

Press the Tab key several times to see all the *editable* text boxes in this dialog box. Note that the Page size and Unit of measure edit boxes cannot be edited directly as text. These two fields are framed in drop-shadow borders, indicating that they contain pop-up lists of choices. The Target printer resolution edit box can be edited through the keyboard, but you can also choose from a pop-up list of choices—as indicated by the right-pointing arrow next to the text in the drop-shadowed box.

You can change the page size by positioning the pointer over the first Page size edit box (showing the page size by name) and holding down the mouse button to display and choose from a pop-up list. Alternatively, you can change the size by typing new numeric values in the Custom page size edit boxes on the second line in the dialog box. Use the second method in the next step.

Step 4

Press the Tab key until the first editable text box is highlighted—the first edit box of the Custom page size measurements. If you are working with the original program defaults, the edit box shows 612 points. Change this to 720. Do not press Enter or Return yet.

Figure 2.5 Highlight and change the first Custom page size measurement edit box

Notice that the radio button next to the Custom page size automatically becomes highlighted.

Step 5

Change to Wide Orientation by clicking the word Wide or the radio button to the left of the word.

Step 6

Position the mouse pointer over the Unit of measure edit box and hold down the mouse button to display the pop-up list of choices, then drag the mouse down to highlight Inches and release the mouse button.

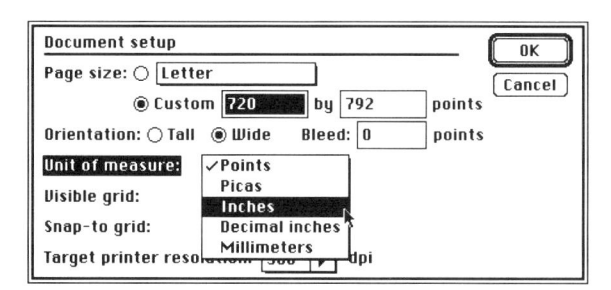

Figure 2.6 Select inches as the unit of measure

Notice that the measurements shown in the dialog box are converted from points to inches.

Step 7

Position the pointer over the first Page size edit box and hold down the button to display the pop-up list of standard page sizes, and choose Letter.

Notice that the measurements next to the Custom page size settings change automatically, and the radio button next to Letter becomes highlighted.

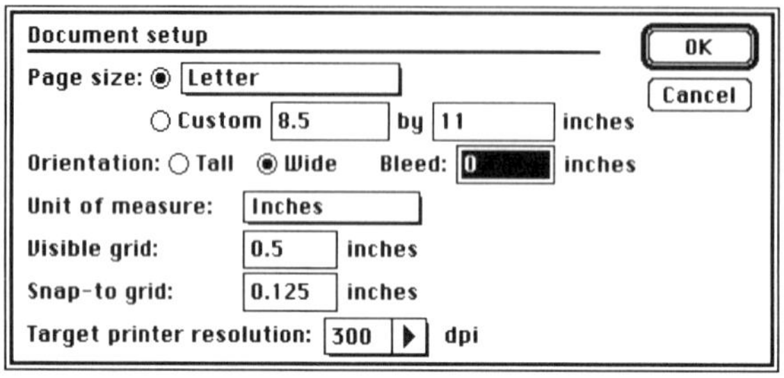

Figure 2.7 Document setup for this exercise

The rest of the entries in this dialog box are described in the sections on the New command and the Document setup command in Chapter 14.

Step 8

Click OK or press Return to close the dialog box and open a new document.

The Document Window

After you enter the initial specifications in the Document setup dialog box, or when an existing document is open, Aldus FreeHand displays a page in the document window.

A quick look at the document window and the palettes on the screen will give you an idea of the versatility of Aldus FreeHand. If you are examining the document window for the first time, choose View ➤ Magnification ➤ Fit in window (if it is not already in Fit in window view) and follow the descriptions in the following sections.

NOTE

We use the ➤ symbol to indicate a menu ➤ command ➤ submenu sequence throughout this book. You choose a command from a submenu by first positioning the mouse on the menu bar at the top of the screen to open the first menu, then dragging down the menu to highlight a command with a right-pointing arrow next to it. This opens the submenu. Still holding down the mouse button, drag down the submenu to highlight the command you want and then release the mouse button.

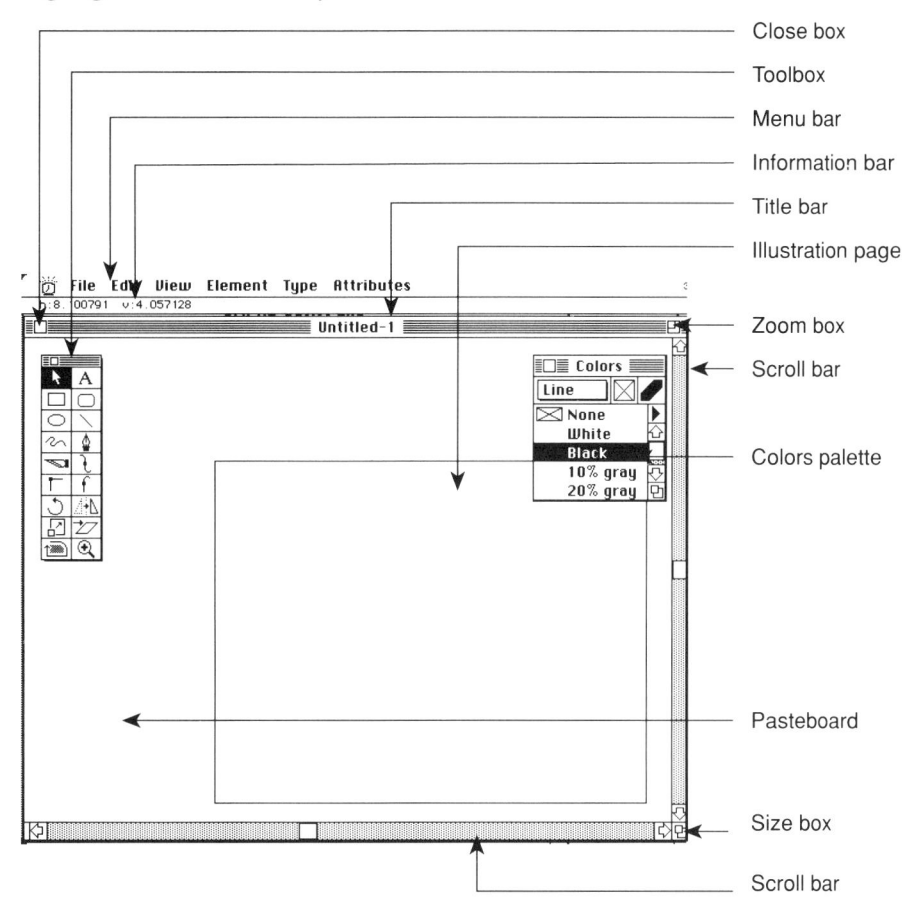

Labels on figure (top to bottom): Close box, Toolbox, Menu bar, Information bar, Title bar, Illustration page, Zoom box, Scroll bar, Colors palette, Pasteboard, Size box, Scroll bar

Figure 2.8 After the Document setup dialog box is closed, Aldus FreeHand displays a blank page

The document window has a *title bar* showing the name of the document and includes a *close box* and a *zoom box*. The *pointer* shows the current position of the mouse and is used for selecting commands and objects on the page or pasteboard.

The *page image* shows the edges of the paper. The area surrounding the page serves as a *pasteboard* for storage of text and graphics while you work. You can use this area as an active storage area while you are

24 Using Aldus FreeHand 3.0

building the artwork, or you can use it as a more permanent storage area for the document—an alternative to using the Scrapbook and other sources for commonly-used elements.

Tools

Aldus FreeHand's Toolbox is much like a conventional artist's assortment of drawing tools. But pens, rulers, protractors, and knives are replaced by icons, which you select to perform the artist's work.

Step 1

If the Toolbox is not already displayed on your screen, you can display a hidden Toolbox by choosing View → Windows → Toolbox when the Toolbox command is not checked (that is, when the Toolbox is not displayed).

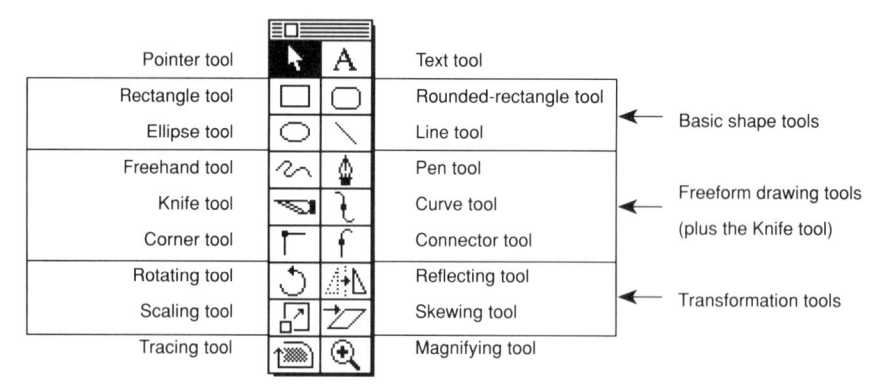

Pointer tool		Text tool
Rectangle tool		Rounded-rectangle tool
Ellipse tool		Line tool
Freehand tool		Pen tool
Knife tool		Curve tool
Corner tool		Connector tool
Rotating tool		Reflecting tool
Scaling tool		Skewing tool
Tracing tool		Magnifying tool

Basic shape tools

Freeform drawing tools (plus the Knife tool)

Transformation tools

Figure 2.9 The Toolbox

The Toolbox is a separate window on the screen. You can drag the Toolbox by its title bar to any position on the screen. You can also close the Toolbox by clicking its close box or by choosing View → Windows → Toolbox. To redisplay the Toolbox after you close it, choose View → Windows → Toolbox.

Some of the tools are used in this tutorial, and all of the tools are explained in detail in Chapter 12 of this book.

The Information Bar

The information bar (usually positioned just below the menu bar) displays information about the current position of the mouse pointer or the currently active item on a page. This information will change dynamically as you move, scale, or otherwise change an active item.

Step 2
If the information bar is not already displayed on your screen, you can display a hidden information bar by choosing View ➤ Windows ➤ Info bar when the Info bar command is not checked (that is, when the information bar is not displayed).

Step 3
Move the mouse and see how the numbers on the information bar change to reflect the current position of the mouse pointer on the screen.

The measurements on the information bar reflect the mouse pointer position with respect to a *zero point* on the rulers, as described next.

Using the Rulers

Step 4
Choose the Rulers command from the View menu (⌘R) if it is not already active. The Rulers command displays a horizontal ruler (along the top of the document window) and a vertical ruler (down the left side of the window).

The unit of measure shown on the rulers is the same as that selected in the Document setup dialog box, displayed whenever you choose the New command or the Document setup command from the File menu. In this case, the rulers show inches, since that was what you chose when you started this document (if you have been following this tutorial).

The rulers—and the information bar—measure position from a zero point, normally the bottom left corner of the page.

Step 5
Move the mouse around to see how markers on the rulers reflect the current mouse position.

26 Using Aldus FreeHand 3.0

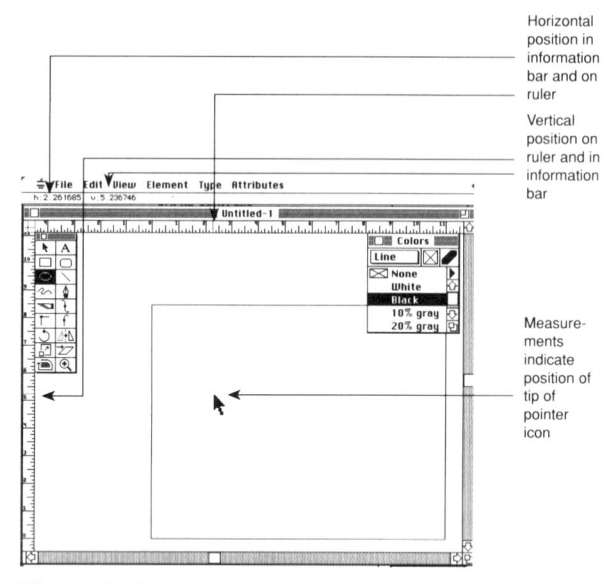

Figure 2.10 The information bar and markers on the rulers reflect the current mouse position

TIP

You can change the zero point by positioning the mouse pointer over the intersection of the rulers at the top left corner of the page and dragging new axes onto the pasteboard or the page.

Displaying Palettes

Step 6

If the Colors palette is not already displayed on your screen, display it now by choosing View → Windows → Colors (⌘9).

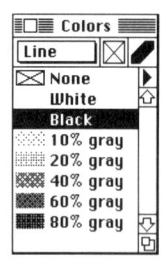

Figure 2.11 The Colors palette

There are two more palettes that you can display—the Layers palette and the Styles palette. These palettes are described in detail in Chapter 13.

Windows and palettes can be moved and sized on the screen. You can have more than one document *window* open at a time, but the active document window will usually display *on top of* any other document windows (unless you have arranged them side-by-side). If you close a document window, you are closing the document. *Palettes*, on the other hand, are always displayed on top of the active window, and each palette is related to the active document only. You can close any palette without closing the active document.

Step 7

Make the Colors palette smaller by positioning the mouse pointer over the size box at the lower right corner of the palette and dragging it. Move the Colors palette to the top right corner of the screen by positioning the mouse pointer over the title bar and dragging it.

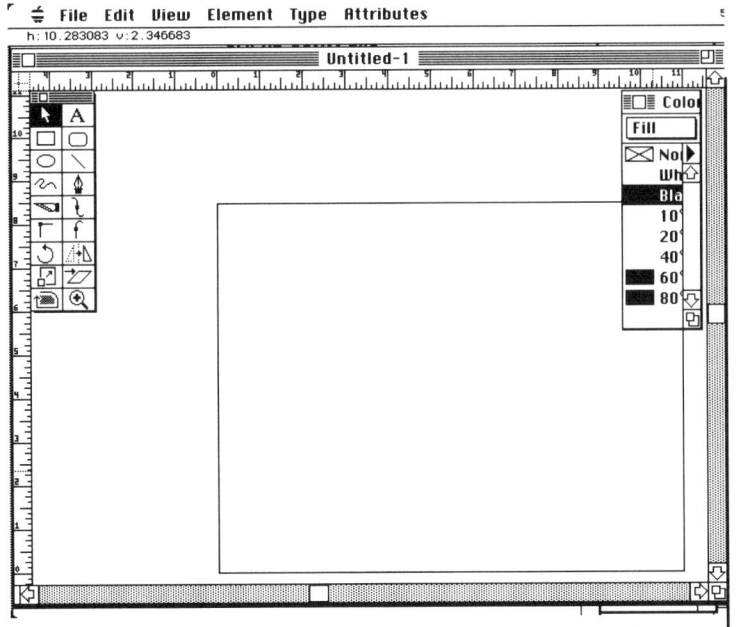

Figure 2.12 The Colors palette made smaller and moved

Examining the Menus

You have already used some of FreeHand's commands in the previous steps. All of FreeHand's menus and commands are described in detail in Part IV of this book, but we summarize them here to give you a quick overview of FreeHand's features.

As you read the next descriptions, feel free to open the menus on your screen and choose commands that are followed by an ellipsis (…) to examine their dialog boxes. Click Cancel to close any dialog box.

Using the Help Function

Three types of on-line help are offered through Aldus FreeHand. First, the Help command in the Apple menu offers a list of Help topics if the Help file is in the folder with the FreeHand program.

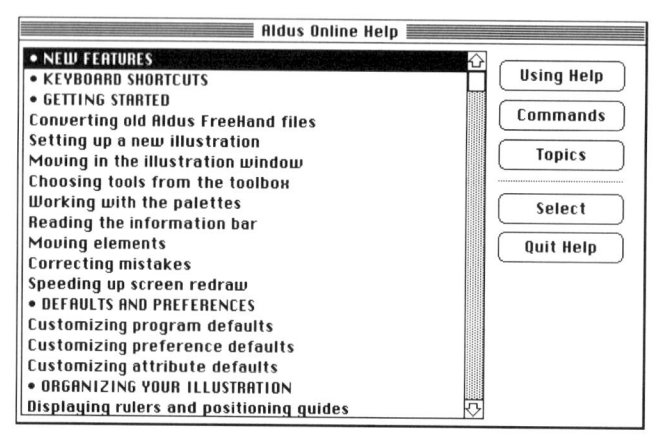

Figure 2.13 The Help topics listed in the Help dialog box

The About FreeHand command in the Apple menu tells you what version of the program you are using. Knowing the version of your program is important if you use the telephone hotline offered by Aldus to resolve problems with FreeHand. (This service, available to registered owners, is well worth the subscription fee if you plan to do a great deal of production with FreeHand.)

Another source of help is the Help button in the Page Setup and Print dialog boxes. This is a standard Macintosh function that displays Help information specific to the dialog box in which you are working.

The File Menu

The File menu includes commands that are common to most Macintosh applications, such as New, Open, Close, Save, Save as, Page Setup, Print, and Quit. FreeHand adds a Revert command that lets you cancel any changes you made to the document since you last saved it. The Place and Export commands let you import graphics from other applications or export the FreeHand artwork into other formats. The Document setup and Page Setup commands allow you to change physical attributes of the artwork such as page size. The Preferences command lets you change how FreeHand displays elements on the screen (without affecting how they print).

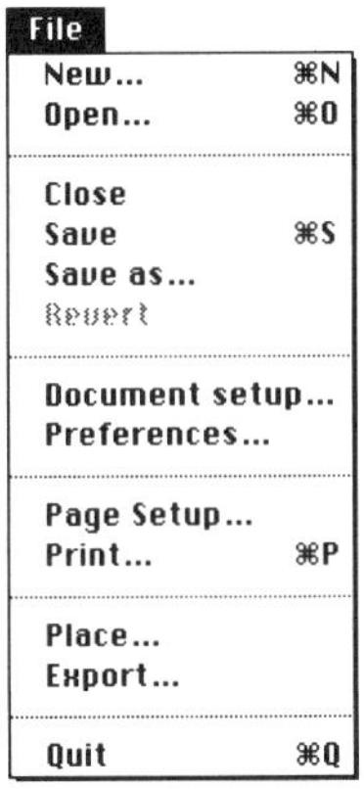

Figure 2.14 The File menu

The Edit Menu

The Edit menu includes commands that are common to most Macintosh applications, such as Undo, Cut, Copy, Paste, Clear, and Select all. FreeHand adds commands that let you cut the *contents* of an object and paste a selection *into* an object, thereby creating a mask or a clipping path. Other commands in this menu let you either duplicate or clone an object (shortcuts for Copy and Paste), move an object by a distance you specify numerically, or repeat the last change (Transform again).

Figure 2.15 The Edit menu

The View Menu

The View menu commands change the size of the page view in the document window, switch between viewing the artwork as it will print (Preview) and viewing the artwork as a system of lines and curves (keyline), and hide or display other elements (palettes, rulers, and non-printing guides) on the screen. You can also determine whether elements will "snap to" points on other elements, guides, or the invisible grid as you create or move them on the screen. None of these commands affects how the document looks when it is printed.

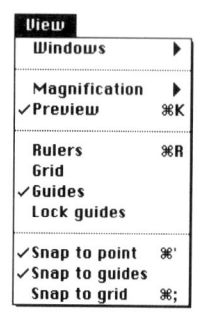

Figure 2.16 The View menu

The Element Menu

The Element menu includes commands that let you rearrange the stacking order of elements within a layer (Bring to front, Bring forward, Send backward, and Send to back).

The Element info command yields a dialog box that shows characteristics specific to the *type* of element that is selected, letting you view or change the size and position of basic shapes like rectangles, or close open paths, or change brightness settings for imported TIFF graphics. (See the description of the Element info command in Chapter 14 for details.) The Points command lets you convert a point from one type to another—such as convert a corner point to a curve point. (See the description of the Pen tool in Chapter 12 for details.)

The Lock command prevents an object from being moved. The Group command creates a relationship between several objects—though you can still select and change individual items within a group. The Unlock and Ungroup commands let you reverse actions taken with the Lock and Group commands.

The Alignment command helps align several objects horizontally and/or vertically. The Blend command creates a series of objects that fall between two selected objects, with gradual changes of shape or color. The Constrain command yields a dialog box that lets you constrain basic shapes to a specific axis.

The Join elements command can be used to "fuse" two overlapping endpoints on an open path, or two endpoints of two paths. The Join elements command also lets you create "windows" in solid objects by joining two objects, thus creating composite paths. The Split element command separates the objects that compose a composite path.

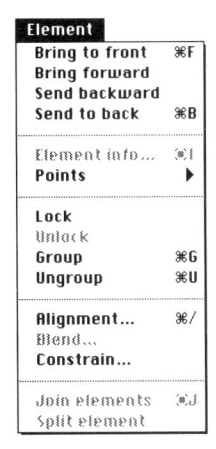

Figure 2.17 The Element menu

The Type Menu

The commands in the Type menu affect text that you type in FreeHand. The Font, Size, Leading, and Type style commands all lead to submenus that let you select individual specifications quickly, or you can use the Type specs command to display a dialog box and set all these characteristics at once. Special effects offered in FreeHand 3.0 include setting fill and stroke (outline) characteristics separately, creating Inline type (in which characters are outlined by one or more bands of white), and zoom text (a three-dimensional appearance).

FreeHand incorporates sophisticated typographic controls such as letter and word spacing (Spacing command), horizontal scaling (expanded or condensed text), and baseline shift (for creating superscripts and subscripts). The Alignment command lets you justify text as well as set it to align left, right, centered, or vertically.

The Convert to paths command lets you convert any text to graphic objects that can then be manipulated like any path drawn with FreeHand's graphics tools. This means you can create custom logos and special effects other than those available through the Effect command submenu.

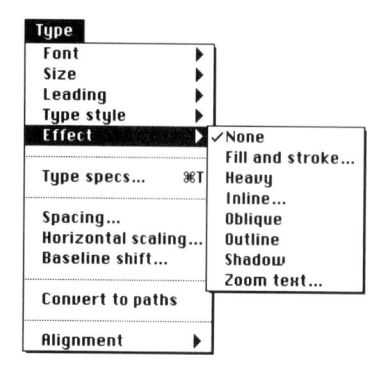

Figure 2.18 The Type menu

The Attributes Menu

The Attributes menu commands change the fill and line style (stroke) of elements created using FreeHand's drawing tools, set the halftone screen resolution and style for imported bitmapped graphics, and set notes that will appear in the PostScript code (a useful tool for those who work directly with the PostScript language).

The Colors and Styles commands let you create new colors and define styles (collections of characteristics that can be named and applied in one step through the Styles palette, instead of making all of the needed settings in the Fill and line and Halftone screen dialog boxes). The line weights listed in the Attributes menu are shortcuts for the line weight specification that can be made in the Fill and line command dialog box.

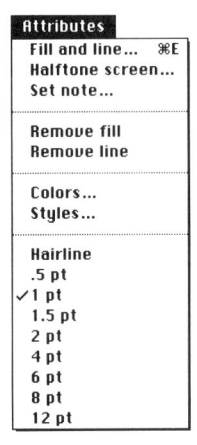

```
Attributes
 Fill and line...   ⌘E
 Halftone screen...
 Set note...
 
 Remove fill
 Remove line
 
 Colors...
 Styles...
 
 Hairline
 .5 pt
✓1 pt
 1.5 pt
 2 pt
 4 pt
 6 pt
 8 pt
 12 pt
```

Figure 2.19 The Attributes menu

Using Tools and Commands

In addition to examining the tools, commands, palettes, and windows on the screen, you can learn more about the basic principles and terminology of FreeHand by creating a simple example of FreeHand artwork. The next sections take you through the steps in producing the artwork shown on the next page. In the process, you will be introduced to some of the basic operations and vocabulary terms used throughout this book.

Figure 2.20 Artwork created in FreeHand

Using the Rectangle Tool

In the next steps, you will use the Rectangle tool to draw two squares, using the rulers and the information bar as guides in determining the position and size of the squares.

Step 1

If you have not been following this tutorial from the beginning and the rulers are not displayed on your screen, choose Rulers from the View menu (⌘R) now, before you draw the rectangle—or simply use the information bar as a guide in positioning the pointer as described in the next steps. It is not important that you draw the elements precisely as described here, but it is important to know that FreeHand offers you all the tools you need if you *want* to be precise in drawing.

Click once on the Rectangle tool to select it, and position the crossbar pointer near the upper left corner of the page. The figure shows the pointer at the 7-inch mark on the vertical ruler (the ruler on the right side of the window), and the 3-inch mark on the horizontal ruler (at the top of the window).

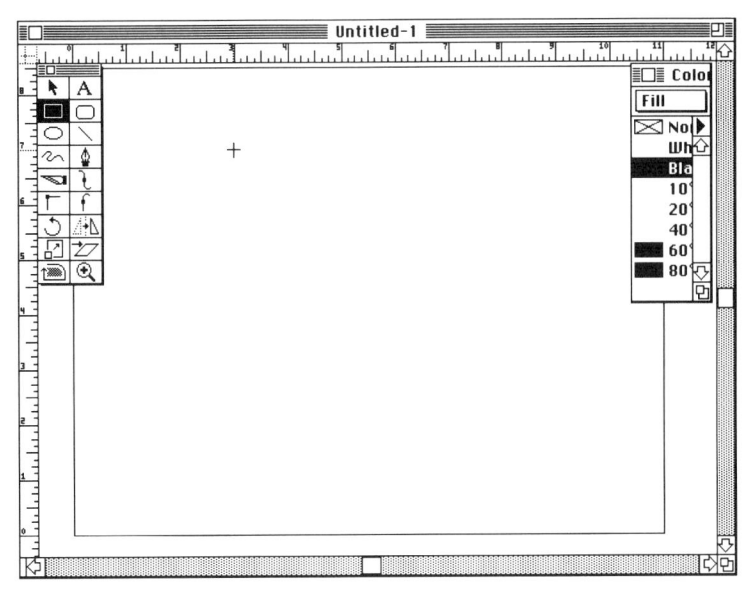

Figure 2.21 The Rectangle tool selected, and the pointer at the 7-inch mark on the vertical ruler, 3-inch mark on the horizontal

Step 2

Hold down the mouse button and drag the pointer—do not release the mouse button until you go through this quick exercise:

As you drag with the mouse, notice that the information bar changes to show the changing width and height of the rectangle. The center of the rectangle is indicated by a small black X on the screen.

While still dragging with the mouse, hold down the Shift key—this forces the rectangle to be a perfect square, regardless of where you drag the pointer. While still dragging the mouse, release the Shift key to see how the shape changes.

Finally, hold down the Shift key and release the mouse button when the square is approximately 5 inches on each side—as indicated on the information bar and by the ruler line position indicators. (If you cannot get the mouse pointer to stop at exactly the measure you intend, it might be because Snap to grid is active, forcing the pointer to stop at fixed increments as you drag. Again, do not worry about matching our measurements precisely in this case, but do read about the Snap to commands in Chapter 14 if you want to work with precision on your own artwork.)

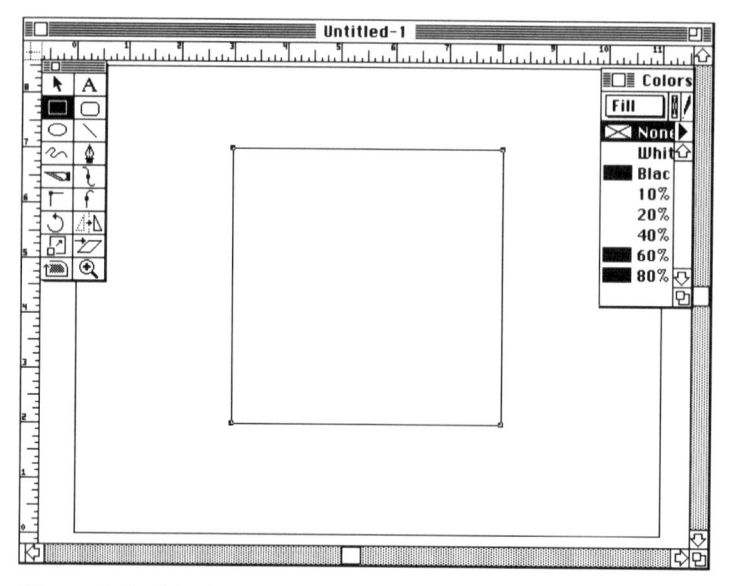

Figure 2.22 5-inch square rectangle on the screen

Notice that the rectangle displays four "handles"—small black squares at the corners, indicating that it is *selected* or *active* on the screen. The square should be a thin black line with no fill. If the square you have drawn has a fill, choose Remove fill from the Attributes menu.

Step 3

Use the same technique to draw a second square starting at 6 inches on the vertical ruler, 4 inches on the horizontal ruler. Release the mouse button when the Shift key is down and the square is approximately 3 inches on each side.

Chapter 2. Basic Concepts   37

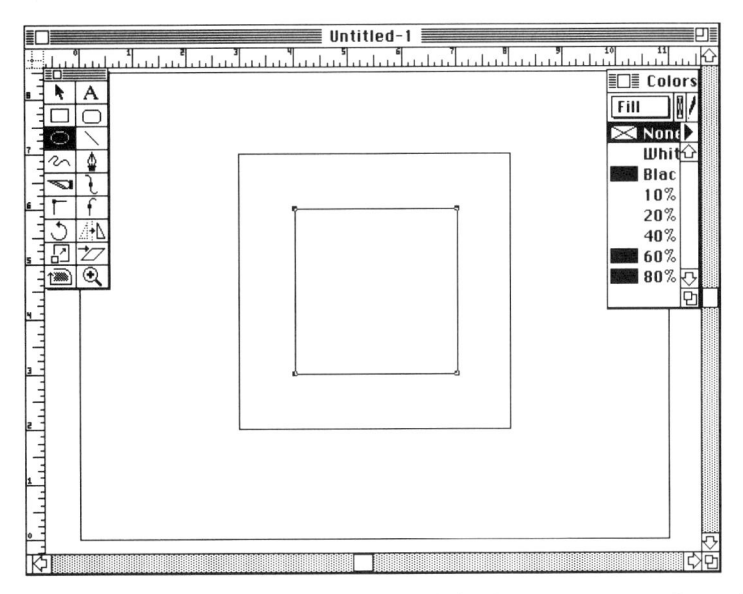

Figure 2.23 3-inch square inside the 5-inch square rectangle on the screen

Now the new rectangle displays four handles, indicating that it is *selected* or *active* on the screen, and the first rectangle is no longer selected.

Using the Pointer Tool

As long as the mouse pointer looks like a crossbar, every time you press the mouse button and drag you will start drawing another rectangle. To *change* a rectangle that you have already created, you must switch to the Pointer tool.

Step 4

Click once on the Pointer tool in the Toolbox, then position the pointer on a side of the smaller square and drag it to move it. The pointer changes to a four-pointed arrow icon as you click and hold down the mouse button with the pointer positioned on an edge of the rectangle. Do not release the mouse button until you go through this quick exercise:

As you drag with the mouse, notice that the information bar changes to show the changing position of the rectangle as it moves. While still dragging, hold down the Shift key to move the rectangle along a 45-degree angle; then release the Shift key to see how the position changes.

When you release the mouse button, choose Undo move elements immediately from the Edit menu (⌘Z).

You can use the Undo command to successively undo the most recent previous actions—up to eight previous steps, or as many as you specify through the Preferences command (described in Chapter 14).

Step 5

Position the pointer on a corner of the smaller square and drag it to change the size of the square—notice that an X appears in the center of the rectangle while you are dragging. Do not release the mouse button until you go through this quick exercise:

As you drag a corner, notice that the information bar changes to show the changing size of the rectangle. While you are still dragging, hold down the Shift key to maintain the square shape; then release the Shift key to see how the size changes.

When you release the mouse button, choose Undo scale elements immediately from the Edit menu (⌘Z).

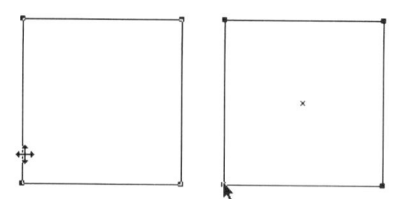

Figure 2.24 Drag a border to move an object (left), drag a handle to change the size or shape (right)

Using the Duplicate Command

There are several ways of copying objects in FreeHand: you can use the Copy and Paste commands, the Duplicate command, or the Clone command. Each of these commands, and the differences among them, are explained in detail in Chapter 14. In the next step, we use the Duplicate command because that leads to several other commands that we want to show you, but the Clone command could have been used here to save one or two steps—see Chapter 14 for why.

Step 6

Click the smaller square with the pointer to select it (if it is not already selected), then choose Duplicate from the Edit menu (⌘D).

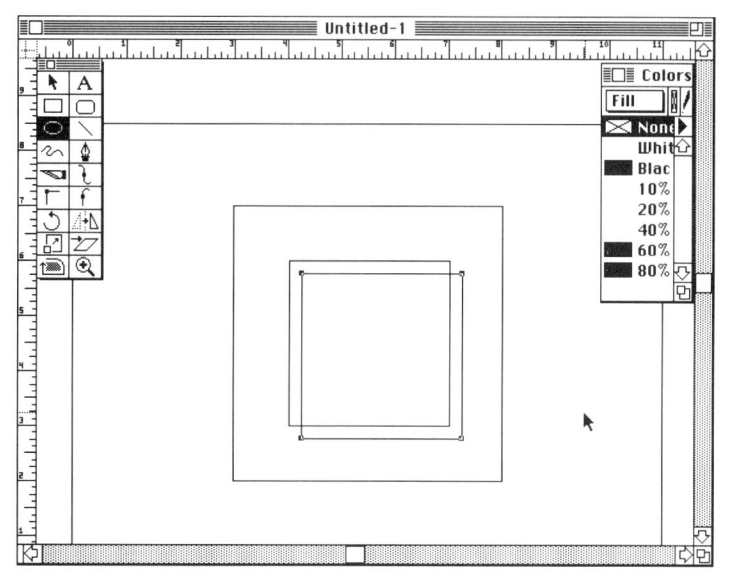

Figure 2.25 The Duplicate command creates a copy next to the original

Using the Rotating Tool

There are two ways to rotate an object: numerically (as we do in the next step) or visually. Both methods are described in detail in Part IV.

Step 7

With the duplicate rectangle selected (that is, with the handles displayed), click the Rotating tool in the Toolbox (↻), then hold down the Option key and click once anywhere on the screen to display the Rotate dialog box.

Step 8

Type "45" in the Angle edit box, and click Center of selection (if it is not already selected), as shown in the figure below.

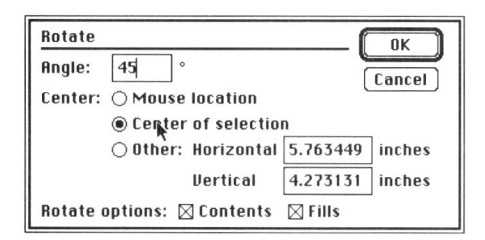

Figure 2.26 Rotate dialog box is displayed when you Option-click with the Rotating tool pointer on the screen

Step 9
Click OK to close the dialog box.

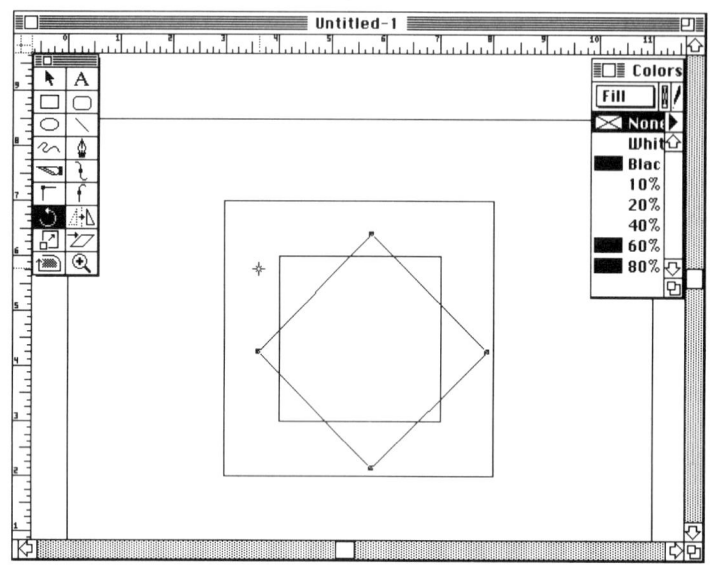

Figure 2.27 Rotated square

Temporarily Selecting the Pointer Tool

Because the Pointer tool is used so frequently, FreeHand offers a method for temporarily selecting the tool, so you can activate it for use and then quickly revert to the previous tool selection.

Step 10
With the Rotating tool still selected, hold down the Command key to get the Pointer tool. Holding down the Command key, position the pointer on any side of the rotated square and drag it to the center of the large square.

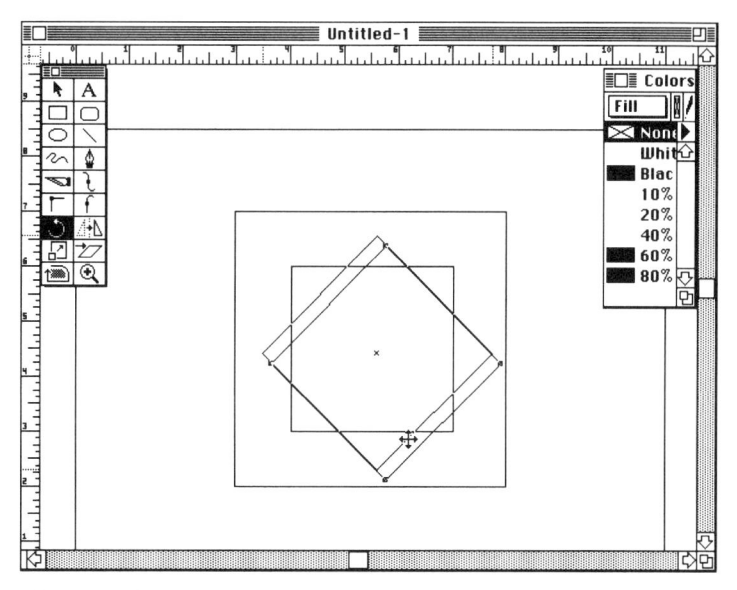

Figure 2.28 Roughly centered squares

Using the Align Command

If you are very careful, you might be able to center two or three objects by dragging them on the screen, but FreeHand offers a much quicker and precise method of aligning objects—the Alignment command.

Step 11

Hold down the Command key to get the Pointer tool, and drag a selection marquee to surround all three squares and select them. (Methods of selecting objects are described in detail in Chapter 12 in the description of the Pointer tool.)

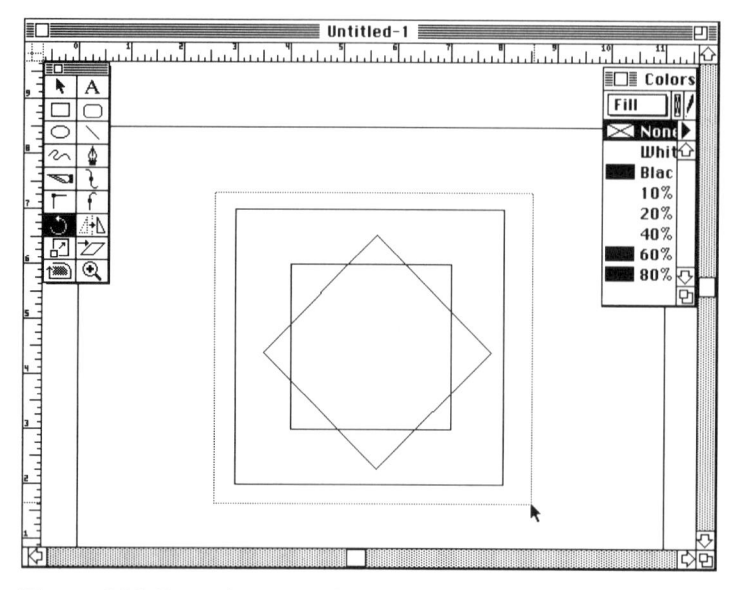

Figure 2.29 Dragging the pointer to select objects

Step 12

Choose Alignment from the Element menu (⌘/) to display the Alignment dialog box, then click Align Elements, Vertical Align Center, and Horizontal Align Center as shown in the next figure.

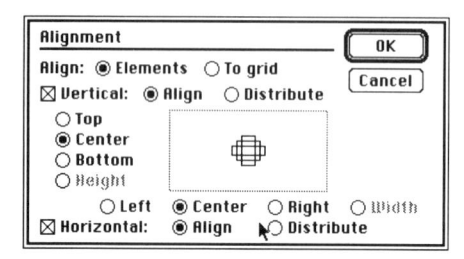

Figure 2.30 The Alignment dialog box set to align the centers of all elements

Step 13

Click OK or press Return to close the dialog box.

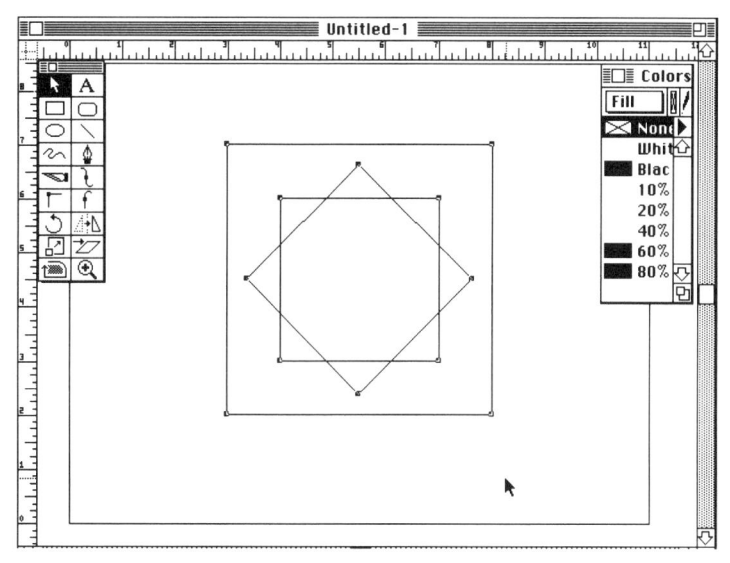

Figure 2.31 All objects aligned to a common center point

Shading Objects

Step 14
Press Tab to deselect everything, then hold down the Command key to get the Pointer tool and click the big square once to select it.

Step 15
With the big square selected, click once on the Fill indicator in the Colors palette (or choose Fill from the pop-up menu at the upper left of the palette). (If the Colors palette is not already displayed, you can display it now by choosing View ➤ Windows ➤ Colors or by pressing ⌘9. If the Colors palette is too narrow and does not display the Fill indicator, drag the size box in the lower right corner of the palette to enlarge it.)

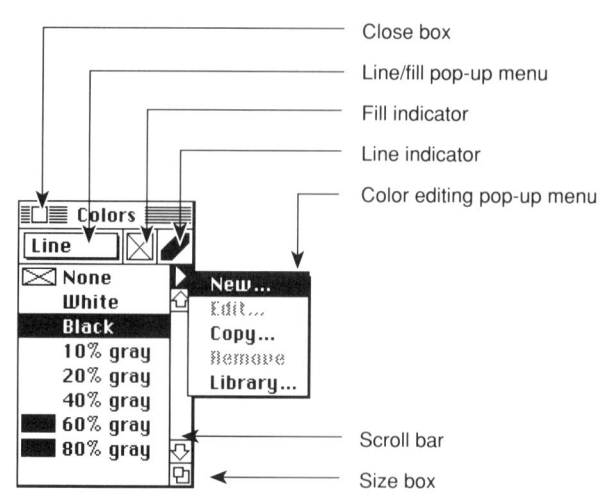

Figure 2.32 Click the Fill indicator in the Colors palette

Step 16

Click Black in the Colors palette to make the fill of the large square black. (If the rectangle does not fill with black, make sure Preview is checked in the View menu, and choose Preview if it is not checked.)

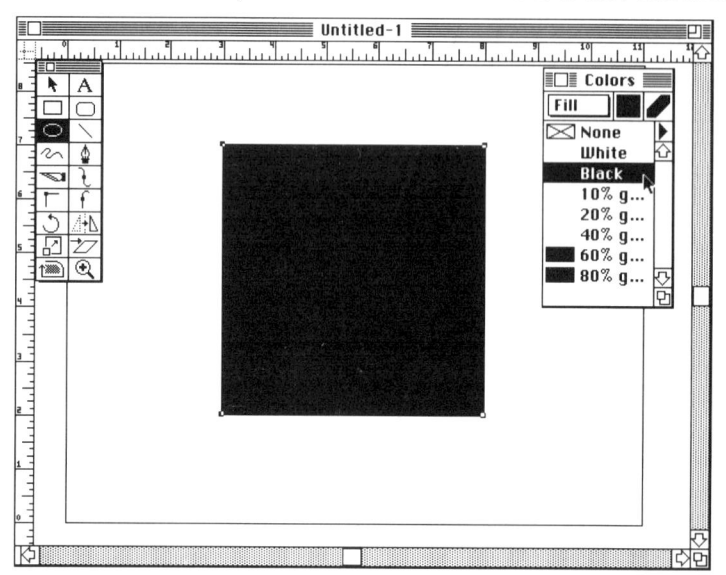

Figure 2.33 The black square hides the other two squares

The black square hides the other two squares, even though it is actually *below* them in stacking order (since it was the first one created), because the other two squares have black borders and *no* fill. There are several ways to make the hidden squares visible, as demonstrated by the next steps.

Preview

Up until now, you have been working in Preview mode, where the artwork is displayed on the screen exactly as it will appear when printed. FreeHand offers the option of viewing artwork in keyline mode—a wireframe view of all elements without representing their actual border and fill patterns or colors.

Step 17

Pull down the View menu and see that Preview is checked. Highlight Preview and release the mouse button to turn Preview off. All three squares are displayed in outline only. An X marks their common center point (since they were aligned to the same center point in step 12).

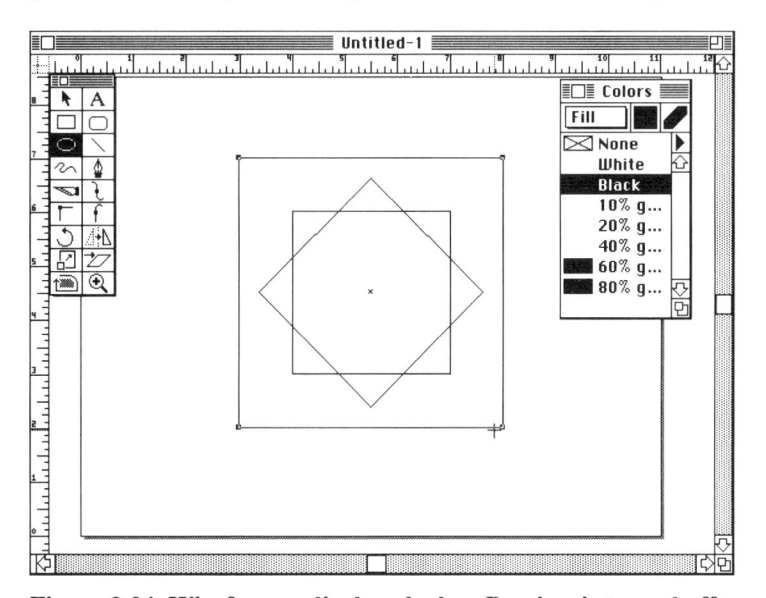

Figure 2.34 Wireframes displayed when Preview is turned off

Step 18

Press the Tab key to deselect the large square. Pressing the Tab key always deselects all objects. Then hold down the Command key to get the Pointer tool, and hold down the Shift key as you click once on each of the two small squares to select them. Holding down the Shift key lets you select more than one object at a time.

Step 19

With the two small squares selected, click once on the Fill indicator in the Colors palette (if it is not already selected, as indicated by the word "Fill" at the top left of the palette), then click White in the Colors palette to make the fill of the small squares white.

Choose Preview from the View menu (⌘K) to turn Preview back on and view the artwork as it will appear when printed.

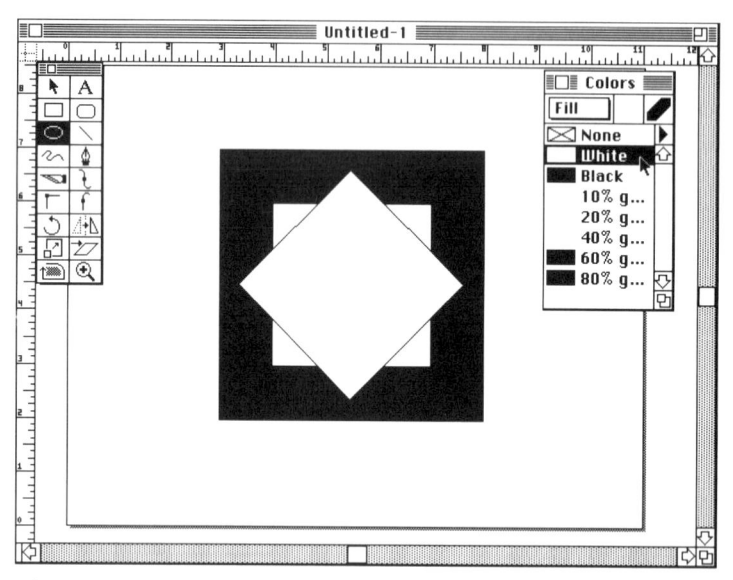

Figure 2.35 Artwork in Preview mode

Save—Often

We have been working on artwork that has not yet been saved—indicated by the fact that the title bar shows it as "Untitled." This means that the artwork is stored in the computer's memory, but not yet on a disk. If the power should fail suddenly, you would lose all of the work you have done so far. It's a good idea to save your documents often while you work.

Step 20

Choose Save from the File menu (⌘S). The first time you use this command, the Save document as dialog box is displayed. Type "Practice Artwork" (or whatever name you choose) in the dialog box. You can choose the drive and folder in which to store the document using the techniques described in Chapter 14 in the description of the Save as command. Format options are also described in Chapter 14.

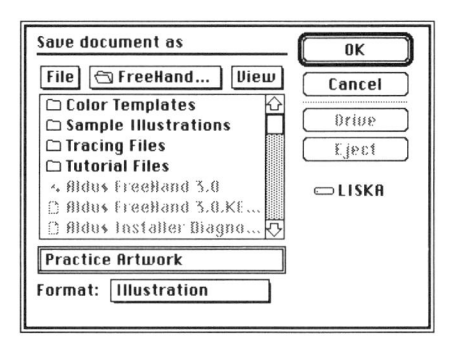

Figure 2.36 The Save document as dialog box

Step 21
Click OK or press Return to close the dialog box.

Using the Text Tool

Step 22
Click the Text tool in the Toolbox, then position the I-beam pointer (I) in the center of the three squares and click to display the Text dialog box.

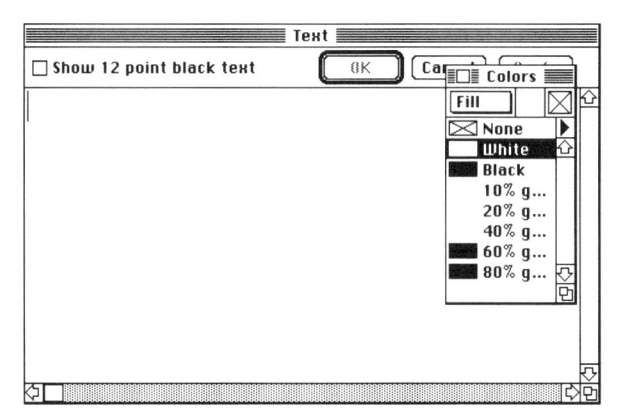

Figure 2.37 The Text dialog box is displayed when you select the Text tool and click on the page

Step 23

The Colors palette displays on top of the Text dialog box (if they overlap), because colors can be applied to text as well as graphics.

With the Fill indicator still selected in the Colors palette from previous steps, click Black in the Colors palette before typing any text.

TIP

If the text you type is "invisible" in the Text dialog box, it is probably because White fill is selected in the Colors palette. You can make the text visible by clicking the Show 12-point black text option at the top of the Text dialog box, or by selecting the text and changing the color. If the text you type is invisible on the page, either White fill is selected or the text is on an invisible layer—see the description of the Layers palette in Chapter 13.

Step 24

Type your initials. It does not matter whether you type a period after each initial, or whether you type them in all caps—these are your own design decisions.

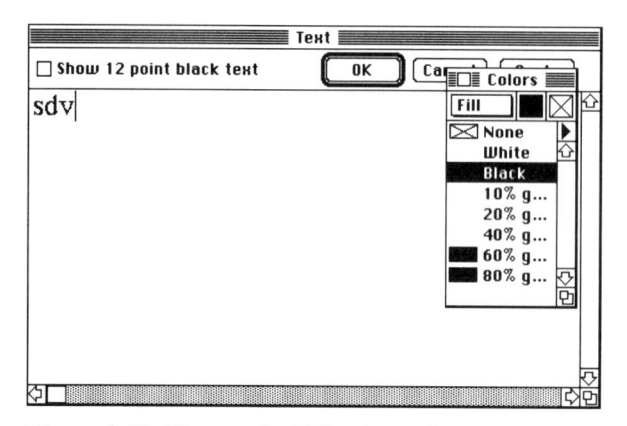

Figure 2.38 Change the Fill color to Black and type your initials

Step 25

Click OK or press Enter to close the dialog box. (This is the only dialog box in which pressing Return does *not* close the box—instead, pressing Return adds a carriage return and moves the text cursor to a new line.)

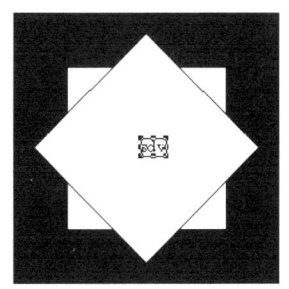

Figure 2.39 Text displayed on the page

Notice that the text is selected, as indicated by a visible frame with six handles. This frame disappears when text is deselected, as you will notice later in this tutorial.

Selecting and Editing Text

Step 26

Make sure that the text of your initials is selected, that is, framed in a box with eight handles. If it is not, activate the Pointer tool—either by holding down the Command key or by clicking the Pointer tool in the Toolbox—and click once on the text to select it.

CAUTION

You cannot select the text on the artwork with the I-beam pointer (that is, when the Text tool is active). If you try to click the text in the artwork, a blank Text dialog box will again be displayed for you to type new text. If you open this dialog box by mistake, simply click Cancel to close the dialog box, then select the text with the Pointer tool.

Step 27

Choose Type specs from the Type menu (⌘T) to display the Type specifications dialog box. Make the text 72-pt bold by making choices from the Size and Style pop-up menus. Choose center alignment by clicking the Center icon—the second alignment icon in the dialog box (▤). Select any font you wish from the Font pop-up menu. Then click OK.

(As described earlier in this chapter, any dialog box edit box that is framed by a drop-shadowed box is a pop-up menu. You display the menu by positioning the pointer over the right-pointing arrow in the Size edit box, or over the text in the Style edit box, then dragging to highlight your desired selection and releasing the mouse button.)

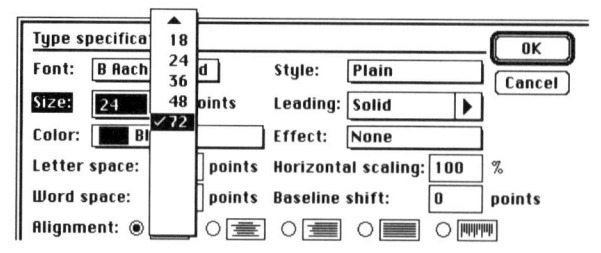

Figure 2.40 Type specifications dialog box with Size pop-up menu

Next you will edit the text that you have already typed. Remember that you cannot select text on the artwork with the I-beam pointer. Hold down the Command key to get the Pointer tool, or select the tool from the Toolbox, then double-click the text with the Pointer tool to display the Text dialog box with the text you have typed. Add your middle initial (if you did not type it already) or remove it if you did type it. Do not close the dialog box until the next step.

You edit text in the Text dialog box the same way you edit text on the desktop (such as file names and folder names) or in most Macintosh applications. Position the I-beam pointer within a line of text and click once to position the pointer for inserting text. Double-click a word to select the whole word, or drag the I-beam pointer over a range of characters to select them, and then type to replace the selection. The Text tool and the Text dialog box are explained in detail in Part IV.

Step 28

In the Text dialog box, drag the I-beam pointer over the text to select it, then choose Inline from the Effect command submenu in the Type menu. The Inline dialog box lets you set the widths of the background and stroke of the Inline type, but for now simply click OK to close the dialog box and accept the default settings.

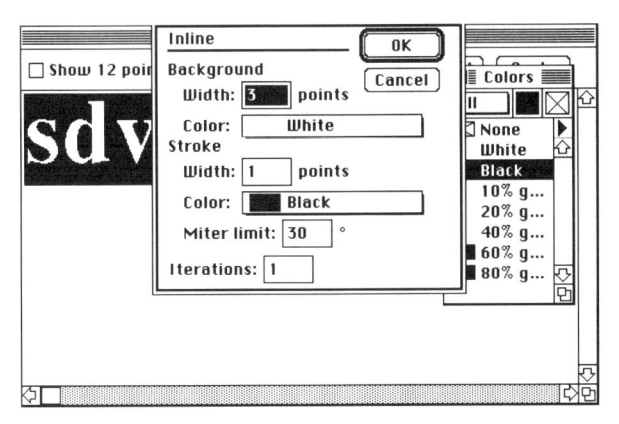

Figure 2.41 Inline type dialog box

When you close the Inline dialog box, you do not see the Inline type effect in the Text dialog box. Close the Text dialog box by clicking OK or pressing Enter to see the Inline type effect on the artwork.

Notice that there are often two or more ways of performing the most common operations in FreeHand. You can format type using submenus of commands in the Type menu, or you can make the same selections in the Type specifications dialog box. You can apply these commands to whole blocks of text selected on the artwork with the Pointer tool, or you can apply the specifications to selected characters only in the Text dialog box.

Step 29

Activate the Pointer tool using any of the techniques you have learned and drag the text to the center of the squares.

Figure 2.42 Text centered in rectangles

Step 30

In the current Fit in window view, the Inline type effect looks like a gray shadow around the type (if it shows at all). Enlarge the view by holding down the Command key and the Space bar to get the Magnifying tool (🔍), and click twice on the text in the artwork to enlarge the view.

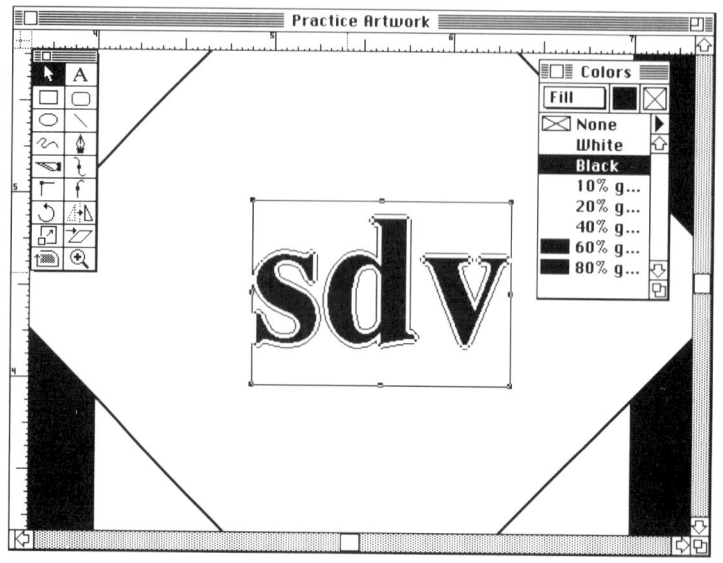

Figure 2.43 Enlarged view of text

You can now see that Inline type is type with an outline around it.

Save

Step 31

Choose the Save command from the File menu, or use the keyboard shortcut, ⌘S.

Remember that when you used the Save command for the first time you got a dialog box that asked you to name the file and tell FreeHand where to save it. Subsequently, whenever you use the Save command FreeHand simply updates the same file. If you want to save the file again without overwriting the first file, you can use the Save as command, as described in Chapter 14.

Print

Step 32

If you have a printer hooked up to your system, choose the Print command from the File menu (⌘P) and then click OK or press Return to close the dialog box and accept all of the defaults for printing.

Figure 2.44 The Print dialog box

The Print command and all of the dialog box options are explained in detail in Chapter 14.

Quit

Step 33

Whenever you want to stop using FreeHand, choose Quit from the File menu or use the keyboard shortcut, ⌘Q.

If you have not saved your work, FreeHand will prompt you to do so whenever you quit the program.

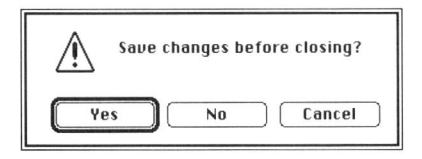

Figure 2.45 Prompt asking if you want to save your latest changes

Step 34

Click Yes to save the changes you have made since the last Save, or click No—do not save the latest changes to the artwork—if you want to cancel any changes you have made since you last saved the artwork. The previous version will still remain on disk.

Summary

You should now be familiar with some of the basic concepts and terminology that you will encounter in learning FreeHand.

The next part of this book presents descriptions of techniques that you can use to create artwork in FreeHand. These techniques are grouped by category (alignment, lines, shapes, etc.).

CAUTION

In addition to the Rectangle tool that you used in earlier steps of this tutorial, the drawing tools in FreeHand include the Rounded-rectangle tool and the Ellipse tool (which operate the same way as the Rectangle tool), the Freehand tool, the Pen tool, the Curve tool, the Corner tool, and the Connector tool. If you are not already familiar with these tools, we recommend that you study and try the methods of using these tools as described in Part IV before attempting some of the techniques described in Part II.

■ Part II ■

Techniques

This part of the book presents over 72 different techniques for achieving specific effects that can be applied to a wide range of applications. Variations of these techniques can be used to create the particular effects you wish to apply in your own artwork.

These chapters are not intended to be read or followed sequentially. We recommend that you simply skim through these chapters, quickly looking at the illustrations for each technique, so you become familiar with the information vailable here. Then, look up techniques as needed while you are developing your own artwork.

If you are using FreeHand for the first time we recommend that you read and try the procedures described in Chapter 11 for using the tools, especially the pen tool, before going through these chapters.

The techniques are divided into seven basic categories:

CHAPTER	DESCRIPTION
3. Lines and Curves	Techniques for creating dotted lines, lines with a hand-drawn look, and parallel curves.
4. Shapes	Techniques for creating arrows, bar charts, organization charts, pie charts, polygons, symmetrical designs, objects that share irregular borders, star shapes, and solid objects with "see-through" holes cut out of the center.
5. Three-Dimensional Effects	Techniques for drawing cubes, coils, drop shadows, flowers, and highlights.
6. Fills and Patterns	Techniques for creating custom fill patterns, blending colors, masking, and using a custom paint palette for quickly selecting the Fill and Line Color settings you want to use repeatedly in developing complex or multiple pages of artwork.

7. Working with Text	Techniques for aligning text in tabular columns, horizontally and vertically, and on a curved path.
8. Alignment and Spacing	Techniques for aligning objects, measuring objects, and creating grids as backgrounds for artwork that requires careful alignment.
9. Working in Layers	Techniques for working in layers, including creating compound lines, hiding parts of artwork, and creating overlays.

3

Lines and Curves (Paths)

FreeHand (like other PostScript-based drawing applications) calls any line or curve a *path*. Paths may be composed of both curved and straight line segments, and may be open (lines or curves) or closed (shapes). An *open* path has two endpoints; a *closed* path or solid shape has no endpoints—all points are connected to each other. The anchor points along curves usually have *curve handles*. Each of these elements is shown in the figure below.

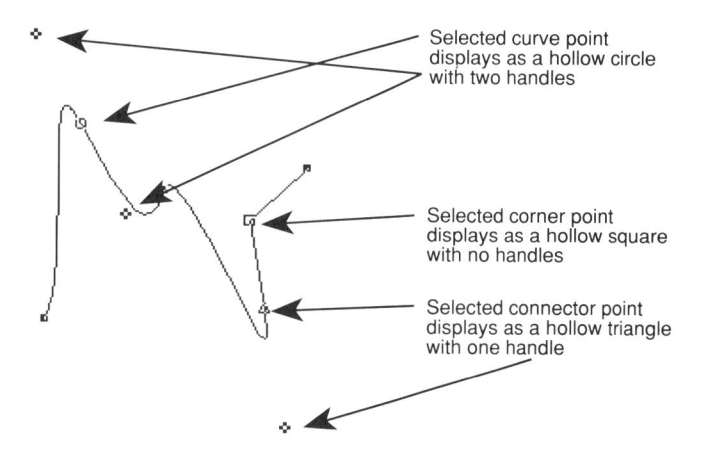

Selected curve point displays as a hollow circle with two handles

Selected corner point displays as a hollow square with no handles

Selected connector point displays as a hollow triangle with one handle

The drawing tool descriptions in Chapter 12 explain how to create and modify paths. This chapter summarizes the basic steps in drawing a line or curve and then goes beyond the basics by describing how to create special effects related to the appearance of the *line* (i.e., not the *fill*).

Techniques described in this chapter include:

- Drawing Curves and Lines
- Dashed and Dotted Lines
- Compound Lines
- Compound Dashed Lines
- Compound Arrows
- Using Dashed Lines as Rectangles and Ellipses
- Ribbons
- Parallel Curves
- Hand-Drawn Looks (3 techniques)
- Quadrille Rules

These effects can be applied to open or closed paths, but techniques more specific to closed paths are described in the next chapter, "Shapes (Closed Paths)." We recommend that you review this chapter so you are familiar with the range of possibilities in creating lines and curves, then refer back to this chapter and the reference chapters in Part IV as needed when you are creating an illustration.

Drawing Curves and Lines

FreeHand has four freeform drawing tools that can be used to draw curves and lines. The Freehand tool and the Pen tool are the most commonly used, and these are supplemented by the Curve tool, the Corner tool, and the Connector tool. These tools and the types of paths they create are described thoroughly in Chapter 12, the reference chapter on tools. Here we simply summarize the methods of drawing complex curves by manually drawing eight familiar symbols composed of simple lines and curves: the numbers 1 through 8.

This is not a lesson in creating your own numerals—you can use text more easily for that. It just so happens that the numbers offer a range of challenges in using the Pen tool: straight lines, curves, corner points, open paths, and closed paths. By following these steps, you should learn enough to be able to draw any path you can imagine.

In all of these steps, you can work at any scale you like, but choose a magnification such that the number you are creating fills as much as one-fourth of the screen—roughly centered.

The Number 1: Straight Lines

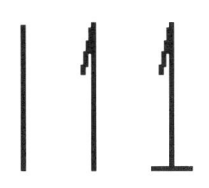

The number 1 is the simplest to draw: Select the Line tool (\) and Shift-drag the mouse vertically (leftmost figure). You can select any line width you wish from the Attributes menu. The numbers at left use a 2-point line weight.

If you want to be more formal, you can use the Pen tool to create a number 1 with a serif at the top (on previous page). First select the Pen tool ( ) and click once on the page in the document window to position the endpoint of the serif. Then release the mouse button and move the pointer up and to the right (diagonally) and click again to create the point at the top of the number. Next, move the pointer down and click again to create the bottom of the number. When you are finished, press Tab to deselect all points.

NOTE

The Line tool can only create straight lines with two endpoints, i.e., a single-segment path. The Pen tool can create single-segment straight lines or lines that are joined to other straight-line segments or curve segments.

The most formal number 1 includes a serif at the bottom of the number as well as the top (rightmost figure, previous page). With the Pen tool still selected, and no points selected, click once to the left of the bottom point of the number, and hold down the Shift key (to force the serif to be horizontal) as you click again to the right of the number.

NOTE

Holding down the Shift key constrains movements to 45-degree angle increments.

This number 1 is now composed of two paths. If you want to be able to move them and transform them as a unit, you can use the Pointer tool to select them both and then use the Group command from the Element menu (⌘G).

The Number 2: Mixed Curves and Straight Lines

The number 2 is a curved line connected to a straight line. You can try drawing this number with the Freehand tool, but you might find this difficult to control precisely (see the figure on the left). A better way is to use the Pen tool, as described in the next steps.

1

For the purposes of following this exercise, make the grid visible (if it is not already displayed as a pattern of dots on your screen) by choosing Grid from the View menu. Use the Magnifying tool (or the 100% or 200% option from the Magnification command submenu in the View menu) to enlarge your view of the grid on the page.

2

Select the Pen tool and position it on the page in the document window as you would if the pointer were truly a pen in your hand and you wanted to draw the number 2—at the top left end of the number. In this case, position it on a visible point of the grid.

Hold down the mouse button and drag the mouse straight up, to the next grid point, then release the mouse button. You will not see a line segment on the page until you position a second point. (By the way, it does not matter exactly what size numbers you create in this exercise, so it does not matter what your grid increments are, or what magnification you are working in.)

3

Next, position the pointer two grid points to the right of the first point, then hold down the mouse button and drag down. As you drag, you will see a curved line segment forming between the two points. You can change the shape of the curve by changing the distance and direction of the drag—and you can experiment as much as you like so long as you are holding down the mouse button. You can see that you are also affecting two curve handles as you drag—the handle of the segment you can see changing as you drag is at the other end of a tangent line from the point you are dragging. The point you are dragging is the curve handle for the next segment you will create. Release the mouse button when the pointer is approximately one grid point below the curve point you are creating.

4

Next position the pointer two grid points below the first point and simply click—this creates a corner point at the base of the number.

NOTE

A corner point can join two straight line segments, as you did at the top of the number 1, or a curve segment and a straight segment, as you are about to do now, or two curve segments, as you will do in creating the number 3. The difference between a curve point and a corner point is that the direction handles for the two curves extending from a curve point are always at the end of a straight-line tangent to the curve point (and if you change the angle of one of the direction levers, the opposite handle also moves), whereas the two handles of a corner point can be moved independently of each other.

5

Finally, hold down the Shift key as you click two grid points to the right of the last point. The Shift key forces a horizontal line. The figure on the left shows the path with black points where you positioned them. The last point is a hollow square indicating that it is selected.

6

Press Tab to deselect all points before going on to a new element. (Otherwise, the next point you position with the Pen tool will be connected to this endpoint of the number 2.) The path shows no points when it is deselected.

The Number 3: Two Curves with a Corner Point

The number 3 is composed of two curve segments, joined by a corner point in the middle where the direction of the lines changes abruptly.

1

Begin this number as you did the number 2. Select the Pen tool and position it on the page in the document window at the top left end of the number. Hold down the mouse button and drag the mouse straight up one grid point, then release the mouse button. (Again, it does not matter exactly how far you drag the mouse.)

Next, position the pointer two grid points to the right of the first point, then hold down the mouse button and drag down one grid point and release the mouse button. As you drag, you will see a curved line segment forming between the two points.

2

Next, position the pointer one grid point down and to the left of the last point—halfway between the two first points and below them—and hold down the mouse button as you drag about one-half the distance between grid points to the left. *Do not release the mouse button yet!* (If you release the mouse button by accident, you should press Tab to deselect all points and start drawing the number again from scratch. See "Pen Tool" in Chapter 12 for a detailed description of how to edit a path as you are working.)

Still holding down the mouse button, hold down the Option key and drag to the right, one-half the distance between grid points after the point. By holding down the Option key, you are dragging the direction handle for the outgoing curve segment only—the direction point for the incoming curve segment remains unchanged. This will have the effect of changing a curve point to a corner point, to create the sharp corner at the center of the number 3, but you will not see the corner until you position the next point. Release the mouse button when the two direction handles for the point are in approximately the same position.

NOTE

After positioning a point with the Pen tool and dragging a direction handle, holding down the Option key and dragging in another direction changes a curve point to a corner point as you are drawing. This enables you to move the outgoing segment's direction handle independently of the incoming segment's handle.

3

Position the pointer on the fourth point of the number 3—two grid points below the second point you positioned—and drag down one grid point.

4

Finally, position the fifth and last point two grid points to the left of the fourth and drag up one grid point.

5

Press the Tab key to deselect all points.

The Number 4: 45-Degree Angles

The number 4 can be created as a single open path or as two open paths. The next steps take you through both variations, using the Shift key to force 45-degree lines as appropriate.

1

To create the number 4 as two open paths, the mouse follows the pattern of movement commonly used in printing the number 4 by hand. Select the Pen tool and click once at the top of the 4. Then move the pointer down and to the left and click again. Next, hold down the Shift key (to force a horizontal line) and click to the right. This forms the "L" component of the number.

2

Press the Tab key to deselect all points, then click the Pen tool again at the top of the number, and hold down the Shift key to force a vertical line as you click the bottom of the number.

Press the Tab key to deselect all points.

3

To combine the two elements, hold down the Command key (to activate the Pointer tool) and the Shift key (to multiple-select objects), and click each element of the number. Then choose the Group command from the Element menu (⌘G).

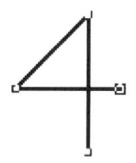

4

If you want the number to be a single open path, select the Pen tool and start drawing at the bottom of the number. Click once to position the bottom point, hold down the Shift key to force a vertical line and click to position the top point. Hold down the Shift key to force a 45-degree line and click to the left of the middle of the vertical line. Then hold down the Shift key to force a horizontal line and click to the right of the vertical line.

Press the Tab key to deselect all points.

The Numbers 5 and 6: Review the Principles

The numbers 5 and 6 can be created using techniques you have already learned in drawing numbers 1 through 4. They are drawn here, however, to practice the principles learned in the previous steps and to demonstrate the creation and use of direction handles in more detail.

1

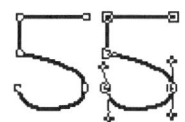

The simplest number 5 is composed of three corner points and two curve points. Use the Pen tool to click the first point at the top right of the 5. Shift-click the second and third points (to force a horizontal and a vertical line), drag down the fourth point, and drag up the last point. The figure on the left shows the resulting number with the path selected (to show the points) and with the points selected (to show the direction handles).

NOTE

When you click on a path to select it with the Pointer tool, all points along the path are displayed. When you click on a point to select it, the selected point shows handles. The handles of corner points are inside the hollow point.

2

If you want to change the shape of a path, you can select one of its points with the Pointer tool (to display the curve handles) and move the handle. You can change the depth of the curve by extending or shortening the direction levers (i.e., the distance of the handle from the point). You can change the angle of the curve by changing the angle of the curve levers. If you move a handle from one side of the point to another, you have the effect of twisting the two curve segments that extend from the point (see figure on the left).

NOTE

You can opt to display or not display the curve levers by checking Display curve levers in the Preferences dialog box, displayed by using the Preferences command in the File menu.

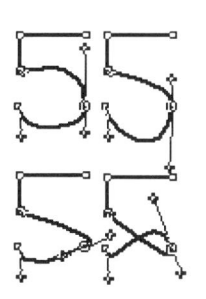

3

You can move the handles of a straight line segment by selecting the point with the Pointer tool, then holding down the Option key and dragging from the center of the point—the first handle you drag out will be the outgoing line segment's handle. You can Option-drag again to get the incoming line segment's handle.

4

Remember to press the Tab key to deselect all points before going on to draw a new element with the Pen tool (or any of the freeform drawing tools).

5

The number 6 is a relatively simple continuous curve with no straight segments or corners. Select the Pen tool and create the top point by positioning the pointer and dragging down and to the left at about a 45-degree angle. You can hold down the Shift key while dragging to force a 45-degree drag.

6

Position a second point directly below the first and drag to the right, holding down the Shift key to force a horizontal drag. Drag as far as you need to in order to get the backbone of the 6 shaped as you like.

7

Finally, position a third point just below the middle of the backbone and drag down and to the left, holding down the Shift key to force a 45-degree drag. Drag as far as you need to in order to get the bowl of the 6 shaped as you like.

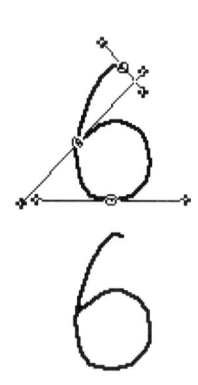

TIP

Position as few points as possible in creating a path. This makes the path easier to edit, and takes up less disk space for storing the file.

8

Press the Tab key to deselect all points before going on to a new element.

The Number 7: Drawn and Traced

All of the numbers we have created are composed of open paths—you can change the thickness, color, and line style of the paths but you cannot fill them with a color or pattern. There is a simple way to create a closed path that outlines an open path—by using the Tracing tool.

In the next steps, you will draw a number 7 as an open path, then use the Tracing tool to create a hollow closed path.

1

To create the number 7 simply select the Pen tool and click three points. You can force 45-degree angles by holding down the Shift key as you click. You can give the number a curved back by dragging the third point instead of clicking. Remember to press the Tab key to deselect all points before starting a new element.

2

Select the path and choose a thick line weight from the Attributes menu.

3

Select the Tracing tool ( ) and drag a selection marquee around the path—the Tracing tool will draw an outline around the path. You can drag the outline away from the original path (or delete the original) and give it different line styles and fills.

The Number 8: Traced Composite Paths

Drawing the number 8 uses the same skills you learned in earlier steps, but we use the number 8 to demonstrate another variation of the effect of the Tracing tool—the creation of several paths that can be joined into a single composite path.

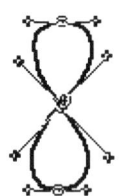

1

Select the Pen tool, position the pointer at the center of the number and drag up and to the left—holding down the Shift key to force a 45-degree drag. Position a second point at the top of the 8 and hold down the Shift key as you drag to the right. Position the third point next to *but not on top of* the first point and hold down the Shift key as you drag down and to the left. Position the next point at the bottom of the 8 and hold down the Shift key as you drag to the right. Position the last point *on top of* the first point and hold down the Shift key as you drag up and to the left.

As soon as you complete the final point that closes the path, the number takes on the current fill pattern.

Chapter 3. Lines and Curves (Paths) 71

NOTE

If you position the third point on top of the first, you close the path prematurely. Delete all the points and start the number again, or see the description of editing techniques under "Pen Tool" in Chapter 12.

2

Next, select the number and choose a thick line weight from the Attributes menu (if it is not still active after creating the number 7). Select the Tracing tool and drag a selection marquee around the number.

The results in this case depend on the fill assigned to the closed-path number 8. To see the results most clearly, drag the traced path(s) away from the original immediately—while they are still selected after the tracing process—using the Pointer tool or the Move command from the Edit menu (⌘M).

If the original number is filled with black or any color or tint (leftmost figure), the Tracing tool outlines the whole figure (rightmost figure). The resulting object takes on the current line style and fill (center figure).

If the original closed path has a fill of None or White (leftmost figure), the Tracing tool traces the outer edge of the 8 plus the inner edges of the two hollow spaces in the 8—thus creating three objects, an outside outline plus two inside outlines (rightmost figure).

3

If you assign a fill to the trace results, all three objects become filled (leftmost figure). You can fill the center holes with white, or you can make them into actual "holes" in the object (rightmost figure) by selecting all three elements and choosing Join elements from the Element menu (⌘J).

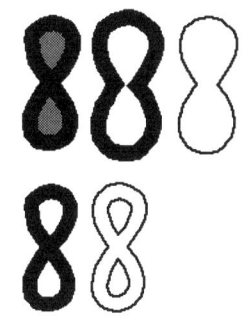

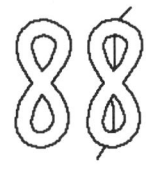

Dashed and Dotted Lines

FreeHand offers nine different dashed line styles (plus a solid line) that you can apply to any path with the Fill and line command. Dashed lines are useful for architectural and schematic drawings, and they provide a great way to indicate movement or sequential steps of a process. Dashed lines can also be used to add tab leaders to tabular text formats.

You can select a dashed line pattern by opening the pop-up menu of dashes in the Fill and line dialog box—that is, choose Fill and line from the Attributes menu (⌘E), select the Basic line style, then position the mouse over the Dash pop-up menu and drag to select one of the dash patterns listed.

You can view and modify the lengths of the dashes and the gaps between them, and create custom dashed lines, by holding down the Option key as you select a dashed line from the pop-up menu of dashes in the Fill and line dialog box. In the Dash pattern dialog box, you can set one or more distances for which the dash is On and set the gap after each dash as the Off distance (see "Fill and line" in Chapter 14). The initial set of lines and their gaps are shown next to an example of each dash pattern in the figure below.

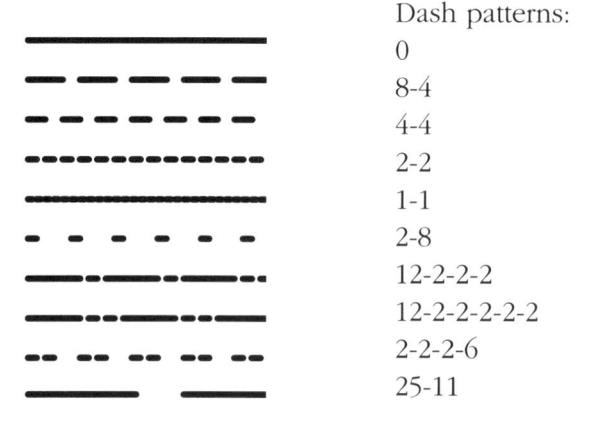

Dash patterns:
0
8-4
4-4
2-2
1-1
2-8
12-2-2-2
12-2-2-2-2-2
2-2-2-6
25-11

The caps you select in the Fill and line dialog box will be applied to the ends of each dash. If you choose the second or third Cap option in the Fill and line dialog box (rounded ends or extended blunt ends), the ends of the dashes will extend into the gap area, thereby making the gap smaller than the distance specified in the Dash pattern dialog box. Notice that most of the original default set of dashed lines have gaps of only 2 points. This means that the gaps will fill in completely when you make dashed lines wider than 2 points and choose rounded ends or extended blunt ends.

TIP

You can make straight lines end on a full dash by making the line length equal to a multiple of the sum of the lengths of the dashes and gaps in the line, minus the size of the last gap. The figure on the left shows a line with a 24-point dash and a 6-point gap drawn in two sizes: 84 points (3*(24+6)-6), and 104 points (not a multiple of the dash/gap size).

You can make lines of perfect squares by making the line weight equal to the dash pattern. The figure at left shows a 24-point line weight and a 24-point dash length with a 6-point gap. The first Cap option in the Fill and line dialog box should be selected (blunt ends).

You can also create custom lines of dots (circles) or squares by following the next steps.

1

Draw a line or shape using one of the freehand drawing tools (i.e., the Line tool, the Pen tool, the Freehand tool, or the Tracing tool). This figure shows a curved line drawn with the Pen tool.

2

With the line still selected, choose Fill and line from the Attributes menu (⌘E) to set Fill to None, Line Color to any percentage of black or a color, and Weight to a point size equal to the width measurement of the dots you wish to create. In this example, we used a weight of 30 points. Click the second choice under Cap (the round ends) for a line of circular dots (top figure), or the third choice (the extended blunt ends) for a line of squares (bottom).

3

Hold down the Option key as you choose any dashed line style from the Dash pop-up menu to get the Line pattern dialog box. In the first On box, type "1" which creates either perfect circles or squares. In the first Off box, type a gap size—making it larger than the point size you chose for the line weight—36 points, for example. All other boxes should show zeros.

CAUTION

If the gap size is equal to the line weight, you create a string of pearls in which each dot touches the next. Smaller gap sizes result in overlapping dots. If you type a number of greater value in the first box, you will get oblong circles and rectangles instead of circles and squares.

TIP

If you use dashed lines a lot you can make them a style, so you can choose them directly from the Styles palette instead of opening the Fill and line dialog box repeatedly. It is a good idea to include the line/gap sizes in the name.

See also "Compound Dashed Lines" in this chapter for examples of layered dashed lines.

Compound Lines

Compound lines consist of two overlapping lines: a black or colored line on the bottom layer, and a slightly thinner, lighter-colored line on top. The lines created by this technique can appear to be one line with a fill color or pattern that is different from the line color at the outer edge of the line—such as the effect shown in the accompanying figure.

The steps listed here create an element composed of a solid black line with a thinner, dashed white line on top, as illustrated in the figure, but you can use the same technique to create a variety of effects.

You can use these types of lines in maps to represent roads or trails or railway lines. You can also use them in line graphs, floor plans, and other schematic drawings. You can apply the same technique to the borders (strokes) of two-dimensional shapes (such as rectangles, circles, or polygons).

1

Use one of the freehand drawing tools to draw the whole path (such as a train line on a map), then choose Fill and line from the Attributes menu (⌘E) to set the attributes of the lower line. The bottom layer in this example has the attributes of 100% black line color, no fill, and 8-point weight. When you are done, click OK.

2

With the line still selected (but no individual points selected), choose Clone from the Edit menu (⌘=) to make a duplicate of the line, layered on top of the first. Set the top line's attributes by choosing Fill and line from the Attributes menu (⌘E). The weight should be lower than the bottom line. In this example we use white line color and 4-point line weight. Use the technique described in "Dashed and Dotted Lines" (the previous technique in this chapter) to create a custom dashed line with 12-point dashes and gaps. Click OK when you are done.

3

Make adjustments to the line weights if necessary to get the look you want. Because the two paths that compose the curving parallel lines overlap precisely, use the following techniques to select and edit lines:

To select the top line only, click with the Pointer tool on the top line.

To select both lines (if you need to move them), hold down the Control key (to select elements under a stack) and the Shift key (to multiple select) as you click with the Pointer tool on any part of the layered lines (see "Pointer Tool" in Chapter 12).

To select the bottom line only, use the technique just described to select both paths, then hold down the Shift key and click the top line to deselect it.

4

You can group the layered lines using Group from the Element menu (⌘G), but you will not be able to change the attributes of the lines globally unless you ungroup and select layers one by one.

5

If you want to add, delete, or move *part* of a route, first select the route lines and ungroup the two layers (if they are grouped) with the Ungroup command from the Element menu (⌘U). Then click the top layer to select it and press the Delete (Backspace) key to remove it. Then edit the bottom layer.

After changing the shape of the bottom line, select it (without selecting individual points) and choose Clone from the Edit menu (⌘=) to make a duplicate of the line, layered on top of the first. Then choose Fill and line from the Attributes menu (⌘E) to set the attributes to a white dashed line.

TIP

Create and print a test sheet to determine what attribute combinations would look best in the size you will use in the final artwork.

See also "Dashed and Dotted Lines," "Compound Dashed Lines," and "Parallel Curves" in this chapter.

Compound Dashed Lines

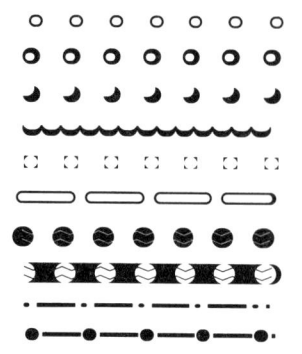

If you combine what you learned about dashed and dotted lines at the beginning of this chapter with the compound line technique, you can create fairly complex line patterns such as those shown in the figure on the left. Rather than go through step-by-step instructions here, we will give you the dash and gap specifications used to create the examples shown here, and you can get the steps from the previous two techniques.

Compound Dashed Line #1

Bottom Line: Black dashed 6-point line with rounded end caps (second Cap option) and a dash size of 1 point and a gap of 20 points.

Top Line: White dashed 4-point line with rounded end caps and a dash size of 1 point and a gap of 20 points.

The result appears to be a dotted line with 4-point white dots bordered by a 1-point black circle, as shown at left.

As long as the dots on each line are spaced the same distance apart, the apparent border size will be one-half of the difference between the line weights of the two lines. In this case, the 2-point difference in dot size yields the effect of a 1-point border. If you wanted a 2-point border, you would need a 4-point difference in line weights, as shown at left when the bottom line is 8 points wide.

Compound Dashed Line #2

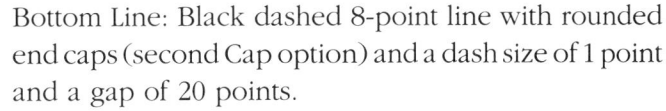

Bottom Line: Black dashed 8-point line with rounded end caps (second Cap option) and a dash size of 1 point and a gap of 20 points.

Top Line: White dashed 8-point line with rounded end caps and a dash size of 1 point and a gap of 20 points, cloned from the first line and then moved up and left 2 pixels. The line was moved by pressing the Up Arrow key twice and the Left Arrow key twice in 100% magnification.

The result is a dotted line with a drop-shadow effect, as shown at left.

Compound Dashed Line #3

Bottom Line: Black dashed 8-point line with rounded end caps and a dash size of 2 points and a gap of 8 points (one of the standard dash patterns that comes with FreeHand).

Top Line: White dashed 8-point line with rounded end caps and a dash size of 2 points and a gap of 8 points, cloned from the first line and moved up 3 pixels.

The result appears to be a line of waves, as shown at left.

Compound Dashed Line #4

Bottom Line: Black dashed 6-point line with extended butt end caps (third Cap option) and a dash size of 1 point and a gap of 20 points.

Top Line: White dashed 6-point line with rounded end caps and a dash size of 1 point and a gap of 20 points.

The result appears to be a line of 6-point white dots on black squares, as shown at left.

Compound Dashed Line #5

Bottom Line: Black dashed 6-point line with rounded end caps and a dash size of 25 points and a gap of 11 points (i.e., the eighth or last dashed line on the normal default menu of dashed lines).

Top Line: White dashed 4-point line with rounded end caps and a dash size of 25 points and a gap of 11 points.

The result appears to be a line of 4-point white lines with rounded ends, framed by a 1-point black border, as shown at left.

Compound Dashed Line #6

Bottom Line: Black dashed 10-point line with rounded end caps and a dash size of 1 point and a gap of 20 points.

Top Line: White wavy line is one of FreeHand's built-in "Custom" line styles: Two Waves. Note that you cannot make a custom line white through the Fill and line dialog box, but you can apply color through the Colors palette.

The result appears to be a line of 10-point black dots with white wave patterns inside each, as shown at left.

NOTE

You cannot see custom line styles on the screen—you have to print them. On-screen, they appear as solid lines.

Compound Dashed Line #7

Bottom Line: Black 10-point line with rounded end caps.

Next Line: White dashed 10-point line with rounded end caps and a dash size of 1 point and a gap of 20 points.

Top Line: Black line one of FreeHand's built-in "Custom" line styles: Two Waves.

Compound Dashed Line #8

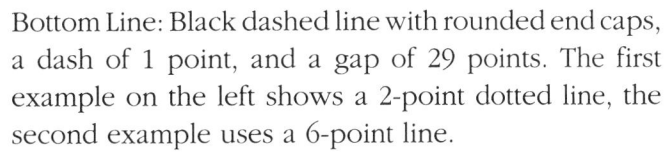

Bottom Line: Black dashed line with rounded end caps, a dash of 1 point, and a gap of 29 points. The first example on the left shows a 2-point dotted line, the second example uses a 6-point line.

Top Line: Black 2-point dashed line with butt end caps (first Cap option), a dash of 20 points, and a gap of 10 points. This line is cloned from the first line and then moved 5 points to the right using the Move command from the Edit menu (⌘M).

TIP

The key to creating lines that overlap but use different dash/gap settings is that the sum of the dash length plus the gap length is the same for both lines—30 in this case. The offset distance is half the gap size of the line that you move.

As you can imagine, there are millions of variations you can create by overlaying lines of different dash patterns and colors, and by overlaying three or more lines at a time.

Compound Arrows

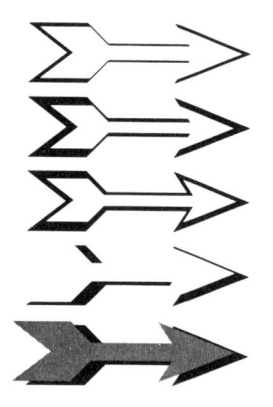

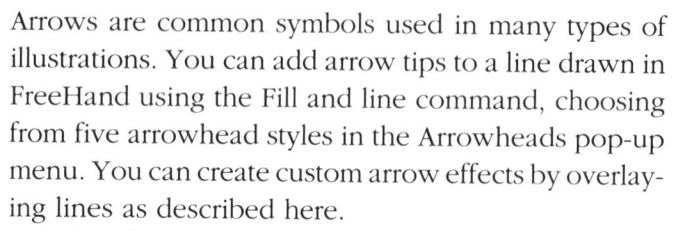

Arrows are common symbols used in many types of illustrations. You can add arrow tips to a line drawn in FreeHand using the Fill and line command, choosing from five arrowhead styles in the Arrowheads pop-up menu. You can create custom arrow effects by overlaying lines as described here.

Rather than go through step-by-step instructions, we will give you the line specifications used to create the following examples. You can get the steps from the compound dashed lines technique described earlier.

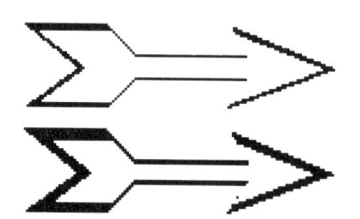

Compound Arrows #1

The simplest custom arrow effect is achieved by overlaying two lines with the same arrow head, but giving the top line a smaller line weight. The top example on the left shows a 10-point black arrow under an 8-point white arrow. The second example shows a 10-point black arrow under a 6-point white arrow.

In both examples, you can see that the lines that frame the length of the arrow appear thinner than the lines at the ends of the arrow. This is a result of how FreeHand creates the arrow tips: the borders along the length of the arrow are *half* the difference between the two line weights, but the borders at each end of the arrow are *equal* to the difference between the two line weights.

Compound Arrows #2

You can get a more even border effect by making the line for the top arrow slightly longer than the bottom line. Taking the two arrows created above, you can lengthen the white arrow in the first example by one point in each direction (i.e., by *half* the difference between the two line weights). You can lengthen the white arrow in the second example by two points in each direction. The results are shown on the previous page.

The easiest way to do this is to start by creating the bottom arrow, then choose Clone from the Edit menu (⌘=) to make a copy on top of it. Choose Fill and line from the Attributes menu (⌘E) to change the top line to white and give it the smaller line weight. Then use the Pointer tool to select the left endpoint of the top line, and press the Left Arrow key to move it one pixel distance while in 100% view.

TIP
In 100% view, one pixel is close to one point on a 72 dpi screen. If the cursor key distance is set at one pixel (through the Preferences command), selected objects move approximately one point each time you press an arrow key.

Compound Arrows #3

The arrows become more dramatic when the overlaid arrow is offset slightly from the one below, creating a drop-shadow effect. In the examples shown at left, the top and bottom arrows are both the same line weights. You can use the Arrow keys as described above to move the top arrow one pixel or point at a time. The effect works best if the top arrow is given a shade of black or a color, rather than made white.

TIP
You can also create arrows as text characters using symbol fonts such as Zapf Dingbats (see figure), or you can create your own arrows using the technique described under "Symmetry" in Chapter 4.

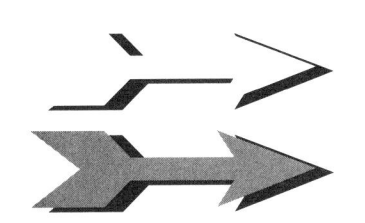

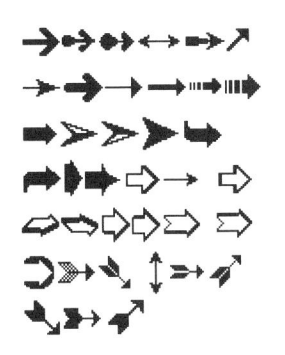

Using Dashed Lines as Rectangles or Ellipses

You can simplify your artwork and save disk space by using dashed lines instead of rectangles or ellipses. This is useful when you want the effect of shaded bands of color as a background to text or graphics. The only limitation is that lines cannot be wider than 288 points, and dashed segments cannot be wider than 200 points.

Here are some examples:

Dashed Lines as Text Background

You can use a dashed line as a decorative background to text. In lists that are printed in a small font, the alternating gray/white bars can actually serve as a reading aid.

In the example shown below, the text is set in 10-point Times and the dashed vertical line is set in 30% gray with 260 points weight (the width of the background for the text). The dash and gap distance are each set at 10 points (so the dashes and gaps coincide with the lines of 10-point text). (See "Aligning Text" in Chapter 8.)

Time	Events	Room
8:00 am	Registration	Lobby
9:00 am	Session 1: *Crisis in Education*	Room A
10:15 am	Break with Coffee and Pastry	Room B
10:45 am	Session 2: *Solutions in the Schools*	Room A
12:00 pm	Lunch with Keynote Speaker	Room C
2:00 pm	Session 3: *Solutions through Media*	Room A
3:15 pm	Break with Beverage Service	Room B
3:45 pm	Session 4: *Solutions at Home*	Room B
5:00 pm	Social Hour	Lobby

Dashed Lines as Grid Elements

In the calendar template shown at left, each week is composed of two overlaid dashed lines. Both lines are set at 72 weight, with 72-point dashes and 12-point gaps. The lower line is tinted 80% gray, the top line 30% gray.

The only other elements in the template are text: one text block for the month, plus seven text blocks for the days of the week. A close-up of the cell for one day is shown at left.

Dotted Lines as Design Elements

You can use the same principles as you learned earlier in this chapter for making compound lines to create design elements composed of large squares or circles. The only difference introduced here is that you must think big. The figure below shows a compound line composed of two 72-point dashed lines with rounded end caps, 1-point dashes, and 90-point gaps.

Ribbons

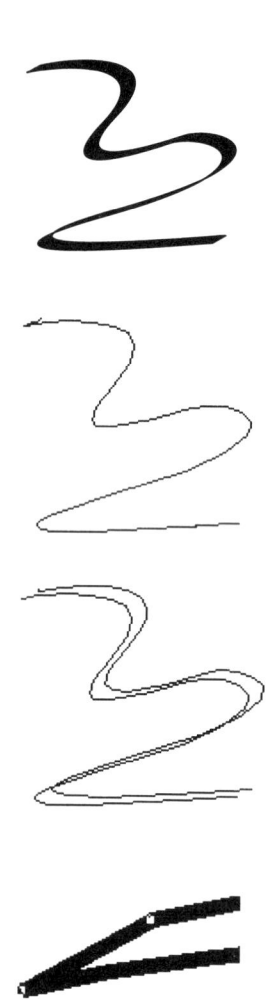

You can create a ribbon effect, or the look of a line created in calligraphy by a pen with a wide flat tip, by offsetting two identical curves as described here. (See the next technique for creating the appearance of two parallel curves that do not cross.)

1

Use one of the freeform drawing tools to draw a curve of the shape you want. The figure here shows a curve drawn with the Pen tool.

2

With the line still selected (but no individual points selected), choose Clone from the Edit menu (⌘=) to make a duplicate of the line. Then use the Pointer tool or the Arrow keys to drag the copy diagonally a short distance.

3

Use the Magnifying tool (holding down the Command key and the Space bar) to zoom into a close-up view of one end of the lines. Select the Line tool and drag a straight line segment from the end of one of the curved lines to the end of the other.

4

Use the Pointer tool to drag a selection marquee to encompass both ends of the line you just created and the endpoints of the curved paths. Then choose Join elements from the Element menu (⌘J).

5

Repeat steps 3 and 4 on the other ends of the curved lines.

6

Use the Colors palette or the Fill and line command from the Attributes menu (⌘E) to assign the line and fill color you wish.

Parallel Curves

Often you will need two parallel lines separated by a specific distance. If there are no curves in the line, you can draw one line and then drag away a copy. Trying to create curved parallel lines using this method poses a problem; the original line and the copy will not run parallel at the curves. As you learned in the previous technique, when a curved line is simply duplicated and moved you get a ribbon effect. Moreover, it is very difficult to place a small, precise distance between each line. This technique provides the solution—and you can make the lines as curved as you like!

Curving parallel lines are often used as the indication of a highway on a map.

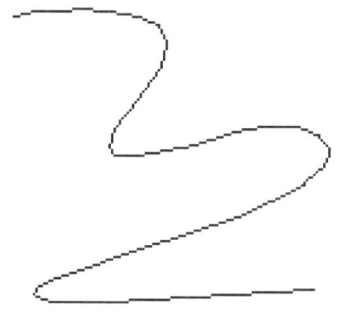

1

Draw a path using one of the freeform drawing tools. This figure shows a curved line drawn with the Pen tool.

2

With the line still selected, choose Fill and line from the Attributes menu (⌘E) to set Fill to None and Line Color to any percentage of black or a color to define the line color as you like. Do not click OK yet.

3

To set the line weight for the parallel lines, you use a formula, as follows. Decide which line weight you want for each parallel line and how many points of space you want between the parallel lines. Double your desired line weight and add in the number of points you want between the parallel lines. For example:

Chapter 3. Lines and Curves (Paths)   89

	2	pts	Line weight for each line
x	2	pts	Times 2
	4	pts	Line weight doubled
+	1.5	pts	Space between lines
	5.5	pts	Total entered as line weight

Type the total into the Weight box—5.5 points in this case—and click OK.

4

With the line selected (but no individual points selected), choose Clone from the Edit menu (⌘=) to make a duplicate of the line, layered on top of the first.

5

With the new copy of the line still selected, choose Fill and line from the Attributes menu (⌘E) and set Line Color to White and Weight to the number of points you decided in step 3 would separate the parallel lines—1.5 points in this case.

6

Make adjustments to the line weights if necessary to get the look you want. Use the selection methods described earlier in this chapter in "Compound Lines." (See also "Pointer Tool" in Chapter 12.)

7

When you have achieved the results you want, use the Pointer tool to drag a selection marquee over the curved parallel line path and choose Group from the Element menu (⌘G). (See "Compound Lines" above for methods of editing the lines.)

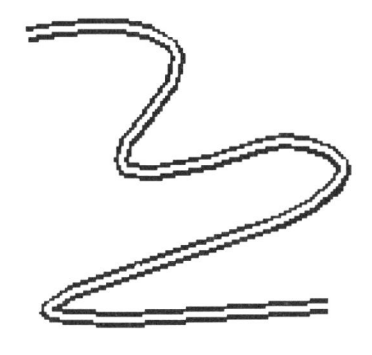

Hand-drawn Look: Method 1

You may want a line that has an uneven, hand-drawn look—one that seems to go from thick to thin, a line you might describe as calligraphic. It is easy to create this effect with FreeHand's layering features. You have complete control of the thickness of the line even after you have drawn it.

You can use this technique to create the effect of a hand-drawn or brush-stroked border around any solid shape (i.e., a closed path).

In this example, you will draw a cartoon balloon with an uneven black border.

1

Using one of the freeform drawing tools or the Tracing tool, create a closed shape, such as the cartoon balloon shape in this figure.

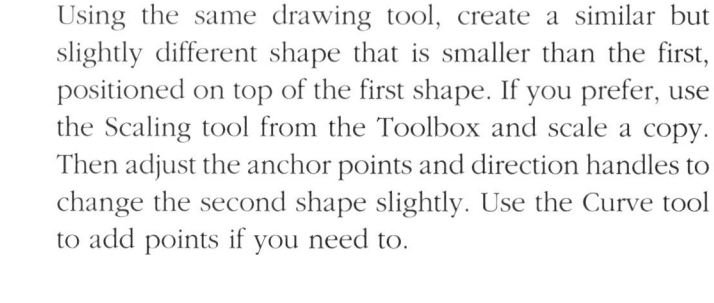

2

Using the same drawing tool, create a similar but slightly different shape that is smaller than the first, positioned on top of the first shape. If you prefer, use the Scaling tool from the Toolbox and scale a copy. Then adjust the anchor points and direction handles to change the second shape slightly. Use the Curve tool to add points if you need to.

3

With the inside shape still selected, choose Fill and line from the Attributes menu (⌘E) to set Fill and line to Basic style, White color (to match your paper color or background). For this effect to work, you usually want to match the fill and line colors to the desired background color. For this demonstration, assume you are drawing on a 30% gray background. Click OK to close the dialog box.

4

Select the larger object and choose Fill and line from the Attributes menu (⌘E) to set the line and fill color to the percentage of black or color that you wish for the hand-drawn line. The figure on the left shows the results when black is selected.

5

Refine the unevenness of the effect by moving the anchor points and direction handles to allow less or more of the black to show.

TIP

Here you have created a shape that can be filled with any color or pattern—it does not really have to match the background. You can also make the center a transparent "hole" by selecting both objects and choosing the Join elements command from the Elements menu (⌘J).

Hand-drawn Look: Method 2

In the preceding technique, you drew lines with a hand-drawn look around a solid shape. In this example, you will use a different technique to create the appearance of hand-drawn lines as open paths.

You can use this technique to add shading effects to solid figures, or to draw complete illustrations. The illustration on the left is composed entirely of elements created using the technique described here. The steps are shown for creating one of the S-shaped highlights near the top of the wing.

1

Using one of the freeform drawing tools or the Tracing tool, draw or trace the line you wish to represent as an open path. This figure shows a hand-drawn curved line drawn with the Freehand tool.

2

Select the Pointer tool and click on the line to select the whole path (without selecting any individual points), then choose Clone from the Edit menu (⌘=) to make a duplicate of the line, layered on top of the first.

3

Drag each anchor point, except the two endpoints, a slight distance away from the first position. Use the Curve tool to add anchor points if you need them.

4

Select both lines and choose Join elements from the Element menu (⌘J). You now have a solid shape, a closed path.

5

With the shape or some part of it still selected, choose Fill and line from the Attributes menu (⌘E) to set the fill to the percentage of black or color you wish the line to be. When you have set the attributes, click OK.

6

Refine the unevenness of the hand-drawn line by adjusting the anchor points and direction handles (see "Pen Tool" in Chapter 12) to create a thicker or thinner line. Use the Curve tool to add anchor points if you need them.

TIP

For a water-color effect where the color fades from dark (where the brush stroke starts) to light (where the stroke ends), choose a graduated fill.

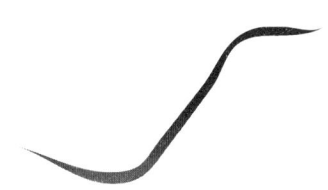

Hand-drawn Look: Method 3

With the Fill and line dialog box it is easy to specify perfectly black, inked lines of any weight. But sometimes you may want a softer, more irregular effect, such as a stipple effect or a sketched or brushed ink look. Here are some tips to help you create these effects in your drawings.

The illustration on the left is composed entirely of elements created with the technique described here. The steps are shown for creating one of the S-shaped highlights near the top of the wing.

1

Draw a line using one of the freeform drawing tools. The figure on the left shows a curved line drawn with the Pen tool.

2

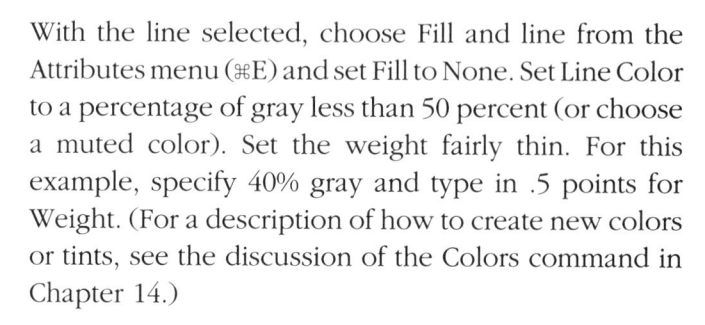

With the line selected, choose Fill and line from the Attributes menu (⌘E) and set Fill to None. Set Line Color to a percentage of gray less than 50 percent (or choose a muted color). Set the weight fairly thin. For this example, specify 40% gray and type in .5 points for Weight. (For a description of how to create new colors or tints, see the discussion of the Colors command in Chapter 14.)

TIP

There are countless variations on the suggestions listed here. You are encouraged to experiment with other paint settings. Create multiple copies of the line and set the line color to different percentages of black (still less than 50%), change the line weights, and try out different end caps.

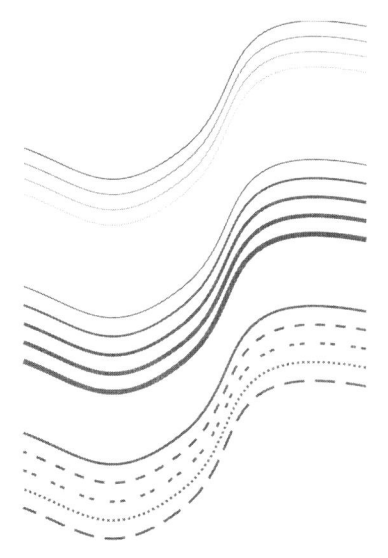

By using different percentages of black (or muted color) and different random dash patterns you can create lines in your final output resembling the etching effect created with a traditional tool called a roulette wheel. Type random values for the dash pattern and gaps. Dash values of 2 points or more will create short dashes. A dash value of 1 point and round end caps will create dots. Use the technique described at the beginning of this chapter for creating custom dashed lines and try entering irregular repeats, such as 1, 5, 1, 5, 2, 1.

Layer two paths with different paint settings over one another (see "Compound Lines" in this chapter).

You will find that thinner lines generally create subtler effects. Subtle line effects are difficult to preview on-screen. You probably will want to print a proof on a LaserWriter, or even a Linotronic, to fine-tune the effect. In either case, you can shorten the cycle of experimentation by setting up a variety of lines on one page and printing them all at once. Then decide which one you will use or modify for use in the final artwork.

See also "Dashed and Dotted Lines" and "Compound Lines" in this chapter.

96 *Using Aldus FreeHand 3.0*

Quadrille Rules

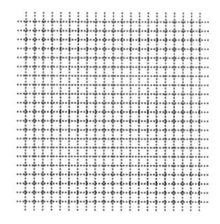

This technique shows you how to create a visible grid of squared rules that is a part of the artwork. You can use this type of grid as a design element or as an integral part of a technical drawing such as a floor plan.

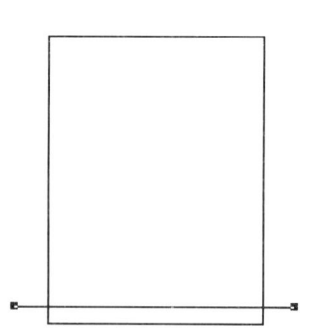

1

Select the Line tool and hold down the Shift key as you drag the mouse to draw a straight line across one of the short sides of the page or drawing area. Make the line at least as long as the long side of the page or drawing area—an 11-inch line across the bottom of an 8.5-inch wide page is shown in the figure on the left.

Note that in steps 1 and 3, the drawing area can be the entire page or a small area on the page. For large pages, perform steps 1 and 3 in the Fit in window view, which you choose from the Magnification command submenu in the View menu or by pressing ⌘W.

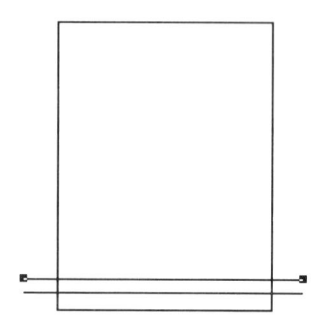

2

Hold down the Command key to get the Pointer tool, and click on the line to select the entire path. Choose Clone from the Edit menu (⌘=) to make a copy of the line, then choose Move from the Edit menu (⌘M) to get the Move dialog box. Select Vertical move by clicking this option, and enter a value in the Distance box (in points) that matches your desired grid size—for example, 36 points (1/2 inch). Click OK to close the dialog box and make a copy of the first line.

3

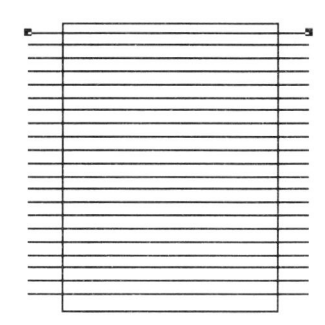

Choose Duplicate from the Edit menu (⌘D) as many times as you need to fill the image area with grid lines.

4

Choose Select all from the Edit menu (⌘A), and choose Group from the Element menu (⌘G). Then choose Clone from the Edit menu (⌘=) to make a copy of the lines. Select the Rotating tool and Option-click on the center of the grid to get the Rotate dialog box. Type "90" (degrees) in the Angle box, and click OK to close the box and rotate a copy of the horizontal lines to create a vertical grid.

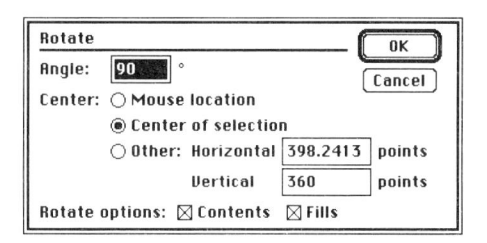

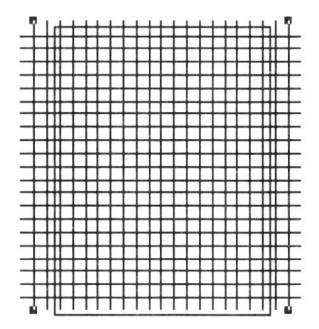

5

While the vertical grid lines are still selected, move them if necessary to center them over the horizontal grid lines.

6

Optionally, you can group or lock the grid (with the Group or the Lock command) or place it on a layer of its own.

4

Shapes (Closed Paths)

Remember that a *closed* path or solid shape has no endpoints—all points are connected to each other. This chapter describes techniques specific to closed paths. Closed paths can also be filled with shades or patterns, as described in Chapter 6.

There are two ways to close an open path. You can choose Element info from the Element menu, then click the check box marked "Closed" to close the path. Or, you can move the endpoints of the path so they are coincident, that is, in exactly the same location, then select both and choose Join elements from the Element menu.

You can also use the Join elements command to join the endpoints of two different paths. Again, the two points must be coincident for the Join elements command to work. There are several ways you can make sure the points are coincident.

- You can set the Snap-to-point distance using the Preferences command from the File menu. A setting of 2 pixels will cause points within 2 pixels of each other to snap together.
- You can use the information bar to get the horizontal and vertical coordinates of a point.
- You can use the Element info dialog box to get the

horizontal and vertical coordinates of a selected point.

- You can use a high magnification when you are moving points to the same location.

As you become familiar with FreeHand, you will find the techniques that best suit your method of working. Techniques described in this chapter include:

- Arrows and Symmetrical Objects
- Tracing Imported Graphics
- Importing Charts
- Drawing Bar Charts
- Drawing Pie Charts
- Organization Charts
- Holes in Solid Objects
- Composite Paths as Masks
- Polygons
- Stars: Method 1
- Stars: Method 2
- Symmetrical Objects
- Radial Symmetry: Method 1
- Radial Symmetry: Method 2
- Shared Borders

Creating Arrows and Symmetrical Objects

Arrows are common symbols used in many types of illustrations. The accompanying figure shows a variety of arrow shapes. You can use FreeHand's built-in arrowheads on lines, use existing arrows from symbol fonts such as Zapf Dingbats, or you can create your own arrows using the technique described here.

This technique can be used to create any symmetrical object.

1

Create the top half of the arrow. Drag a guide from the horizontal ruler to help you align the first and last points, turn on the grid, or use the information bar to make sure that the first and last points lie on the same horizontal line. This figure shows the top half of this arrow created with the Pen tool.

2

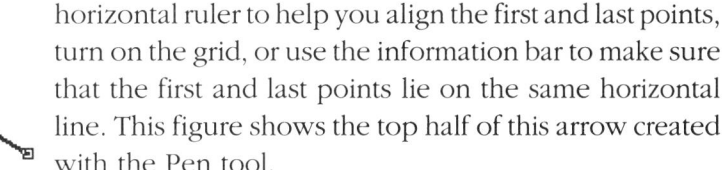

Select the entire element by Command-Option-clicking on the path. Choose Clone from the Edit menu (⌘=) to clone it, then choose the Reflecting tool and Option-click on one of the endpoints of the arrow. Make sure that you Option-click exactly on the endpoint. You can use the coordinates in the information bar as a guide.

3

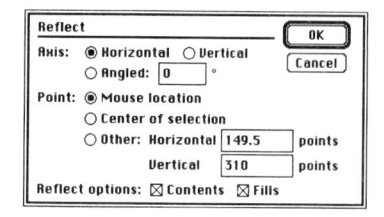

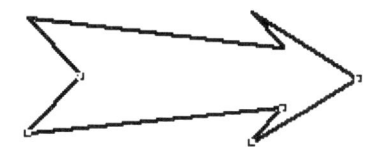

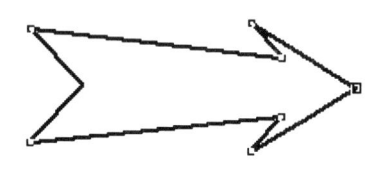

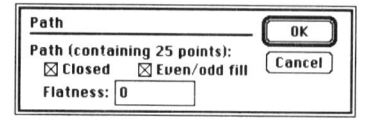

When you Option-click with the Reflecting tool, the Reflect dialog box opens. Select Horizontal from the Axis options and Mouse location from the Point options, then click OK. This flips the clone of the original element across the horizontal axis, creating the bottom half of the arrow.

If the arrow you create in this step is not to your liking, it might be faster to rework half of it, then delete the unchanged half and go back to step 2.

4

Press Tab to deselect everything. Then hold down the Command key to get the Pointer tool, and drag a selection marquee (see the description of Pointer tool in Chapter 12) around one pair of the common points where the two paths join, in this case, the tip of the arrow. Choose Join elements from the Element menu (⌘J) to join the pair. If your endpoints were *exactly* coincident, the two paths become a single closed path.

However, your endpoints may not be exactly coincident, in which case, the path will be open. To close the path, choose Element info from the Element menu (⌘I). Click the Closed option in the Element info dialog box, and click OK to close it.

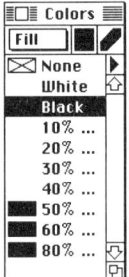

5

To fill the arrow, click the Fill indicator in the Colors palette, then click Black in the palette. If the arrow does not appear filled, you either did not close the path, or you are in keyline view instead of Preview. Choose Element info from the Element menu (⌘I) to see if the path is filled, or press ⌘K to switch from keyline to Preview mode.

6

To make the arrow longer or shorter, select the points at one end with the Pointer tool. Hold down the Shift key after you start to drag the point horizontally. The point selected for adjusting in this example is the tip of the arrow.

NOTE

Be sure to select all of the points that compose the tip of the arrow or the base of the arrow when stretching it longer or shorter. Otherwise, you will distort the shape of the arrow.

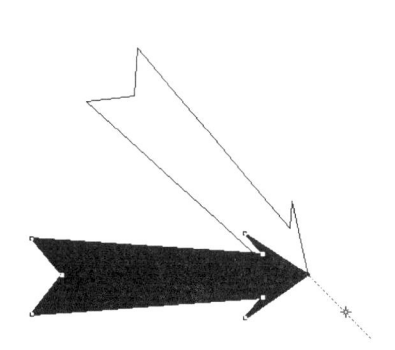

7

To rotate the arrow: click with the Pointer tool anywhere along the path to select it; select the Rotating tool; put the starburst pointer at the tip of the arrow; and drag to rotate the arrow.

Tracing Imported Graphics

You can use the Tracing tool to trace any element in FreeHand—objects that have been created in FreeHand or objects that have been imported. The basic functioning of the Tracing tool is detailed in Chapter 12, but here we describe the steps in importing and then tracing bitmapped or PICT or EPS graphics from other sources.

1

Import the image you want to trace using the Place command from the File menu. Tracing works best with high-contrast black-and-white images. If you want to trace a grayscale TIFF image, you will get better results if you convert it to black-and-white first.

2

If you do not want the image being traced to print, put it on a non-printing background layer. Otherwise, put it on a foreground layer and make that layer inactive, so that you don't accidentally change the image to be traced, then press Tab to deselect it.

3

Double-click the Tracing tool in the Toolbox to open the Trace dialog box, and set the options you want. Check Tight if you want the trace as accurate as possible. This works best with TIFF images scanned at a high resolution. If you leave this option unchecked, the Tracing tool traces images at 72 dpi, which uses less memory and traces faster.

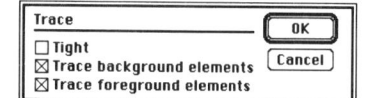

4

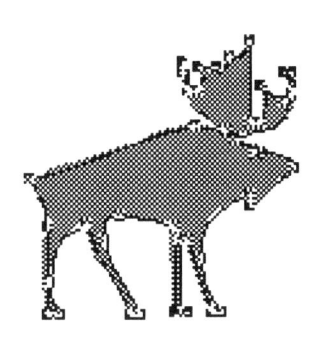

Make sure that the current active layer is different from the one that contains the image to be traced, then drag the Tracing tool pointer diagonally to surround the image with a marquee. FreeHand traces the image, and displays the resulting path or paths with all points displayed.

5

Choose Group from the Element menu (⌘G) to group the selected paths to avoid accidentally moving a single point. If you want to edit the path, you can Option-click with the Pointer tool to select single points in the group.

6

To see the traced version clearly, either make the layer with the original image invisible, delete the original image, or delete the layer on which it resides.

Importing Charts

You can import charts created in PICT format by spreadsheet and charting programs. If you do not need to edit the chart, you can either import it using the Place command from the File menu, or paste it into FreeHand from the Clipboard. This technique assumes that you want to use FreeHand's tools to enhance the chart.

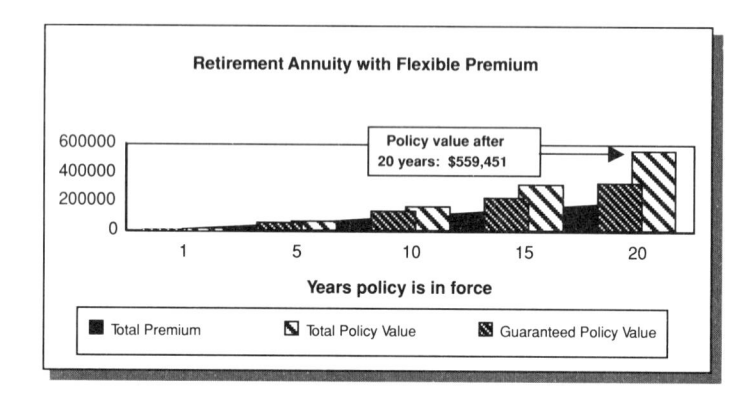

1

Create the chart in a spreadsheet or charting program, then save it as a PICT file.

TIP

Microsoft Excel cannot save charts in PICT format. To import a chart from Excel in an editable format, select the chart in Excel, then hold down the Option key and choose Copy from the Edit menu. Paste the chart into a program that lets you save in PICT format, such as MacDraw or Canvas, then save it in PICT format.

2

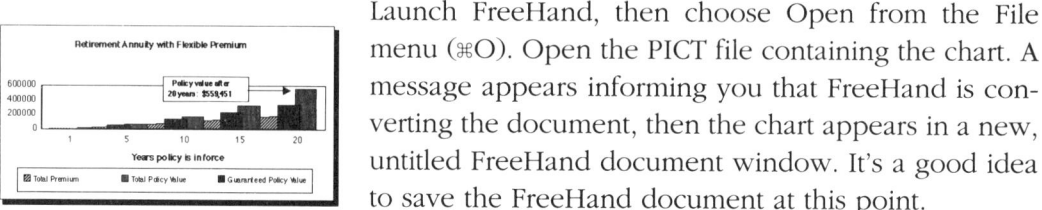

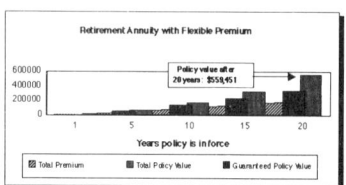

Launch FreeHand, then choose Open from the File menu (⌘O). Open the PICT file containing the chart. A message appears informing you that FreeHand is converting the document, then the chart appears in a new, untitled FreeHand document window. It's a good idea to save the FreeHand document at this point.

3

Now you can use any of FreeHand's tools and commands to make enhancements to the chart. For example, you can apply custom colors, or rotate axis labels at an angle to fit longer labels into the available space.

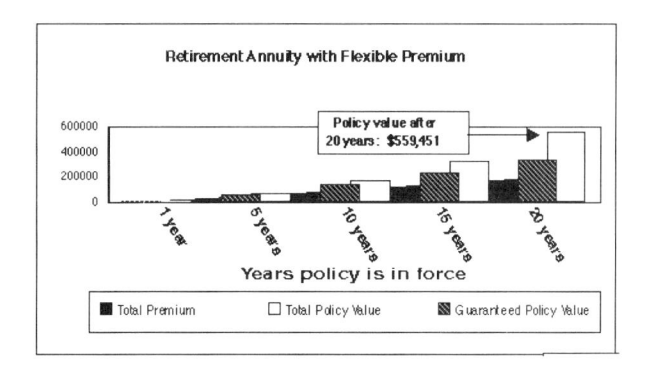

TIP

When you work with bar charts that contain groups of bars, you can group the bars together with the key in the legend (the small square in the legend that is the same color as the bars). That way, you can apply the same fill and line attributes to the entire set of bars and the legend with a single command.

Drawing Bar Charts

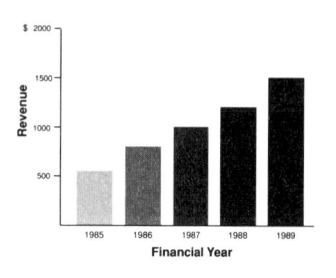

Bar charts, like the one shown in the figure, are probably the single most common form of business graphics. Here is a technique for quickly producing a series of bars, scaled to accurate dimensions.

1

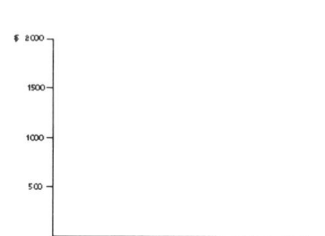

Use the Pen tool with the Shift key to draw two straight lines that will serve as the chart's two axes. Set tick marks to represent the increments you wish to show (see "Dividing Equally" in Chapter 8). Add text to label each tick mark. This figure shows increments of $100 along the vertical (y) axis, labeled in $500 increments.

2

Decide how wide you want to make your bars. Using the Rectangle tool, draw a rectangle the width of one bar, and the height of one unit on the vertical scale, or a decimal multiple of one unit (that is, ten units, one hundred units, one thousand units, and so on). For this example, make the height of the basic bar (the bar you will scale) equivalent to $1,000. You can draw this rectangle visually on the screen, or choose Element info from the Element menu (⌘I) and specify precise dimensions in the Element info dialog box.

It does not matter what the exact size of your basic unit is in points or inches, so long as you know it represents 1, 10, 100, or 1,000 chart units, and it matches the scale you have set up on the axes.

If you want groups of bars or three-dimensional bars, align the first group, or add dimension and shading to the first bar, *before* you go on to step 3.

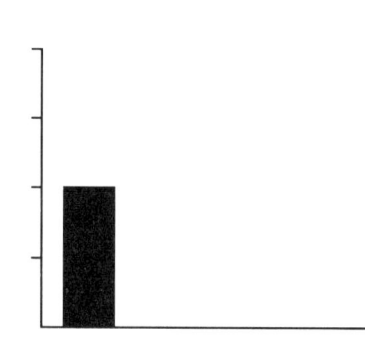

3

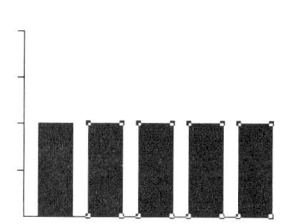

Make as many copies of this basic unit as you need bars by choosing Clone from the Edit menu (⌘=) and dragging the clone with the Shift key held down so it is aligned along the horizontal axis. Use the Duplicate command from the Edit menu (⌘D) to create additional copies spaced equally apart. In this example, create four copies of the basic bar, spaced about 1/4 inch apart.

4

Select the Scaling tool and, one by one, click to select each bar, then Option-click the Scaling tool on the bottom edge of the bar. When the Scale dialog box appears, click Other under the Scaling options, enter 100% in the Horizontal box, and the appropriate percentage in the Vertical box. Click Mouse location under the Center options. The table below shows the values to use in scaling for this example.

BAR #	DESIRED VALUE	VERTICAL SCALE
1	$550	55%
2	$800	80%
3	$1,000	100%
4	$1,200	120%
5	$1,500	150%

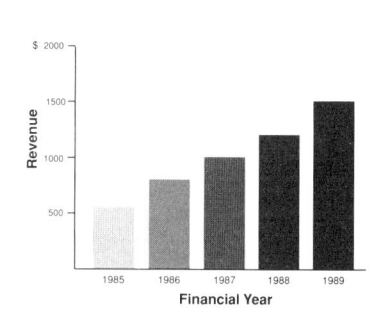

5

Finish the chart by filling the bars and adding a title, legend, and caption, if appropriate.

See also "Drop Shadows #1 and #2," and "Cubes #1 and #2," in Chapter 7, "Aligning Objects" and "Dividing Equally," in Chapter 8, and the Maps in Chapter 11.

Drawing Pie Charts

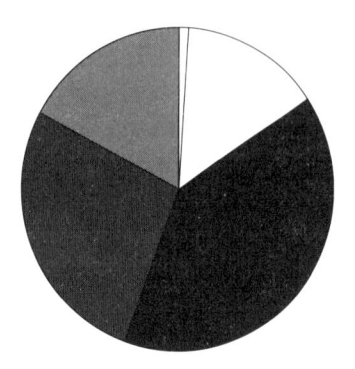

Pie charts, such as the one shown in the figure, are a common form of business graphics. Here is a technique you can use to divide a pie quickly, with wedges scaled to accurate dimensions.

1

First switch from Preview mode to keyline view (⌘K), then use the Ellipse tool with the Shift key to draw a perfect circle. Click the Pen tool once on the center of the circle, then with the Shift key held down, click on the top of the circle, which forces a straight line. This draws a radius at twelve o'clock. Your drawing should look like the one in the figure.

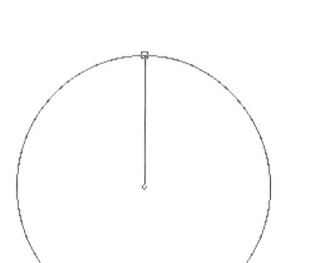

TIP

When you use the Ellipse and Rectangle tools in keyline mode, the center point of the shape is visible as a small x. Use keyline whenever you need to align something to the center of an ellipse or rectangle.

2

Determine the number of degrees of the circle for each slice of the pie you wish to divide based on the formula:

Degrees = (value of slice/total value of pie) X 360
or
Degrees = Percent share of slice X 360

In this example, you derive degree values for each slice based on the desired dollar amount, shown in the following table:

Chapter 4. Shapes (Closed Paths) 111

SLICE #	DESIRED VALUE	RELATIVE %	DEGREES
1	$55	1.00%	3.6
2	$800	14.54%	52.36
3	$1,000	18.18%	65.45
4	$1,200	21.82%	78.54
5	$1,500	27.27%	98.18
6	$945	17.19%	61.87
Totals	$5,500	100.00%	360.0

3

Select the radius with the Pointer tool. Choose Clone from the Edit menu (⌘=) to clone it. Then select the Rotating tool and Option-click on the anchor point at the center of the circle. This opens the Rotate dialog box. Type the number of degrees assigned to the first pie slice in the Angle box, -3.6 in this case, and click Mouse location under the Center option.

Entering a positive number will position the slice counterclockwise from the radius; a negative number will position the slice clockwise from the radius. Click OK to close the Rotate dialog box and rotate the clone of the radius the indicated number of degrees. This figure shows the result of the -3.6° angle rotation.

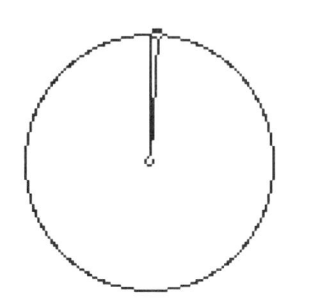

4

Continue adding each slice of the pie. Clone the most recently rotated radius by choosing Clone from the Edit menu) (⌘=). Option-click the Rotating tool on the center point and enter the appropriate number of degrees for each new slice. Make sure that you click Mouse location as the center of rotation in the Rotate dialog box. After you have created all the slices, your pie chart looks like the one in this figure.

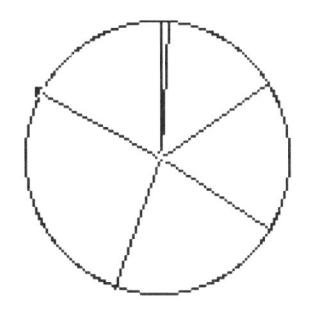

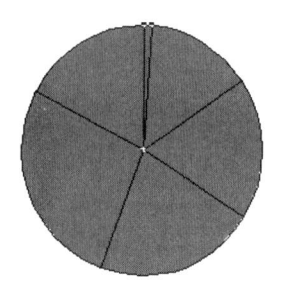

If you want to shade each slice differently, go on with the next steps. Otherwise, if you want all slices shaded the same, choose Select all from the Edit menu (⌘A), and then set the desired line and fill using the Colors palette. Switch to Preview mode (⌘K) to see the fill and line you applied.

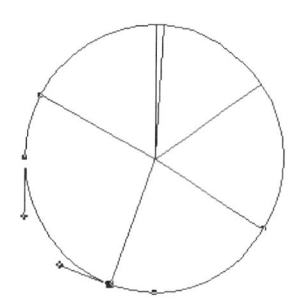

5

In the next steps, you are going to make each slice of pie a closed path, composed of two radii and an arc, to be able to assign each slice a different fill.

Select the circle and choose Ungroup from the Element menu (⌘U). Select the Knife tool and cut the circumference at each point where a radius hits it. You may want to use the ⌘Space bar shortcut to zoom in so you cut the circle at the right points.

6

To join two radii and an arc to make each slice of pie a closed path, you will first join a radius and an arc, then use the Element info command to close the path.

To create the first slice, Shift-click on a radius and the adjacent arc of any pie wedge. Then choose Join elements from the Element menu (⌘J) to join the radius and the arc into a single open path. Finally, close the path by choosing Element info from the Element menu (⌘I) and clicking to check the Closed option. FreeHand automatically draws a second radius to convert the open path into a closed slice of the pie.

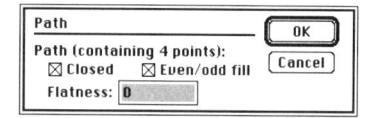

Repeat step 6 for each slice of the pie. You may have difficulty selecting the final radius, because it lies behind an already-completed slice of the pie. In that case, select the completed slice and choose Send to back from the Element menu (⌘B) to send the completed slice behind the radius you want to select. Then select the final radius and arc and choose Join elements from the Element menu (⌘J) to join them. Close the slice by choosing Element info from the Element menu (⌘I) and checking Closed in the Element info dialog box.

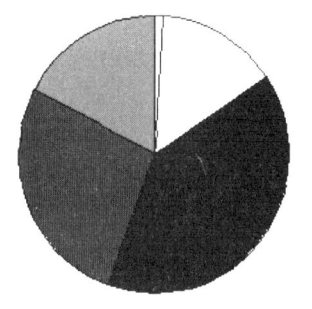

7

Finally, use the Colors palette to set the fill and line of your choice for each slice. This figure shows the example pie chart with different fill settings for each slice.

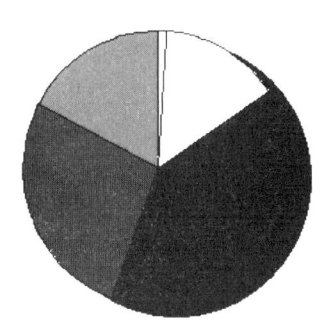

TIPS

If you want a three-dimensional pie, use the Pointer tool to Option-drag a copy of the circle before you cut it with the Knife tool in step 5, and position the copy a short diagonal distance from the pie. Use the Colors palette to give the copy a line and fill, then choose Send to back from the Element menu (⌘B) to put the new circle behind the pie chart.

See also the techniques in the next chapter that describe three-dimensional effects to learn how to achieve this more realistically, or if you want each slice exploded with a three-dimensional effect.

You can also use any of the transformation tools (Scaling, Rotating, Reflecting, and Skewing tools) to make the pie more interesting.

See also "Cubes #1 and #2," in Chapter 7 and "Aligning Objects" and "Dividing Equally" in Chapter 8.

114 Using Aldus FreeHand 3.0

Organization Charts

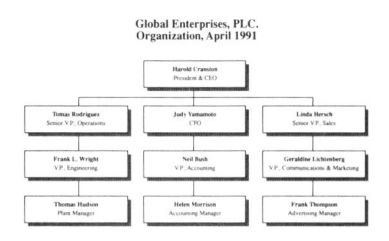

Organization charts, such as the one shown in the figure, are a very common form of business graphics. Here is a technique for quickly producing an organization chart.

1

Use the Text tool to type the text of the longest name and title or department that will appear in the organization chart. These can be typed in one text block. Choose Type ➤ Alignment ➤ Align center, and choose the font and size you want using the Type specs command from the Type menu (⌘T). Position the text block in the upper-left portion of the page, so that you leave room to create duplicates both below and to the right.

NOTE
These text elements need not reflect reality—the person whose name you type need not hold the title or be in the department you type—but they must have as many characters as the longest entries in the chart.

2

Use the Rectangle tool to draw a rectangle around the text, and choose Fill and line from the Attributes menu (⌘E) or the Colors palette to set the Fill to White and the Line to the shade you want. Then use the Send to back command from the Element menu (⌘B) to place the filled rectangle behind the text. This rectangle and the text form the basic element used throughout the chart. If you want to add a drop shadow or a three-dimensional effect to the rectangle, do so *before* you go on to step 3.

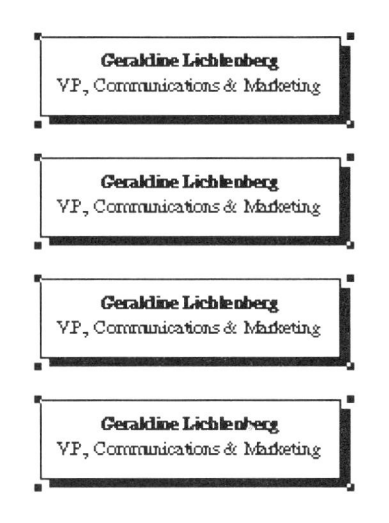

NOTE

The fill of the rectangle can be white or any percentage of black or a color, but it cannot be set to None or the lines drawn in step 7 will be visible behind the text.

When you have completed the basic unit, choose Select all from the Edit menu (⌘A) to select all of the elements, then use the Group command from the Element menu (⌘G) to group all of these basic elements, including the text.

3

Working in Fit in window view (choose View → Magnification → Fit in window or press ⌘W), make as many copies of this basic unit as you need for the organization chart. Use the Pointer tool to select the grouped rectangle and text. Choose Clone from the Edit menu (⌘=) to make a clone, then Shift-drag to align the clone horizontally or vertically. Make as many additional copies as required by pressing ⌘D (Duplicate from the Edit menu).

If you will be making several columns of entries, it is a good idea to create one column by dragging a clone of the first box into the second position and then using the Duplicate command to create additional copies spaced equally apart. In this example, create three copies of the basic element, spaced about 1/4 inch apart, for a total of four boxes in the column.

Then use the Pointer tool to select the whole column and choose Clone from the Edit menu (⌘=) to clone the whole column. Shift-drag the clone to create the second column, then use the Duplicate command from the Edit menu (⌘D) to create the subsequent columns. If the columns require unequal numbers of elements, use the one with the largest number as the base, then delete the extras from the clones.

4

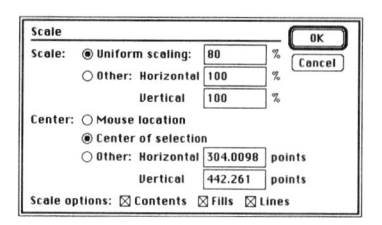

If the final layout is too large to fit on one page, you can use the Select all command from the Edit menu (⌘A) and use the Scaling tool with the Option key to reduce the size of the chart (including the size of the type).

5

Once you have the overall chart arranged on the page, use the Text tool to add a chart title and caption (if appropriate).

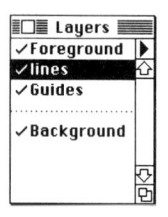

6

Press Tab to deselect all elements, then create a new drawing layer by choosing New from the Layers palette pop-up menu. Name the new layer and drag it into position in the Layers palette so it is behind the Foreground layer, on which all the elements in the artwork currently reside. Make the new layer the current drawing layer.

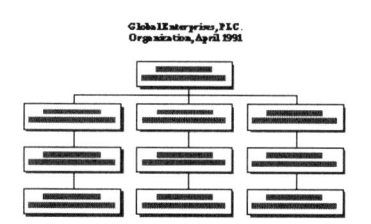

7

Use the Line tool with the Shift key to draw straight lines from the center of each rectangle to the center of adjacent rectangles or to adjoining lines that indicate the structure of the organization.

You can start by drawing a long path from the top box down through the longest column, then add other lines to connect the other columns.

8

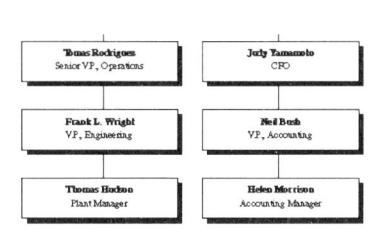

Finally, use Select all from the Edit menu (⌘A) and the Ungroup command from the Element menu (⌘U) to select all of the elements and ungroup them. Use the Magnifying tool to change to a magnified view of the top of the chart. Press Tab to deselect everything, then one by one, double-click each text element with the Pointer tool, then change the boilerplate text to the appropriate name, title, and department in each box on the chart.

See also "Cubes #1 and #2" in Chapter 7 and "Aligning Objects" and "Grids #1 and #4" in Chapter 8.

Holes in Solid Objects

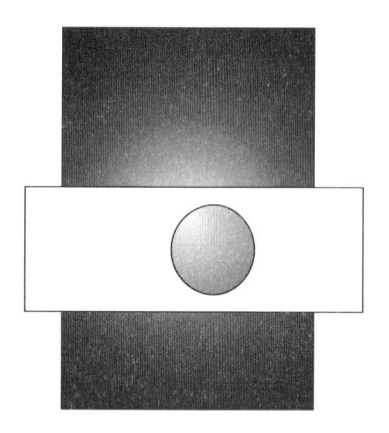

You can always make a solid shape appear to have a hole in it by drawing the hole and giving it a fill of white. But what if you want the hole to be transparent to objects below it? You can use the Join elements command from the Element menu to create this effect.

This effect is most commonly seen in the holes inside closed letters of the alphabet—something that FreeHand does automatically when you convert type to paths using the Convert to paths command—but you can use the technique described here to combine any two closed, ungrouped paths.

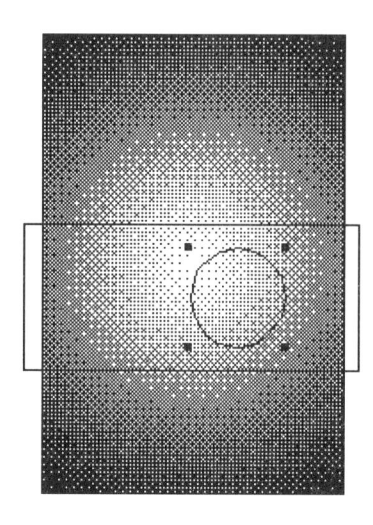

1

First create the background that you want to appear through the hole. In this case, we used the Rectangle tool to draw a rectangle, then gave it a radial fill from 10% gray to 80% gray.

Next, create the object with the hole as two paths: the outer edge and the shape of the hole. In this example, the outer edge is a rectangle created with the Rectangle tool. The circle just right of center is the shape of the hole, created with the Ellipse tool and the Shift key.

2

Select both objects and choose Ungroup from the Element menu (⌘U). You cannot join grouped elements to make a composite path.

3

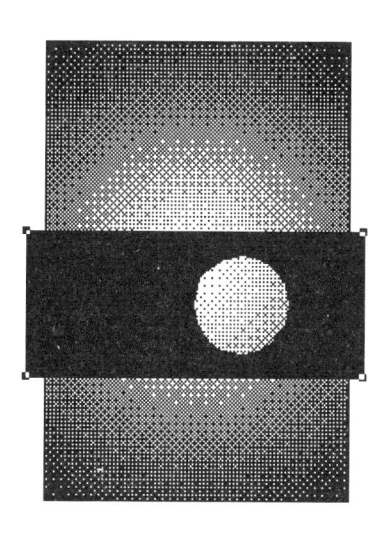

With both objects selected, choose Join elements from the Element menu (⌘J). The objects now form a single composite path. Then use the Colors palette to apply a black fill to the composite path. The background radial fill shows through the hole.

4

To edit either shape, select points by Option-clicking with the Pointer tool.

See also "Composite Paths as Masks" in this chapter.

Composite Paths as Masks

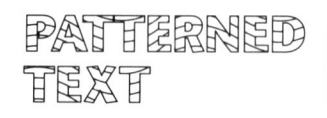

You can use a path to mask other elements using the Paste inside command. However, this results in a complex file that takes considerable time to print. In many cases, you can use composite paths to achieve the same effect, with substantially shorter printing times. In this example, type converted to paths is used as the mask, but you can use this technique with any shape.

1

First create the image that you want to mask. In this example, we created a simple pattern by cloning, moving, and duplicating a wavy line, but the masked image can be any combination of elements created in FreeHand, or imported from another program, including imported scanned images.

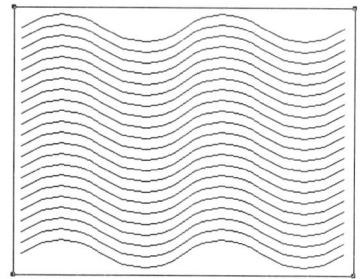

2

Select the Rectangle tool, draw a rectangle that covers the entire page, then choose Ungroup from the Element menu to ungroup it (⌘U). This rectangle will form the background of the finished artwork. For now, leave it unfilled so you can see the image that will be masked.

3

Create the mask. In this example, we converted a text block to a composite path using the Convert to paths command from the Type menu, but you can use any ungrouped path as a mask.

TIP

If you want to use two or more non-contiguous paths as a mask, create them, then join them into a single composite path by selecting them and choosing Join elements from the Element menu (⌘J). The Convert to paths command does this automatically with the individual characters in a block of type.

4

Position the masked image and the mask relative to one another so the parts of the image you want to be visible are positioned behind the mask. Then select the mask and the background rectangle, and join them into a composite path using the Join elements command from the Element menu (⌘J).

5

Apply the fill and line attributes of your choice to the composite path. If you want a white background with no border, apply a fill of White and a line of None. In this example, we gave the background a white fill and a black line. The masked image now shows through the mask. The visual appearance is identical to that obtained by pasting the image inside the mask, but this method takes far less time to print.

TIP

If you want the mask, but not the background rectangle to have a line, select the mask by Option-clicking with the Pointer tool, choose Clone from the Edit menu (⌘=) to make a clone, then apply the line attributes of your choice to the clone.

122 Using Aldus FreeHand 3.0

Polygons

You can use the technique described here to draw any polygon shape with equal-length sides all around—equilateral triangles, pentagons, hexagons, or polygons with seven or more sides. (You can use the Rectangle tool instead of this technique to draw perfect squares.) A five-sided polygon (pentagon) is created in this example.

1

Use the Line tool with the Shift key to draw a straight vertical line like the one shown in the figure on the left.

2

With the line still selected, use the Clone command from the Edit menu (⌘=) to make a duplicate of the line, layered on top of the first. Next, select the Rotating tool and Option-click the pointer at the bottom point of the line. In the Rotate dialog box, enter the number of degrees yielded by the following formula:

360 ÷ (number of sides to the polygon)

For example, enter 72 degrees for a five-sided polygon, 60 degrees for a six-sided polygon, and so on.

For a five-sided polygon, type "72" (for 72°) into the Angle edit box of the Rotate dialog box, select Mouse location under Center, then click OK to close the dialog box and rotate the copy of the line.

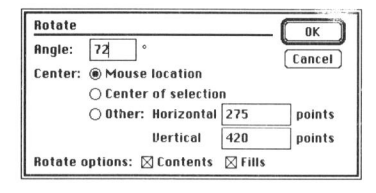

3

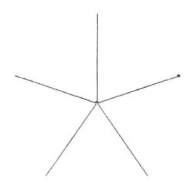

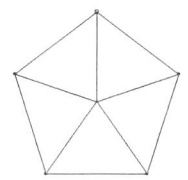

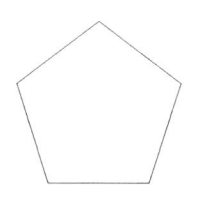

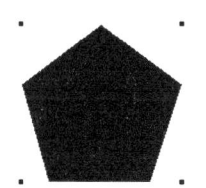

With the rotated copy selected, choose Duplicate from the Edit menu (⌘D) three times. You now have five lines radiating from a common center.

4

Use the Pen tool to draw the polygon by clicking on the outer endpoint of each line.

5

Press Tab to deselect everything. Then, holding down the Command, Option, and Shift keys, click once on each of the five lines to select them, and press Delete (Backspace). The five lines are deleted, leaving the polygon.

6

Choose Fill and line from the Attributes menu (⌘E) and give the polygon your desired line and fill settings. In this example, the polygon has a 100% black fill and a 60% gray line color with a weight of 5 points.

7

Optionally, you can use the Pointer tool to select the object and choose Group from the Element menu (⌘G). This way, you can easily select, move, or scale the object without distorting the shape.

Stars: Method 1

You can use the technique described here (and the next one) to draw any star shape—five-pointed, six-pointed, or more.

1

Use the Line tool with the Shift key to draw a straight vertical line like the one shown in the figure on the left.

2

With the line selected, choose Clone from the Edit menu (⌘=) to make a duplicate of the line, layered on top of the original. Select the Rotating tool and Option-click at the bottom point of the line. In the Rotate dialog box, enter the number of degrees yielded by the following formula:

  360/(number of points on the star)

This yields 72° for a five-pointed star, 60° for a six-pointed star, and so on.

Type "72" (for 72°) into the Angle edit box of the Rotate dialog box, and select Mouse location as the Center, then click OK to close the box and rotate the copy of the line.

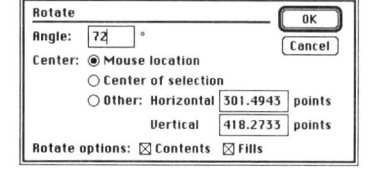

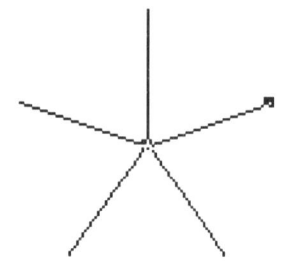

3

With the rotated copy selected, choose Duplicate from the Edit menu (⌘D) three times. You now have five lines radiating from a common center.

4

Select the Pen tool and carefully click on every other outer endpoint to produce a straight line connecting them. Be sure to click and release the mouse button on each point without dragging.

For a five-pointed star, start by clicking the top point, then click the lower left point. Proceed to the upper right point and click, then move over to the upper left point and click. Then move to the lower right point and click, and finally, complete the star and close the path by once again clicking at the top point.

For stars with an odd number of points, clicking every other point will always result in one closed path, such as the seven- and nine-pointed stars shown in the figure on the left.

For stars with an even number of points, clicking every other point will yield two paths. For a six-pointed star, click on every other point to draw two triangles. For an eight-pointed star, click on every other point to draw two squares. These and other variations are shown in the figure on the left.

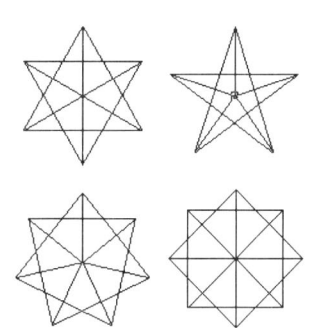

5

Press Tab to deselect everything. Then, holding down the Command, Option, and Shift keys, click once on each of the five original lines that were used as guides to select them, and press Delete (Backspace). The five lines are deleted, leaving the star.

6

If you want a solid shaded star with no line color (or line color the same as the fill), choose Fill and line from the Attributes menu (⌘E) to assign the star your desired fill attributes, and give the line the same attributes or assign None to the line. For stars with an odd number of points, select the star and choose Element info from the Element menu (⌘I), then click the Odd/even fill option to uncheck it.

If you would like to be able to outline the outside edge of the star with a different color, go on to step 7.

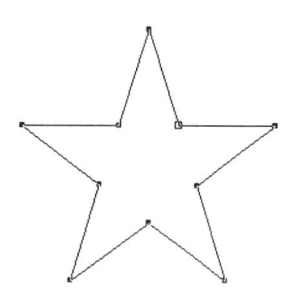

7

In a magnified view, use the Knife tool to cut lines that cross inside the shape, then choose Cut from the Edit menu (⌘X), or press Delete (Backspace) to delete the inside line segments. Bear in mind that you will need to use the Knife tool twice at each location where the paths overlap, once to cut the line in front, and a second time to cut the line behind. Use the Join elements command from the Element menu (⌘J) to join corresponding inside points.

8

You can now choose Fill and line from the Attributes menu (⌘E) to set a different line and fill for the star shape. In this example, the star has a 100% black fill and a 60% gray line color with a weight of 5 points.

9

Optionally, you can use the Pointer tool to select the object and choose Group from the Element menu (⌘G). This way, you can easily select, move, or scale the object without distorting the shape.

Stars: Method 2

You can use the technique described here to draw any star shape, but here you have more control over the length of the points than with the previous technique.

1

Use the Line tool with the Shift key to draw a straight vertical line. With the line selected, choose Clone from the Edit menu (⌘=) to make a duplicate of the line, layered on top of the original. Select the Rotating tool and Option-click at the bottom point of the line. The Rotate dialog box appears.

Enter the number of degrees yielded by the following formula:

360/(number of points on the star)

This yields 72° for a five-pointed star, 60° for a six-pointed star, and so on.

Type "72" (for 72°) into the Angle edit box of the Rotate dialog box, and select Mouse location as the point of rotation, then click OK to close the box and rotate the copy of the line.

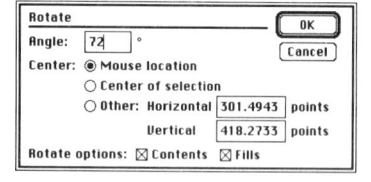

2

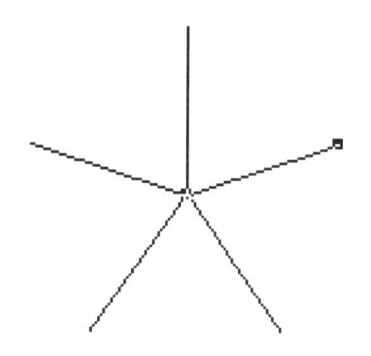

Choose Duplicate from the Edit menu (⌘D) three times (or more if you are creating star shapes with more than five points). You now have five lines radiating from a common center.

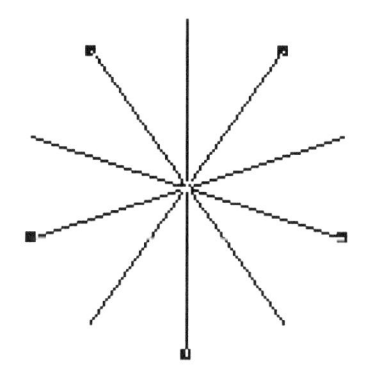

3

Use the Select all command from the Edit menu (⌘A) and then choose Clone from the Edit menu (⌘=) to make a duplicate of the lines. Then select the Rotating tool and Option-click on the common center points. Type *half* the number of degrees you typed in step 2—36 for a five-pointed star—in the Rotate dialog box, and select Mouse location as the point of rotation. Click OK to close the box and rotate the copy of the lines. This yields ten lines radiating from a common center.

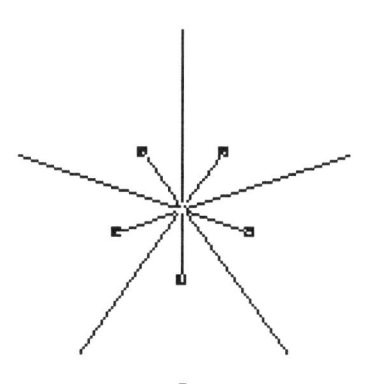

4

With the copied lines still selected, select the Scaling tool and Option-click on the common center points.

With the Uniform scaling option selected, type "40" into the percentage box of the Scale dialog box, click Mouse location for the center of transformation, then click OK.

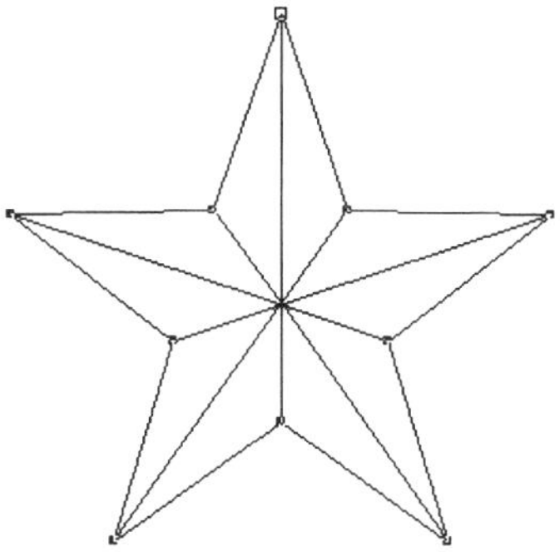

5

Select the Pen tool and connect the outer endpoints sequentially with careful clicks of the mouse in a clockwise or counterclockwise sequence. Be sure to click and release the mouse button on each point without dragging. Complete the star by clicking at the point where you started.

6

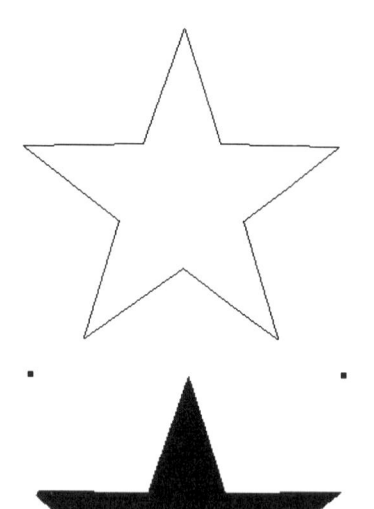

Press Tab to deselect everything. Then, holding down the Command, Option, and Shift keys, click once on each of the ten lines that were used as guides to select them, and press Delete (Backspace). The lines are deleted, leaving the star.

Be sure that only the original lines used as guides are selected before you remove them.

7

Choose Fill and line from the Attributes menu (⌘E) to set the fill and line of the star as you wish.

TIP

The percentage reduction you enter in step 5 determines the sharpness of the points. The greater the percentage reduction, the sharper the points. The figures on the facing page show the results of different reduction settings.

Chapter 4. Shapes (Closed Paths)   *131*

85%

75%

65%

55%

40%

30%

25%

20%

15%

Symmetrical Objects

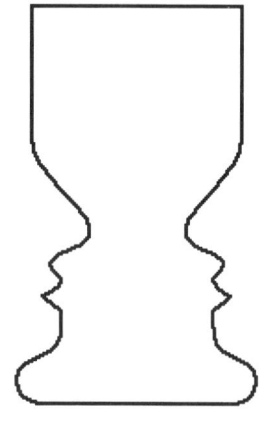

The technique described here can be used to create any symmetrical object in which one half is an exact reflection of the other. The accompanying figure shows a goblet created for this example.

1

Create the left or top half of the object (depending on the axis of symmetry). The figure on the left shows the left half of a goblet created with the Pen tool.

2

With the drawn element selected (but no individual points selected), choose Clone from the Edit menu (⌘=) to make a duplicate of the object, layered on top of the first.

3

Select the Reflecting tool, then hold down the Option key and click on one of the two endpoints. When you Option-click with the Reflecting tool, the Reflect dialog box opens. Select Vertical axis reflection and reflect around the Mouse location, then close the dialog box by clicking OK. This creates a mirror image—in this case, the right half of the goblet.

If the object you create in this step is not to your liking, delete one half and rework the other half of it, then go back to step 2.

4

When you have achieved the results you wish, select an adjacent endpoint from each half by dragging with the Pointer tool, and choose the Join elements command from the Element menu (⌘J) to join the pair.

5

Optionally, you can use the Pointer tool to select the object and choose Group from the Element menu (⌘G). This way, you can easily select, move, or scale the object without distorting the shape.

See also "Radial Symmetry: Method 1" and "Radial Symmetry: Method 2" in this chapter.

Radial Symmetry: Method 1

Radial symmetry describes any object composed of a single shape that is repeated in a pattern around a central point. An example of radial symmetry is a flower, such as the one shown in the accompanying figure. In this technique, the Rotating tool is used to create simple patterns in which the shapes do not need to meet precisely at the edges—that is, they can overlap, or there can be gaps between them.

You can use this technique to create any radially symmetrical design that allows some gap or overlap between the units of the design.

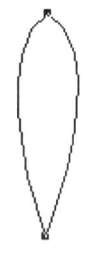

1

Create an object that will become the basic unit of the radial design, using whatever tool is appropriate. In this example, use the Pen tool to create a petal-shaped object, as in the figure on the left.

2

With the object selected (but no individual endpoints selected), choose Clone from the Edit menu (⌘=).

3

Select the Rotating tool and Option-click the point you want to use as the center of the design—in this case, the base of the petal. In the Rotate dialog box, enter the number of degrees yielded by the following formula:

Degrees = 360°/(number of repeated units)

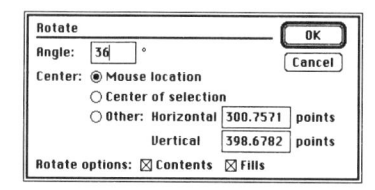

In this example, you want ten units, so type "36" as the number of degrees (360 divided by 10). Other common values are shown in the following table:

Number of Repeated Units in Circle	Degrees
2	180
3	120
4	90
5	72
6	60
7	51.43
8	45
9	40
10	36

Select Mouse location as the point of rotation, and click OK to close the Rotate dialog box to make a rotated copy of the cloned object. Next, use the Duplicate command from the Edit menu (⌘D) until the circle is complete—eight more copies in this example.

4

Optionally, choose Select all from the Edit menu (⌘A) and Group from the Element menu (⌘G) to group the objects that make up your shape.

TIP

Once you create a design, you can create many variations by scaling, overlaying, and/or skewing the object. The figure at the left shows three copies of the flower petals scaled progressively smaller, with variations in the fill and line color for each group of petals in the object.

Radial Symmetry: Method 2

This second technique for creating radially symmetrical designs is more controlled than the first, creating shapes that meet precisely at the edges, such as the one shown in the accompanying figure.

This technique can be used to create any radially symmetrical design.

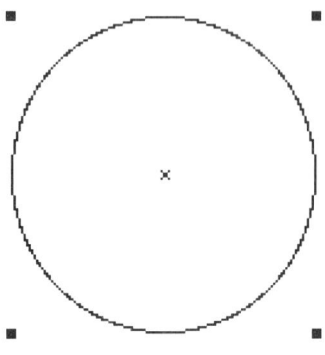

1

Switch to keyline mode (⌘K), then use the Ellipse tool with the Shift key to draw a circle (as shown in the figure on the left) whose center will be the center of the radial design and whose circumference will cross through the radial elements.

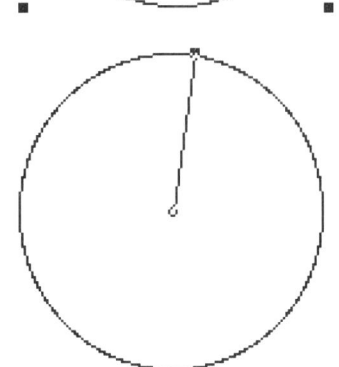

2

Use the Line tool to draw a radius of the circle. In this example, the radius is just past the 12 o'clock position. With the radius selected, choose Clone from the Edit menu (⌘=).

3

Select the Rotating tool, and hold down the Option key as you click on the center of the circle. The Rotate dialog box appears.

In the Angle edit box of the Rotate dialog box, type the number of degrees yielded by the following formula:

Degrees = 360°/(number of repeated units)

See the table in "Radial Symmetry: Method 1."

Chapter 4. Shapes (Closed Paths) 137

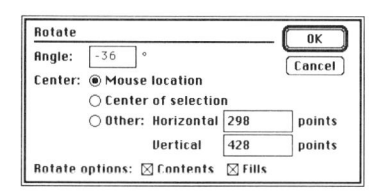

In the example shown here, there are 10 repeated units, so enter "–36" for the angle. Positive numbers rotate elements counterclockwise, and negative numbers rotate them clockwise. Select Mouse location as the point of rotation, then click OK to close the box and rotate the copy of the radius.

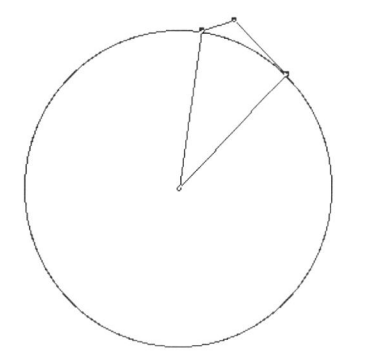

4

Create a closed shape that will become the basic unit of the radial design, using the two radii as guides for the edges of the shape. In this example, use the Pen tool to draw an irregular polygon.

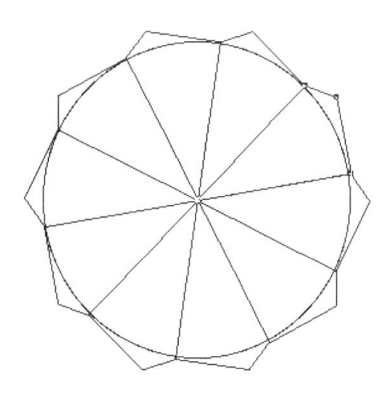

5

With the object selected, choose Clone from the Edit menu (⌘=). Then with the cloned copy of the basic radial element selected, select the Rotating tool and Option-click the center of the circle. In the Angle edit box of the Rotate dialog box, type the number of degrees you used in step 3 (-36°), and select Mouse location as the point of rotation. Click OK to close the dialog box and rotate the clone. Use the Duplicate command from the Edit menu (⌘D) as many times as needed to complete the design.

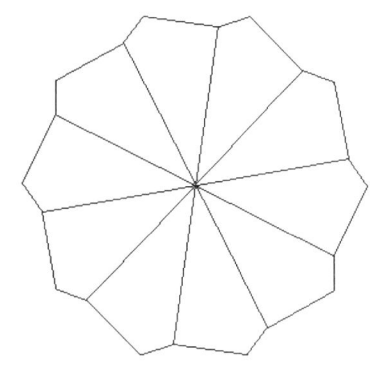

6

Control-click with the Pointer tool to select the original circle and the two radii you used as guides, then press Delete (Backspace) to delete them. Then select the remaining objects and choose Group from the Element menu (⌘G). Switch to Preview mode (⌘K) and use the Colors palette to apply a line and fill of your choice.

Shared Borders

Separate shapes that share common irregular edges—that must fit together like jigsaw puzzle pieces—are a common drawing situation. Individual countries, states, or counties on a map are typical example. This simple technique shows the most efficient way for you to handle this drawing situation.

Perfect for map work, this technique also proves useful for illustration styles that simulate dimension by using shapes of various gray fills.

1

Using one of the freehand drawing tools, draw a shape with an irregular path similar to the figure on the left. Then with the object selected (but no individual points selected), choose Duplicate from the Edit menu (⌘D). Drag the copy away from the original object.

2

Select the Knife tool and click at two points on the duplicate path. The line length between these two cuts will become the new common border. The figure on the left shows the cut segment separated from the object.

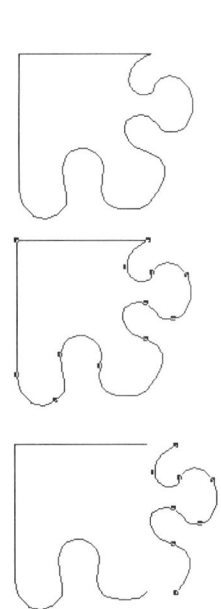

Chapter 4. Shapes (Closed Paths) *139*

3

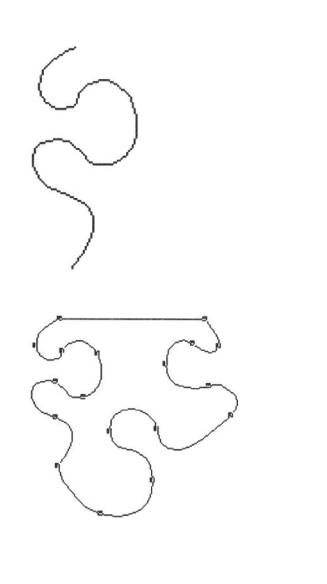

Delete the segment that you do not need—the segment that will not be part of a shared border.

4

Choose the appropriate tool and finish drawing the adjoining shape, beginning by selecting an endpoint of the shared border line segment.

5

When you finish drawing, drag the two shapes into position. The two shapes will have identical common borders and will fit together perfectly.

See also "Knife Tool" and "Pen Tool" in Chapter 12.

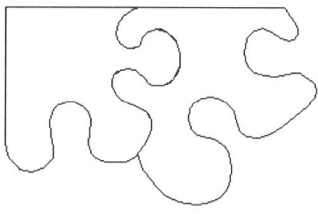

5

Three-Dimensional Effects

This chapter describes techniques that simulate three-dimensional objects. Three-dimensional effects can be achieved through use of perspective and shading.

Techniques described in this chapter include:

- Coils and Springs
- Cubes: Method 1
- Cubes: Method 2
- Cubes: Method 3
- Interlocking Objects
- Cylinders
- Drop Shadows: Method 1
- Drop Shadows: Method 2
- Flower Petals
- Highlights

Coils and Springs

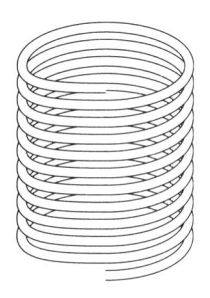

Coils and springs are common parts of mechanical devices and appear in many technical drawings, but they can be difficult to create unless you know the right techniques. Using the technique described here, you will draw a coil like the one pictured in the figure.

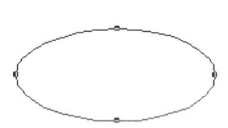

1
Use the Ellipse tool to draw an ellipse. Then ungroup the object using the Ungroup command from the Element menu (⌘U).

2
Select the lowest anchor point on the ellipse, then choose Split element from the Element menu to split the path at that point.

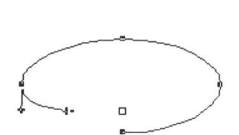

3
Press Tab to deselect everything, then hold down the Command key to get the Pointer tool, select one of the two anchor points created by the split, and move it slightly up or down. You can drag it with the Shift key held down to constrain the movement to vertical, use the Move command from the Edit menu, or use the Arrow keys on the keyboard.

You can refine the shape by moving the next anchor point (along the line from the lower of the two severed points) down about half the distance of the first movement.

4

Use the Fill and line command from the Attributes menu (⌘E) to set the line of the ellipse to black with a weight of 10 points (or any thickness you desire) for the coil.

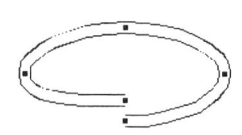

5

With the path selected, choose Clone from the Edit menu (⌘=) to place a copy in front of the original. With the copy selected, choose Fill and line from the Attributes menu (⌘E) to give the copy a line of white with a weight of 8 points (or two points less than the weight selected in step 4).

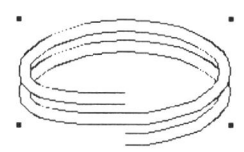

6

Select both paths and group them using the Group command from the Element menu (⌘G). Choose Clone from the Edit menu (⌘=) to make a clone of the group, then move the clone up (if you want the viewing perspective to be from the top of the coil) or down (if you want the viewing perspective to be from the bottom) to meet the first coil. The easiest way to do this is to drag the clone with the Pointer tool until it is approximately in place, then make fine adjustments with the arrow keys.

Press ⌘D (Duplicate from the Edit menu) to create as many additional loops of the coil as you wish. In this figure, there are a total of eleven loops in the coil.

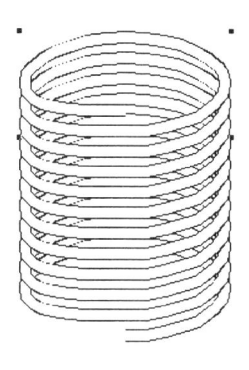

Cubes: Method 1

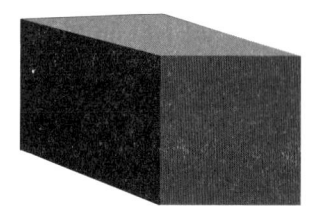

You can use the simple, visual approach shown here to build a six-sided wire-frame cube.

You can also use this approach to create three-dimensional objects with rectangular sides, like the drawing in the accompanying figure.

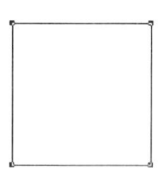

1

Use the Rectangle tool with the Shift key to draw a square like the one in the figure on the left. (Recall that holding down the Shift key with the Rectangle tool forces a perfect square.) Then choose Ungroup from the Element menu (⌘U) to ungroup the square.

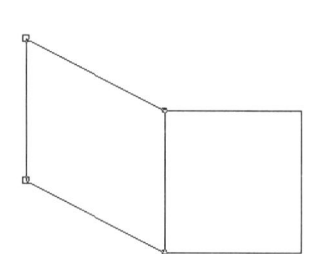

2

Select the square, choose Clone from the Edit menu (⌘=) to make a clone, and Shift-drag the clone to the left. Position the clone against the first square so they share a border.

Then select the two leftmost anchor points on the left square and move them up slightly at a diagonal, holding down the Shift key or using the Up Arrow key if you want to maintain isometric dimensions.

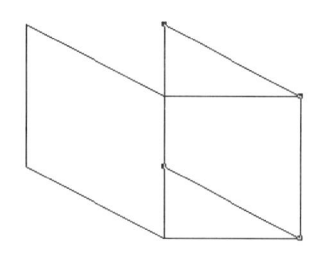

3

Select the object you just changed into a parallelogram. Choose Clone from the Edit menu (⌘=) to make a clone, then drag the clone into position to meet the right edge of the first square.

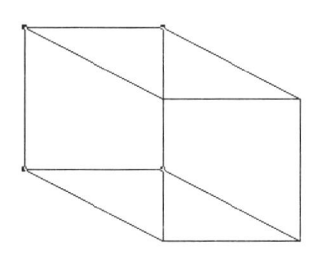

4

Select the first square. Use the Clone command from the Edit menu (⌘=) to make a clone, then drag the clone into position as the fourth side (the rear).

TIP

If you have difficulty aligning the various anchor points precisely, you can select each point, choose Element info from the Element menu (⌘I), then type the desired location for the point into the horizontal and vertical position edit boxes in the Element info dialog box.

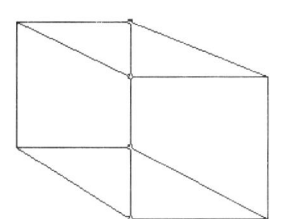

5

To create true perspective, select the anchor points at the upper, backmost edges of the cube by dragging a selection marquee around the top rear edge, then hold down the Shift key as you drag them down slightly. Then select the left rear anchor points of the cube and drag them right slightly.

6

To add to the sense of depth, use the Pen tool to draw a polygon that matches the top side of the cube. You can then shade each of the three "visible" sides (since only three sides would be visible if the object were solid) with a different shade. If one of the "invisible" sides shows through, select the face of the cube through which it shows and choose Bring to front from the Element menu (⌘F).

When the cube is complete, select the entire object and use the Group command from the Element menu (⌘G) to make it a single object.

Cubes: Method 2

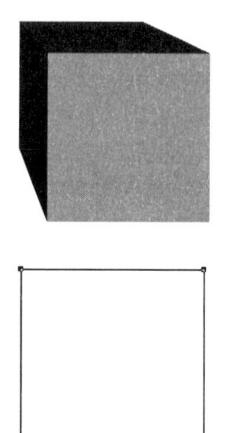

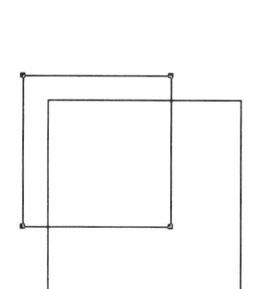

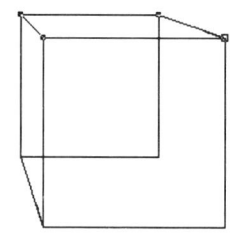

You can use this technique to create three-dimensional objects with irregular sides.

1

Use the Rectangle tool to draw a rectangle, then choose Ungroup from the Element menu (⌘U) to ungroup it.

2

To make one smaller copy of the rectangle, choose Clone from the Edit menu (⌘=) to make a clone, then select the Scaling tool. Option-click with the Scaling tool to open the Scale dialog box. Click Uniform scale and enter 75%, and leave Center of selection as the point of transformation.

With the copy selected, position it so it overlaps the first rectangle.

The positioning of the smaller rectangle will determine the apparent length of the box as well as the viewer's perspective. For example, if you position the smaller rectangle above the larger one, the cube will appear deep and will be viewed from an overhead perspective; if you position the smaller rectangle to overlap the larger rectangle, as in this example, the perspective will be nearly head-on.

3

Select the Pen tool and draw polygons that match the two new "visible" sides of the cube (since the front of the cube is already a closed path, you need not recreate it).

4

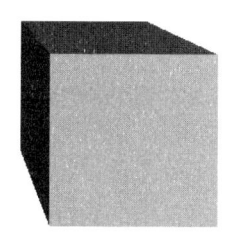

To add to the sense of depth, you can use the Fill and line command from the Attributes menu (⌘E) to set a gray fill (that is, some percentage of black) to shade each side. If one of the "invisible" sides shows through, select the face of the cube through which it shows and choose Bring to front from the Element menu (⌘F).

5

When the cube is complete, select the entire object, and use the Group command from the Element menu (⌘G) to make it a single object.

See also "Cubes: Method 1," and "Highlights" in this chapter, and "Custom Grid #1—Perspective" in Chapter 8.

Cubes: Method 3

Packaging design often calls for accurate three-dimensional perspective views of rectangular-sided objects such as boxes. This technique lets you create accurate three-dimensional perspectives for several common engineering views by creating the sides of the box as rectangular objects, then scaling, skewing, and rotating them into place around a common point. One advantage of this technique is that any text on the package remains editable, even though it has been transformed, so you can create designs before the text has been finalized, then edit the text as necessary.

1

Create the side, front, and bottom faces of the package as rectangular objects with their sides touching, as if the package were flattened. Then use the Group command from the Element menu (⌘G) to group all the elements on each face, so you have three grouped objects, one for each face. Use rounded caps and joins for the line attributes of each rectangle to avoid "spikes" at the corners of the finished package. Then select each grouped side, choose Element info from the Element menu (⌘I) and click to check the Group transforms as a unit option. If you do not do this, the text will not transform along with the rest of the group.

2

Use the Select all command from the Edit menu (⌘A), then Option-click with the Scaling tool at the point where all three faces touch. This point of "mutual intersection" is the origin point for all the transformations used in this technique, so you may want to make a note of its vertical and horizontal coordinates. In the Scale dialog box, click Scale Other, enter scaling values of 100% Horizontal and 86.602% Vertical, and click Mouse location as the point of transformation, then click OK.

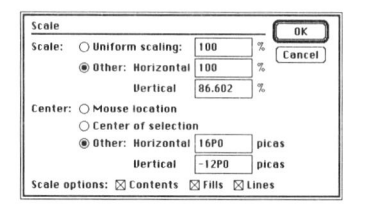

TIP

If you find it difficult to click precisely on the origin point for the transformations, you can type the coordinates into the other edit boxes in the Scale, Skew, and Rotate dialog boxes.

3

Select the group that comprises the side of the package, then Option-click the Skewing tool at the point of mutual intersection. In the Skew dialog box, enter a skew value of -30° along the horizontal axis and click Mouse location as the point of transformation, then click OK. Then Option-click the Rotating tool at the same point, click Mouse location, and rotate the side surface 90°.

You will repeat the process of skewing and rotating the two remaining surfaces, using the values given below.

4

Select the group that comprises the front of the box, then Option-click the Skewing tool at the point of mutual intersection. Enter a skew value of 30° along the horizontal axis. Click Mouse location as the point of transformation, then click OK. Next, Option-click the Rotating tool at the point of mutual intersection, enter a rotation value of 30°, click Mouse location as the point of transformation, then click OK.

5

Select the group that comprises the bottom of the box, then Option-click the Skewing tool at the point of mutual intersection, enter a skew value of -30° along the horizontal axis, click Mouse location as the point of transformation, then click OK. Finally, Option-click the Rotating tool at the point of mutual intersection, enter a rotation value of 30°, and click Mouse location as the point of transformation, then click OK.

6

If the final illustration is too large to fit on one page, you can use the Select all command from the Edit menu (⌘A) and use the Scaling tool to reduce the size of the package (including the size of the type). Similarly you can use the Select all command and then use the Pointer tool to move the package to the center of the page. Once you have completed the package, you should group it with the Group command from the Element menu (⌘G) to avoid inadvertently separating the components.

The transformation values given here produce an isometric view. The values for some other common views are listed in the table below. Note that, while an isometric view uses the same vertical scaling percentage for each face, some of the other views require different scaling percentages for the different faces, so they must be scaled separately.

View	Face	Vertical Scale	Shear	Rotate
Axonometric	Side	70.711%	-45°	90°
	Front	100%	0°	45°
	Bottom	70.711%	-45°	45°
Isometric	Side	86.602%	-30°	90°
	Front	86.602%	30°	30°
	Bottom	86.602%	-30°	30°
Dimetric	Side	96.592%	-15°	90°
	Front	96.592%	15°	60°
	Bottom	50%	-60°	60°
Trimetric	Side	96.592%	-15°	90°
	Front	86.602%	30°	45°
	Bottom	70.711%	-45°	45°
Trimetric	Side	96.592%	-15°	90°
	Front	70.711%	45°	30°
	Bottom	86.602%	-30°	30°

See also "Cubes: Methods 1 and 2" in this chapter and "Custom Grid #1—Perspective" in Chapter 8.

Interlocking Objects

You can use FreeHand's stacking and layering features to produce series of interlocking objects. This example shows how to create a series of interlocking circles, but you can use this technique with any shape, including freeform paths and type converted to paths.

1
Working in 100% view, use the Ellipse tool with the Shift key to draw a circle 30 points in diameter. The information bar gives you the diameter of the circle as you drag the Ellipse tool. Then ungroup the circle using the Ungroup command from the Element menu (⌘U), and give it a black 6-point line and no fill using the Fill and line command from the Attributes menu (⌘E).

2
Choose Clone from the Edit menu (⌘=) to clone the circle, and use the Move command from the Edit menu (⌘M) to move the clone 20 points horizontally.

3
Select the first circle you drew, use the Clone command from the Edit menu (⌘=) to clone it, and give the clone a 4-point white line and no fill using the Fill and line command from the Attributes menu (⌘E). With the white circle selected, hold down the Shift and Control keys and click on the circle to add the black circle behind it to the selection. One sign that both circles are selected is that the anchor points are no longer visible. Two selected points at the same location "cancel each other out" on the screen, but both are in fact selected. With both circles selected, choose Group from the Element menu (⌘G) to group the black and white circles.

4

Press ⌘Space bar and click on the second circle to zoom in to a magnified view, then Command-click on the second circle to select it. Use the Knife tool to cut the second circle at the left and right anchor points, then press Tab to deselect everything.

5

Select the upper segment of the right circle, then use the Clone command from the Edit menu (⌘=) to clone it, and give the clone a 4-point white line and no fill using the Fill and line command from the Attributes menu (⌘E).
 With the white segment selected, press the Shift and Control keys and click on the segment to add the black segment behind it to the selection. Next, choose Group from the Element menu (⌘G) to group the black and white segments.

6

Select the lower segment of the right circle, then choose Clone from the Edit menu (⌘=) to clone it, and give the clone a 4-point white line and no fill. With the white segment selected, hold down the Shift and Control keys and click on the segment to add the black segment behind it to the selection. Next, choose Group from the Element menu (⌘G) to group the black and white segments.

7

Press Tab to deselect everything, then go to the Layers palette, choose New from the palette's pop-up menu, and position the new layer behind the foreground layer. Then select the group that now comprises the lower segment of the right circle, and click the new layer's name in the Layers palette to send the segment to the new layer. You now have two interlocking circles.

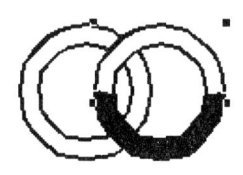

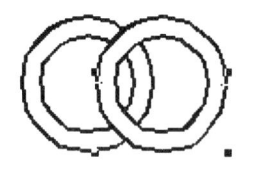

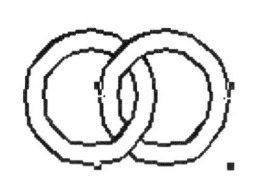

8

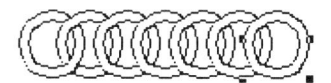

If you want to produce additional circles, first determine how many additional circles you want to make. Then choose Clone from the Edit menu (⌘=) to clone the group that comprises the upper segment of the right circle. Use the Move command from the Edit menu (⌘M) to move the clone 20 points horizontally. Press ⌘D (Duplicate from the Edit menu) to produce the desired number of additional copies. Then select the group that comprises the lower segment of the circle and repeat the process. You now have the desired number of circles, but they do not overlap correctly.

9

Starting at the third circle from the left, select the group that comprises the lower half of the circle and choose Send to back from the element menu (⌘B) to send it to the back of the layer. Then repeat this process for the lower halves of the remaining new circles, working from left to right.

NOTE

On the screen image, you may notice small breaks in the circles where the segments meet, but the art will print correctly.

Cylinders

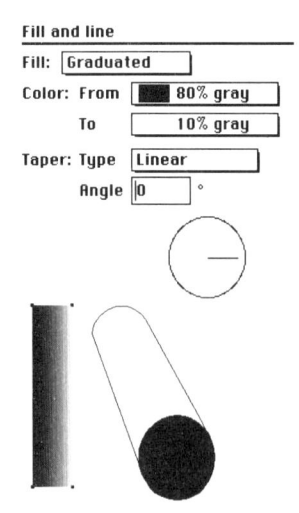

This technique uses graduated fills and clipping paths to produce realistic highlights on curved surfaces. The example used here is a cylinder, but you can adapt this technique to produce shading on any curved surface.

1

First use the Ellipse tool to draw an ellipse that will form the face of the cylinder. The ellipse should be almost a perfect circle. How far out of round you draw it depends on the perspective view you want to achieve. In this example, the ellipse is slightly taller than it is wide. Give the ellipse a line of None and a fill of 80% gray using either the Fill and line command from the Attributes menu (⌘E) or the Colors palette.

2

Next, draw the shape of the shaft using the Pen tool. For now, give it no fill and a fine black line. You will remove the line later, but for now the line lets you see the shape.

3

Use the Rectangle tool to draw a rectangle the same height as the shaft of the cylinder, and approximately half its width. Then choose Ungroup from the Element menu (⌘U) to ungroup the rectangle. Use the Fill and line command from the Attributes menu (⌘E) to give the rectangle a line of None, and a horizontal graduated fill from 80% gray at the left to 10% gray at the right.

4

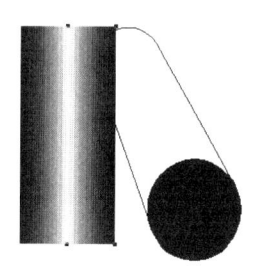

With the rectangle selected, choose the Clone command from the Edit menu (⌘=) to clone it. Then select the Reflecting tool and Shift-click on the lower-right corner of the clone to reflect it around the vertical axis. Finally, select both rectangles and choose Group from the Element menu (⌘G) to group them.

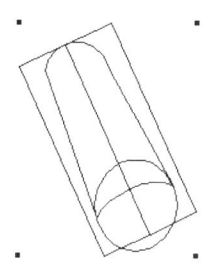

5

With the Rotating tool, rotate the grouped rectangles to the same angle as the shaft of the cylinder. Then drag the group into position so it covers the shaft completely, with the highlight in the center positioned over the center of the shaft. You may want to switch to keyline view (⌘K) to do this.

6

With the grouped, rotated rectangles selected, choose Cut from the Edit menu (⌘X) to cut them to the Clipboard. Then select the shaft of the cylinder and choose Paste inside from the Edit menu.

7

If necessary, select the ellipse that forms the face of the cylinder, and choose Bring to front from the Element menu (⌘F) to bring it to the front. Then drag a selection marquee around the entire cylinder, and choose Group from the Element menu (⌘G) to group it.

Drop Shadows: Method 1

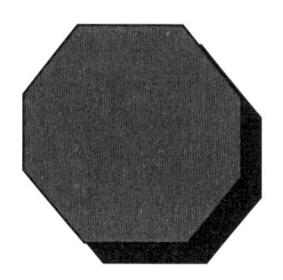

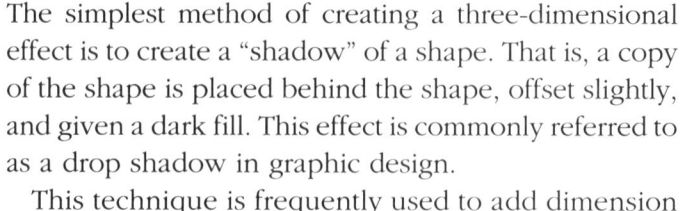

The simplest method of creating a three-dimensional effect is to create a "shadow" of a shape. That is, a copy of the shape is placed behind the shape, offset slightly, and given a dark fill. This effect is commonly referred to as a drop shadow in graphic design.

This technique is frequently used to add dimension or visual interest to conceptual illustrations such as bar charts and organization charts. You can add special effects to any illustration by using this three-dimensional technique on text, borders, and other two-dimensional objects.

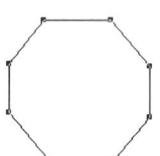

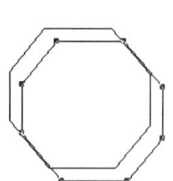

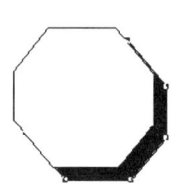

1

Create an object using whatever tool is appropriate. In this example, use the Pen tool to draw a polygon. You can use the visible grid as an alignment aid.

2

Use the Pointer tool to select the object, then choose Duplicate from the Edit menu (⌘D) to create a duplicate that is slightly offset diagonally from the original.

3

With the duplicate still selected, choose Send to back from the Element menu (⌘B). Then use Fill and line from the Attributes menu (⌘E) to add shading to the shadow, or apply a fill and line using the Colors palette.

See also "Drawing Bar Charts" and "Organizational Charts" in Chapter 4, "Cubes: Methods 1 and 2," and "Drop Shadows: Method 2" in this chapter.

Drop Shadows: Method 2

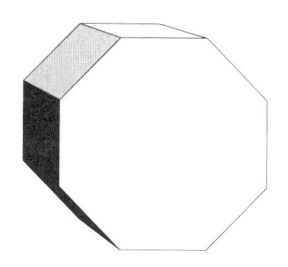

The three-dimensional objects you can create with Aldus FreeHand are not truly three-dimensional; you cannot rotate a drawing of a house to see a front view and a back view. But you can create a third dimension visually using the technique described here.

Besides adding dimensions to create representation of solid objects such as boxes, buildings, and books, you can add special effects to any illustration by using this three-dimensional technique on text, borders, and other two-dimensional objects.

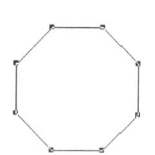

1

Create an object using whatever tool is appropriate. In this example, use the Pen tool to draw a polygon. You can use the visible grid as an alignment aid.

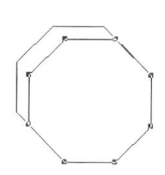

2

Use the Pointer tool to select the object, then choose Duplicate from the Edit menu (⌘D) to create a duplicate that is slightly offset diagonally from the original.

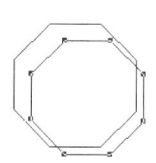

3

With the duplicate still selected, select the Scaling tool from the Toolbox. Click in the center of the duplicate, then Shift-drag to scale the object slightly smaller than the original object. Then, with the duplicate still selected, choose Send to back from the Element menu (⌘B).

4

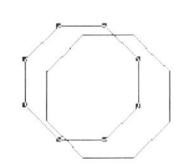

Position the smaller polygon as shown in the figure on the left by dragging it with the Pointer tool. The position of the smaller polygon determines the point of view in the perspective illusion. Experiment with other positions if you like.

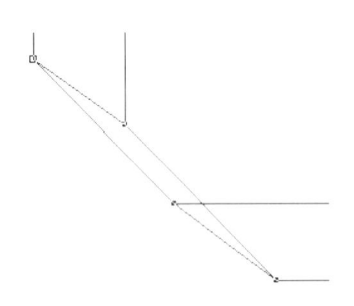

5

Using the Pen tool, draw polygons between each set of corresponding anchor points to form the sides of the object. If you work in keyline mode at high magnification, you will find it is easier to place the points precisely at the corners of the two original polygons.

6

If you want to add shading to each face, use Fill and line from the Attributes menu (⌘E) to add shading to the three-dimensional faces of the object, or apply a fill from the Colors palette.

In this figure, use a fill of 100% black for the bottom face, 80% gray for the next face, 40% gray for the next face, and 20% gray for the top face. Finally, select the small polygon and press Delete (Backspace) to delete it.

See also "Cubes: Methods 1 and 2" in this chapter and "Custom Grid #1—Perspective" in Chapter 8.

Flower Petals

Flowers are certainly among the most common objects rendered as artwork. Here is a simple technique for creating flowers like the one pictured in the accompanying figure.

You can use variations on this technique to draw other types of flowers, including roses, chrysanthemums, and other more complicated varieties.

1

Draw one petal that you will use as the basic unit. Select the petal and choose Clone from the Edit menu (⌘=) to make a clone. Then select the Rotating tool and Option-click the base of the petal. In the Rotate dialog box, enter the number of degrees yielded by the following formula:

Degrees = 360°/ (number of petals)

In this example, you will want 36 units; so you will type "10" as the number of degrees (360 divided by 36). (See also "Radial Symmetry: Methods 1 and 2" in Chapter 4.)

Click Mouse location for the center of rotation, then click OK to close the Rotate dialog box and rotate the cloned petal. Use Duplicate from the Edit menu (⌘D) to complete the flower.

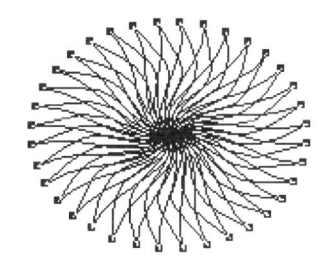

2

Scale the flower nonproportionally. Choose Select all from the Edit menu (⌘A) or drag a selection marquee around all the petals to select the flower. Then select the Scaling tool, click near the bottom left edge of the petals, and drag diagonally to achieve an effect similar to the one shown in the figure on the left.

3

With the Pointer tool, select and move the points at the outside tip of each petal by a small amount to create a more natural, organic look.

4

You can create more complex arrangements of petals by scaling the first set to smaller sizes and overlaying several additional sets. To do this, select the whole flower with the Pointer tool and choose Clone from the Edit menu (⌘=) to make a clone. Then select the Scaling tool, click the center of the flower as the transformation point, and drag until the smaller set of petals is the size you wish.

For a more realistic effect, use Group from the Element menu (⌘G) and the Rotating tool to rotate each set slightly.

TIP

You can use this technique with a wide variety of fills. For example, you can apply a graduated fill to the basic petal you create in Step 1, before cloning and duplicating it. That way, the gradation of color goes from the center of the flower to its edge. Or you can use the Join elements command from the Element menu to make the basic flower you create in Steps 1–3 a composite path rather than a group. Then you can apply a radial fill to the whole flower. You will have to use the Element info command from the Element menu, and then uncheck the Even/odd fill option to avoid holes appearing where the petals overlap. With either of these treatments, experiment with the color of the line as well. Start with a color that is midway between the starting and ending colors of the fill.

See also "Radial Symmetry: Methods 1 and 2" in Chapter 4.

Highlights

You can make highlights easily, quickly, and accurately with FreeHand using the Blend command. Remember that the Blend command blends not only different paint attributes, but different shapes as well. This allows you to blend and highlight gradations between two shapes as diverse as an ellipse and a rectangle, or two colors as different as black and white.

Highlights are usually not the same shape as the object being highlighted. With FreeHand it is possible to blend smoothly disparate shapes to create more realistic three-dimensional shading effects.

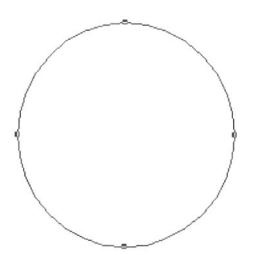

1

The object to be shaded is a perfect circle, shown in the figure on the left. To create the circle, use the Ellipse tool with the Shift key to constrain the object to a perfect circle. With the object selected, choose Ungroup from the Element menu (⌘U).

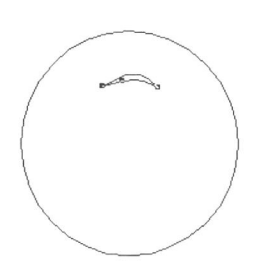

2

Now you will draw the shape of the highlight that would appear if the object were truly three-dimensional and lighted from a single source. Use the Pen tool to draw a crescent shape, which is the natural highlight for a sphere.

Normally, you could create a crescent shape with only two anchor points, one at each end. But since you will be blending this crescent into the circle, you want to add one more anchor point as a reference point for the blend, halfway along the inside edge of the crescent.

Position the crescent inside the circle, so that the bottom anchor point of the circle, the center of the circle, and the anchor point halfway along the inside edge of

162   Using Aldus FreeHand 3.0

the crescent lie approximately in a straight line. The crescent should be about halfway between the center and the edge of the circle.

3

With the Pointer tool, select the crescent shape inside the circle and choose Fill and line from the Attributes menu (⌘E). Fill the crescent with a light color or a light gray and click OK. Then select the circle, choose Fill and line again (⌘E), and this time set the fill to a darker shade of the same color, and click OK.

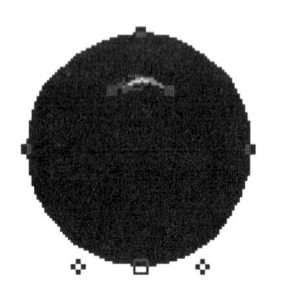

4

Use the Select all command from the Edit menu (⌘A) to select both objects. Then hold down the Shift key, and click to select the bottom anchor point of the circle, and the anchor point halfway along the inside of the crescent. These act as reference points for the blend.

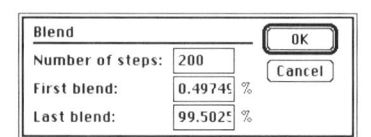

5

Now you are ready to blend. Choose Blend from the Element menu. The Blend dialog box appears. Type the number of blend steps you would like the transformation to use. The more steps you request, the smoother the blend. In this example, we used 200 steps. After selecting the number of blend steps, click OK.

The more blend steps you use, the larger and slower the file will be. Usually no more than 30 blends are needed to yield a smooth transition on a laser printer, and fewer blends are needed when the objects are small, but more blends are needed for high-resolution imagesetter output. See Chapter 6 for information on calculating the optimal number of blends.

6

If you have a 24-bit color monitor, preview the blend with the monitor set to millions of colors. On an 8-bit color or grayscale monitor, you will see distinct bands, but these will be less obvious on printed output from a laser printer, and unnoticeable on output from a high-resolution imagesetter.

You may need to try a couple of different blends to create the most effective visual illusion and highlight. Experiment by choosing different points to blend. Do not forget that blending is affected by the pair of reference points you choose initially. Successful illusion blending happens when you choose two points that have a smooth and direct transition path.

6

Fills and Patterns

Any closed path can have a fill that is different from the border around it. (Fills assigned to open paths do not appear until the path is closed.) You can create and assign fills through the Colors palette, through the Colors command in the Attributes menu, or through the Fill and line command in the Attributes menu. These basic functions are described in Chapter 13 (in the sections on the Colors and Styles palettes) and in Chapter 14 (in the sections on the Fill and line command, the Colors command, the Styles command, the Paste inside command, and the Blend command).

In this chapter, we briefly summarize the methods of filling a closed path and then go on to some of the more difficult or unusual uses of these functions. Topics covered in this chapter include:

- Applying Fills
- Using Custom Fills
- Using the Styles Palette
- Creating Color Templates
- Copying Colors from One Document to Another
- Creating a Color Library
- Creating Optimal Blends
- Blending for Spot Color Separation

- Blending to Create New Colors or Grays
- Clipping Paths as Masks
- Masking to Change Fills
- Masking to Create Highlights
- Off-center Radial Fills
- Patterns #1—Discrete Objects
- Patterns #2—Continuous Symmetry
- Patterns #3—Continuous Asymmetry

Applying Fills

This section offers a quick summary of the methods of applying fills to a closed path.

Using the Colors Palette to Fill an Object

The simplest way to fill an object with a color is through the Colors palette.

1

First select the object(s) to be filled. You can apply the same fill to more than one object at a time through the Colors palette.

2

Choose View ► Windows ► Colors to display the Colors palette if it is not already displayed—or use the keyboard shortcut ⌘9.

3

Click a color listed in the palette.

If the color you wish to apply is not visible in the palette, use the scroll bars to view additional colors, or drag the size box at the lower right corner of the Colors palette to enlarge it.

If the color you wish to apply is not listed on the palette, you can create it as a new color following the procedure described in the discussion of the Colors palette in Chapter 13, or copy it from another document or a color library as described later in this chapter.

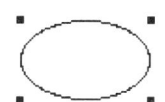

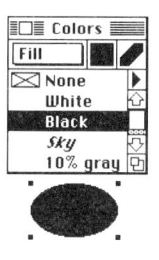

If the selected object does not fill with the selected color, either the object was not really selected (i.e., does not show handles or points) or the element is not a closed path. You can close it by choosing Element info from the Element menu (⌘I) and clicking Closed path if it is not already checked.

See also the description of the Pen tool in Chapter 12 for methods of closing a path.

Filling an Element through the Fill and Line Dialog Box

The Fill and line dialog box offers a greater variety of fill options than does the Colors palette.

1

First select the object(s) to be filled. You can apply the same fill to more than one object at a time through the Fill and line dialog box only if all of the objects have the same fill and line specifications to begin with. Otherwise, to change the fill of two objects that currently have different fills, you need to select them one at a time and go through the next steps for each.

2

Choose Fill and line from the Attributes menu (⌘E) to display the Fill and line dialog box.

3

Select the type of fill from the Fill pop-up menu. The figure on the left shows the pop-up menu in the dialog box.

4

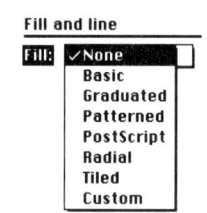

The rest of the options in the dialog box change depending on the type of fill you select—and each of these options is described in detail in Chapter 14 in "Fill and line." Click OK to close the dialog box when you have made additional selections appropriate to the type of fill you have chosen. The figure on the left shows the results when default settings are accepted for a Basic Black fill (top), a Black-to-White Graduated fill (middle), and a Black-to-White Radial fill (bottom).

Tiled and custom fills are described later in this chapter as well as in Chapter 14.

Filling an Element through the Styles Palette

If you have defined styles that include fill specifications, you can fill an object through the Styles palette. The Styles palette is described in detail in Chapter 13, and additional suggestions for creating a Styles palette are given later in this chapter. If you already have created a style, you can apply it following these steps.

1

First select the object(s) to be filled.

2

Choose View ➤ Windows ➤ Styles to display the Styles palette if it is not already displayed—or use the keyboard shortcut ⌘3.

3

Click a style listed in the palette.

If the selected object does not show the fill, either the object is not really selected, the path is not closed, or the style you applied has no fill specifications associated with it.

Using Custom Fills

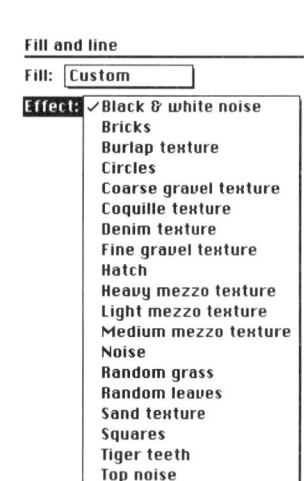

Fill and line
Fill: Custom
Effect: ✓ Black & white noise
Bricks
Burlap texture
Circles
Coarse gravel texture
Coquille texture
Denim texture
Fine gravel texture
Hatch
Heavy mezzo texture
Light mezzo texture
Medium mezzo texture
Noise
Random grass
Random leaves
Sand texture
Squares
Tiger teeth
Top noise

FreeHand comes with 19 custom fills that become available in the Effect pop-up menu when Custom is selected as the Fill in the Fill and line dialog box. Whenever you choose a custom fill, FreeHand displays a dialog box that lets you change the appearance of the fill. These basic functions are described in detail in the Fill and line command description in Chapter 14.

Custom fills appear on the screen as a pattern of "c"s when applied to an object—you cannot see the fill until you print it. This can be inconvenient when you want to change the default settings for the fill. Here we present a handy reference table that shows what each of the custom fill samples look like with the default settings.

TIP

It is a good idea to add to the Styles palette custom fills that you have modified (as described in the next technique), so you can easily apply them to other objects without remembering how they were modified.

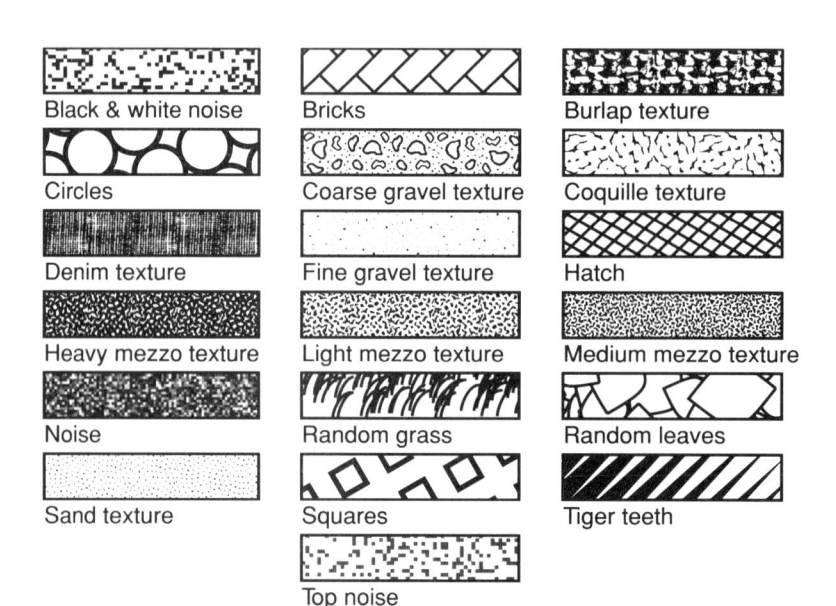

Black & white noise | Bricks | Burlap texture
Circles | Coarse gravel texture | Coquille texture
Denim texture | Fine gravel texture | Hatch
Heavy mezzo texture | Light mezzo texture | Medium mezzo texture
Noise | Random grass | Random leaves
Sand texture | Squares | Tiger teeth
Top noise

Using the Styles Palette

If you know that you will be using certain attributes—such as colors, fills, or stroke combinations—repeatedly in a drawing, it is useful to create a Styles palette of your choices. Chapter 13 describes how to create and use a Styles palette. Here we briefly summarize those steps, then eulogize several benefits of using a Styles palette in your work.

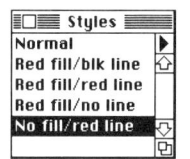

1

You display the Styles palette by choosing View → Windows → Styles or by pressing ⌘3.

2

One way to define a style is to first select an element that has already been set up with the attributes that you want to use in the style, then choose New from the Styles palette pop-up menu. Type the name of the new style in the Styles dialog box, click Apply, then click OK to close the dialog box and apply the style to the selected element.

3

To apply a style to an object through the Styles palette, first select the object, then click the name of the style you wish to apply in the Styles palette.

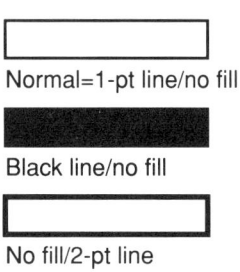

TIP

If you work in a group where different Styles palettes are shared, or if you switch between different Styles palettes often, it is a good idea to print a reference sheet. Draw a series of ellipses or rectangles, and assign each with the attributes you want using the Styles palette. Using the Text tool, label each object with the style name and a brief description.

Normal=1-pt line/no fill

Black line/no fill

No fill/2-pt line

No fill/hairline

172 Using Aldus FreeHand 3.0

Creating Color Templates

FreeHand comes with four color templates, called *Bright Template, Pastel Template, Earth Template*, and *Corporate Template*. You can use one of these templates in creating your own artwork by using the Open command from the File menu (⌘O) to open the template (stored in the *Color Templates* folder, in the *Aldus FreeHand 3.0* application folder) and then starting your artwork from scratch as a new, untitled document.

You can create your own custom color templates using the technique described here. You can also copy colors from a template or document into any other FreeHand document using the technique described following this one ("Copying Colors from One Document to Another").

Follow these steps to create your own custom color template:

1

Start a new document and create an object for each color in the palette that you will create. The objects can be lines, rectangles, ellipses, text, or any other path or imported graphic. The figure on the left shows three ellipses.

2

Use the Colors command from the Attributes menu, or the New command from the Colors palette's pop-up menu, to display the Colors dialog box and create each color you want in the palette.

TIP

You can create a color template by opening a new document and creating all your colors through the Colors dialog box, without adding any objects and

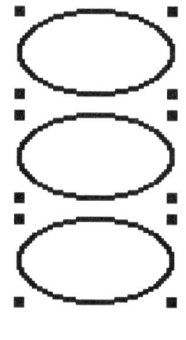

Chapter 6. Fills and Patterns   173

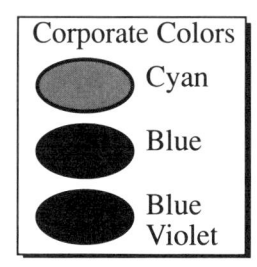

applying the colors, but you miss the advantage of being able to print a color test sheet or reference sheet, as suggested in Step 4.

TIP

You can instead create a color template by opening an existing document that includes all the colors you want in the template, select and delete all the artwork, then save the empty file as a template (Step 5).

3

Assign each color as a Basic Fill color to each of the objects you created.

4

Optionally, print a proof sheet or reference sheet on a color printer. This is a good idea if several people will be sharing the same custom Colors palette, or if you will be using many different Colors palettes.

TIP

For a reference sheet, it is helpful to add a heading on the page that identifies the template name, and to add text labels next to each colored object, identifying the name of the color and (optionally) the composition.

5

Move the color objects off to the side—beyond the page margins of the artwork—and save the document in the Template format (an option in the Save document as dialog box).

TIP

You can change the default color template by opening a new document and creating all your colors through the Colors dialog box, then saving the document as a template file with the name *Aldus FreeHand Defaults* and storing it in the *Aldus FreeHand 3.0* application folder.

174 Using Aldus FreeHand 3.0

Copying Colors from One Document to Another

You do not need to create colors from scratch every time you open a new document. If you want to use all the same colors that you used in a previous document, either create a template from the artwork (see the first Tip in the previous technique), or copy one or more of the colors from the existing artwork into the new document, as described here.

1

Open the FreeHand document that uses the colors you want to copy. Select an object that uses the color you want (or select several objects of different colors to copy more than one color at a time), and choose Copy from the Edit menu (⌘C).

TIP

If the objects that use the color you want are very large or complex or grouped, you can create a simple object such as a line and assign it the color you want from the Colors palette, or create a rectangle or ellipse and assign two colors to the same object—one to the line and one to the fill. You can store three colors in any closed path by assigning one to the line, and two to a graduated fill. The figure below shows the Fill and line dialog box with three colors assigned to one object.

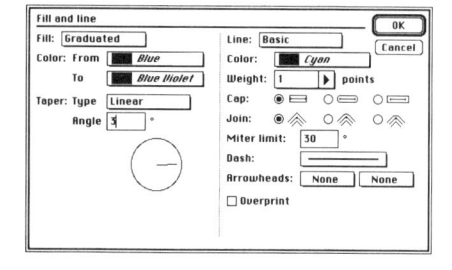

2

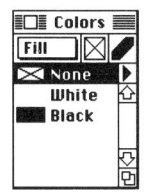

Open a new document or the document into which you wish to copy the colors, and choose Paste from the Edit menu (⌘V). The pasted object's colors are automatically added to the Colors palette. The figure on the left shows the Colors palette of a document before (left) and after (right) objects with new colors were pasted into the document from another FreeHand document.

TIP

If the objects you copy from Artwork #1 use colors with the same names as colors in Artwork #2—the document you paste them into—the pasted objects will take on the color definitions set up in Artwork #2.

See also "Creating a Color Library," the next technique.

176 Using Aldus FreeHand 3.0

Creating a Color Library

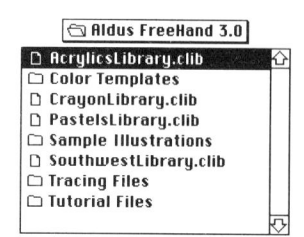

FreeHand comes with a color library called *CrayonLibrary.clib*, that contains process color formulas for the colors commonly included in a box of 64 crayons. The use of this library is described in detail in the Colors palette description in Chapter 13. You can also create your own custom color libraries using the technique described here.

TIP

You might wonder why you would bother going through the next steps to create a color library when you can create the color easily in FreeHand. The answer is that it is easier to add colors to a palette from a library than to copy colors from one FreeHand document to another (described in the previous technique).

A color library is a text file that can be created or edited using any word-processing application—or using PageMaker and exporting the text as a text-only file. You can learn a lot about a color library by opening the *CrayonLibrary.clib* that comes with FreeHand. An excerpt from that file is shown below:

header lines	>	ColorLibrary 1.0
		% These are from the 64 crayon box - sharpener NOT included
		LibraryType Crayon Colors
		BeginColorDefs
color definitions	>	name=(Apricot) cmyk=(.0, .15, .3, .0) rgb=(1.0, .85, .7)
		name=(Aquamarine) cmyk=(1.0, .1, .1, .0) rgb=(.0, .9, .9)
		name=(Bittersweet) cmyk=(.15, .7, 1.0, .0) rgb=(.85, .3, .0)
		...(60 lines omitted here)...
		name=(Yellow Orange) cmyk=(.0, .35, 1.0, .0) rgb=(1.0, .65, .0)
end of file marker	>	**EndColorDefs**
		EndColorLibrary

The lines shown in bold must appear in any color library file. They include two header lines: one that identifies this as a color library ("ColorLibrary 1.0"), and a line that signifies the start of the color definitions ("BeginColorDefs"). Two footer lines are also required: "EndColorDefs" and "EndColorLibrary." These lines must be typed as shown here—with no spaces between the words.

Between these two lines you type the color definitions. These too must follow a very strict form. In the next line, the unchanging elements are shown in bold, the variable elements are shown in italics:

name=(*Apricot***) cmyk=(***.0, .15, .3, .0***) rgb=(***1.0, .85, .7***)**

The color name that you type in parentheses after "name=" will be the name that appears in the Colors palette when you copy this color into an illustration. The four numbers that you type in parentheses after "cmyk=" are the percentages of cyan, magenta, yellow, and black that compose the color—0%, 15%, 30%, and 0%, respectively, in this example. The three numbers that you type in parentheses after "rgb=" are the percentages of red, green, and blue that compose the color—100%, 85%, and 70% in this example.

The steps below demonstrate one method of creating a color library.

1

Before you define the color library, you need to know what percentages to assign to the color model. One way to do this is to use a color reference book that shows colors and gives their percentage components for the RGB and CMYK color models. Another way is to define a color in FreeHand—using the Colors command from the Attributes menu or the New command from the Colors palette pop-up menu to get the Colors dialog box. The figures below show the Colors dialog box for a new color named "Blue Violet," first with the RGB color model selected and then with the CMYK color model selected.

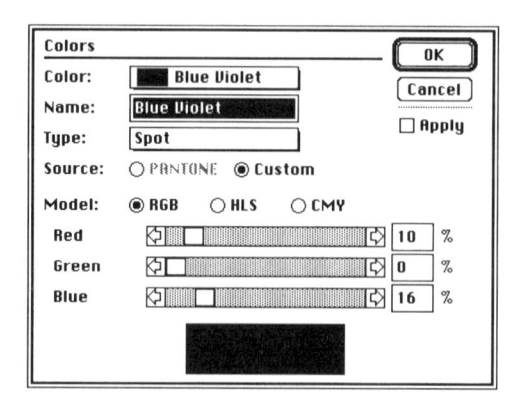

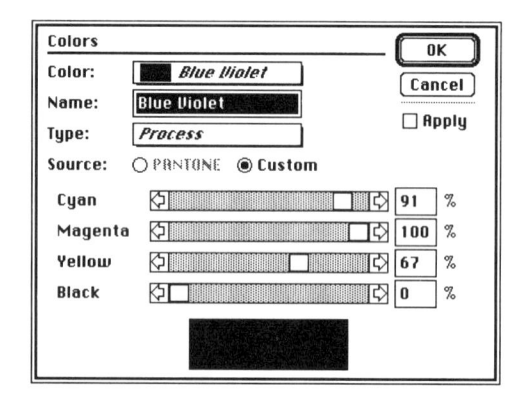

Make a note of the percentages of colors used in the two models before closing the Colors dialog box and quitting FreeHand (or switching to the text editing application through MultiFinder).

TIP

Colors display most accurately on the screen and in dialog boxes when the monitor is set to 256 colors (through the Control Panel in the Apple menu). If your monitor is set to 16 colors, the colors on the screen and in the Colors palette will not be as accurate as the colors displayed in the Colors dialog box (when editing a color or creating a new color).

TIP

Whether you use a color reference book or create the color in FreeHand to get the percentages, you cannot know exactly how the color will print until you go through the steps of printing the actual inks on paper. If the exact color is important to you, it is worth the trouble and expense of printing a Matchprint or Cromalin color proof of color samples before you apply them to artwork and produce color separations for offset printing.

2

Using any text editing application, start a new file and type the header lines:

ColorLibrary 1.0
BeginColorDefs

3

Type the lines that define the new colors. The order that you type them here will be the order in which they appear in the Select library color(s) dialog box, the Colors dialog box, and the Colors palette.

name=(Earth) cmyk=(.3, .6, 1.0, .1) rgb=(.6, .3, .0)
name=(Sky) cmyk=(.5, .3, .15, .0) rgb=(.5, .7, .85)
name=(Water) cmyk=(.90, .20, .56, .0) rgb=(.1, .5, .44)

They need not be in alphabetical order—although that is the most common order used. You might prefer to list them by color groups, or list them in rainbow-color sequence:

name=(Red) cmyk=(.12, 1.0, 1.0, .0) rgb=(.88, .0, .0)
name=(Orange) cmyk=(.0, .4, 1.0, .0) rgb=(1.0, .6, .0)
name=(Yellow) cmyk=(.0, .0, 1.0, .0) rgb=(1.0, 1.0, .0)
name=(Green Yellow) cmyk=(.2, .0, 1.0, .0) rgb=(.8, .0, 1.0)
name=(Green) cmyk=(1.0, .18, 1.0, .0) rgb=(.0, .82, .0)
name=(Green Blue) cmyk=(1.0, .4, .37, .0) rgb=(.0, .6, .63)
name=(Blue) cmyk=(.71, .70, .21, .0) rgb=(.29, .30, .79)
name=(Blue Violet) cmyk=(.91, 1.0, .67, .0) rgb=(.09, .0, .33)
name=(Violet Blue) cmyk=(.8, 1.0, .67, .0) rgb=(.2, .0, .33)
name=(Violet Red) cmyk=(.1, 1.0, .0, .0) rgb=(.9, .0, 1.0)

You need not include all color models in a color definition, and the color models can be specified in any order (i.e., you can type the RGB color model specifications first and the CMYK model second). If you omit the RGB definition, the color will be grayed out (not available) when you select Spot color in the Select library color(s) dialog box (Step 7). If you omit the CMYK definition, the color will be grayed when you select Process color in Step 7.

NOTE

If you specify both the CMYK and the RGB color models, but the percentages entered for one do not yield the same color as the percentages entered for the other, the CMYK color model will take precedence.

4

Type the two lines that are required to end the file:

EndColorDefs

EndColorLibrary

5

Save the file as text only, with a ".clib" extension at the end of the file name.

6

To add a color from the library to a FreeHand document, choose Library from the pop-up menu on the Colors palette, and choose a library name from the list.

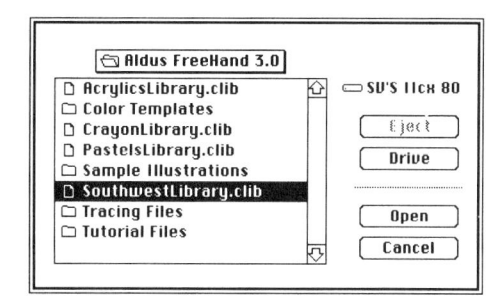

CAUTION

If you get an error message when you try to open a library that you just created, open the library using your text editing application and review every line against the guidelines given here. Since a library is computer code, everything must be entered exactly as described. Even an extra space in one of the first two lines can result in an error.

7

Click Process or Spot to select the model in which FreeHand will store the color, then Shift-click each color name you want to add to your document and click OK.

NOTE

Colors from the library that have the same name as colors in the document's Colors palette will not be listed in the Select library color(s) dialog box.

8

The selected colors will be added to the end of the list in the Colors palette. You can rearrange the colors in the list as described for the Colors palette in Chapter 13.

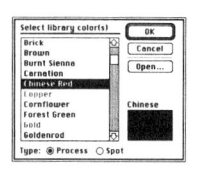

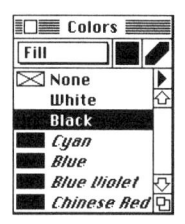

Creating Optimal Blends

The Blend command is often used to create a series of graduated colors as part of the artwork—as an alternative to specifying a graduated fill through the Fill and line dialog box. In this usage, you want to create blends that have smooth blends between colors, without the distinct "bands" of color that can result when you specify too few steps in the Blend dialog box. At the same time, you do not want to create so many blend steps that you increase the file size without improving the result.

NOTE

Creating gradual fills with blends makes a file larger than if the same effects are created using the Graduated fill option in the Fill and line dialog box. For example, a file with an empty rectangle took 3,580 bytes of space. The same rectangle saved with a graduated fill took 3,592 bytes (only 12 bytes added by the fill). The same graduated effect created as a blend composed of nine rectangles took 5,072 bytes (nearly 1,500 bytes added). The figure on the left shows a rectangle created using a graduated fill (left) and the same area created as a blend composed of nine rectangles (right).

NOTE

The color changes created by a graduated fill might not appear the same as the color changes created by blending on a low resolution monitor, or when colors are set to less than 256 through the Control Panel, but they should look similar when printed.

TIP

As a general rule, it's a good idea to use graduated fills instead of blends where possible. When you must use blends to create an airbrush effect—when you want the shades of color to meet along a curved edge rather than the straight bands created by graduated fills, for example, calculate the optimum number of steps in the blend using one of the two formulas presented in the next steps.

1

Create the two objects to be blended. Use the Colors palette or the Fill and line command from the Attributes menu (⌘E) to define the attributes for each object. If these are closed paths, set the line color to None or make it the same color as the fill.

TIP

If you are blending two rectangular shapes, use a straight line set to a wide weight instead of drawing two rectangles to minimize the file size. For instance, nine 16-point wide rectangles that composed a blend (left) took up 4,902 bytes, whereas the same blend effect composed of 16-point wide lines (right) took up only 4,502 bytes.

2a

If the two corresponding points that you intend to select in the blending process are less than an inch apart, use this formula to calculate the optimum number of blend steps:

> Number of steps = 2 X distance (in points) between corresponding reference points identified in the blend.

For example, if the selected reference points in the two blend elements are 60 points apart, as in the figure in Step 4, the optimal number of steps in blending is 120. If you cannot figure out how far apart the elements are (using the rulers), see "Measuring with a Point" in Chapter 8.

2b

Over distances larger than an inch, other factors that come into play besides the distance between elements include printer resolution (dpi), line screen frequency (lpi) specified as the Screen ruling in the Halftone screen dialog box (displayed by choosing the Halftone screen command from the Attributes menu), and the percentage of color change between elements.

The formula for calculating the optimal number of blends over distances larger than one inch becomes:

Number of steps = (dpi/lpi)² X (% change in color).

For example, if you are printing at 300 dpi with a 60 lpi screen ruling specification and a 10% change in color, the optimal number of steps is 3 (i.e., 300/60=5, 5 squared = 25, 10% of 25 is 2.5, rounded to the next highest integer = 3).

Aldus has made this calculation easy by providing a FreeHand document in the *Aldus FreeHand 3.0* application folder called *Blend Table* which you can print as a reference sheet. It has optimal blends already calculated for 260 different dpi/lpi/%-change combinations.

Determine the degree of color change by selecting each object in turn and choosing Colors from the Attributes menu to open the Colors dialog box and view the color composition under the process color model (CMYK). Make a note of each process color's percentage, and see which process color undergoes the greatest percentage change between the two elements.

For example, let's say the two colors have the compositions shown in the following table. The color change percentage that you use in the above formula would be 100%—the change in yellow.

Component	Color 1	Color 2	Difference
Cyan	10%	40%	30%
Magenta	30%	80%	50%
Yellow	0%	100%	**100%**
Black	15%	40%	25%

3

Calculate the band width that will result: divide the distance between the two reference points that you will identify in blending the elements by the estimated number of blend steps. The result is the approximate size of the color bands that will result from the blend. A .5-point band yields the highest quality possible with current printing technologies. If the band width is smaller than .5 point, you can probably use fewer steps in the blend. A one-point band yields good quality at most resolutions, and you can get by with larger band sizes if your final art is to be printed at a low (300 dpi) resolution. Beyond a point, however, large bands become visible. If you are blending open paths, the line weight should not be smaller than the band width.

Adjust the number of blend steps or the line weights as appropriate.

4

Use the Pointer tool to select the two objects. If they are rectangles or ellipses created with FreeHand's basic shape tools, choose Ungroup from the Element menu (⌘U) to ungroup them. Then select two corresponding points on each of the objects. To select a point, first click on the object with the Pointer tool to select the object, then click on a point. (See "Blend" in Chapter 14. Remember that objects must be ungrouped, and corresponding points must be selected on closed paths, in order to be blended.)

5

Choose the Blend command from the Element menu and specify the number of steps calculated in Step 2.

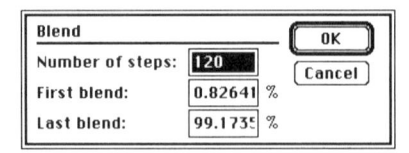

```
Blend
Number of steps: 120        OK
First blend:    0.82641 %   Cancel
Last blend:     99.1735 %
```

6

Print the blend to check the results.

TIP

You will see that the gradations of the fill appear smoother on high-resolution printers than they do on the screen. The banding that appears on the screen (at 72 dpi) will dissipate when the blend is printed at higher resolutions (such as a 300 dpi laser printer). Banding that might appear from a 300 dpi laser printer will dissipate when printed on an imagesetter at 1,200 dpi or more.

7

If the printed results are not acceptable, you can decrease banding by increasing the printer resolution, or modify the artwork using one of these techniques:

The Blend command automatically groups the two original objects with the resulting blended object(s). You can change the result by selecting the group and choosing Element info from the Element menu (⌘I) to get the Blend dialog box and then increasing the number of steps.

You can decrease the line frequency by selecting the grouped, blended objects and choosing Halftone screen from the Attributes menu and specifying a higher value for Screen ruling.

You can increase the percentage in color change by changing the color composition of one or both elements. Option-click one of the original objects and use the Colors palette or Fill and line from the Attributes menu (⌘E) to change the color or tint of the object. The color in the blended objects will change automatically if you have not ungrouped the set.

You can use the Ungroup command to ungroup the blended objects, delete the objects created by the blend, and move the two original objects closer together. Then use the Blend command again.

TIP

If the file takes too long to print or is too large, you can decrease the printing time or the file size by using fewer blend steps, but you will need to compensate by making one or more of the adjustments suggested in Step 7.

TIP

The Blend command always creates *process* colors when two objects of different colors are blended—even if spot colors were assigned to the original objects. It is a good idea to specify process colors for the original elements (and all other elements in artwork that contain color blends) so you can print only four color separations. Otherwise, you will need to print four color separations plus a separation for each spot color used. If you want to blend colors for spot color printing, use the "Blending for Spot Color Printing" technique, described next.

Blending for Spot Color Separation

The Blend command always creates process colors when two objects of different colors are blended—even if spot colors were assigned to the original objects. It is a good idea to specify process colors for the original elements (and all other elements in artwork that contain color blends) so you can print only four color separations. Otherwise, you will need to print four color separations plus a separation for each spot color used. If you want to blend colors for spot color printing, you can use the technique described here instead of using the Blend command.

1

Create two objects that overlap to the limits of where you want the two spot colors to blend or overlap. The figure on the left shows two triangles with a partial overlap.

2

Put the object(s) on different layers—one for each spot color. (This is not essential to the result, but it will simplify your work tremendously.) The figure on the left shows the two layers side by side, even though the objects actually overlap in the artwork, as shown in Step 1.

3

Assign each object a graduated fill. Specify each gradation from a spot color to a light *tint* of the same color, or to white. The darker end of the gradation of the first spot color should be the light end of the gradation for the second spot color, as shown in the figure on the left.

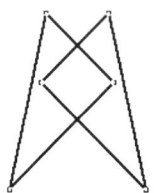

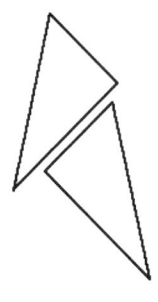

4

Choose Print from the File menu (⌘P). In the Print dialog box, click Print as Separations, then click the Change button under the Options label at the bottom left corner.

5

In the Print options dialog box, check Crop marks, Separation names, and Registration marks. Then click each color name and set each to Overprint ink (to prevent knockouts). Press Return twice to close both dialog boxes and print the separations.

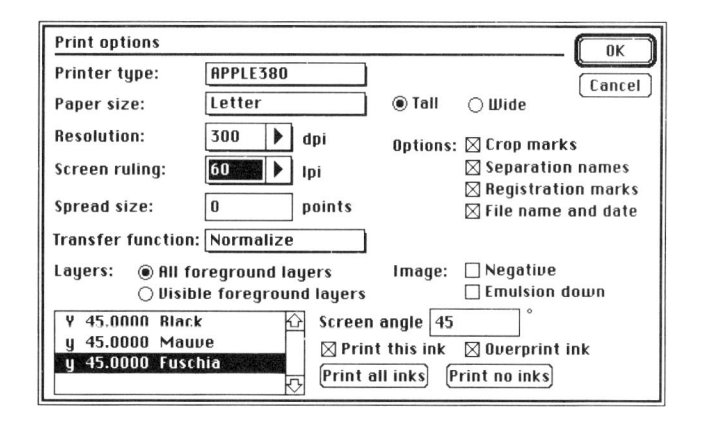

```
Print options                                              OK
Printer type:    APPLE380                               Cancel
Paper size:      Letter           ● Tall    ○ Wide
Resolution:      300   ▶ dpi      Options: ☒ Crop marks
Screen ruling:   60    ▶ lpi               ☒ Separation names
                                           ☒ Registration marks
Spread size:     0       points            ☒ File name and date
Transfer function: Normalize
Layers:    ● All foreground layers    Image: ☐ Negative
           ○ Visible foreground layers        ☐ Emulsion down
  Y 45.0000 Black            Screen angle 45
  y 45.0000 Mauve            ☒ Print this ink  ☒ Overprint ink
  y 45.0000 Fuschia          [Print all inks]  [Print no inks]
```

TIP

You will not be able to print accurate color proofs or composites, because the "white" end of the graduated fill is not transparent.

See the K2 Skis example in Chapter 10 for another method of printing spot colors that blend into each other.

Blending to Create New Colors or Grays

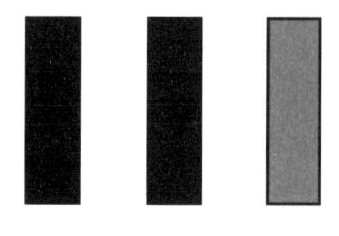

The "Creating Optional Blends" technique showed you how to use the Blend command to add gradations of color. This technique uses the Blend command to generate a new color automatically. This is useful when you want a color that is exactly halfway between two PMS colors, two process colors, or two gray fills. This is a good alternative to defining a new color numerically or visually through the Colors dialog box, especially if you do not have a color screen.

The result of the example you create here appears as shades of gray as shown in the accompanying figure.

1

Draw two objects (closed paths) and use the Colors palette or the Fill and line command from the Attributes menu (⌘E) to assign them the two fill colors (or grays) you wish to blend. In the figure on the left, two rectangles are assigned different percentages of black fill.

2

Use the Pointer tool to select the two objects. If they are rectangles or ellipses created with FreeHand's basic shape tools, choose Ungroup from the Element menu (⌘U) to ungroup them. Then select two corresponding points on each of the objects. (See "Blend" in Chapter 14. Remember that objects must be ungrouped, and corresponding points must be selected on closed paths, in order to be blended. To select a point, first click on the object with the Pointer tool to select the object, then click on a point.)

3

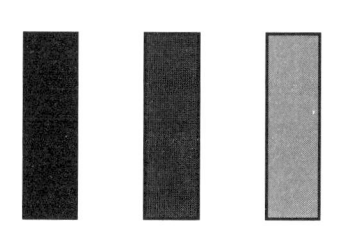

Choose the Blend command from the Element menu and specify 1 (one) step of blending between your two colors. By leaving the defaults, the first blend to 50% and the last blend to 50%, you will produce a new color that is exactly halfway along the spectrum between the two starting colors. This same procedure can be used to create automatically colors that are 1/3, 1/4, 1/5, or even 1/400 of each other simply by increasing the number of steps or by adjusting the percentages entered in the Blend dialog box.

Click OK in the Blend dialog box. The Blend command will produce the midway color and fill a new object with that color automatically in the active window.

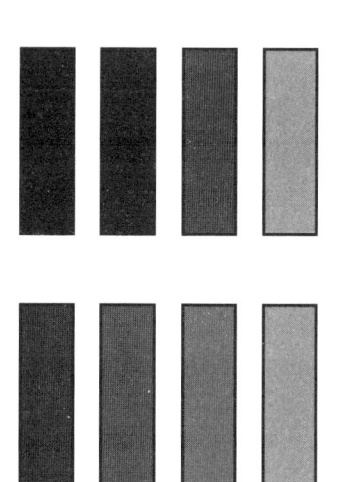

4

The Blend command automatically groups the two original objects with the resulting blended object(s). You can change the result by selecting the group and choosing Element info from the Element menu (⌘I) to get the Blend dialog box and change the number of steps or the percentages.

You can also change the result by Option-clicking one of the original objects and using the Colors palette or Fill and line from the Attributes menu (⌘E) to change the color or tint of the object. The color in the blended objects will change automatically if you have not ungrouped the set.

You can also change the result by ungrouping the set and changing individual elements, as described in the next step.

5

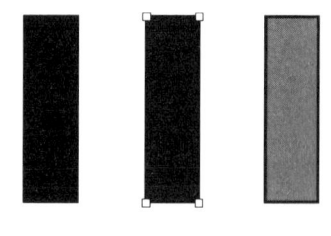

To view the composition of the new color or tint created by the Blend command (i.e., the cyan, magenta, yellow, and black percentage attributes), and to add it to the Colors palette, first select the group created by the Blend command and choose Ungroup from the Element menu (⌘U). If the blend yielded more than one new object, the new set will still be grouped—you can select individual objects by Option-clicking them with the Pointer tool.

6

When you have selected one object created by the blend, choose Fill and line from the Attributes menu (⌘E), then position the pointer on the Fill color edit box to open the pop-up menu, and release the mouse button to get the Colors dialog box showing the new color's composition.

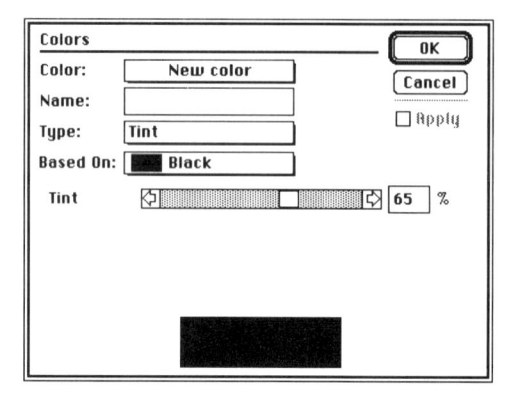

Notice that the new color created by the Blend command does not have a name, and does not appear in the Colors palette. You can give it a name by typing in the Name edit box, and the color will be available through the Colors palette. You can also change the color composition by changing the percentages assigned in the Colors dialog box.

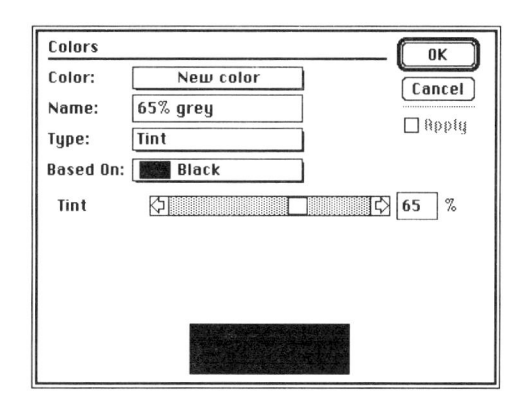

```
Colors                                    OK
Color:      New color
Name:       65% grey                     Cancel
Type:       Tint                         ☐ Apply
Based On:   ■ Black
Tint        ◁▓▓▓▓▓▓▓▓▓▓▓▓▓▷  65 %
```

TIP

FreeHand displays colors best when the monitor is set to display 256 or millions of colors. If your monitor is set to 16 colors, the colors you see on the page and in the Colors palette will not be as accurate as when they are displayed in the Colors dialog box or printed in color. If the colors that result from the blending in this technique are not what you expect, you can view the color more accurately by:

- Changing the monitor to 256 or millions of colors through the Control Panel, or
- Selecting the element whose color you wish to view, choosing Fill and line from the Attributes menu, and holding down the mouse button on the Colors pop-up menu to get the Colors dialog box displaying the color more accurately (see Chapter 13).

Clipping Paths as Masks

A shape that lets you see through to background elements that fall within its borders is called a mask in traditional graphic design, or a clipping path in PostScript terminology. This technique describes how to use a closed path as a clipping path.

TIP

You can also use a composite path as a mask, as described in Chapter 4. In general, artwork that uses clipping paths as masks may take longer to print than artwork that uses composite paths to create the same effect. Nevertheless, some artwork will require clipping paths to achieve effects that would be difficult or impossible using composite paths. See also the description in Chapter 10 of the wine label artwork that uses composite paths instead of a clipping path.

1

Create the artwork that you want to view through the clipping path. The figure on the left shows a simple beach scene with water, sand, and a palm tree at sunset. (See "Compound Dashed Lines" in Chapter 3 for an example of creating waves.)

2

Create the object that you want to serve as the clipping path. Position the clipping path over the artwork so the artwork appears inside the frame of the clipping path exactly as you want it to appear. The edges of the circle will define the clipping path that will frame the artwork. The figure on the left shows a circle centered over the artwork.

3

Select all of the artwork except the circle and choose Cut from the Edit menu (⌘X) and then select the circle and choose Paste inside from the Edit menu. The beach scene becomes masked by the circle, yielding the effect of a beach scene in a circular frame.

4

To edit the beach scene, select the circle and choose Cut contents from the Edit menu. The artwork will return to the state it was in Step 2. You can edit the artwork as you like and then repeat Step 3.

You can apply a fill color to clipping paths, and the color or tint will appear as the background to the artwork inside the path—this is how the figure at the beginning of this technique was created.

TIP

You can use this same technique to mask text objects or imported TIFF or EPS graphics. You can also mask areas of artwork that contain other clipping paths.

See also "Composite Paths as Masks" in Chapter 4, and "Join elements" in Chapter 14.

Masking to Change Fills

Besides using clipping paths to give artwork a special border or shape, as in the previous technique, you can use a clipping path to create the effect of changing fills in an object that crosses over different background shapes. In this example, text overlaps black and white areas. The masking technique is used to put white text over the black background and black type over the white background.

1

Type text and position it over a changing background. The figure on the left shows black type that has been rotated and skewed and positioned to overlap a black palm tree.

2

Select the text and choose Clone from the Edit menu (⌘=). Make the text white. The easiest way is to simply click White in the Colors palette, but you can instead use the Type specs command from the Type menu and change other attributes at the same time.

3

Select the white text and choose Cut from the Edit menu (⌘X), then select the black object (the tree in this case) and choose Paste inside from the Edit menu. The result is text that appears to change from black to white as it crosses different background shapes.

Masking to Create Highlights

You can use a clipping path to make an object appear to change fill or stroke color and thereby create shadows or highlights. In this example, a ray of moonlight is highlighted in water.

1

Begin with the water and moon used in the beach scene started a few techniques earlier. (See "Compound Dashed Lines" in Chapter 3 for an example of creating waves.)

Use one of the drawing tools to outline the area you wish to highlight or shadow. In this case, the Pen tool is used to draw a polygon in the shape that moonlight might appear reflected on water.

2

Select the object to be highlighted and choose Clone from the Edit menu (⌘=).

Choose Fill and line from the Attributes menu (⌘E) to change the attributes of the copied object(s)—making them darker to create a shadow effect, or lighter to make a highlight.

In this case, the black lines that are layered below each white line are changed to a 40% black tint.

3

With the changed objects selected, choose Cut from the Edit menu (⌘X), then select the highlight shape and choose Paste inside from the Edit menu.

4

Finally, with the highlight shape selected, change the line color to None—either by clicking the Line indicator and None in the Colors palette, or by choosing Fill and line from the Attributes menu (⌘E).

Off-center Radial Fills

Radial fills are normally centered within the object they fill. You can use the masking feature described in the previous techniques to create off-center radial fills. This is useful in creating realistic shading effects.

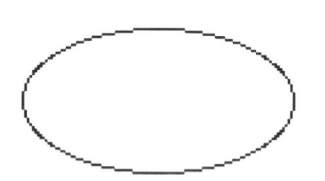

1

Create the object you want to fill with an off-center radial fill. The figure on the left shows a simple ellipse.

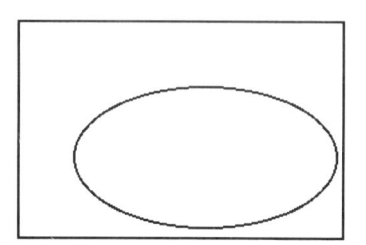

2

Draw a rectangle to surround the object you created in Step 1. The center of the rectangle should align with the point that you want to be the center of the radial fill in the ellipse, and the ellipse should fall completely within the borders of the rectangle.

3

With the rectangle selected, choose Fill and line from the Attributes menu (⌘E) and specify a radial fill. In this example, we filled from white to black to get a white center. Click OK to close the dialog box.

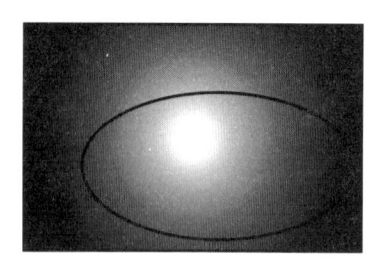

4

With the rectangle selected, choose Send to back from the Element menu (⌘B) so you can see the ellipse, and adjust the position of the ellipse so the center of the radial fill is exactly where you want it in the ellipse.

5

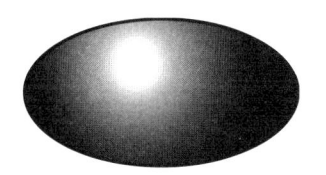

With the rectangle selected, choose Cut from the Edit menu (⌘X) and then select the ellipse and choose Paste inside from the Edit menu. The rectangle becomes masked by the ellipse, yielding the effect of an off-center radial fill in an ellipse.

See also "Highlights" in Chapter 5. See Henk Dawson's globe in Chapter 10 for an alternative method of creating off-center radial fills.

Patterns #1—Discrete Objects

Pattern repeat and all its nuances can be a difficult concept. Until you can see the result of a simple graphic repeat, you are not sure it is what you want. With traditional pen-and-ink methods, creating a pattern repeat could be a costly and time-consuming exercise, often producing unexpected results. Aldus FreeHand automatically generates repeating *tiles* of a pattern for you to see. The program does the tough work and all you have to do is decide whether you like the results.

Besides creating your own custom fill patterns for charts or graphs or any shape, you can use FreeHand's pattern feature in designing fabrics or wallpapers. Here is one example of how to build a simple pattern of non-overlapping elements. (See "Patterns #2—Continuous Symmetry" for a description of how to create tiles with cross-over patterns.)

1
Create an object that you wish to fill with a custom pattern. The figure on the left shows a rectangle.

2
Build a basic tile design with one of the drawing tools. The figure on the left shows a heart shape. This is the shape that will be repeated in a pattern.

3
Select the object(s) that are to compose the pattern—the heart in this case—and choose Cut or Copy from the Edit menu (⌘X or ⌘C).

4

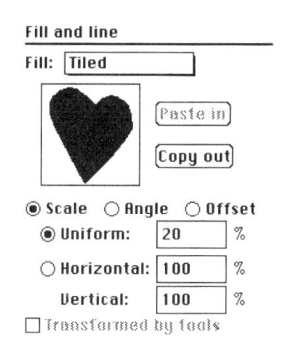

Select the object you wish to fill with the new pattern—the rectangle in this case—then choose Fill and line from the Attributes menu (⌘E). Choose Tiled from the Fill pop-up menu, then click the Paste in button to paste the object(s) you copied in Step 3 into the tile window.

You can make adjustments to the scale, angle, and offset as described in the section on the Fill and line command in Chapter 14. In this case, we scaled the heart to 20% of its original size. Click OK to close the dialog box.

Normally, FreeHand will create a rectangular "tile" that is the exact size of the artwork you create.

TIP

If you want space between the tile elements, create a rectangle surrounding and larger than the tile element. If you do not want the fill or border of the tiling rectangle to be part of the pattern, choose Fill and line from the Attributes menu and assign a Fill and Line of None. Include this rectangle in your selection in Step 3.

To produce an opaque background, you can assign a color or fill to the tiling rectangle—and choose the Send to back command before doing Step 3.

The figures show three tile sizes at the far left—one the size of the heart and two others created by surrounding the heart with a rectangle. The resulting patterns are shown at the right of each tile example.

5

Now that you have created the pattern, you can fill any new shape with it by making it a style in the Styles palette. Select the element that has already been filled with the tiled pattern, then choose New from the Styles palette pop-up menu, type the name of the new style in the Styles dialog box, and click Apply. Click OK to close the dialog box and apply the style to the selected element. Do not click Apply if you do not want the element to be affected by changes you make to that style later. In either case, the appearance of the element does not change when you first create the style, but the style name is added to the Styles palette. (See the Styles palette description in Chapter 13.)

6

You can edit the pattern by changing the artwork that you used originally to create the first pattern tile, then repeating Steps 3, 4, and 5, giving the revised pattern a new style name. You will have to use the Styles palette to apply the revised pattern to the artwork. You cannot edit a pattern and change the artwork simultaneously (as you can with custom colors).

7

When you are satisfied with the pattern design, you can delete the tile artwork; the pattern will remain stored with the current file. If you want to edit the tile later, you can retrieve it by selecting an object filled with the pattern, choosing Fill and line from the Attributes menu (⌘E), clicking Copy out, closing the dialog box, and choosing Paste from the Edit menu (⌘V). This creates a copy of the original tile artwork, which you can edit to create a new pattern.

8

You can change many aspects of your fill without redrawing a tiling element. To do so, select an object filled with the pattern, then choose Fill and line from the Attributes menu (⌘E) to return to the Fill and line dialog box. Change the Scale, Angle, or Offset specifications, or click Transformed by tools at the bottom of the dialog box. After closing the dialog box, use one of the transformation tools to rotate, scale, skew, or reflect the selected object—the pattern changes too. Repeat Step 5 to create a new style based on the changed pattern.

CAUTION

Tiled fills increase the printing time. You can minimize printing time if you keep tiles simple, avoid using elements created with a clipping path as the tile, and scale and transform the tile elements (scale and rotate them) *before* making them a pattern (instead of scaling and rotating through the Fill and line dialog box).

See also "Patterns #2—Continuous Symmetry."

Patterns #2—Continuous Symmetry

The previous technique described how to create a simple pattern that is not continuous. In other words, the graphics of the pattern did not overlap the edges of the tiling rectangle. The process is a bit more complicated if you want to create continuous patterns, requiring that the graphics flow in a continuous connection from one tile to another. The technique described here can be used to create tiles that form a continuous, symmetrical pattern.

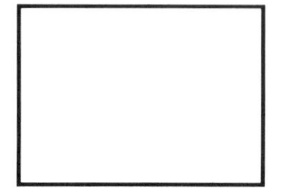

1

Create an object that you wish to fill with a custom pattern. The figure on the left shows a rectangle.

2

Create a symmetrical design with one of the drawing tools. A symmetrical design is one in which the top half is a mirror image of the bottom half, and the left half is a mirror image of the right half. The figure on the left shows a symmetrical design composed of five interlocking circles.

3

If you are using one of FreeHand's basic shape tools to create the objects—the Rectangle tool, Rounded-rectangle tool, or Ellipse tool—you must select the objects and choose the Ungroup command from the Element menu (⌘U) before using the Knife tool in Step 5.

4

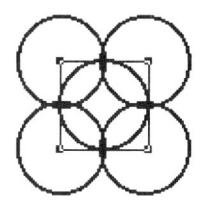

Using the Rectangle tool, draw a rectangle over the area you would like to use as a pattern fill. To have the design cross over from one tile to another and line up well, position your rectangle so its center point precisely matches the center of the symmetrical design.

5

Use the Magnifying tool to zoom in to a maximum magnification of the objects, and use the Knife tool to cut each line where it crosses the rectangle: Select an object with the Pointer tool, then click on the point you want to cut with the Knife tool. (See the description of using the Knife tool in Chapter 12.)

TIP
To make this step easier, you can drag ruler guides to meet the edges of the rectangle, and select Snap to guides from the View menu. It might also be easier to work with Preview turned off.

CAUTION
Cuts made with the Knife tool will snap to points, grids, and ruler guides if these options are activated in the View menu. It is a good idea to turn the Snap to guides option on if you use ruler guides to help align the cuts, but turn all other snap to options off when you use the Knife tool, or the cut points might not appear where you intend.

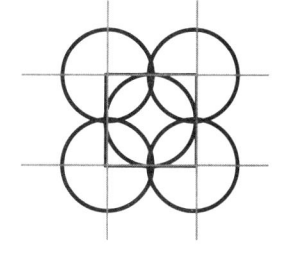

6

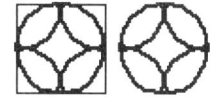

Select and delete all of the elements that fall outside the rectangle. Check to make sure your cut points meet the edges of the rectangle, then delete the rectangle.

7

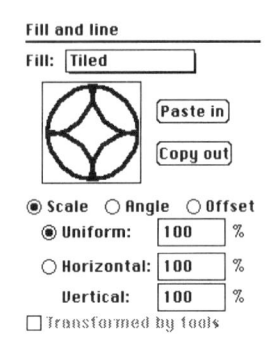

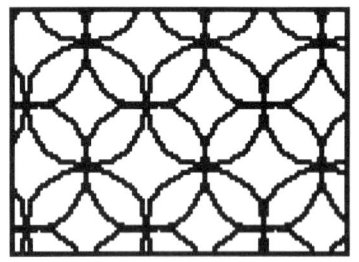

Select the object(s) that are to compose the pattern and choose Cut or Copy from the Edit menu (⌘X or ⌘C).

8

Select the object you wish to fill with the new pattern, then choose Fill and line from the Attributes menu (⌘E). Choose Tiled from the Fill pop-up menu, then click the Paste in button to paste the object(s) you copied in Step 3 into the tile window.

You can make adjustments to the scale, angle, and offset as described in the section on the Fill and line command in Chapter 14. Click OK to close the dialog box.

9

Now that you have created the pattern, you can fill any new shape with it by making it a style in the Styles palette. Select the element that has already been filled with the tiled pattern, then choose New from the Styles palette pop-up menu, type the name of the new style in the Styles dialog box, and click Apply. Then click OK to close the dialog box and apply the style to the selected element. Do not click Apply if you do not want the element to be affected by changes you make to that style later. In either case, the appearance of the element does not change when you first create the style, but the style name is added to the Styles palette. (See the Styles palette description in Chapter 13.)

10

You can edit the pattern, and create new styles for each pattern change, as described in the previous technique (Steps 6, 7, and 8).

TIP

You can achieve different results in the overall pattern by changing the size of the rectangle. The figure below shows three variations in the size of the rectangle and the resulting patterns.

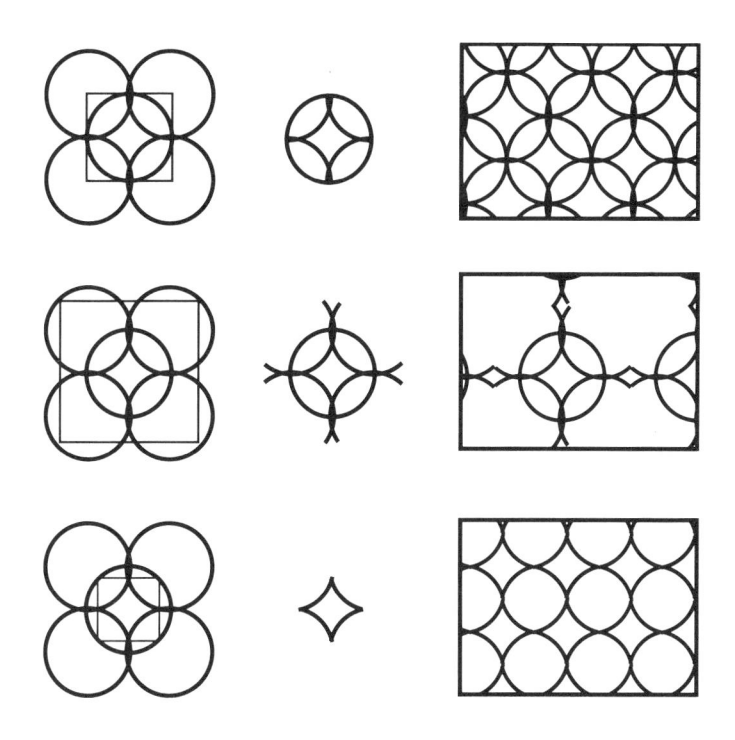

TIP

Create more intricate symmetrical designs by drawing one quadrant of the design and using the Reflecting tool to create the other four quadrants.

Patterns #3—Continuous Asymmetry

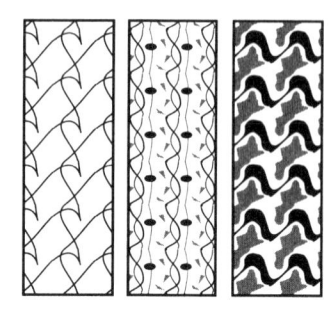

The previous technique described how to create a continuous, symmetrical pattern. The technique described here can be used to create a continuous pattern from an asymmetrical or amorphous design.

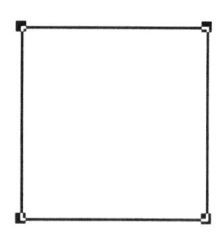

1

Select the Rectangle tool and hold down the Shift key as you draw a perfect square the size of the tile you wish to create. (You can draw a larger square if you like to work with larger elements at first, then scale the tile contents down before using them in a pattern.)

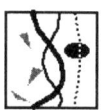

2

Create a tile design inside the square with any of the drawing tools. No paths should cross the borders of the tiling square. Paths must touch the edges of the square, however, if you want the effect of a continuous pattern. You can make this easier by dragging ruler guides to match the edges of the tiling square. (If no paths touch the borders of the tiling square, you are creating the type of pattern described in "Patterns #1—Discrete Objects.")

If you can apply all of the guidelines listed in the next step while you are drawing, all the better. Otherwise, you can just play with a design in this step and then refine it by editing as described in Step 3.

The figure on the left shows three tile designs composed of paths drawn with the Freehand tool: three squiggly open paths with the same line weight and color, three squiggly paths with different line weights and colors (plus some floating elements), and a pattern that includes a closed, filled path.

3

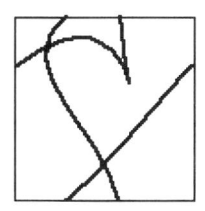

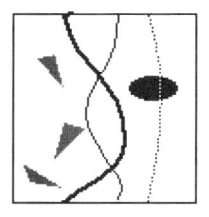

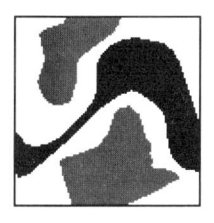

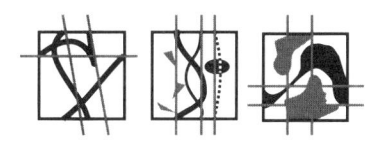

Edit the design(s) following these guidelines:

Make sure that the same number of points touch the top of the tiling rectangle as touch the bottom, and that the same number of points touch the left edge of the tiling rectangle as touch the right edge. In other words, if the design touches the top edge at three points, you want the bottom of the rectangle to be touched at three points also.

Additional precautions are required if all the design elements do not share the same stroke and fill. For example, if three lines touch the top border and use three different line weights or styles, the three lines that touch the bottom border must have the same sequence of line styles.

If any fill patterns will be used, the edges of any filled shape must touch a border with an even number of points and touch with the same number of points on the opposing sides of the tiling rectangle.

4

Next, you want lines that cross the left edge of the rectangle to match the vertical position of lines that cross the right edge, and lines that cross the top edge of the rectangle to match the horizontal position of lines that cross the bottom edge. This will make the lines that cross from one tile to the next meet.

TIP

This step is simplified if you drag ruler guides to cross opposing sides of the rectangle, and select Snap to guides from the View menu. It might also be easier to work in a magnified view with Preview turned off.

TIP

For smooth transitions from one tile to the next in the final pattern, you want the handles of the points that fall opposite each other to be parallel.

5

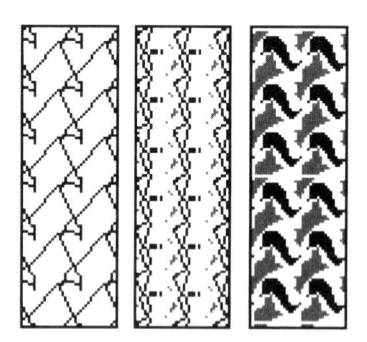

Delete the tiling rectangle—or use the Colors palette to set the Fill and line to None—then select the object(s) that are to compose the pattern and choose Cut or Copy from the Edit menu (⌘X or ⌘C).

6

Select the object you wish to fill with the new pattern, then choose Fill and line from the Attributes menu (⌘E). Choose Tiled from the Fill pop-up menu, then click the Paste in button to paste the object(s) you copied in Step 5 into the tile window.

You can make adjustments to the scale, angle, and offset as described in "Fill and line" in Chapter 14. Click OK to close the dialog box.

7

You can edit the pattern, as described in the technique "Patterns #1—Discrete Objects" (Steps 6, 7, and 8).

8

Once you have created a pattern you like, you can fill any new shape with it by making it a style in the Styles palette. Select the element that has already been filled with the tiled pattern, then choose New from the Styles palette pop-up menu. Type the name of the new style in the Styles dialog box, click Apply, then click OK to close the dialog box and apply the style to the selected element. Do not click Apply if you do not want the element to be affected by changes you make to that style later. In either case, the appearance of the element does not change when you first create the style, but the style name is added to the Styles palette. (See the Styles palette description in Chapter 13.)

See also "Patterns #1" and "Patterns #2."

7

Working with Text

Aldus FreeHand enables you to set type with precise typographical controls. Besides controlling the spacing between letters, words, and lines, you can use FreeHand's transformation tools to scale, rotate, reflect, stretch, and shrink text just as you can any other graphic element. You can also create special effects using FreeHand's commands for text formatting or by converting the text to outlines and manipulating the fill and line characteristics.

The tools and menu commands that control text are described in detail in Chapters 12 and 14. In this chapter, we summarize the basic steps and go on to demonstrate a few techniques that combine different tools and commands to achieve specific results with text.

Techniques covered in this chapter include:

- Typing, Editing, and Formatting text
- Aligning Text—3 Methods
- Joining Text to a Curved Path
- Importing Text from Other Applications
- Overprinting Text in Color Separations
- Creating "Hidden Notes" in the Artwork
- Converting Text to Paths

Typing, Editing, and Formatting Text

> Reservations
> Requested
> It's a good idea to call at least *two weeks ahead* for reservations. This resort is extremely popular during the summer months.

The process of typing, editing, and formatting text is described in detail in Chapter 12 in the "Text Tool" section. If you have never worked with FreeHand or a text editor before, you should read Chapter 12 first before trying the techniques described in this chapter. If you have worked with text in any program before, this quick summary should be enough to get you started with FreeHand, and familiarize you with some of the options for text that are described later in this chapter and in Chapters 12 and 14.

1

To type new text on the page, click the Text tool (⌘A) in the Toolbox, then position the I-beam pointer (⌘I) on the page and click or drag with the mouse to display the Text dialog box.

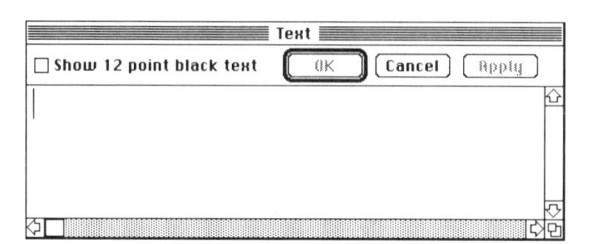

2

When you type in this dialog box, you can force a new line by pressing the Return key. Otherwise, text wraps automatically to fit the width of the text block you created by dragging the I-beam pointer on the page, but you will not see the line breaks in the Text dialog box.

In this dialog box, you can edit the content of the text or use commands from the Type menu to format selected parts of the text.

You select text in the Text dialog box the same way you select text on the desktop (such as file names and folder names) and in most Macintosh applications—by clicking, double-clicking, or dragging the I-beam pointer (see Chapter 12).

You can use the Colors palette or commands from the Attributes menu to format selected portions of the text.

You can kern (i.e. reduce or increase) the space between individual letters in the Text dialog box (see Chapter 12).

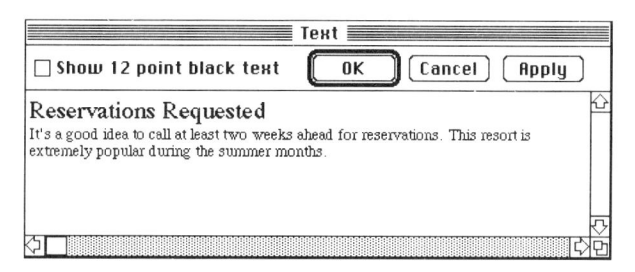

3

You must click OK or press Enter to close the Text dialog box. When you close the Text dialog box, the text appears on the page framed in a box with eight handles, indicating that the text is selected. This box disappears when the text is deselected.

4

When you first close the Text dialog box, the text is selected on the page, i.e., it is framed in a box with eight handles. Otherwise, to select text on the page you must activate the Pointer tool—either by holding down the Command key or by clicking the Text tool in the Toolbox.

When you click the Pointer tool once on the text to select it, you can use any of the Type menu commands

214   *Using Aldus FreeHand 3.0*

*Reservations
Requested
It's a good idea to call at
least two weeks ahead for
reservations. This resort is
extremely popular during
the summer months.*

to format the entire text block; you can use available commands in the Element and Attributes menus to change the stroke and fill of the text; and you can use the transformation tools to rotate, reflect, enlarge, or skew the text. You can also use the Convert to paths command to convert the text to graphic elements that you can then modify with the freeform tools.

You can also change the color of the text with the Colors palette. Normally in this palette, the Line of text is set to None. You cannot change this with the Colors palette unless you specify a visible stroke for the text using the Fill and stroke command from the Effect command submenu in the Type menu.

5

You can drag the handles of selected text to change the size of the text block and simultaneously change the size of the text or change the letter spacing or line spacing (to make it fit the new text block size). (See "Text Tool" in Chapter 12.)

6

Click with the Pointer tool twice on the text (or click once and then choose the Element info command from the Element menu) to display the Text dialog box and edit the text or format selected portions of text.

Aligning Text Blocks: Method 1

Monday
Tuesday
Wednesday
Thursday
Friday

Aldus FreeHand 3.0's enhanced features for handling text enable you to create long text blocks and mix fonts within a text block, and the Alignment command submenu in the Type menu lets you set text to be flush right, flush left, centered, or justified. If your text is in a single text block, you can use these alignment commands as described in Chapter 14.

However, if you choose to create a series of *separate* text blocks that fall on the same vertical line, you can align them using one of the next two techniques. The basic strategy in aligning text along a vertical axis is to clone the first text object and drag it into the second position while holding down the Shift key to force alignment, then use the Duplicate command to align additional copies. You can then edit the copied blocks.

1

Select the Text tool and click on the screen where you wish the text to start. Type the text in the Text dialog box. Choose commands from the Type menu to format the text as you like.

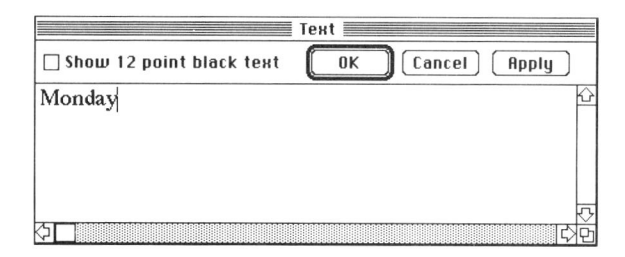

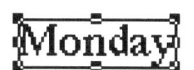

Monday

Click OK to close the dialog box.

CAUTION

Be sure to choose the correct type specifications (font size, style, and so on) before you go on to Step 2. If you change the specifications of the blocks *after* you align them, you may have to realign each one.

Monday
Monday

2

With the text block selected, choose Clone from the Edit menu (⌘=). Then hold down the Command key to get the Pointer tool, and drag the text block down. Hold down the Shift key to align the text as you release the mouse button.

Monday
Monday
Monday
Monday
Monday

3

Choose the Duplicate command from the Edit menu (⌘D) to create new text objects spaced the same distance apart.

Monday
Tuesday
Wednesday
Thursday
Friday

4

Double-click the text with the Pointer tool to get the Text dialog box and edit the new blocks of text as needed.

Aligning Text: Method 2

'91 '92 '93 '94

This technique for aligning text involves the Alignment command, and can be used to align a series of text blocks vertically or horizontally.

1

Create the text blocks using the Text tool, roughly positioning them where you wish them to be on the screen.

The figure on the left shows four separate text blocks. Notice that they are not exactly aligned.

2

Select all of the text blocks by using the Pointer tool or the Select all command from the Edit menu (⌘A), or by dragging the selection marquee around the text (see "Pointer Tool" in Chapter 12).

3

With all of the text blocks selected, choose Alignment from the Element menu. To align objects along a horizontal axis, as in this example, click Align: Elements, Vertical: Align, Bottom, and Horizontal: Distribute, Width. To align objects along a vertical axis, click Vertical: Distribute, Height, and Horizontal: Align, Left. (See Chapter 14 for a detailed explanation of the Alignment dialog box options.)

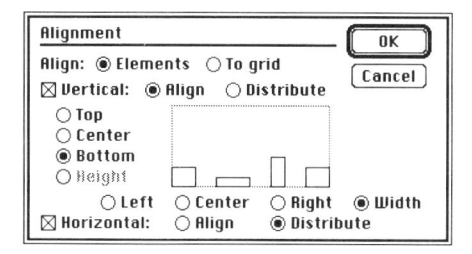

Click OK to close the dialog box.

See also "Aligning Text Blocks: Method 1", and "Tabular Text" in this chapter and "Grid: Methods 1–4" in Chapter 8.

Aligning Text Blocks: Method 3

TV Sports Audience

Event	Men	Women
Super Bowl	47	36
World Series	51	39
Breeders Cup	40	43
Basketball	54	31
Bowling	44	43
Golf	53	39
Tennis	44	42

Aldus FreeHand does not have tab settings as word processors do, but the technique described here can be used to create the appearance of tabular material. The different columns of text need not be set in the same font.

This technique is useful whenever you need to create columns and rows of text that are aligned horizontally as well as vertically.

The basic strategy in setting up columns of text is to create the column that will use the largest font first, and then copy that column and change the type specifications (if necessary) to create all other columns.

1

Select the Text tool and click on the screen where you wish the text to start. Type the column that will use the largest font first. Press Return to start new lines or rows. Choose commands from the Type menu to format the text as you like. Set the alignment to left, centered, or right, as appropriate for this column. Click OK to close the dialog box.

2

With the text block selected, choose Clone from the Edit menu (⌘=). Then hold down the Command key to get the Pointer tool, and drag the text block to the right. Hold down the Shift key to align the text as you release the mouse button.

3

Choose the Duplicate command from the Edit menu (⌘D) to create new text objects spaced the same distance apart.

4

Double-click the text with the Pointer tool to get the Text dialog box and edit the new blocks of text as needed. You can change alignment (left, centered, right) and the font and the point size of the type, but do not change the leading between lines if you wish to maintain horizontal alignment between columns of text.

5

After you have typed all of the columns, adjust the space between the columns. Use the Pointer tool with the Shift key held down to drag each column left or right to refine the overall layout of the columns.

6

Once you have typed and aligned all of the text blocks, select them all and use the Group command from the Element menu (⌘G) to group them so they will stay in alignment when you move them.

TIP

Be sure to set up the column with the largest font size before you go through this procedure. Otherwise, the lines of text might run into each other when you set up columns that call for larger type, and you will have to change the leading for all of the columns.

Joining Text to a Curved Path

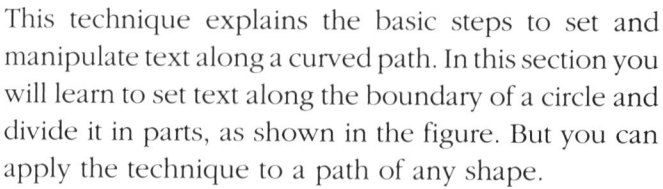

This technique explains the basic steps to set and manipulate text along a curved path. In this section you will learn to set text along the boundary of a circle and divide it in parts, as shown in the figure. But you can apply the technique to a path of any shape.

This technique is especially useful for logos, labels, maps, and other applications that require text to follow an arbitrary path. You can also use this technique to create custom curves composed of symbols from Zapf Dingbats or other fonts.

1

Use the Ellipse tool to draw an ellipse or a circle. (Recall that you can use the Shift key with the Ellipse tool to create perfect circles.) The curvature of the circle can be adjusted by selecting the circle and dragging a corner handle (if the path is grouped—as are all closed paths created with the basic shape tools) or by selecting and moving anchor points with the Pointer tool (if the path is not grouped).

2

If you have created the path with the Ellipse tool or with one of the other basic shape tools, choose Ungroup from the Element menu (⌘U) before joining the text to the path (Step 4).

NOTE

You can join text to a grouped path, but some of the results in the steps described next will not be the same for a grouped path as for an ungrouped path. For example, if the ellipse is not ungrouped (using the Ungroup command from the Element menu) before the elements are joined, the truncation described in Step 5 will be from the left or the text might overlap instead of truncate.

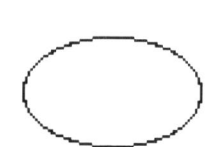

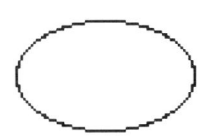

INNER CAFE

3

Select the Text tool from the Toolbox. Then click on the page and begin typing. The text will appear in the Text dialog box as you type. Choose commands from the Type menu to format the text as you like. Click OK to close the dialog box.

4

Use the Pointer tool to select both the text and the ellipse, then choose Join elements from the Element menu (⌘J). The ellipse disappears and the text takes on the shape of the curve. The position of the text is determined by the alignment of the text as set through the Alignment command submenu in the Type menu:

- Text aligned left (top figure) begins at the first point on the path. If the path is an ellipse created with the Ellipse tool and then ungrouped, the first point is at the leftmost point.
- Text aligned right (second figure) ends at the last point on the path—this is the same as the first point on a closed path.
- Centered text (third figure) is centered between the two ends.
- Justified text (fourth figure) is squeezed or expanded to fit the space.

NOTE

If the path was a grouped object created with one of the basic shape tools, the text is positioned at the top of the path regardless of the alignment setting (as in the figure on the left).

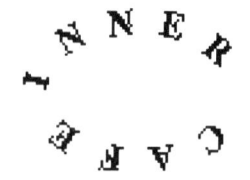

222   *Using Aldus FreeHand 3.0*

TIP

You can get even spacing between letters of justified text joined to an ellipse by ending the text with a non-breaking space (Option-Space bar). The ellipse must be drawn from the top right to the bottom left. The figure on the left shows justified text with a non-breaking space at the end.

TIP

When the two elements are first joined, they are automatically selected as indicated by visible handles (if the path was grouped before the two elements were joined) or anchor points (if the path was not grouped). Once you deselect the object, you can select it again by clicking on the *path*—not on the text. If you cannot find the path (because it is not visible), try dragging the Pointer tool to surround the object with the selection marquee.

5

You can change the shape of the curved path by clicking on it and dragging a handle (if the object is grouped) or an anchor point (if it is an ungrouped path).

If the path is shorter than the text, the overflow text is "hidden" (i.e., does not display). The alignment of the text (set by the Alignment command from the Type menu) determines what part of the text is hidden:

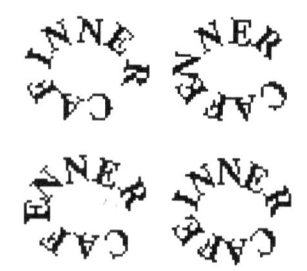

- Text aligned left (top left figure) is truncated from the right.
- Text aligned right (top right figure) is truncated from the left.
- Centered text (bottom left figure) is truncated from both ends.
- Justified text (bottom right figure) is squeezed to fit the space.

INNER

CAFE

6

To force all or part of the text to the bottom of the ellipse, use the Return key to force a line break before the text you want on the bottom. (Text on the third line and beyond will not display along the path.)

If you did not enter the carriage return when you typed the text, you can do so after joining the text to the path by selecting the object, choosing the Element info command from the Element menu (see next step), then clicking the Edit Text button to get the Text dialog box.

7

You can reposition the text in other ways through the Element info dialog box. Select the object by clicking on the path and choose Element info from the Element menu (⌘I) to display the Text along a path or the Text on an ellipse dialog box. You can instead Option-double-click the path with the Pointer tool to display the Element info dialog box. (In either case, the text must not be grouped to the path, or you must subselect the text by Option-clicking it with the Pointer tool for the Element info command to work this way.)

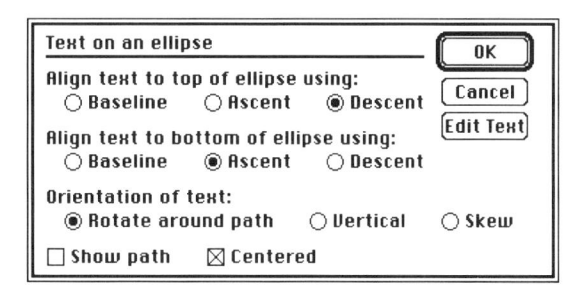

```
┌─────────────────────────────────────────────────┐
│ Text on an ellipse                    [   OK   ]│
│ Align text to top of ellipse using:   [ Cancel ]│
│   ○ Baseline   ○ Ascent   ● Descent             │
│ Align text to bottom of ellipse using: [Edit Text]│
│   ○ Baseline   ● Ascent   ○ Descent             │
│ Orientation of text:                            │
│   ● Rotate around path   ○ Vertical   ○ Skew    │
│ ☐ Show path     ☒ Centered                      │
└─────────────────────────────────────────────────┘
```

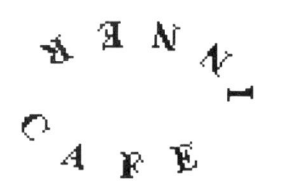

The Element info dialog box entries are explained in detail in the discussion of the Element info command in Chapter 14, but we show two examples here. The figures on the left show text on an ellipse set to vertical orientation (top) and skewed orientation (bottom). Skewing actually creates a three-dimensional wrap around a circular path.

8

To make the text run inside or below the path, select the Reflecting tool and click once on the object.

TIP

You can also arrange text along a path to create custom curves composed of symbols from Zapf Dingbats or other fonts.

CAUTION

You can separate text from the path by choosing Split element from the Element menu; and the text goes back to its original location on the page before the paths were joined. If you use the Split element command and the text seems to vanish from the screen, it is probably because the original location of the text is beyond the current window on the page—either because the text was originally far from the path to which it was joined or because you moved the element after joining it to the text.

Importing Text from Other Applications

You can copy text from another application into FreeHand by using the Copy and Paste commands. (You cannot use the Place command, which imports graphics only.) The basic steps and a few examples are shown here.

1

The one real object of education is to leave a man in the condition of continually asking questions.
—Bishop Creighton

Open the application that contains the text you wish to copy, select the text to be copied, and choose Copy from the Edit menu (⌘C). The figure on the left shows text selected in Microsoft Word.

2

Quit the application and open a FreeHand document (or switch to the FreeHand document under MultiFinder), then select the Text tool and click on the page to open the Text dialog box.

In this step, you can instead double-click existing text in the FreeHand document to open a Text dialog box that has some text already entered.

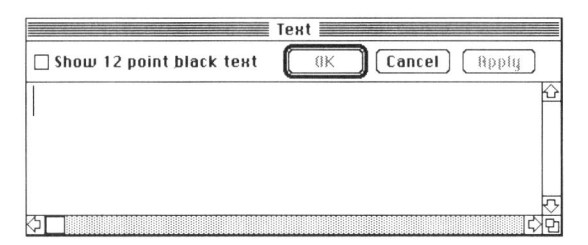

3

Choose Paste from the Edit menu (⌘V) to insert the copied text at the insertion point. The following figures show the same text copied in Step 1 from Microsoft Word and pasted into an empty Text dialog box (below) and displayed on the page (below and to the left).

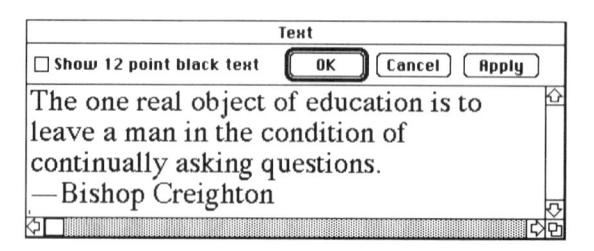

```
                           Text
☐ Show 12 point black text    [ OK ]  [ Cancel ]  [ Apply ]
The one real object of education is to
leave a man in the condition of
continually asking questions.
—Bishop Creighton
```

The one real object of education is to leave a man in the condition of continually asking questions.
—Bishop Creighton

Click OK to close the dialog box. Imported text takes on the default type specifications when pasted into an empty text box, or the type specifications of the surrounding text when pasted into existing text.

Overprinting Text in Color Separations

When elements of different colors overlap, FreeHand normally knocks out the background color when printing spot color separations. It is a good idea to force text to overprint background colors—especially text in small point sizes—in order to compensate for slight misregistration problems. You do this by checking Overprint for the stroke in the Fill and stroke dialog box, displayed by choosing Fill and stroke from the Effect command submenu in the Type menu. Examples of text printed with and without this option (with a deliberate misregistration of one point) are shown below.

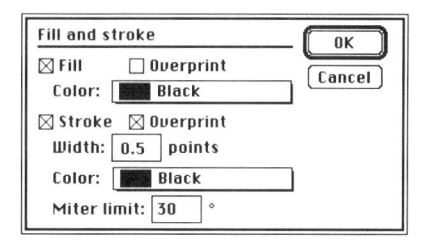

Black Text with Stroke Overprinting Gray Field

In this first example, 12-point Times text is set in a rectangle that is filled with a 40% gray tint. Overprint is checked in the Fill and stroke dialog box.

Black Text with Background Knocked Out

In the second example, Overprint is *not* checked in the Fill and stroke dialog box. In printing, the two plates were off register by 1 point.

(Since we expected perfect registration in printing this book, we simulated this effect here by setting the same type in white under the black type, then moved the black type 1 point diagonally along a 45-degree angle.)

Creating "Hidden" Notes in the Artwork

BULLET COLORS:
Red for PR department items
Blue for Corporate news items
Yellow for Personnel dept

In working with complex illustrations that involve many grouped objects and layers, you can type notes about how the file is organized for your own reference or for others who might need to edit the artwork later.

This technique is especially useful if you are working in a group where work on a single illustration is shared among several people, or when you are working on many different, complex illustrations that you must modify over a period of time. Hidden notes can also be helpful on a boilerplate document that will be "cloned" to create many illustrations in a series, as in this example.

BULLET COLORS:
Red for PR department items
Blue for Corporate news items
Yellow for Personnel dept

1

Use the Text tool to type notes (such as instructions about alignment or how the artwork is organized) as text, directly on the artwork. These can be typed in one area on a page of the document that is not used by the artwork, or they can be scattered around on the artwork, with each note close to the object(s) it addresses.

2

Open the Layers palette by choosing View ➔ Windows ➔ Layers (⌘6). Select all of the notes and click the Background layer in the Layers palette to place the text on a non-printing layer. (Be sure that the Background layer is visible—i.e., checked in the Layers palette. See the description of using the Layers palette in Chapter 13.)

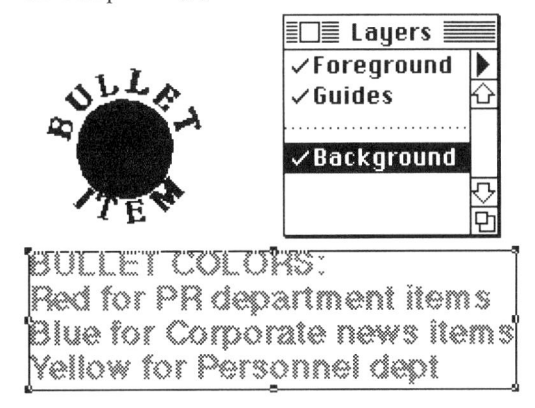

TIP

Use a small font that is easy to read on the screen. To fit many notes in a small space, you can make the font as small as 2 points so the notes will be readable on the screen only at the highest magnification.

Converting Text to Paths

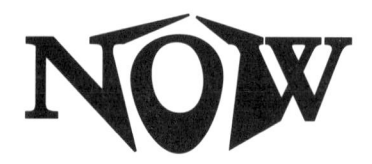

The Convert to paths command lets you convert a selected text object into a composite path. You can then edit the character shapes, or use the composite path to mask other objects. This command, and the conditions under which it is available, is covered in Chapter 14. We briefly summarize the steps in converting text to a path here, and then show some examples of when this is useful.

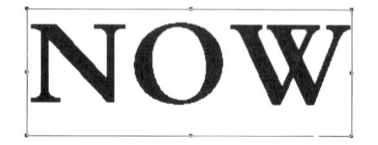

1

Select the text object you want to convert to a composite path, then choose Convert to paths from the Type menu. For the Convert to paths command to work, the printer fonts for the selected text must be in the System on your Macintosh; the ones resident in your printer are not sufficient. The figure at left shows text before (above) and after (below) using the Convert to paths command.

The selected text object is converted to a composite path, and each character is also a composite path. This means that the bowls in the characters will be holes through which you can see elements below.

2

You can apply colors to the line and fill to text converted to paths with the Colors palette, just as you can apply colors to the fill of normal text and to the line of text formatted using Type ➔ Effect ➔ Fill and stroke. You will notice, however, that the stroke width specified with the Fill and stroke command for text prints much thinner than the same line width specified through the Fill and line command for graphics. The figure on the left shows text (above) and paths (below) formatted with a 1-point stroke or line and a 40% gray fill.

You can also use commands not normally available for text objects—from the Attributes menu, or from the Styles palette—to change the appearance of the text that has been converted to paths. For example, you can apply custom line styles or custom fills to paths, such as the Medium mezzo texture used as fill in the figure on the left.

3
You can use the text shapes as clipping paths—filling the text with graphics or with other text. The figure on the left shows an abstract design composed using FreeHand's drawing tools (above) pasted inside the text shapes (below).

(See "Clipping Paths as Masks" in Chapter 6, and the section on the Edit menu's Paste inside command in Chapter 14. See the description of the wine label in Chapter 10 for using text as a clipping path to create custom inline type.)

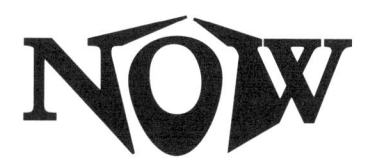

4
If you want to manipulate individual characters, you can subselect them by Option-clicking them with the Pointer tool, or you can choose Split element from the Element menu to turn the characters into independent composite paths.

Once you have selected an individual character, you can change the shape of the path by moving the points or direction handles (see Chapters 2, 3, and 12).

For more information on composite paths, see "Join elements" in Chapter 14.

TIP
Text converted to paths is no longer a font. You can deliberately convert text to paths so you can take the artwork from one system to another and print it easily without worrying about what fonts are installed on each system. This is a good idea if the artwork includes very few words in a rarely available font, but it will increase the file size in direct proportion to the amount of text.

8

Spacing and Alignment

Traditionally, the process of making sure that all elements lined up properly required a large percentage of the time spent in developing a complex illustration. The alignment of objects had to be carefully thought out before pen or brush touched paper. With Free-Hand, you can think through the alignment requirements before you start an illustration, or you can simply begin illustrating and move objects into alignment later. This is one of the outstanding advantages of using a computer.

FreeHand offers several aids in aligning objects to each other or to an axis, including the information bar (which shows position of objects as you create or move them), the rulers, ruler guides, a grid, the Alignment command, and the Constrain command. These basic features are described in Chapter 2 (Basic Concepts) and in Part IV (Tools, Palettes, and Commands Reference).

This chapter offers some suggestions on using FreeHand's alignment aids, and adds a few additional methods of aligning objects. We recommend that you first review this chapter so you are familiar with the tools and tricks available for aligning objects, then refer back to this chapter and the reference chapters in Part IV as needed when you are creating an illustration.

Topics covered include:

- Using Rulers and Guides
- Using the Grid System
- Custom Grid #1—Perspective
- Custom Grid #2—Page Layout
- Aligning Objects
- Measuring with a Point
- Dividing Equally
- Creating Spacing Guides

Using Rulers and Guides

FreeHand lets you create non-printing guidelines on the page that help you align objects: If Snap to guides is chosen (i.e., checked) in the View menu, the ruler guides have a snap-to effect on objects and the cursor when they come within three pixels of the guide (or whatever distance you specify through the Preferences command).

You can position ruler guides on a page before you create objects, and use the snap-to effect of the rulers to help position the pointer when you start a new element. You can also position ruler guides at any time and use them as guides for dragging existing elements into alignment, as described in the next steps.

1

Create the objects using whatever tools are appropriate, positioning them roughly where you wish them to be on the screen.

The figure on the left shows four squares created with the Rectangle tool. Notice that they are not exactly aligned.

2

Choose Rulers from the View menu (⌘R) to display the rulers (if they are not already displayed), then position the mouse pointer over the horizontal ruler at the top of the page and drag a horizontal ruler guide onto the page. (It does not matter what tool is selected.)

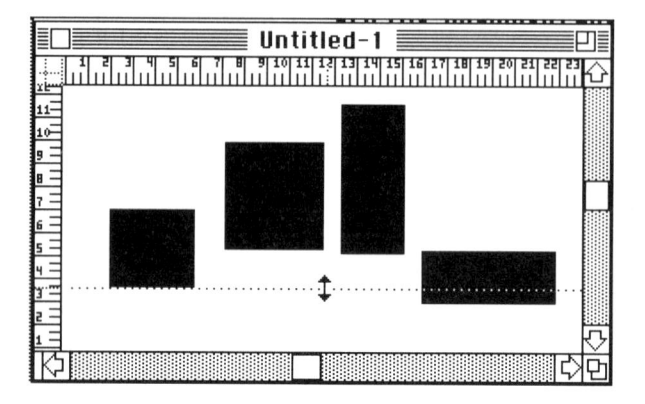

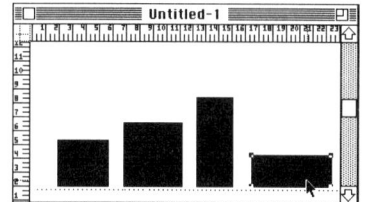

3

Press the Command key to get the Pointer tool if it is not already selected, and drag each object to touch the alignment guide. If Snap to guides is checked in the View menu, the snap-to effect will help you align the objects against the ruler guide in any magnification. However, it might help to first select the Magnifying tool (or hold down the Command key and the Space bar) and click on the objects you wish to align, to invoke a magnified view.

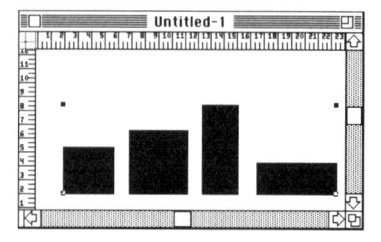

4

Once you have positioned all of the objects, you can select them all and use the Group command in the Element menu (⌘G) to group them and thereby keep them in alignment when you want to move them as a unit.

TIP

You can use ruler guides to create a complete grid system before starting an illustration, and save a document with the ruler guides only as a template for creating a series of related illustrations.

TIP

You can also use ruler guides to help align the Knife tool when you are cutting an object in half.

See also "Using the Grid System," "Custom Grid #1–Perspective," and "Custom Grid #2–Page Layout" in this chapter.

Using the Grid System

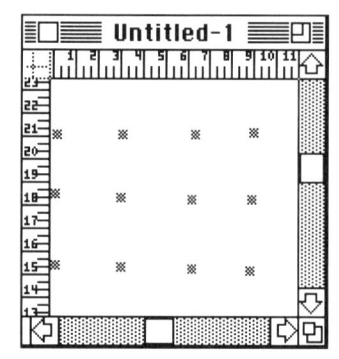

All FreeHand drawings have a grid that you can use to align objects. The distance between alignment points of the grid is first determined by the entries you make in the Document setup dialog box, displayed when you choose the New command or the Document setup command from the File menu.

You can make the grid visible or invisible on the screen by choosing the Grid command from the View menu. You can turn the snap-to effect of the grid on or off by choosing Snap to grid from the View menu. You can make an element align to the grid by dragging it close to a grid point (when Snap to grid is on) or by using the Alignment command.

Each of these commands is described in Chapter 14, but here we review all the steps involved in using a grid.

1

To set up the grid dimensions, display the Document setup dialog box. You can do this by choosing the New command from the File menu (⌘N) to start a new document, or by choosing Document setup from the File menu to change the grid on the current document.

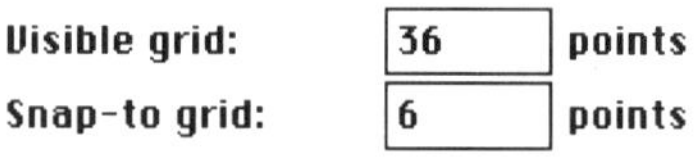

In the Document setup dialog box, you can specify a Visible grid that is different from the Snap-to grid. The normal default sets a 36-point (1/2 inch) visible grid and a 6-point (1/12th inch) snap-to grid. A 6-point grid is the smallest practical grid size when the snap-to distance is 3 points (the normal default in the Preferences dialog box).

You can accept the defaults or change the grid size, then click OK to close the dialog box.

2

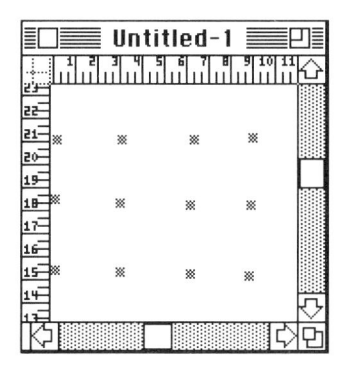

Make the grid visible on the screen by choosing the Grid command from the View menu (if it is not already checked).

CAUTION

The visible grid can become invisible in reduced views. For example, a 6-point visible grid is only visible in views of 200% or higher magnification. A 13-point grid is the smallest visible at 100% magnification. The smallest grids visible at 50%, 25%, and 12.5% are 25 points, 50 points, and 100 points, respectively.

3

Turn the snap-to effect of the grid on by choosing Snap to grid from the View menu (if it is not already checked). The snap-to effect will come into play when you are creating or moving an object—turning it on or off does not move any objects that are already positioned on the page.

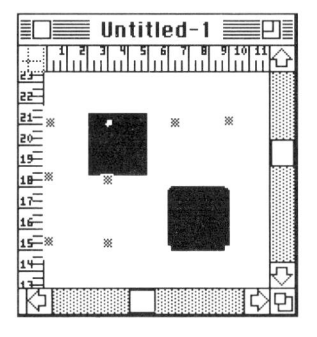

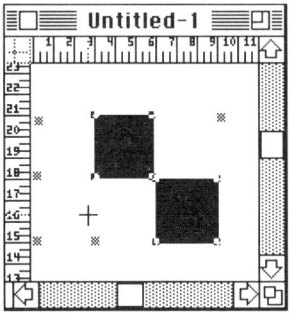

4

When Snap to grid is on, the mouse pointer will automatically snap to the nearest grid point when you are drawing an object with one of FreeHand's drawing tools.

The figure on the left shows a rectangle drawn when Snap to grid is off (above) and when it is on (below). The visible dots in these figures correspond to the snap-to grid dimensions set in the Document setup dialog box.

5

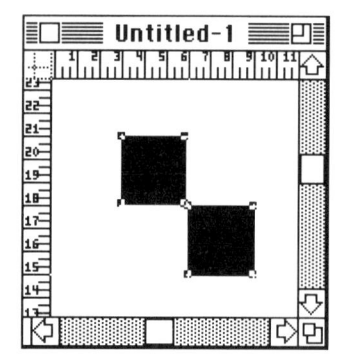

You can make an element that is on the page align to the grid by dragging it close to a grid point (when Snap to grid is on) or by using the Alignment command from the Element menu and choosing the Align To grid option in combination with Vertical and/or Horizontal alignment specifications. The figure below shows the Alignment dialog box settings and the figure on the left shows the resulting movement of the rectangle that was off the grid in Step 4.

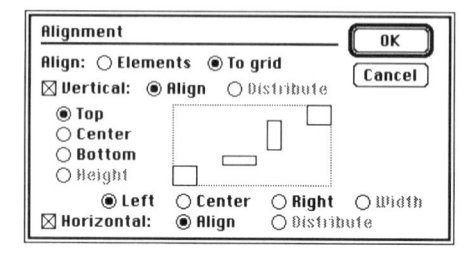

TIP

In general, use the snap-to effect of the grid when you want to align elements at fixed intervals or create elements of fixed sizes. Use ruler guides when you want to align elements horizontally or vertically but *not* at fixed intervals.

See also "Using Rulers and Guides" earlier in this chapter.

Measuring with a Point

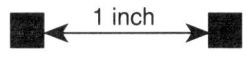

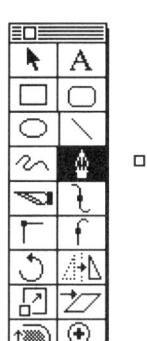

Here is a quick and effective way to measure distance and angle. You can measure the size of an object you have drawn, or measure the distance between objects, or measure empty space in the drawing window (to plan the position of the next object you create).

1

Create a single anchor point by clicking the Pen tool once on the page, as the figure on the left shows. This point will be your measuring point.

2

Using the Pointer tool, click on and move the point to a starting place for measuring, as shown in the figure on the left.

3

Select the point again and move it across the page the distance you would like to measure. If you are measuring a horizontal or vertical distance, hold down the Shift key to constrain your movement and measurement along 45-degree angles.

4

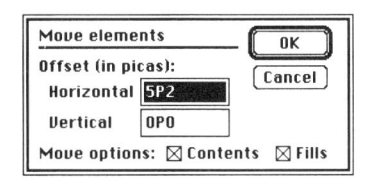

Choose the Move command from the Edit menu (⌘M) to view the Move dialog box. The distance and angle that you moved the point will be shown here.

Custom Grid #1—Perspective

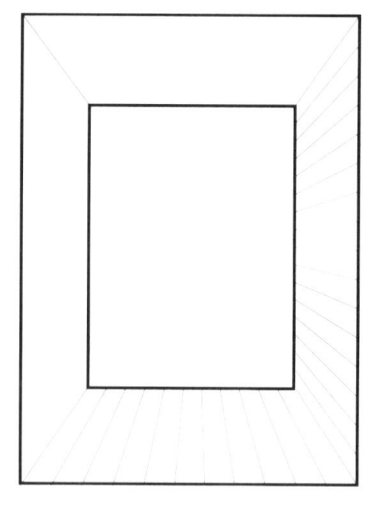

Often you will need to have an accurate grid or guidelines to follow in an illustration. For instance, some artists like to create custom guidelines. Or maybe you have a custom grid for your newsletter. If the grid is composed of horizontal and vertical lines, you can use ruler guides or the invisible grid system described in the previous two techniques. If you want a grid that uses diagonal lines, use the technique described here. This technique enables you to create a grid that shows perspective, like the one shown in the accompanying figure.

You can use this grid as a guide for illustrations that show one-point perspective of single objects, or for several objects that will appear to be standing beside each other. Examples of two-point perspective are given at the end of these steps.

1

Use the Rectangle tool to draw a rectangle the size of the finished illustration. In the figure on the left, the size of the rectangle is the size of the page.

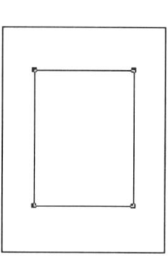

2

With the rectangle selected, choose Clone from the Edit menu (⌘=), then drag a corner handle to make the copy smaller. Position the smaller rectangle inside the first rectangle. In the figure at left the smaller rectangle is centered within the larger one, but this is not a requirement. The position of the inner rectangle determines the perspective (see the tip at end of this technique).

3

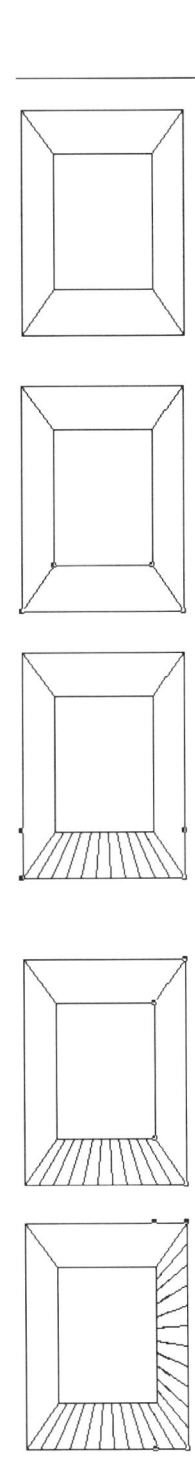

Use the Line tool to connect corresponding corners of each rectangle with straight lines, as shown in the figure on the left.

4

Use the Blend command to add more grid lines for depth: First select the lines in the bottom corners to select them both.

Then choose the Blend command from the Element menu and enter a number of blend steps equal to the number of additional lines you wish to create—10 in this example.

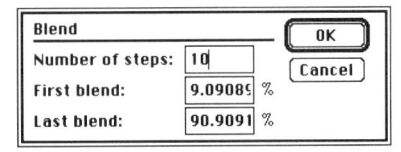

Blend		
Number of steps:	10	OK
First blend:	9.0908 %	Cancel
Last blend:	90.9091 %	

Click OK to create the intermediate lines.

5

With the blended set still selected, choose Ungroup from the Element menu (⌘U), then press Tab to deselect all objects. Shift-click to select the two lines in the right corners of the rectangles as shown in the figure on the left.

Again choose the Blend command from the Element menu and enter a number of blend steps equal to the number of additional lines you wish to create—10 in this example.

Click OK to create the intermediate lines.

TIP

To keep the grid as simple as possible, add grid lines only to two sides, such as the bottom and right sides of the rectangles, as shown in the figure on the left.

6

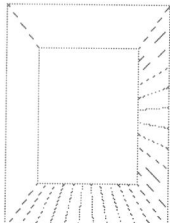

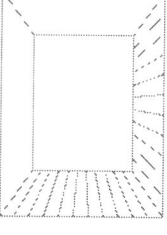

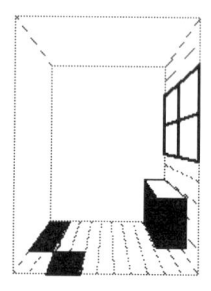

Next, move the lines to the Background layer: Open the Layers palette (if it is not already open) by choosing View ➤ Windows ➤ Layers (⌘6). Choose Select all from the Edit menu (⌘A) to select the guide lines. Click the Background layer in the Layers palette to place the lines on a non-printing layer. (Be sure the Background layer is visible—i.e., checked in the Layers palette. See the description of using the Layers palette in Chapter 13.)

7

In drawing three-dimensional objects, use the diagonal depth lines as guides in drawing the side walls of the object, but maintain horizontal and vertical lines for the front face of the object. For example, in the figure on the left, the front and back faces are normal rectangles, but the side walls follow diagonal grid lines.

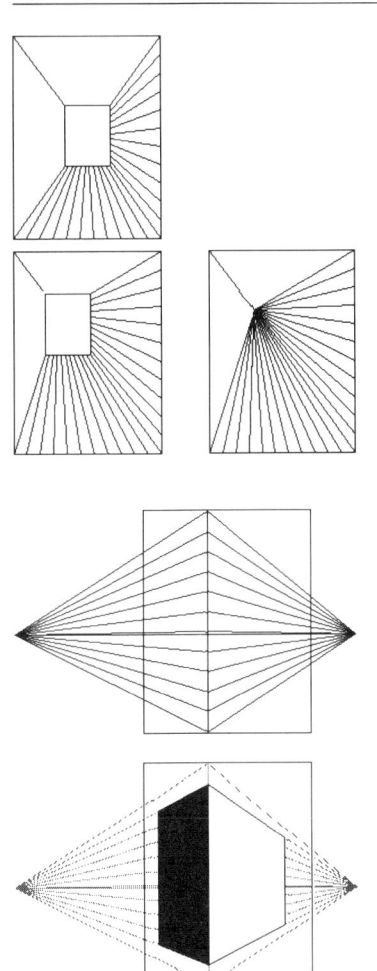

TIP

The positioning of the smaller rectangle will determine the viewer's perspective—identified by the grid lines that are closest to horizontal.

Also, the smaller the rectangle you make in Step 2, the deeper the perspective will seem. The extreme version—where all the lines converge at a point (i.e., the smallest possible rectangle)—demonstrates why this is called one-point perspective. The point at which the lines converge is called the vanishing point.

You can use the same technique to create two-point perspective using two vanishing points. The vanishing points can extend into the pasteboard area, as shown in the figures on the left.

The two vanishing points usually fall along the same horizontal line. As with one-point perspective, the viewer's perspective is identified by the grid lines that are closest to horizontal.

See also "Cubes: Method 3" in Chapter 5.

Custom Grid #2—Page Layout

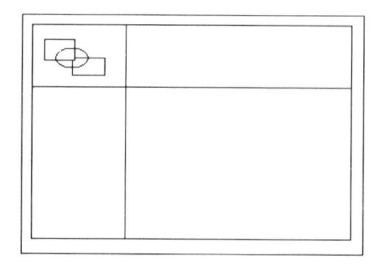

You can use the grid shown in the accompanying figure to create a series of illustrations that must all conform to the same page layout specifications—such as a series of handouts for a presentation, or a series of product specification sheets for your company's product line. Then use this grid as a template for creating each page as a separate FreeHand document.

You can use this technique to create any template system for consistent page layout, such as a series of ads, a series of overheads or slides, or a series of charts.

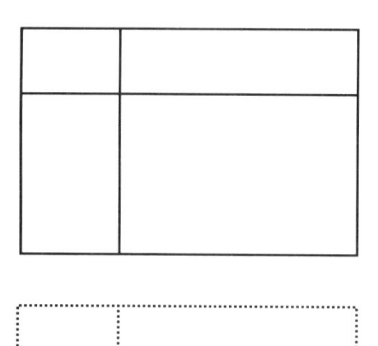

1

Determine the basic "grid" of the page layout and sketch it with the Line tool and/or the Rectangle tool.

2

Open the Layers palette (if it is not already open) by choosing View ➤ Windows ➤ Layers (⌘6). Use the Select all command from the Edit menu (⌘A) to select the entire grid. Click the Background layer in the Layers palette to place the grid on a non-printing layer. (Be sure that the Background layer is visible—i.e., checked in the Layers palette. See the description of using the Layers palette in Chapter 13.)

3

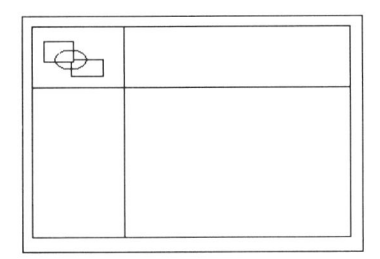

Press Tab to deselect all elements, then click the Foreground layer in the Layers palette to make that the active layer. Add any ruled lines and standing text that are intended to print on every page. Use Select all from the Edit menu (⌘A) and Lock from the Element menu to lock the objects in place so they will not be selected or moved as you work, or move them to a layer of their own.

4

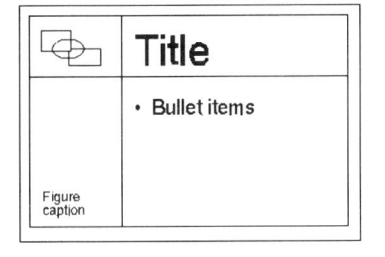

Add dummy text blocks that will change on each page, and move them into their fixed positions. The figure on the left shows dummy text blocks.

The position of the dummy text blocks will remain the same in all files based on this template, but the content will be altered for each page. Therefore, you do not want to lock the objects, but it is a good idea to put them on a layer of their own.

5

Save the file as a template document that you can use repeatedly.

See also "Creating Spacing Guides" in this chapter.

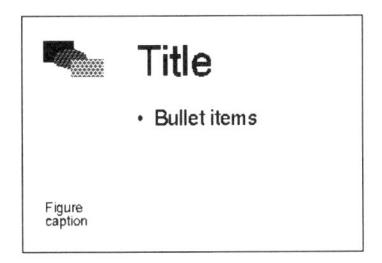

Aligning Objects

Any illustration that is composed of more than one object, such as the series of squares illustrated in the accompanying figure, probably calls for careful alignment procedures. Besides using the grid and ruler guides or the Alignment command (described in Part IV) to help in aligning objects, there's a convenient way of aligning objects by Shift-dragging a clone of the first object and then using the Duplicate command (described here).

1

Create the first object using whatever drawing tool is appropriate (Freehand tool, Tracing tool, Pen tool, Text tool, Line tool, Rectangle tool, or Ellipse tool). For example, use the Rectangle tool to create a rectangular object, as shown in the figure on the left.

2

If subsequent objects are to be identical, select the first object (but be sure no individual points are selected) and choose Clone from the Edit menu (⌘=). Drag the cloned object to the new position, holding down the Shift key to align the object as you release the mouse button.

3

Choose Duplicate from the Edit menu (⌘D) to align another copy of the object the same relative distance apart. Press ⌘D for each additional copy you wish to make.

4

Modify the copied objects as appropriate *after* you have created the set of aligned copies.

5

Once you have edited all of the objects, you can select them all and use the Group command in the Element menu (⌘G) to group them and thereby keep them in alignment when you want to move them as a unit.

See also "Using Ruler and Guides," "Using the Grid System," "Custom Grid #1–Perspective," and "Custom Grid #2–Page Layout" in this chapter, and "Aligning Text: Methods 1 and 2" in Chapter 7.

Dividing Equally

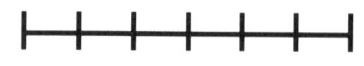

You may find it necessary to divide a shape or a line into a specific number of segments. Even dividing something in half can be difficult if you rely on the rulers or the information bar as your only aids. With the following technique, you do not need to actually calculate the divisions; FreeHand does it for you.

Common applications for this technique include dividing lines and shapes for technical or architectural drawings or creating grids and guidelines for templates and artwork. This is also a useful aid in creating forms.

1

For this exercise, first use the Line tool with the Shift key to draw a horizontal line of any length. This is the line you will divide into equal segments.

2

Use the Line tool to draw a short vertical line. With the Snap to point option turned on, snap this vertical line to one endpoint of the horizontal line. (You might want to magnify your view of the artwork to do this.)

3

With the vertical line still selected, choose Clone from the Edit menu (⌘=), then hold down the Command key to get the Pointer tool. Drag this cloned line to the opposite endpoint of the horizontal line and snap once again, holding down the Shift key to align the second tick relative to the first tick along the horizontal axis as you release the mouse button.

4

Using the Pointer tool, Shift-click both vertical lines to select both lines.

5

Choose the Blend command from the Element menu to display the Blend dialog box, and type a number that is one less than the number of parts you would like. For example, if you would like to divide the line into six equal parts, type "5" for the number of steps. Click OK. In this example, five dividers are added at six equal intervals between the two end lines.

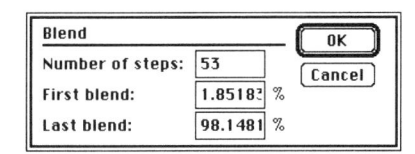

```
Blend
Number of steps: 53         OK
First blend:    1.8518 %    Cancel
Last blend:     98.1481 %
```

TIP

This procedure adds dividers but does not actually break the horizontal line into segments. If you want to break up the horizontal line into separate parts, you can use the Knife tool.

See also "Measuring with a Point" earlier in this chapter.

Creating Spacing Guides

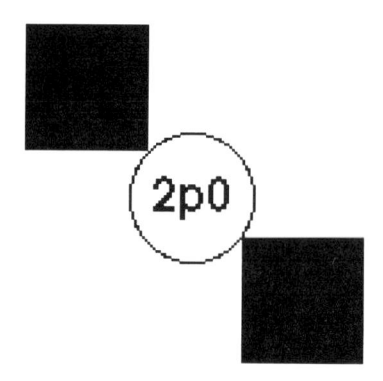

It is a good idea to apply consistent standards for spacing between objects in an illustration. Here is one technique that supplements the ruler and the information bar by storing the spacing information as part of the artwork, in the form of a graphic object that is on the non-printing background layer.

This technique is especially useful when you need to create a series of illustrations that meet consistent standards for spacing between objects or between graphic elements and text elements.

1

Select the Ellipse tool and drag the mouse on the page to draw an ellipse of any size. Hold down the Command key to get the Pointer tool (or select the Pointer tool in the Toolbox) and Option-double-click on the ellipse to get the Ellipse dialog box. Enter the values that yield the same height (difference between Top and Bottom values) and width (difference between Left and Right) to draw a perfect circle. The value should match the space that you wish to make consistent between objects.

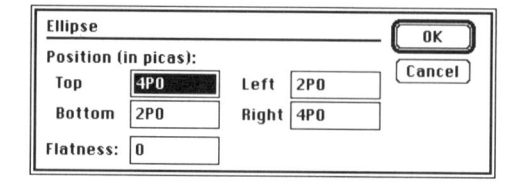

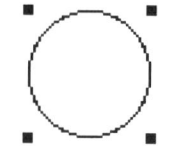

2

Choose Fill and line from the Attributes menu (⌘E), and set the Fill to None and the Line Weight to Hairline (.25 points) or thinner—if the line is thick, it might interfere with precise measurements. Click OK to close the dialog box.

3

If you need more than one spacing guide to measure different distances, type a text label for each guide using the Text tool. Group the label with the circle by selecting the guide object and the text and choosing Group from the Element menu (⌘G).

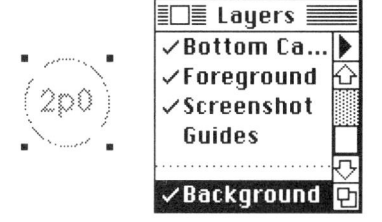

4

Open the Layers palette (if it is not already open) by choosing View ➤ Windows➤ Layers (⌘6). Select the spacing guide(s) and click the Background layer in the Layers palette to place the spacing guides on a non-printing layer. (Be sure the Background layer is visible—i.e., checked in the Layers palette. See the description of using the Layers palette in Chapter 13.)

5

Whenever you need to position two objects next to each other, drag the circle to meet one edge of one object, then bring the second object to meet the opposite edge of the circle.

TIP

By using a circle instead of a line or a rectangle as a measuring guide, you can measure distances consistently at any angle—not only vertical and horizontal distances.

By placing the spacing guides on a background layer, you can keep them as part of the artwork but they will not print.

See also "Using the Grid System," "Custom Grid #1–Perspective," "Custom Grid #2–Page Layout," and "Measuring with a Point" in this chapter, and " 'Hidden' Notes" in Chapter 7.

9

Working in Layers

In FreeHand, as in all object-oriented drawing applications, you can make one object overlap another, and you can rearrange this layering sequence using the Send to back, Bring to front, Send backward, and Bring forward commands. In addition, FreeHand lets you create named layers within the artwork and manipulate them through the Layers palette. This is a tremendous productivity tool for working with complex illustrations.

Any named layer can include objects that overlap each other—so in effect you are creating layers within layers. To simplify our descriptions in this chapter, we have used the word "layers" to describe the named layers listed in the Layers palette, and the word "levels" to describe the overlapping sequence of objects within one layer.

The Layers palette is described comprehensively in Chapter 13, and the Send to back, Bring to front, Send backward, and Bring forward commands are detailed in Chapter 14. In this chapter, we extol the benefits offered by FreeHand's layering feature, then describe some of the specific uses of this feature, including:

- Rearranging Overlapping Objects Within a Layer
- Managing Overlapping, Identical Objects
- Layering Overlapping, Identical Objects
- Layering Spot Color Separations
- Layering Different Type Specifications
- Layering to Produce Overhead Transparencies

Benefits of Working in Layers

The first two techniques in this chapter show how overlapping objects can be managed within one layer. The remaining techniques described in this chapter show you how to manage overlapping objects by putting them on different layers. Although the layering feature existed in earlier versions of FreeHand, the Layers palette introduced with version 3.0 has made this feature much easier to work with.

You can work without ever opening the Layers palette or knowing that it exists, but once you use it you will wonder how you ever lived without it. The Layers palette offers the advantages of (1) letting you make some layers active while the others are visible but not changeable, (2) letting you make some layers invisible while you work on others, (3) letting you print selected layers only, and (4) letting you rearrange layers easily.

There are many reasons for working in multiple layers. A few uses are suggested here, with specific uses demonstrated in the following techniques.

Simplify Complex Artwork

Layering can help simplify complex illustrations. By putting different collections of objects on different layers, you can make layers invisible or unselectable which allows you to easily work on one portion of the artwork at a time. You make a layer invisible by clicking the check mark next to the layer name in the Layers palette. You make it visible again by clicking to the left of the name when no check mark is displayed.

Layers can be set up for related groups of elements, or you could maintain two layers: the Foreground layer with all of the finished art, and a Working layer where you create new elements while the Foreground layer is made invisible or inactive. When you are finished creating an object, you would move the elements from the Working layer to the Foreground.

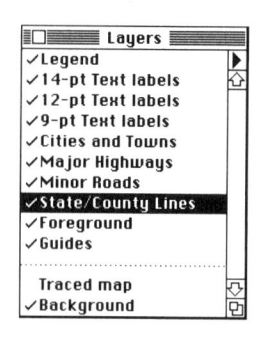

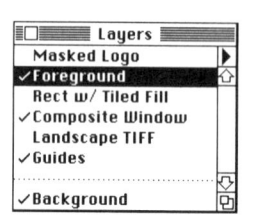

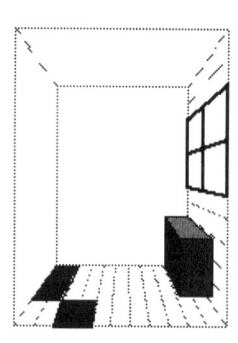

CAUTION

Once an element is sandwiched between other elements in the Foreground layer, do not move it on to another layer just for editing unless you have a way of knowing exactly what elements were above and below it in the Foreground layer.

Save Screen Redraw Time

By dividing complex illustrations into layers, you can save screen redraw time while you are working by making one or more layers invisible. Objects that make especially good candidates for invisible layers include imported TIFF images, objects with tiled fills, and clipping paths with complex contents.

Save Printing Time

You can save printing time with printing drafts of complex illustrations by putting the approved or unchanging elements on layers below the Background and printing only the new or changed elements.

Use the Background Layer for Non-printing Elements

The Background layer is normally set up below the printing line in the Layers palette. Layers below the printing line do not print. Objects on the Background layer appear grayed on the screen, but you can select and edit them as you would objects on any other layer.

You can use the Background layer to store elements that are aids in your work. Several of the techniques described in Chapter 8 suggest putting custom grids and spacing guides on the Background layer. You can also store elements that you have traced—but do not wish to print—on the Background layer.

Create Different Versions of Artwork

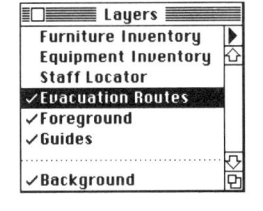

Working in layers, you can create multiple versions of an illustration. For example, the Foreground layer might contain a complex floor plan. You can create a separate layer for a schematic of emergency evacuation routes, another layer for the names of people in each unit or room, another layer for an equipment and furniture inventory of each room, and so on. In printing, you would print the Foreground layer plus only *one* of the other layers.

Rearranging Overlapping Objects Within a Layer

These two techniques are useful whenever you need to rearrange the sequence of three or more overlapping elements that are all on the same named layer (such as the Foreground), like the boxes shown in the accompanying figure.

Method 1: Using the Bring Forward (or Send Backward) Command

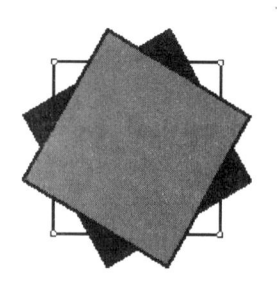

1

Create a series of three or more objects layered on top of one another, like the three overlapping boxes shown on the left, and select the bottom-most object.

TIP
You can select the objects below other objects by finding an exposed edge of the box you wish to select, or you can click through successive levels by holding down the Control key as you click.

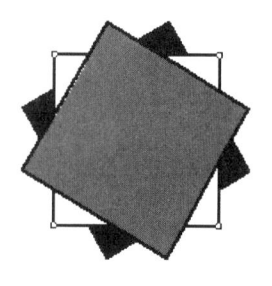

2

To move the bottom box to a new position between the other two boxes, choose Bring forward from the Element menu.

Method 2: Using the Send to Back Command

This alternative is useful when four or more overlapping objects are seriously out of order.

1

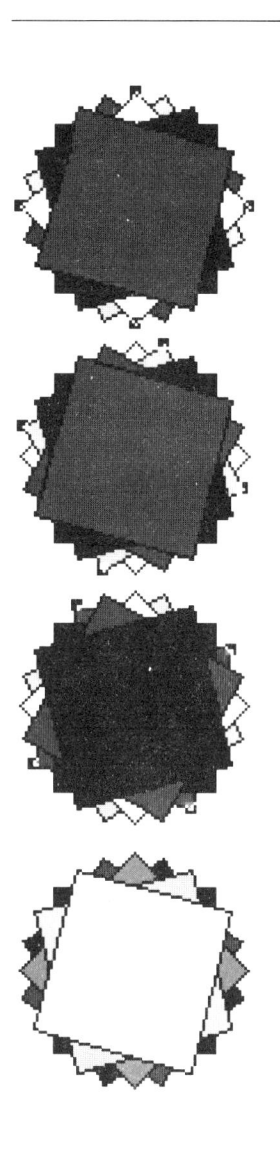

Select the object that you want to end up on top of all the others and choose Send to back from the Element menu (⌘B).

2

Select the object that you want just below the top and choose Send to back from the Element menu (⌘B).

3

Continue selecting objects in your intended top-down order and choosing Send to back from the Element menu (⌘B). The last object you select should be the one you intend to be below all the others. The end result should be the intended sequence of levels.

Managing Overlapping, Identical Objects

You can overlap different objects within one layer. When objects overlap, you can select the objects below other objects by finding an exposed edge of the object you wish to select, or you can click through successive levels by holding down the Control key as you click. If the overlapping objects are identical paths, even if they have different line styles such as the overlapping lines shown at left, there is no exposed edge. It is therefore difficult to know which object you have selected by Control-clicking since the handles do not change as you click through the levels.

Here are two handy techniques for managing overlapping, identical objects.

When There Are Only Two Objects

If there are only two identical overlapping objects, you can easily select and modify the top object by clicking it. To modify the object on the lower layer, click the top object to select it, then hold down the Control key and click again to select the object below. You can make your modifications while the object is more or less hidden by the top object, or you can use the next steps to be more certain of what object is selected and to see the changes more clearly.

1

Select the top object by clicking it, then choose Send to back from the Element menu (⌘B). The appearance of the overlapping objects before and after this rearrangement is shown at left.

2

Click away from the objects (or press the Tab key) to deselect everything, then click again on the overlapping objects to select the one that is now on top, and make your modifications. In this case, the line is changed from black to gray.

3

Select the top object by clicking it (if it is not still selected after the previous step), then choose Send to back from the Element menu (⌘B). The final appearance of the overlapping objects is shown at left.

When There Are Three or More Objects

The problem is more complicated when there are three or more identical overlapping objects, such as the three-part line shown on the left. The next steps make it easy to select and modify each object.

1

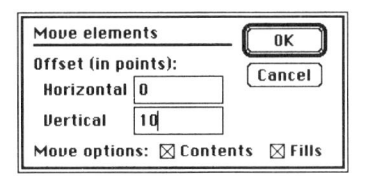

Select the top object by clicking it, then choose Move from the Edit menu (⌘M) and enter a number that is easy to remember—such as 10. Select the direction that will most clearly separate the objects—Horizontal if the objects are vertical lines, Vertical if the objects are horizontal lines. If you move at an angle, you will need to remember the number of degrees you used.

Click OK to close the dialog box and move the object.

TIP

If you are moving objects with a white fill and line, you might want to create a temporary black background rectangle against which you can see the moved objects. Another alternative is to change them to a more visible color before moving them, then change them back to white after replacing all the objects in Step 4.

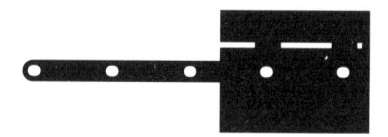

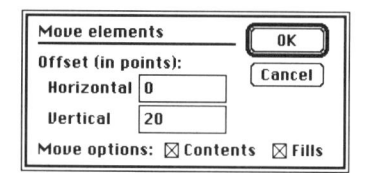

2

Select the second object by clicking it, and repeat Step 1, but this time *double* the numeric values you entered in Step 1. Repeat this for each object in the stack except the last one—keep the object on the lowest level in its original position.

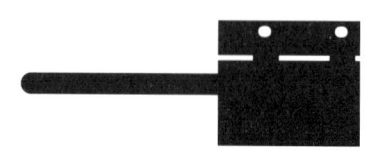

3

Now that the objects are separated, you can easily select and modify each one.

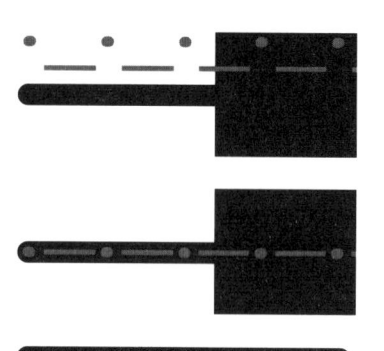

4

When you are finished, select the top object and choose the Move command from the Edit menu (⌘M). This time, enter the *negative* of the same numbers you entered in Step 1 to return it to its former position. Repeat this step for each item you moved.

   See also "Layering Overlapping, Identical Objects," the next technique.

Layering Overlapping, Identical Objects

Here is another solution to the problem posed in the first technique in this chapter, "Managing Overlapping, Identical Objects." In this case, the objects are positioned on different named layers in FreeHand, and managed through the Layers palette. This solution can be useful when there are only two overlapping elements, but its efficiency increases with the number of overlapping elements.

1

Press the Tab key to deselect all elements in the artwork, then choose View → Windows → Layers (⌘6) to open the Layers palette (if it is not already open). Next, choose New from the Layers palette pop-up menu. Create one new layer for each of the overlapping objects.

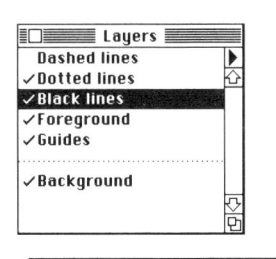

2

Select the top object by clicking it, then click the new top layer. Then click the check mark next to the layer name to make it invisible for the moment.

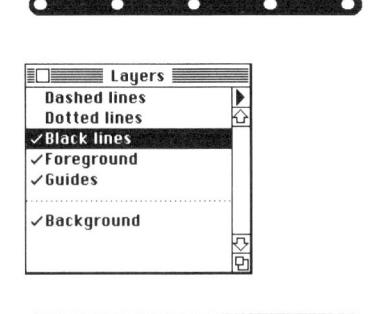

3

Click away from the objects (or press the Tab key) to deselect everything. Click again on the overlapping objects to select the one that is now visible on top, and then click the next layer name. Next, click the check mark next to the layer name to make it invisible.

4

Repeat Step 3 for each of the overlapping objects, then click at the left of each layer name to make them all visible again.

5

To edit an object on one of the layers, you can make all of the other layers invisible by clicking the check marks next to their names, or by choosing Multilayer from the Layers palette pop-up menu to remove the check mark (if one is displayed)—so that only objects on the active layer can be selected. Click the name of the layer that contains the objects you want to edit, then select and modify the elements.

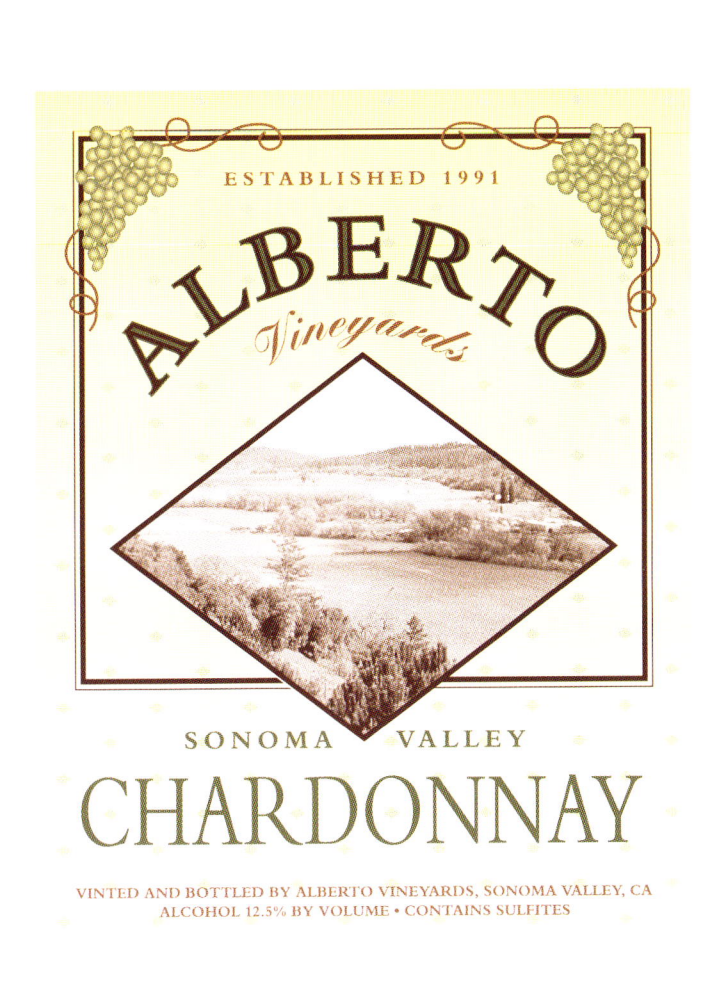

Wine label described in Chapter 10. Reprinted by permission from Susan Equitz.

The High Technology War (detail) decribed in Chapter 10. Reprinted by permission of *U.S. News and World Report.*

K2 ski toe designed in FreeHand, printed as six overlays for spot color production (see Chapter 10 for description). This version was scanned from a slide, manipulated in Adobe Photoshop, and placed as a color TIFF image in Aldus PageMaker for process color printing. Reprinted by permission from K2 Corporation.

San Francisco Bay Area Regional Transit Map (detail) described in Chapter 11. Reprinted by permission from MTC (Metropolitan Transportation Commission).

Seattle Downtown Circulation Map (detail) described in Chapter 11. Reprinted by permission from METRO (Municipality of Metropolitan Seattle).

San Francisco Bay Area Road Map (detail) described in Chapter 11. Reprinted by permission from Eureka Cartography and the *San Francisco Business Times*.

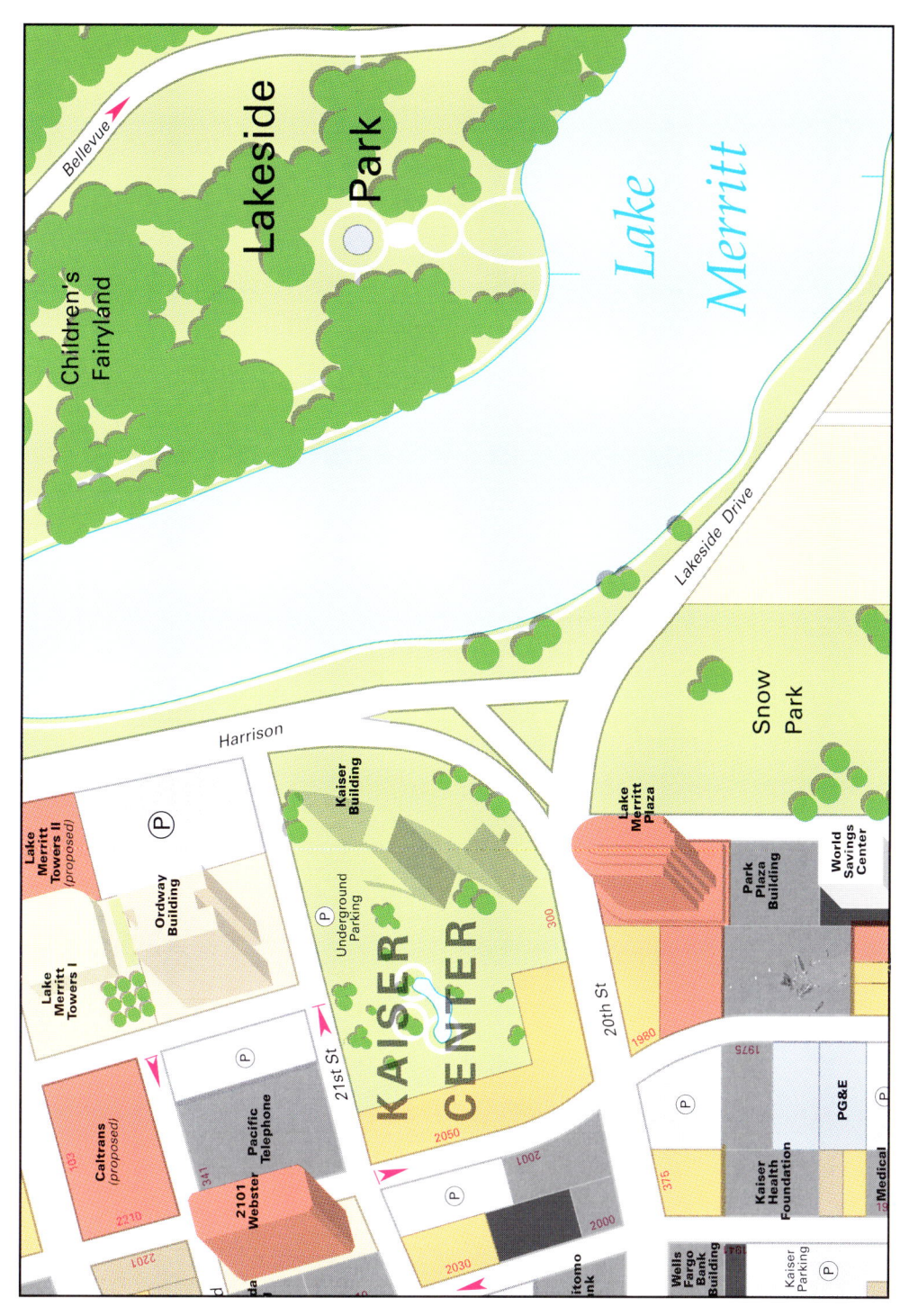

Oakland Downtown Business Development Map (detail) described in Chapter 11. Reprinted by permission from Eureka Cartography and the *San Francisco Business Times*.

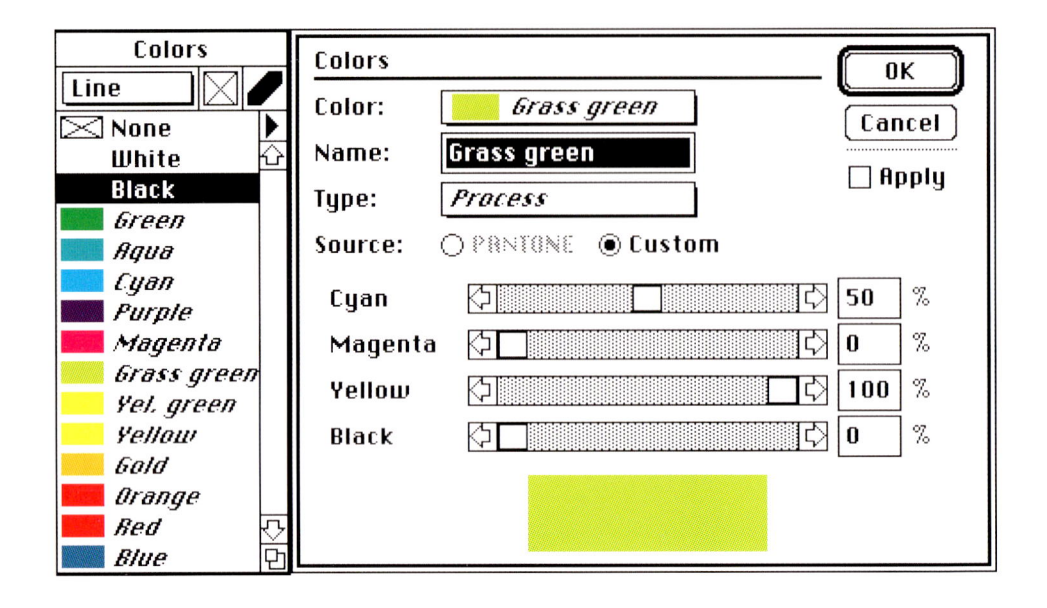

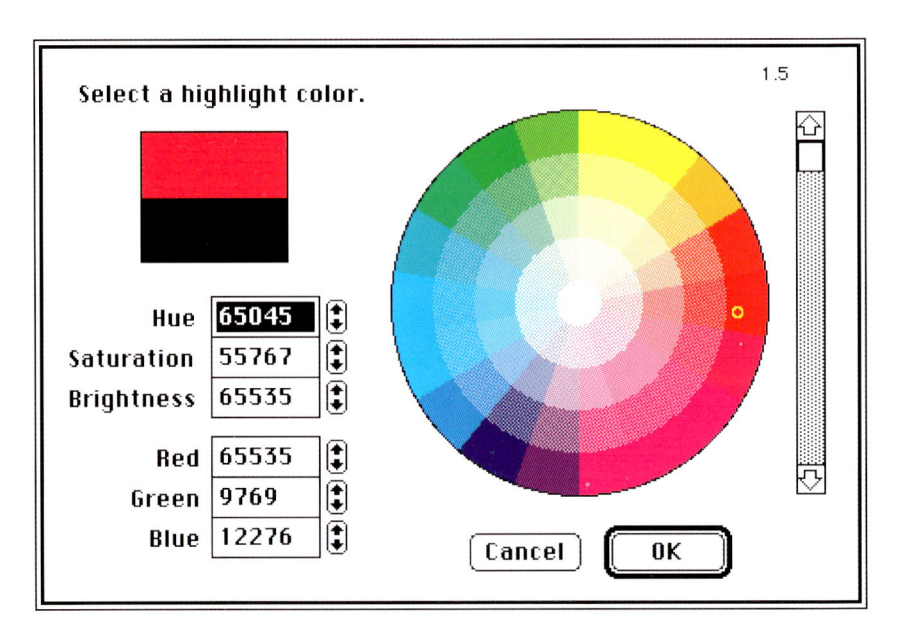

Colors palette and Colors dialog box displayed in FreeHand (top figures) and on-screen color adjusting wheel displayed through the Macintosh Control Panel (bottom figure).

Layering Spot Color Separations

You can assign spot colors to objects, and FreeHand will print spot color separations automatically if you select that option in the Print dialog box. It is not necessary, but it can be useful, to set up all of the elements that share the same spot color on individual layers named for that spot color.

This technique is especially useful if you are working on a monochrome monitor, assigning colors based on PANTONE colors, or working with colors that were originally created on a color monitor. It is also useful if you want to globally change from one color to another without actually redefining colors.

CAUTION

This technique is most applicable to artwork in which the spot colors do not overlap—unless the colors always overlap in the same stacking order.

1

Choose View → Windows → Layers (⌘6) to open the Layers palette, and choose New from the Layers palette pop-up menu. Create one new layer for each of the spot colors.

2

Draw the artwork, using the Colors palette or the Fill and line command from the Attributes menu (⌘E) to assign colors to different parts of the image. After assigning an object a color, click the layer named for that color.

3

If some elements have a different line color from the fill color, add a new layer named for each line-fill color combination and place objects on those layers as appropriate.

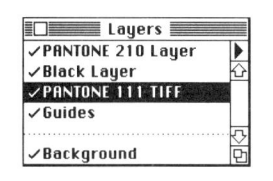

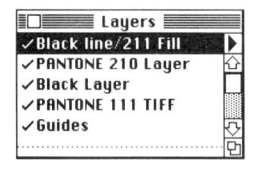

4

To see what elements have been assigned which colors on a monochrome screen, make all of the other layers invisible by clicking the check marks next to their names—leaving only one layer visible at a time. Alternatively, you can choose Multilayer from the Layers palette pop-up menu to remove the check mark (if one is displayed) and turn Multilayer off, so that only objects on the active layer can be selected. Click the name of the layer that contains the objects you want to edit, then choose Select all from the Edit menu (⌘A) to see what elements are selected.

5

To globally change one spot color to another, first select all of the elements on one layer (using one of the techniques suggested in the previous step). Then click a new color in the Colors palette for the line and fill of the selected objects. (You cannot use the Fill and line command to change colors unless all of the objects have the same fill and line style.)

Choose Edit from the Layers palette pop-up menu to change the name of the layer to match the new color assignment.

Layering Different Type Specifications

You can define specific fill and line attributes as styles in the Styles palette, but there is no way to create styles for text formats. If you put text that shares the same type specifications on one layer, you can easily select all of the text at once and change the font, size, style, color, or other type specifications.

This technique is especially useful if you are working with large volumes of text—in maps and technical illustrations.

1

Press the Tab key to deselect all elements in the artwork, then choose View ➤ Windows ➤ Layers (⌘ 6) to open the Layers palette (if it is not already showing). Choose New from the Layers palette pop-up menu. Create one new layer for each different type specification (i.e., each unique combination of choices from the commands in the Type menu).

2

If you have already added text to the artwork, select all of the text objects that share one set of specifications, then click the new layer with that specification name. Repeat this step for each set of like text objects.

As you add new text objects, click the layer named for the new object's type specifications.

3

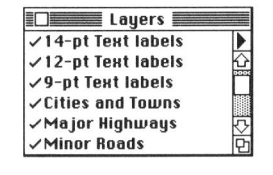

To view and edit text elements that have been assigned a set of common type specifications, make all of the other layers invisible by clicking the check marks next to their names—leaving only one layer visible at a time. Or you can choose Multilayer from the Layers palette pop-up menu to remove the check mark (if one is displayed), so that only objects on the active layer can be selected. Click the name of the layer that contains the objects you want to edit, then choose Select all from the Edit menu (⌘A) and use commands in the Type menu to change the specifications.

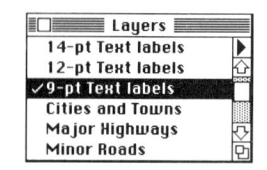

South S.F.

Burlingame

Belmont   Foster City

Los Altos

Layering to Produce Overhead Transparencies

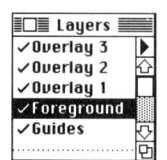

An overhead transparency is a clear sheet of acetate printed with an image and projected onto a screen by a speaker who is giving a presentation to a group. Here is a technique for creating a series of overlays—two or more overhead transparencies with different images that will be laid on top of each other as they are projected during a presentation.

1

Working in the Foreground layer, draw the artwork that will compose the first transparency—the bottom layer when additional transparencies are overlayed during a presentation. Choose Fill and line from the Attributes menu (⌘E) to set the fill and line characteristics of each element, including different colors if you wish.

2

Press the Tab key to deselect all elements in the artwork, then choose View → Windows → Layers (⌘6) to open the Layers palette. Choose New from the Layers palette pop-up menu. Create one new layer for each of the overlays that will be added to the first image.

3

Click the new layer above Foreground in the Layers palette, and draw the artwork that will compose the second transparency—the second layer when the two transparencies are overlayed during the presentation.

Repeat this step for each additional overlay, positioning the artwork for each overlay on a different layer.

4

Print the artwork for each overlay on a separate sheet, in color or in black and white. Do this by first making all layers but one invisible, then printing the visible overlay (⌘P) and clicking the Options button in the Print dialog box. Click Visible foreground layers to activate that option (if it is not already selected), then click OK twice to close the dialog boxes.

An alternative in this step is to rearrange the layers so that only one layer is above the printing line in the Layers palette for each printing. See "Layers Palette" in Chapter 13.

▪ Part III ▪

Case Studies

The impact of desktop publishing on professional publishers, corporate publications departments, and self-publishing associations and individuals is best seen through the experiences of those who have made the transition from traditional methods to electronic publishing over the past few years. Chapters 10 and 11 of this book offer case studies of professional illustrations that were once produced using traditional methods and are now produced using FreeHand. For each example you will find descriptions of how the illustrator organized the artwork and/or handled tricky elements.

CHAPTER	DESCRIPTION
10. Commercial Art	Packaging, informative illustrations, detailed technical illustrations, and a comic strip.
11. Cartography	Four different styles of maps, from large regions to downtown streets.

10

Commercial Art

This chapter presents six case studies of commercial art that were created using FreeHand and collected from a variety of sources. Examples include:

- Alberto Vineyards Wine Label—designed by artist Susan Equitz, including an imported TIFF image and clever customization of text that has been converted to paths
- The High-Technology War—an information graphic from *U.S. News & World Report*
- K2 Skis—artwork that is printed on the ski tops, prepared for spot color production *without* using the built-in color separation function (with good reasons)
- A Comic Strip—conceived and produced by John Laney, incorporating bitmaps with the FreeHand artwork
- Black-and White Artwork—by Henk Dawson, master of highlighting techniques
- Technical Illustrations from Mate Punch and Die Company—realistic representations of industrial tools, including cut-away diagrams

Alberto Vineyards Wine Label

Overview

This wine label, designed by Susan Equitz, demonstrates some of the unique features of FreeHand that distinguish it from most other drawing applications: custom tiled patterns, text along a curved path, incorporation of scanned TIFF images with line art, the ability to cut "holes" within objects to create windows to the layers below, and the ability to convert text to line-art objects. The label was briefly described in Chapter 1, simplified for the general reader, but here we give the details that will thrill advanced users as well as curious novices (see Figure 10.1 and color plate).

Details

The label consists of a scanned image of Sonoma Valley, California, overlayed by a rectangle with a graduated fill and a second rectangle with a custom tiled fill. The TIFF image is visible through a diamond-shaped "hole" in the two rectangles. This effect is created by using the Join elements command to join each rectangle with a diamond-shaped polygon to create a composite path.

Using composite paths is more efficient than the alternative: making a diamond-shaped polygon into a clipping path around the scan by pasting the TIFF *inside* the diamond. Composite paths with see-through areas generally take less time to print than clipping paths. (See Chapter 4 for the steps in using a composite path to mask other elements; see Chapter 6 for the steps in creating a clipping path.)

The tiled pattern in the top rectangle consists of two small diamonds and no other fill, so the pattern is transparent to the graduated fill in a rectangle positioned behind it. The rectangles that compose the double-line black frame within the label are pasted inside the top rectangle, along with the tiled pattern, so the diamond hole cuts across the double-line black frame (see Figure 10.2).

Chapter 10. Commercial Art 277

Grapes are ellipses with radial fill, clustered and grouped

Text of Alberto converted to paths and made into custom inline type

Type joined to an invisible ellipse

Imported scanned image in TIFF format, cropped by a diamond-shaped window through two rectangles

Rectangle with tiled fill of small diamonds and two black-framed rectangles pasted inside, overlayed on rectangle with a graduated fill, both rectangles joined to a diamond to create a hollow area behind the scanned image

ESTABLISHED 1991

ALBERTO
Vineyards

SONOMA VALLEY
CHARDONNAY

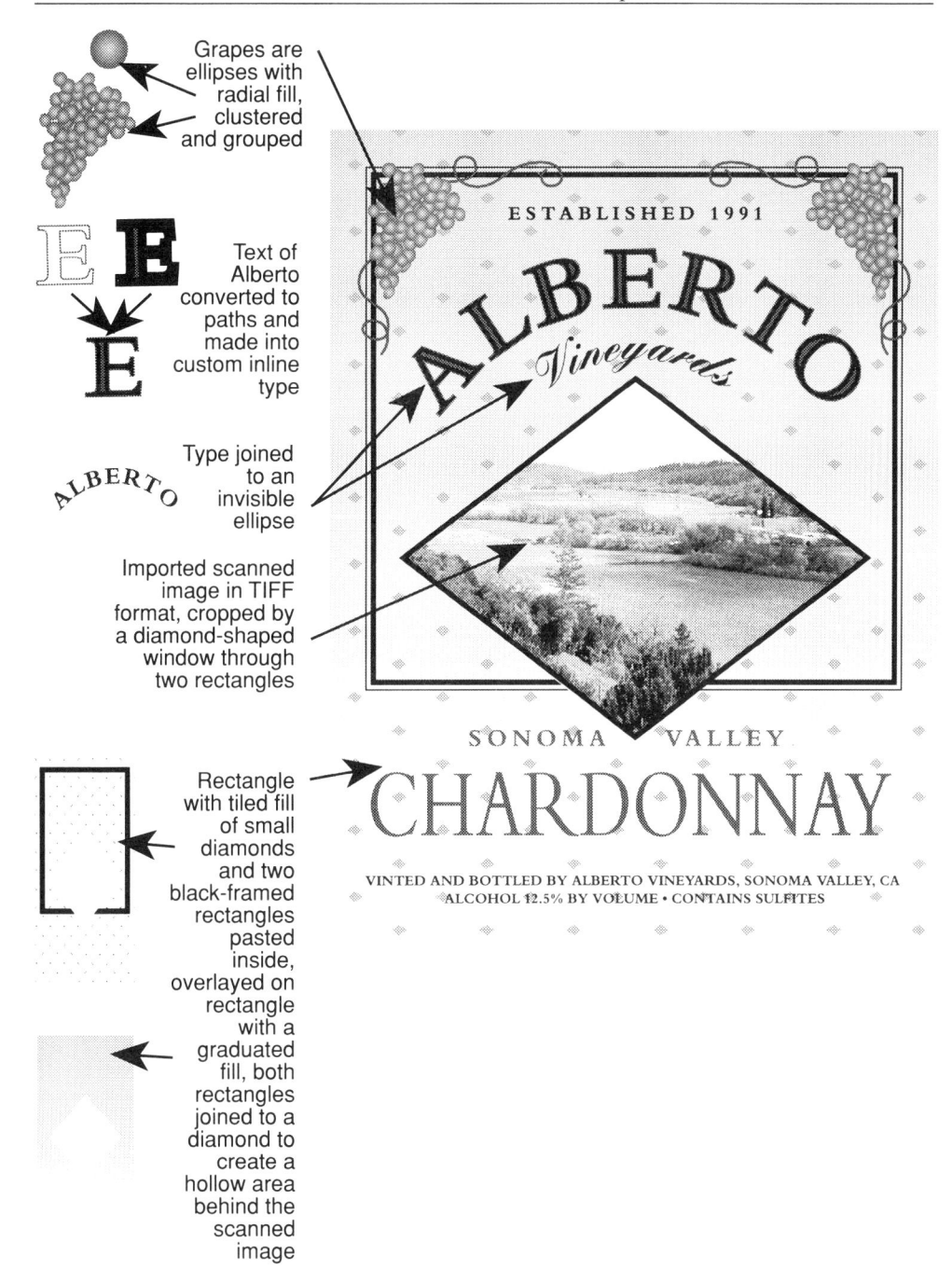

VINTED AND BOTTLED BY ALBERTO VINEYARDS, SONOMA VALLEY, CA
ALCOHOL 12.5% BY VOLUME • CONTAINS SULFITES

Figure 10.1 Wine label designed by Susan Equitz, TechArt, San Francisco

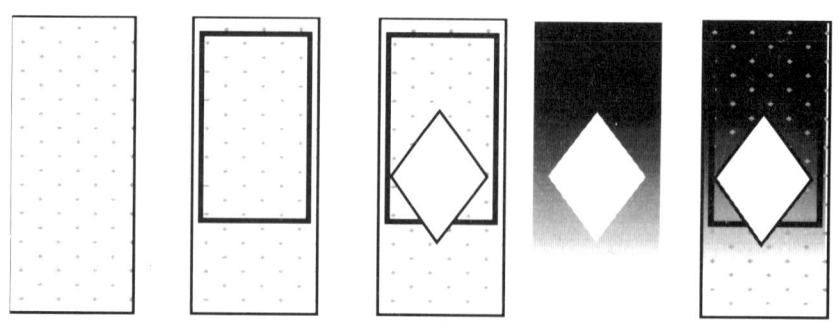

Figure 10.2 Rectangle with diamond fill pattern (left), same rectangle with a smaller rectangle pasted inside (second), and with diamond overlayed then joined to make a composite path (third). Identical rectangle with graduated fill joined with a diamond shape (fourth), and positioned behind the diamond-filled composite (right)

The word "Vineyards" is simply text joined to an ellipse. The word "Alberto" is more complex: It was typed as text and joined to an ellipse, then converted to a graphics object using the Convert to paths command. The Fill and line command was used to set the fill to None and the line to 0.5 picas. The grouped text was then ungrouped to yield individual letters, then the letters were cloned, and the top copy was set to have an olive fill color and a 3.5 pica black line. This made the border around each letter thick, but it had the effect of expanding the letters so they seemed closer to each other. (The effect happens because a 3.5 pica line weight adds 1.825 picas inside the border plus 1.825 picas outside the border of each letter.)

To return the letters to their original distance apart, each individual letter was then cut and pasted inside the matching letter below it, so the matching letter became a clipping path for the letters that were made too fat by thick outlines.

Figure 10.3 Letter with thin outline and no fill, letter with thick outline and light fill, and result when second letter is pasted inside the first

Credits

Designed by Susan Equitz, TechArt, San Francisco

The High-Technology War

Overview

The artists at *U.S. News and World Report* use Aldus FreeHand extensively to produce their information graphics, such as the High-Technology War excerpt shown in this example (see Figure 10.4 and color plate). Their skilled FreeHand artists can produce a complex illustration in two days or less, and they meet faster deadlines by teaming more than one artist on a single illustration.

The artwork is set up for process color separations, which they print directly to film on a Linotronic imagesetter.

Details

The research department and the editorial staff at *U.S. News and World Report* usually provide the technical information needed for an illustration, although the artists may get involved in researching some of the details such as what a particular plane, building, or geographical area looks like.

The artwork for many of the objects in an informational illustration is traced from scanned photographs. This is how the aircraft, tanks, and missiles were created in The High-Technology War illustration. Very often the relevant elements of the photograph are traced (using conventional pencils and tracing paper) and the traced photo is then scanned. This saves disk storage space (since scanned line art takes up less space than grayscale images), and makes it easier to use the Tracing tool to trace only those elements that will be used in the final illustration.

The artwork is designed to fit the page layout. Artists start with a template that shows the grid of a full page. The grid is created with the Line tool and the Rectangle tool as a grid of lines positioned on a nonprinting layer below the Background layer.

280 *Using Aldus FreeHand 3.0*

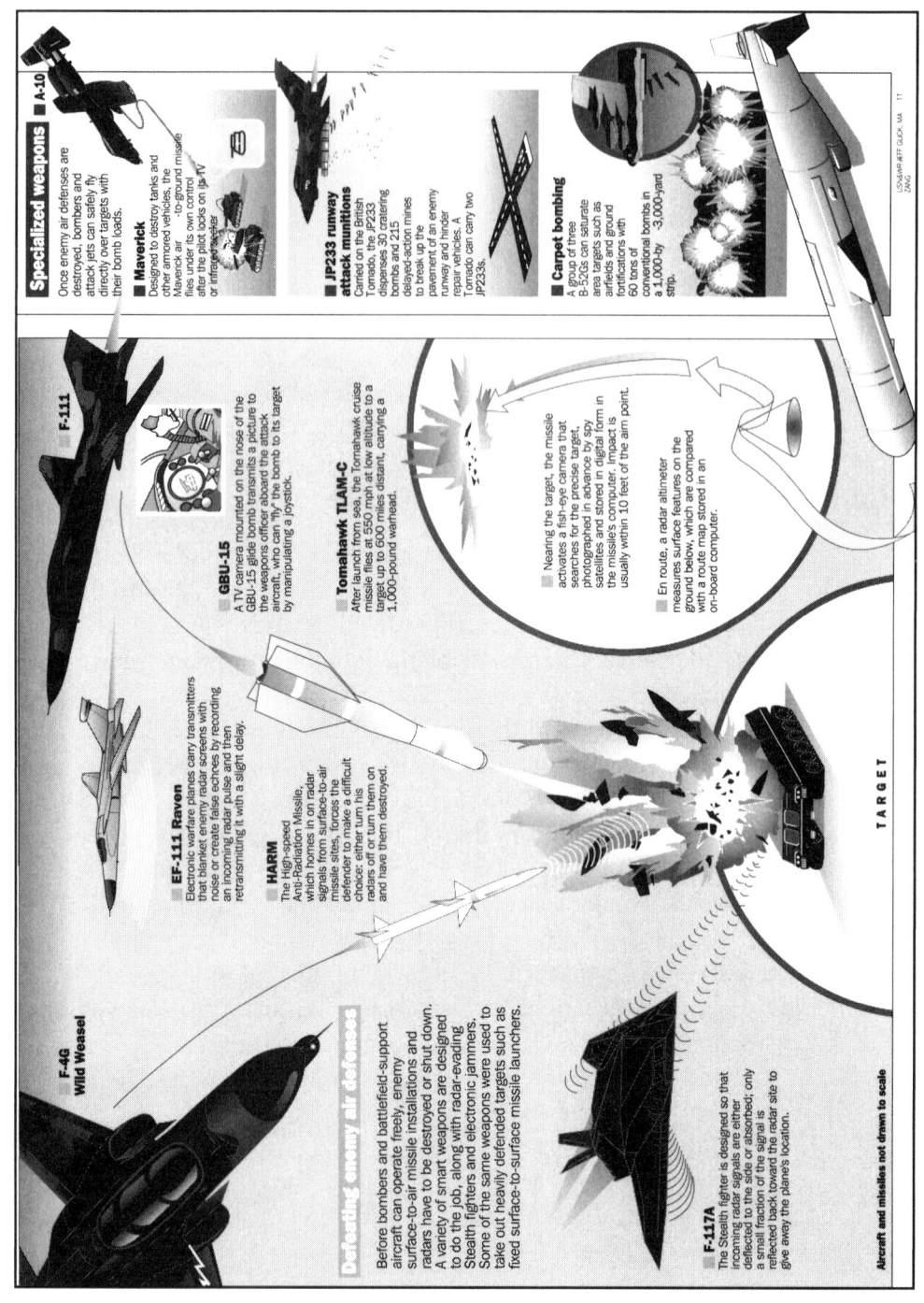

Figure 10.4 The High Technology War (detail). Reprinted by permission of *U.S. News and World Report.*

Figure 10.5 Custom grid of guide lines set on a non-printing layer below the Background

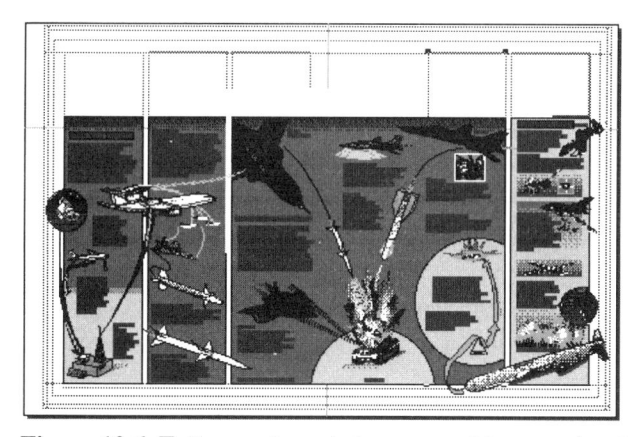

Figure 10.6 Full page layout shows graphic spanning two full pages. See color plate of center panel

All text and ruled lines are set up to print as a fifth color—with black defined as a spot color—and are overprinted on the rest of the process-separated artwork. This makes it easy to make last-minute text changes, a common occurrence in news printing, and to print the negative for the black overprint elements only. Overprinting ruled lines also eliminates some of the problems that can develop if the lines were separated as process black and fell out of register during printing on the high-speed press.

The final artwork is positioned on the page layout in Visionary (a page layout application that enables you to link artwork from desktop computers to the high-end Scitex system for color separations). It is then ported over to a Scitex system for final printing of film negatives, unless the artwork is too complicated or cumbersome. In the latter case, the artwork is printed directly from FreeHand to a Linotronic 1300, and the separations are stripped in to the film for the page layout from the Scitex.

Credits

Reprinted with permission from *U.S. News and World Report,* Washington, D.C. Special thanks to Jeff Glick, Graphics Director, for his time and support.

K2 Skis

Overview

The Art Department at K2 Skis uses Aldus FreeHand to design their ski tops (see color plate). They manage approximately 130 different ski models, and artist Mike Johnson noted that even one third that many would cause a bottleneck in the art department if they were not using computers for the artwork.

The artwork is set up for spot color separations, which they print directly to film on a Linotronic imagesetter. The ski tops are mass-produced using the screen printing process.

Details

Since an adult ski can be over 80 inches long and the maximum length allowed in one FreeHand document is 40 inches (2,880 points), the artists break the artwork for a full ski top into two files—one for the toe and one for the tail of the ski. Instead of creating the artwork for each half as a composite of overlayed elements, the six process colors were handled as six separate pieces of artwork, aligned next to each other (rather than one on top of the other).

There are several good reasons for creating six separate images, not stacked or layered on top of each other:

- Since you cannot see through spot color blends when they overlap on the screen or print as composite, there is no proofing advantage to overlaying the elements. (See "Blending for Spot Color Separation" in Chapter 6.)

- If the separations were printed from a composite, each 3.5-inch-wide ski top would use nearly 480 inches of film when printed to the Linotronic. If the elements for two colors are printed side-by-side on the 12-inch wide film roll, the ski top would require less than 240 inches. This is a considerable savings when you consider that film is about one dollar per foot, that they produce 130 different ski models, and that each model is printed to the Linotronic more than once (for proofing and approval cycles).

284   Using Aldus Freehand 3.0

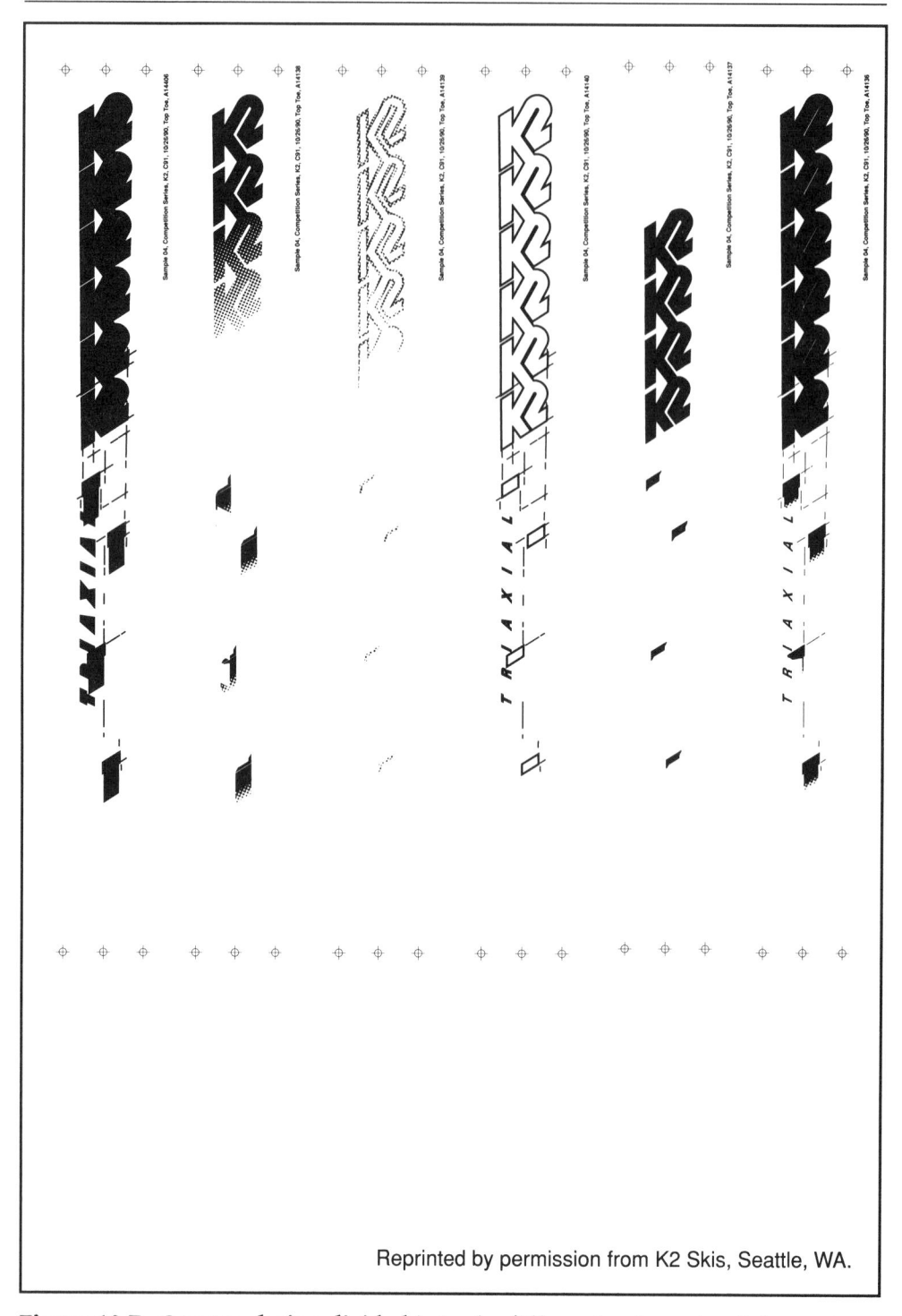

Reprinted by permission from K2 Skis, Seattle, WA.

Figure 10.7   One toe design divided into six different color sets of elements.

For each file, one version of the artwork is created with registration marks added as part of the artwork. The artwork is then cloned to create a version for each spot color to be used, plus one version for a white-ink undercoat below the artwork that will be printed on dark ski tops. (The plastic ski top was dark gray on the skis in this example, and colors were printed over the gray background—see the color pages.) The color separations printed in this example were ocean blue, pearl, fluorescent lava, magenta, and the white underprinter.

In this case, the artist dragged the first cloned copy of the artwork to the right while holding down the Shift key to align the two duplicates horizontally. They were spaced so both fit within a 12-inch width (the width of the paper rolls in the Linotronic imagesetter). The artist then used the Duplicate command to create four more copies, spaced evenly apart. Each cloned copy of the artwork was modified as necessary to create the desired final result, but all versions were defined in shades of black rather than as spot colors, so the six versions of the artwork could be printed out two-up, in 36-inch long rolls, on the 12-inch wide paper or film accommodated by the Linotronic. The print shop was told what spot colors to use for each separation, and sequence to lay them down in.

Credits

Artwork reprinted by permission from K2 Skis, Vashon, Washington. Special thanks to Rich Greene (Graphic Arts Manager) and Mike Johnson (FreeHand artist) for their time and support.

Comic Strip

Description

This full-page comic strip is one of a series published in *MacTech Journal*. The artwork is set up as a 16-by-21 inch page layout, printed reduced in the final form to improve the resolution of MacPaint-format graphics that are included as part of the final artwork.

Details

Most of the line art in this FreeHand document consists of bitmap drawings created using GraphicWorks—a paint program on the Macintosh that can work with layers of bitmapped art the way FreeHand can work with layers of polygons. FreeHand was used to created the final layout, captions, text, panel frames, halftone fills and speech balloons.

The steps in this process were as follows: The figures and layout were first sketched using felt-tipped marker, scaled to final output size. A 200% scan of this sketch was imported into a FreeHand document that is 200% of the final print size. The panel borders and balloons were added on a layer above the scan and a laserprint of each of the frame was made using manual tile option. The scan was discarded and the document with only panels and balloons was saved.

Working on tracing paper on top of the printout, a tighter drawing of the figures was created. (This step allows the composition to take balloon placement and panels shapes into account.) The drawings were made in soft pencil or fine-point marker. The tracings (sometimes more than one for a panel) were scanned and imported into GraphicWorks, where the line art was cleaned up and refined. This was faster and easier than trying to draw each cartoon character with a mouse. The final GraphicWorks image for each panel (without a border) was exported as a 1-bit MacPaint document.

When all the panels are complete, they are placed, one at a time into the FreeHand layout at the default level of 100. The artist set each bitmap to transparent pasted them inside their respective panel borders. Changing the current drawing level to 90, the polygon tool was used to create the halftone fills. (The artist zoomed into 200% and tried to place the point-to-point lines right down the center of the trap lines. He did not use

Chapter 10. Commercial Art 287

Figure 10.8 Comic strip pages by John Laney

Autotrace because it was not accurate enough and what he wanted was just a closed path polygon with no outline.) As each polygon is completed it becomes a closed path and jumps behind the bitmap to layer 90.

Credits

Comic strip concept, script, and artwork by John Laney, Interactive Design, Seattle, Washington. Reprinted with permission from John Laney.

Highlights from Henk Dawson

Description

FreeHand artist Henk Dawson is a master of highlighting, as the four illustrations shown and described here demonstrate.

Details

Most of these illustrations began with a scanned image that was imported into FreeHand and traced manually, using the freeform drawing tools.

A BUILDING

The gradations of color used in the Meydenbauer building are very subtle. They were created as graduated fills ranging from as little as a 10% tint to white in some panels. The final artwork was output on a Linotronic 330 in order to get 3,300 dpi resolution and thereby reduce banding.

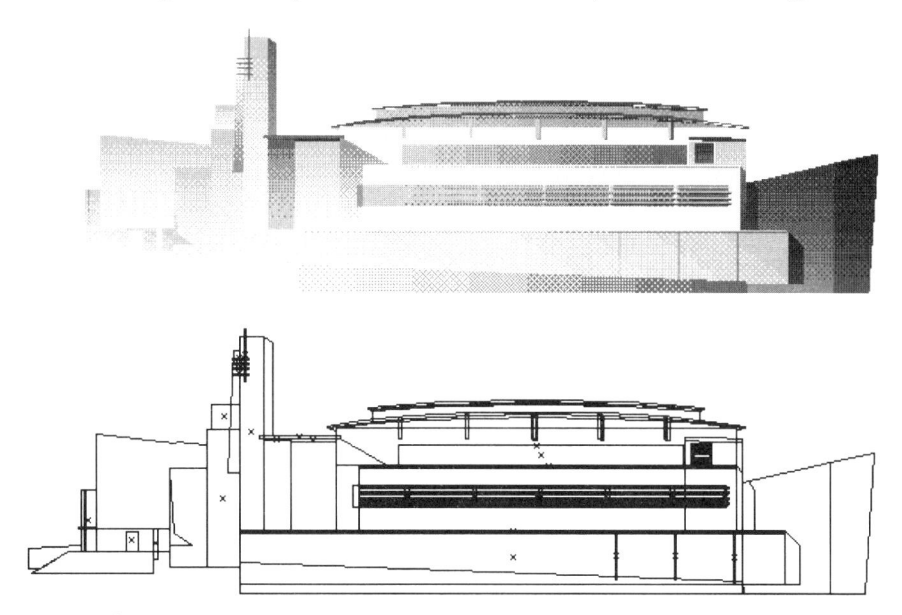

Figure 10.9 Building in Preview (top) and keyline view (bottom)

290   *Using Aldus Freehand 3.0*

Reprinted by permission from the artist

Figure 10.10   Examples of artwork from Henk Dawson.

A MOTOR BOAT

The motor boat scene was created by importing a scanned photo and positioning it on a background layer, where it was used as a guide in creating the final artwork entirely with FreeHand's freeform drawing tools.

The fabulous water trail is composed of a series of wave lines created using the Blend command: First the boat was roughly outlined on a new "water" layer and all other layers were turned off for faster screen redraw and for more convenience in developing the water trails.

For the top wave trail, the inside and outside edges of the water trail were drawn with the Freehand tool; the outer trail was set to a 70% gray fill with no line and the inner trail to 10% gray fill with no line. Then the two paths were selected and the Blend command was used to create ten intermediate trails. The middle and bottom wave trails were created the same way, except the inside path was set to 20% gray for the middle trail and white for the bottom trail, and the middle trail used 15 blend steps. Finally, the water was added as a gray rectangular background to the trails.

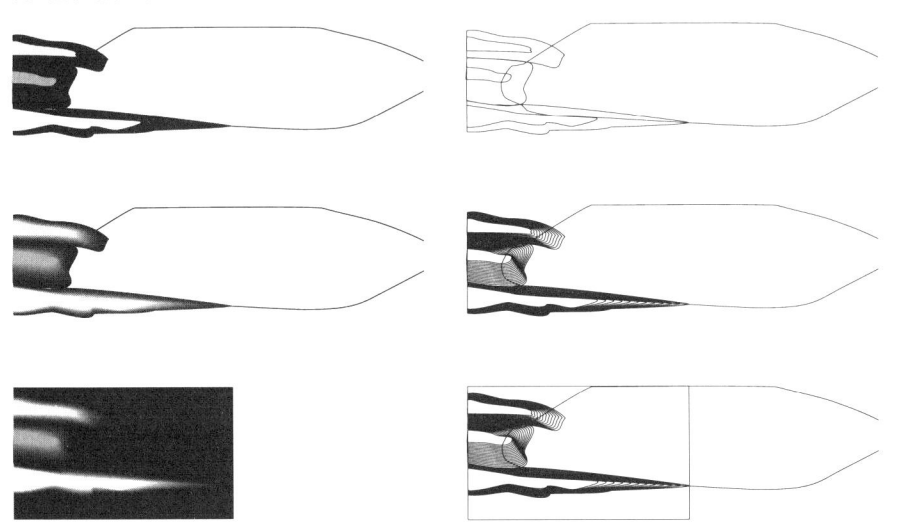

Figure 10.11 Evolution of the water trail in Preview (left) and keyline view (right)

BOAT ENGINE

Henk used a different technique to create the shading effects for the boat engine, shown here in Preview and keyline view. He drew closed paths in the shape of the highlights he wanted, and gave them a graduated fill.

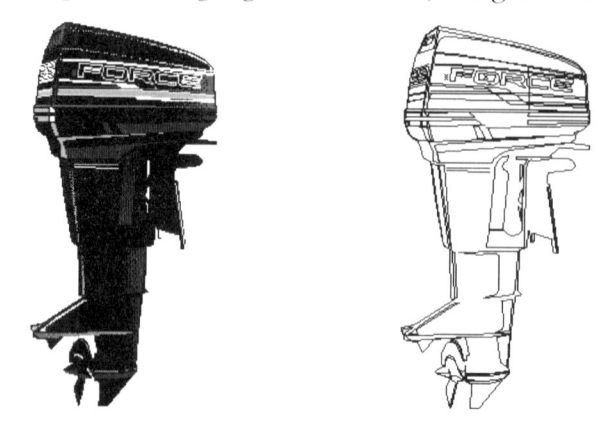

Figure 10.12 Boat engine in Preview (left) and keyline view (right)

GLOBE

The globe is composed of only two paths, each with a radial fill—but Henk used two clever tricks to force the radial fill to appear off-center from the apparent globe center, and to make the radial bands darker over land than over water. The top object is a single closed path that outlines the *water* within the globe. The path is given a radial fill that ranges from White to Pantone Blue 3145 and no line color. Henk then dragged one point away from the globe to move the center of the radial fill—the further away the point, the more off-center the radial fill appears.

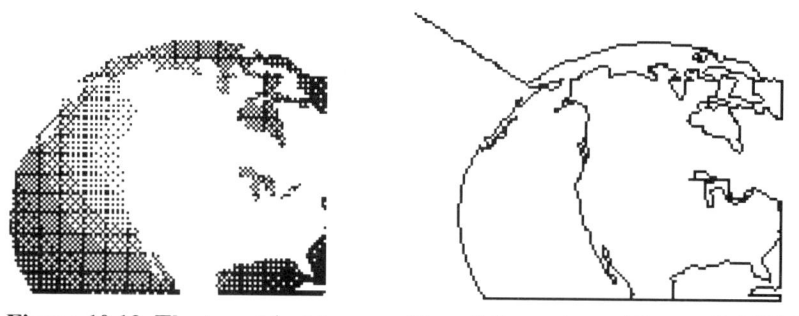

Figure 10.13 The top object is an outline of the water, with a radial fill forced off center by dragging one point away

The bottom object is a closed path that meets the same extreme points as the water object, but omits all other points except as needed to have the shape's edges completely covered by the water's edges. The radial fill of the second object ranges from 20% gray to 80% gray.

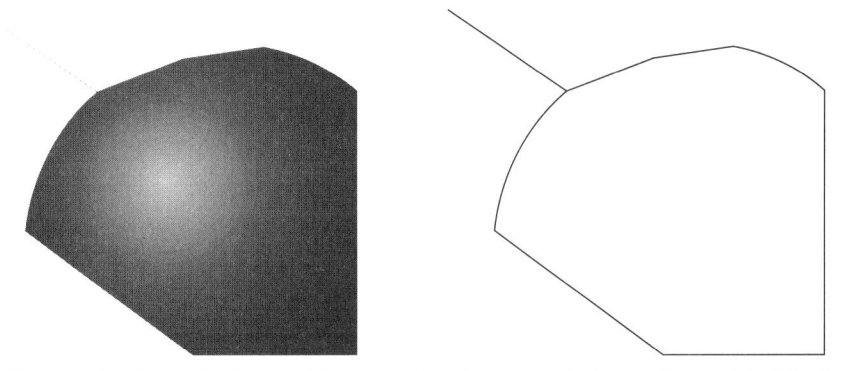

Figure 10.14 **The left object is a rough polygon that shares the right object's extreme points and has a darker radial fill**

When the two objects are positioned one above the other, you perceive the darker radial fill as the land forms. The only objects added in the final art are a rectangle with a graduated fill and three city marks.

Credits

Artwork by Henk Dawson. Reprinted by permission from the artist.

Technical Illustrations from Mate Punch and Die Company

Description

The drawings appeared (along with many others) in a Tooling Overview brochure produced by Mate Punch for Murata Wiedemann NC Punch Presses. All artwork was traced from scanned photographs—but it is the mastery of shading that makes these drawings so realistic.

Detail

The artists for the marketing department at Mate Punch and Die use FreeHand almost exclusively in their work, producing detailed technical illustrations and assembling them into two-page spreads in FreeHand.

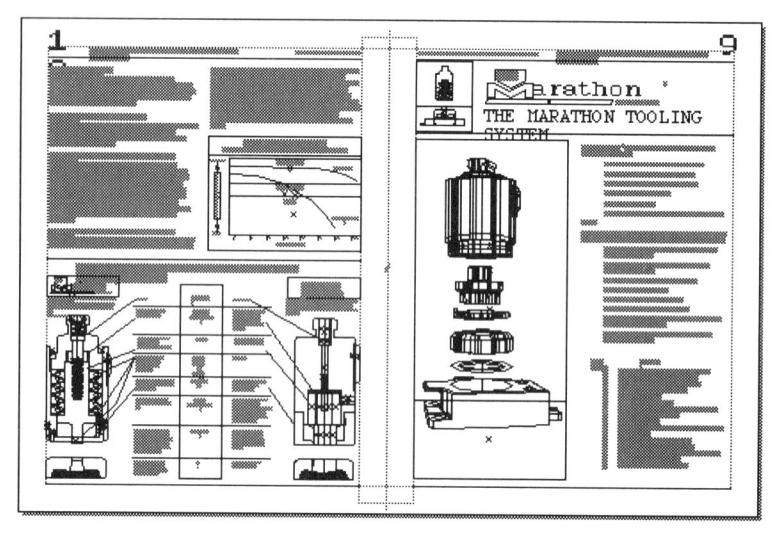

Figure 10.15 Two-page spread of tool catalogue created entirely in FreeHand

Credits

Reprinted by permission from Mate Punch and Die Company, Anoka, Minnesota. Special thanks to Brian Bartness for his time and cooperation.

Chapter 10. Commercial Art   295

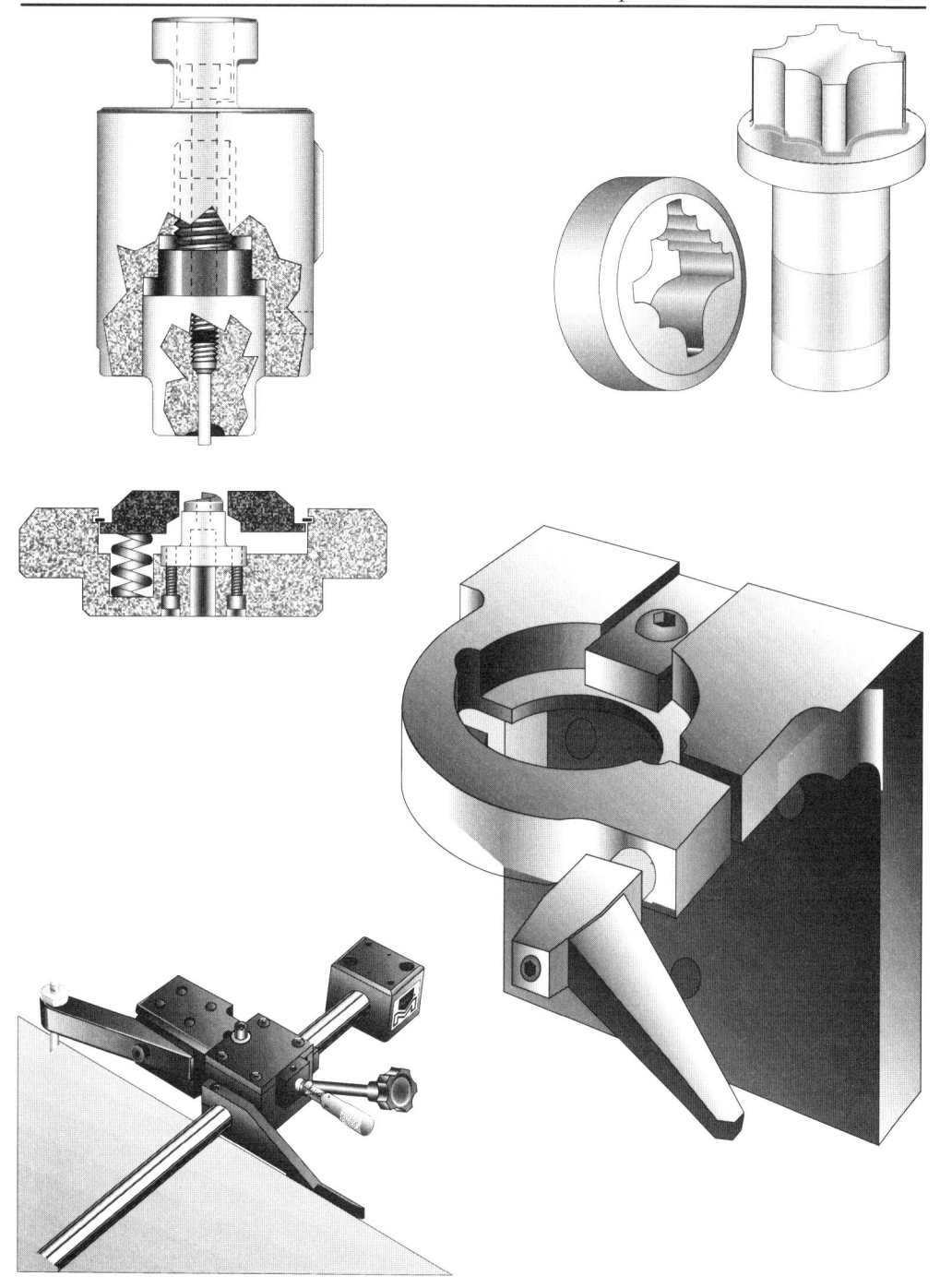

Figure 10.16 Mate punch examples reprinted by permission from Mate Punch and Co., Anoka, MN

11

Cartography

This chapter presents four different styles of maps created using FreeHand and collected from a variety of sources. Examples include:

- San Francisco Bay Area Regional Transit Maps—Style 1, a color-coded guide to public transportation
- Seattle Street Map—Style 2, also color-coded for easy reference
- San Francisco Bay Area Road Map—Style 3, showing major highways in a major urban area, by Eureka Cartography
- Oakland Downtown Business Development Map—Style 4, a detailed view of a downtown area, including three-dimensional aerial views of buildings

San Francisco Bay Area Regional Transit Maps

Overview

This color-coded map of San Francisco Bay Area regional public transport appears on the cover of the 128-page, 5.25-by-8.25-inch Regional Transit Guide and is enlarged to 8.25-by-14.375 inches on an inside fold-out page (see Figure 11.2 and color plate). The original version of this map was designed by Reineck & Reineck (of San Francisco) in 1981 and was created with traditional techniques. Years later, the design was re-created by the in-house graphics department at MTC using Adobe Illustrator, and the maps are now updated using Aldus FreeHand.

Details

There are three tricks in simplifying the production and editing of this complex graphic—all facilitated by FreeHand's system of palettes. The first trick is to name each custom color according to the transit system with which it is identified. This makes it easy for the artists who work on the file, since they are already familiar with the common vocabulary of the transit system so there is no need to invent a new vocabulary of custom color names. An added advantage is that the artists can change the color for a transit system without changing the name.

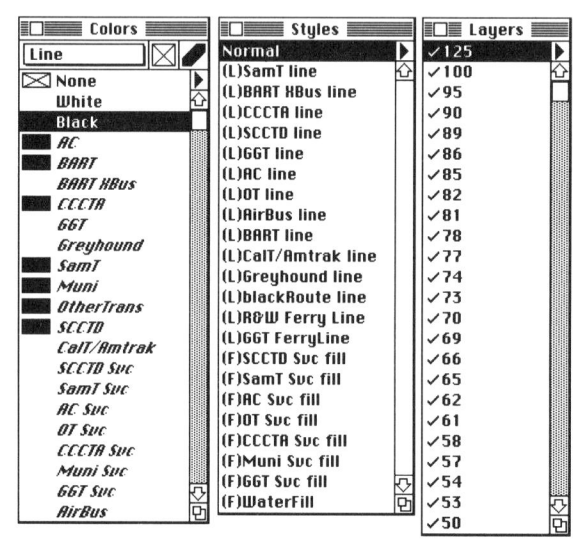

Figure 11.1 The Colors, Styles, and Layers palettes for the MTC transit map

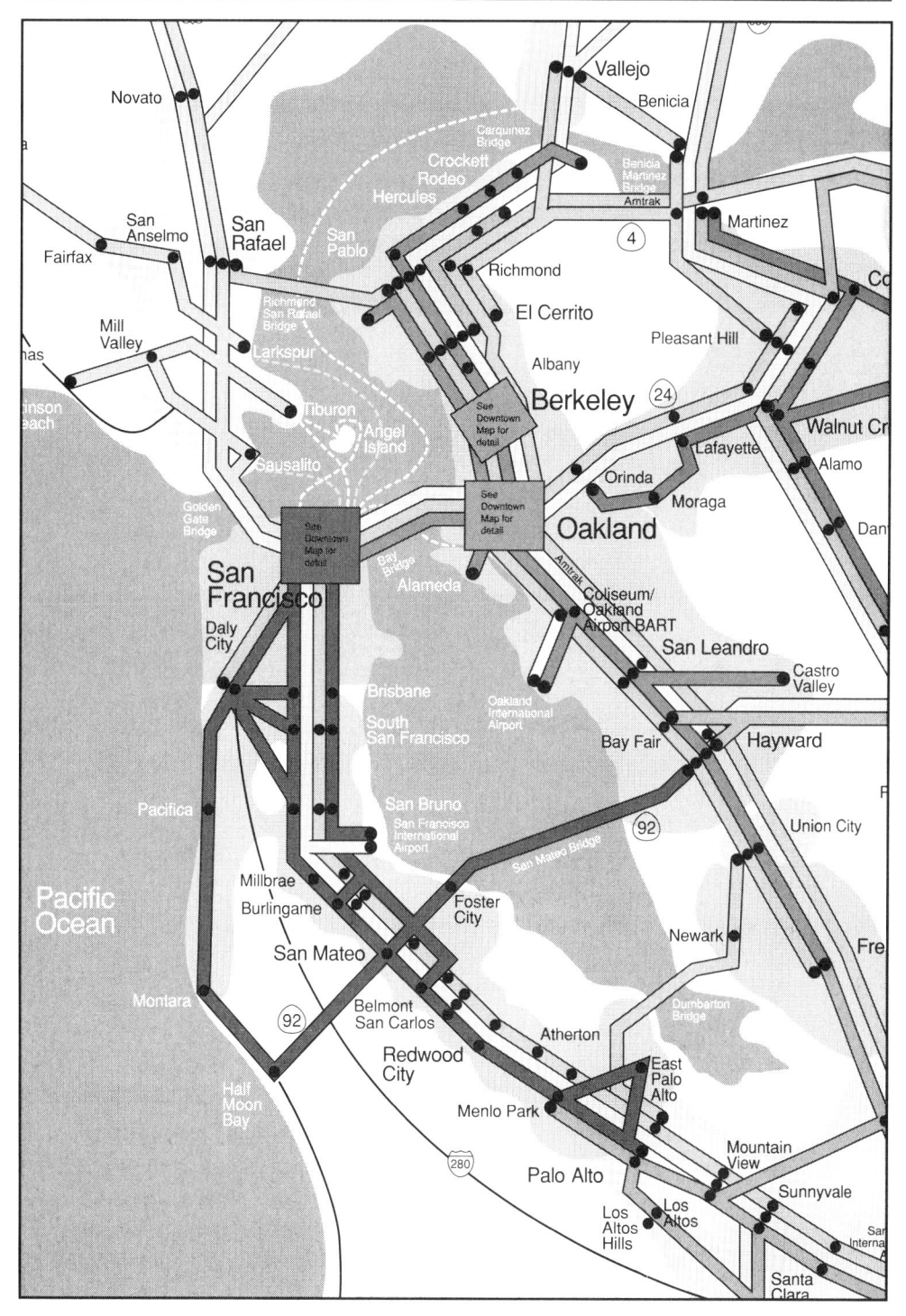

Figure 11.2 San Francisco Bay Area Map (detail)
Reprinted by permission from MTC (Metropolitan Transportation Commission)

The second production trick is to use the Styles palette, again naming styles according to the transit lines to which they apply. (See Chapters 7 and 13 for discussions of how and why to use styles.)

The third production trick lies in the use of layers. The full map can take a long time to display or redraw the screen as edits are made. By putting different categories of the artwork on different layers, the artists can selectively make visible only those layers they are working on, plus the reference layer of highway lines.

Layer contents	Layer number(s)
Type, highway signs, & highway lines	125
Transit stops (Black dots at nodes)	100
Boxes indicating downtown map areas	95
Transit lines (For each operator, colored line is in layer above a thicker black line):	
SamTrans	89-90
BART Express Bus	85-86
CCCTA	81-82
Santa Clara County Transit	77-78
Golden Gate Transit	73-74
AC Transit	69-70
Local bus service	65-66
Oakland Air-BART	61-62
BART line	57-58
CalTrain/Amtrak line	53-54
Greyhound	49-50
Transit service areas	40
Ferry lines:	
Red & White Fleet ferry	26
Golden Gate Transit	25
Water	20

Credits

Reprinted by permission from Metropolitan Transportation Commission (MTC), Oakland, California. Special thanks to Marilyn Reynolds, Manager of Technical Services, Barbara Wilkie, Supervisor of Graphics and production manager on the transit guides, and Peter Beeler, FreeHand artist, for their time and support.

Seattle Street Map

Description

This color-coded Downtown Circulation Map of public transport in Seattle, Washington, is printed as an 8-by-12.75-inch section (see color plate) on a larger folding map that includes the complete transit system.

Details

The basic roads and coastline in the map were originally traced from a scanned aerial map of the area, imported as a TIFF file and later deleted from the artwork. Roads are simply wide white lines. Transit lines are color-coded according to the legend in the lower left corner.

Credits

Reprinted with permission from METRO, Municipality of Seattle, Washington. Special thanks to Carol Mockridge, Leah Clark, and Rheta Deal for their time and support.

Chapter 11. Cartography 303

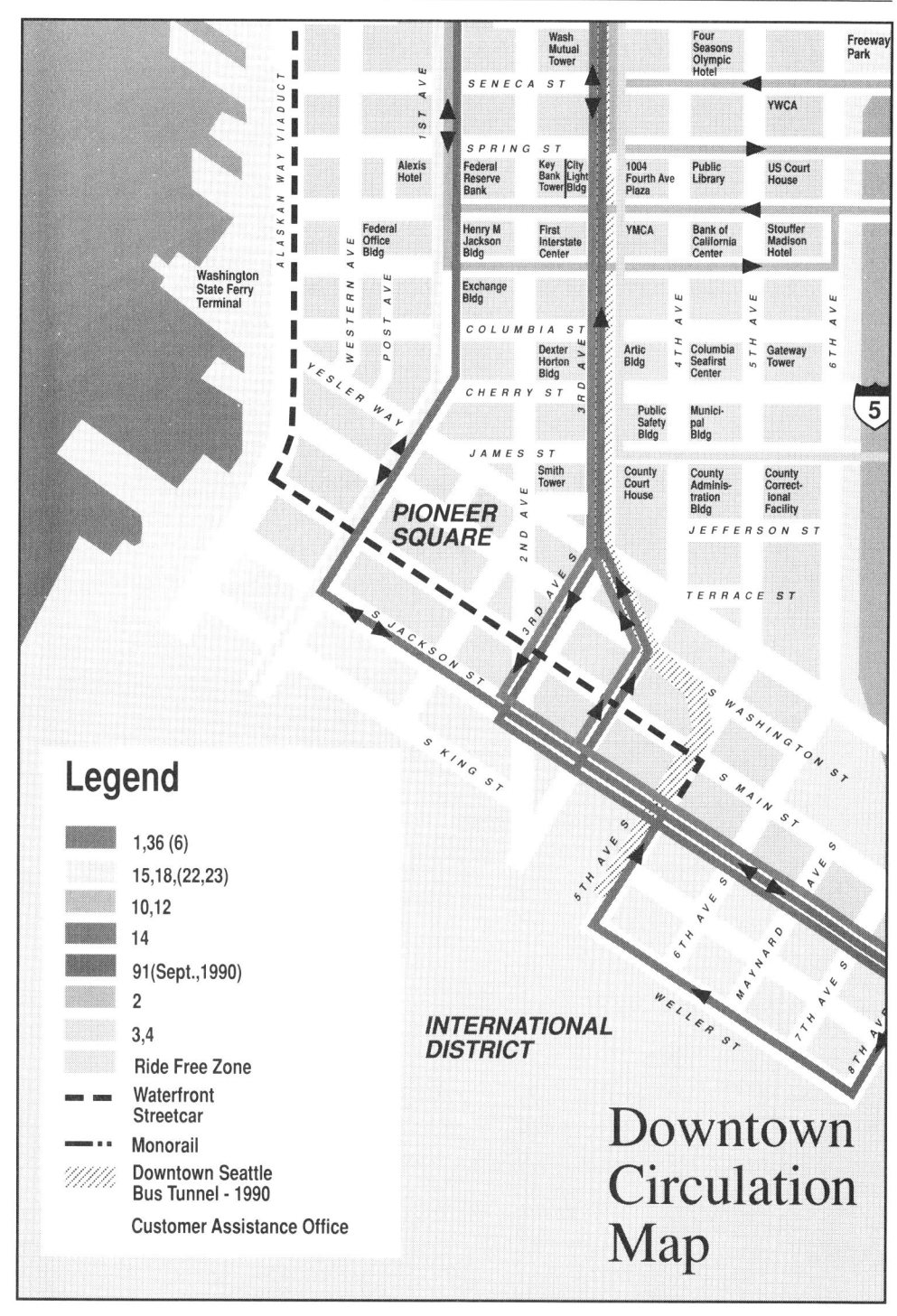

Figure 11.3 Seattle Downtown Circulation Map (detail). Reprinted by permission from METRO (Municipality of Metropolitan Seattle).

San Francisco Bay Area Road Map

Description

This road map of the San Francisco Bay Area (see Figure 11.4 and color plate) appears as a 5.25-by-7.5-inch portion of a 25-by-38-inch poster titled "Corridor 680 South," published by the *San Francisco Business Times*. The full poster won an award in computer innovation from the American Congress on Surveying and Mapping annual design competition.

Details

Eureka Cartography used the same three tricks as in the previous case study to simplify the production and editing of this complex graphic. They named some of the custom colors according to the category with which the color is identified. They used the Styles palette extensively, again naming styles according to the categories of objects to which they apply. They put different categories of the artwork on different layers.

The separate maps that composed the full folded piece were designed so that each map was not larger than 12 inches. This means they could be printed on 12-inch wide rolls of film from a Linotronic imagesetter and stripped together into full poster size.

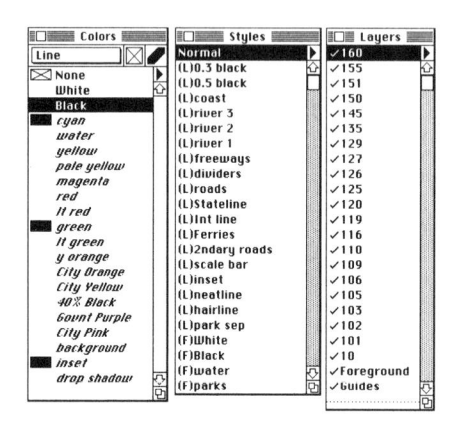

Figure 11.5 The Colors, Styles, and Layers palettes for the S.F. Bay Area Road Map

Credits

Reprinted by permission from Eureka Cartography, Berkeley, California. Special thanks to Neal Dinoff for his time and cooperation.

Chapter 11. Cartography   305

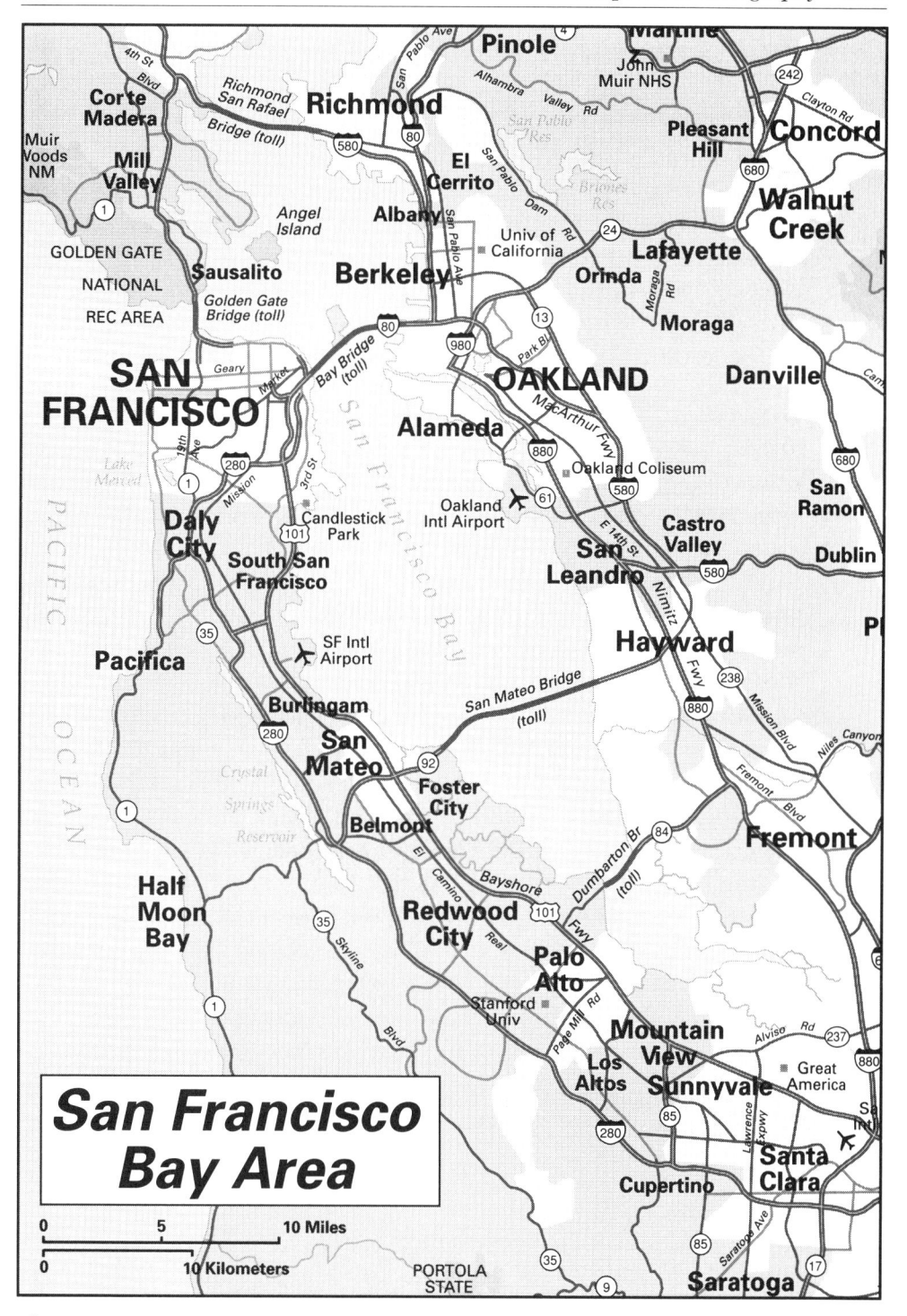

Figure 11.5 San Francisco Bay Area Road Map reprinted by permission from Eureka Cartography

Oakland Downtown Business Development Map

Description

The graphic shown in Figure 11.6 (and in the color plate) is a small fragment from a 25-by-38-inch poster titled Oakland Downtown Business Development Map created by Eureka Cartography for the *San Francisco Business Times* in collaboration with Grubb and Ellis Company.

Details

The artists collected public domain street maps and made pencil tracings of the areas they wished to cover. The traced lines were reduced, scanned, and imported to the Background layer in FreeHand, then traced using FreeHand's freeform drawing tools. The artwork was created as a full-size 25-by-38-inch document.

The initial drawings of the streets and geographical features were printed in tiled pieces and passed on to the real estate firm where detailed notes were added about current land use, current construction and plans, and proposed construction or redevelopment.

In adding details to the artwork, the artists collected aerial photographs, developer's sketches, and prepared their own field drawings. These were used to make pencil drawings of the various buildings which were scanned and placed onto the background layers. They then used the freeform drawing tools to trace three-dimensional representations of the existing buildings.

Because the final separations were printed on a Linotronic 300 with a maximum 12-inch wide roll of film, the streets were intentionally designed to be white so the film could be cut along street lines and pasted together into the final large negative for reproduction.

Because of the extensive collaboration involved, the technical considerations involved in producing artwork for a large poster, and the complexity of the artwork, the full poster took two months to create.

Credits

Map created by Eureka Cartography (Berkeley, California) for the *San Francisco Business Times*. Reprinted by permission from Eureka Cartography and the *San Francisco Business Times*. Special thanks to Neal Dinoff for his time and cooperation.

Chapter 11. Cartography   307

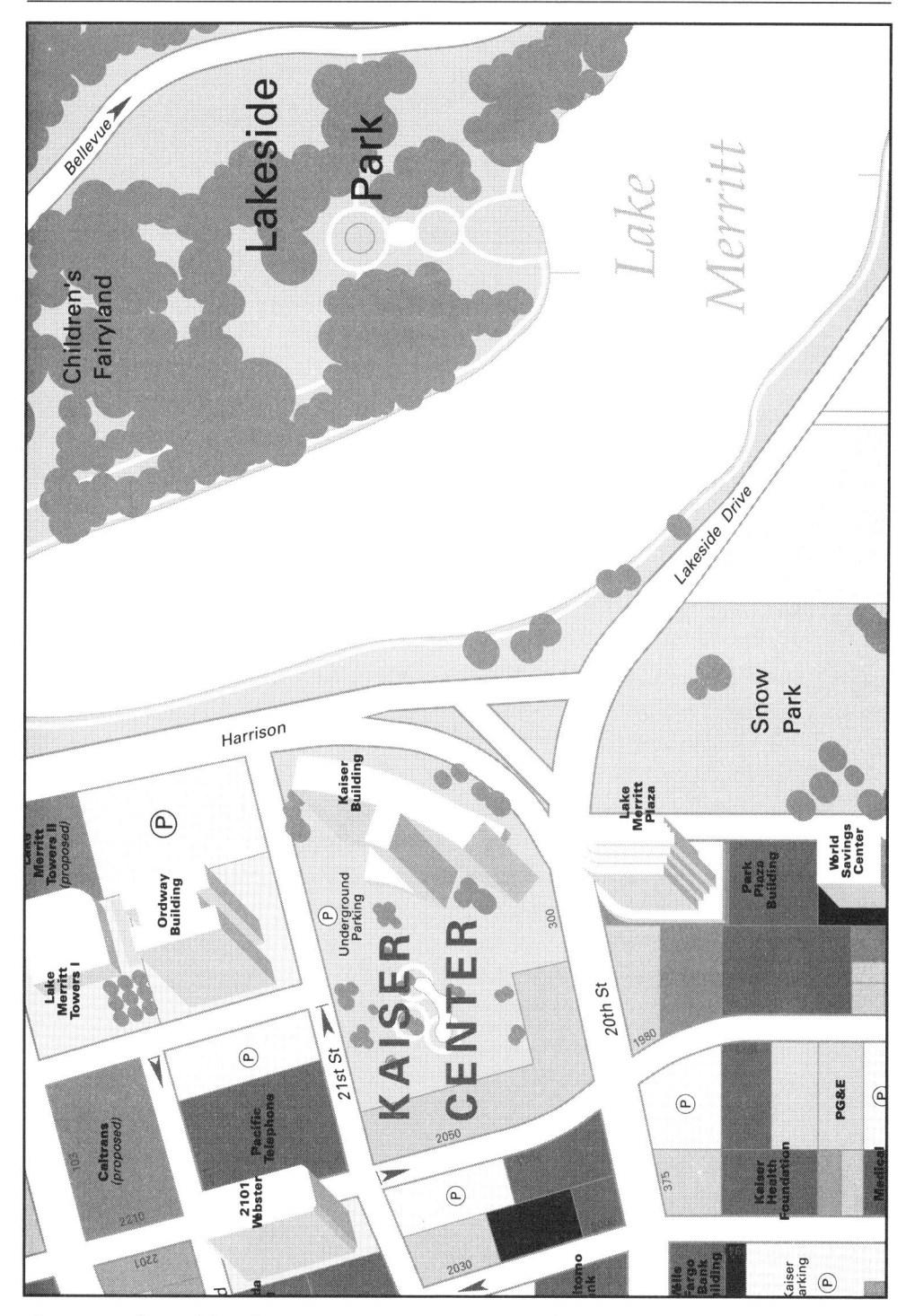

**Figure 11.6   Oakland Downtown Business Development Map (detail)
Reprinted by permission from Eureka Cartography**

■ Part IV ■

Reference

The last three chapters of this book compose a reference section that describes each tool, palette, and command in detail:

CHAPTER	DESCRIPTION
12. The Information Bar and the Toolbox	Describes each tool in the order they appear in the toolbox.
13. The Colors, Layers, and Styles Palettes	The three palettes are described in detail.
14. Menu Commands	Describes each command in the order they appear on the menus.

12

The Information Bar and the Toolbox

The opening screen in FreeHand displays an information bar below the menu titles, plus two movable windows—the Toolbox and the Colors palette—if you are working with the initial defaults that are built into FreeHand. You can also display a Layers palette and a Styles palette. This chapter describes the information bar and the Toolbox in detail. (The next chapter covers the Colors, Layers, and Styles palettes.)

312   Using Aldus FreeHand 3.0

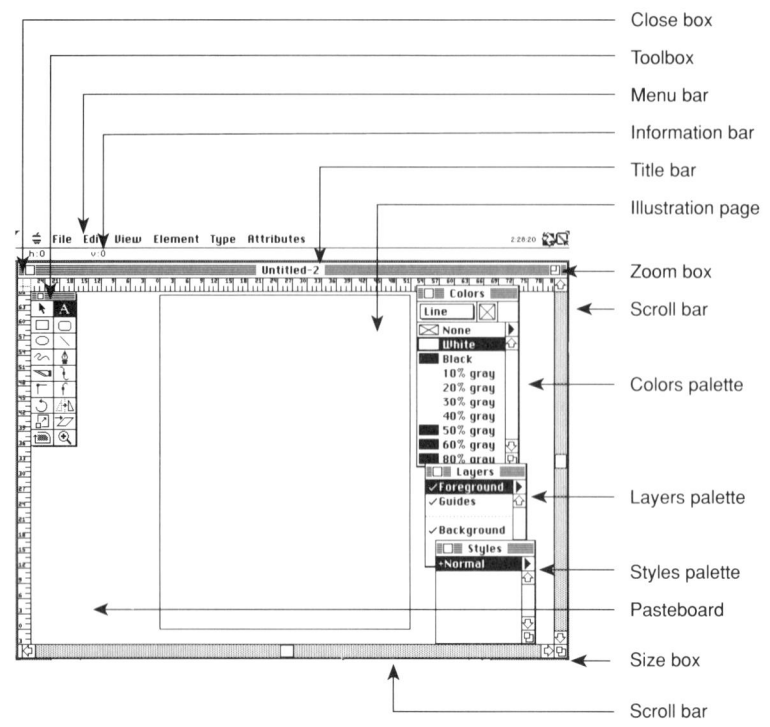

Figure 12.1 Screen displaying a new document window plus the information bar and all working palettes

The information bar displays numerical data about the current position of the cursor or the current size and position of objects as you draw or scale them. The Toolbox offers immediate access to 18 tools that affect how the mouse pointer works.

The information bar can be displayed by choosing Info bar from the Windows command submenu in the View menu.

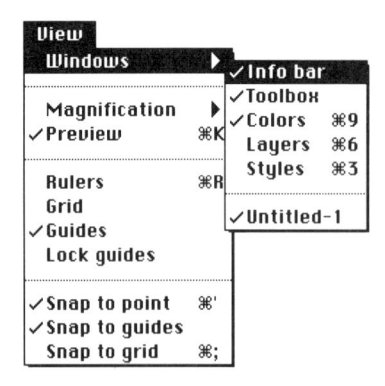

Figure 12.2 The submenu of the Windows command in the View menu

You can close the Toolbox by clicking its close box in the upper left corner of the palette. You can move the Toolbox by dragging its title bar. You can also drag the information bar anywhere on the screen.

When you first start FreeHand or open a FreeHand document, the information bar and palettes are displayed as they were when you last used FreeHand *if* you have chosen the Save palette positions option in the Preferences dialog box (as described in the section on the Preferences command in Chapter 14). If you have chosen *not* to save palette positions, FreeHand displays only the information bar, the Toolbox, and the Colors palette (i.e., the original palette positions set up by Aldus).

The Information Bar

The information bar, displayed just below the menu bar when Info bar is checked in the Windows command submenu in the View menu, shows information about the current position of the pointer or the currently active item on a page. This information changes dynamically as you move, scale, or otherwise change an active item.

If nothing is selected, the information bar displays the current position of the mouse pointer, measured from the zero point on the ruler (normally the lower left corner of the artwork page—see the section on the Rulers command in Chapter 14 for information about the zero point).

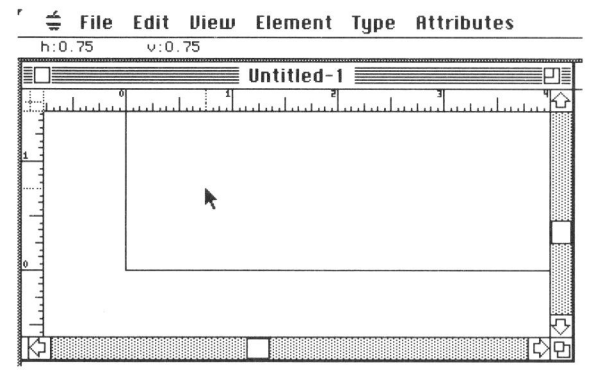

Figure 12.3 Information bar displays position of mouse pointer when nothing is selected

The data shown in the information bar changes when something is selected or when you are drawing or changing an object. When you are drawing or scaling a rectangle or ellipse, the information bar displays the current cursor position plus the height and width of the object. When you

314   Using Aldus FreeHand 3.0

are drawing or scaling a straight line, the information bar displays the current cursor position plus the height, width, length, and angle of the line. When you move any object, the information bar displays the current cursor position plus the horizontal distance, vertical distance, diagonal distance, and angle of the movement. These variations are shown in Figures 12.4 through 12.6.

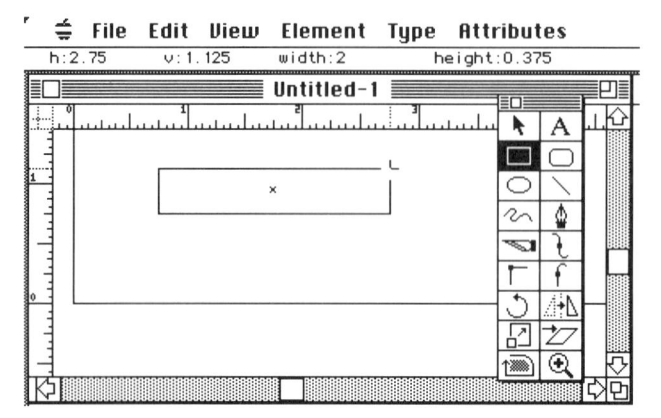

Figure 12.4 Information bar displays position of mouse pointer and height and width of a rectangle or oval as you are drawing or scaling

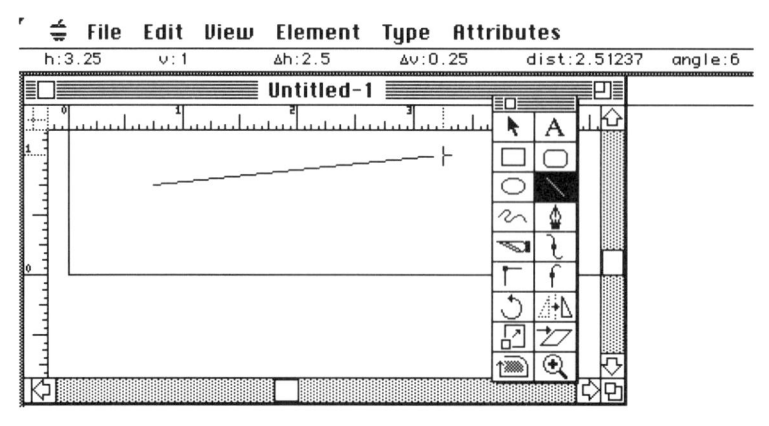

Figure 12.5 Information bar displays position of mouse pointer and height, width, length, and angle of the line as you are drawing or scaling

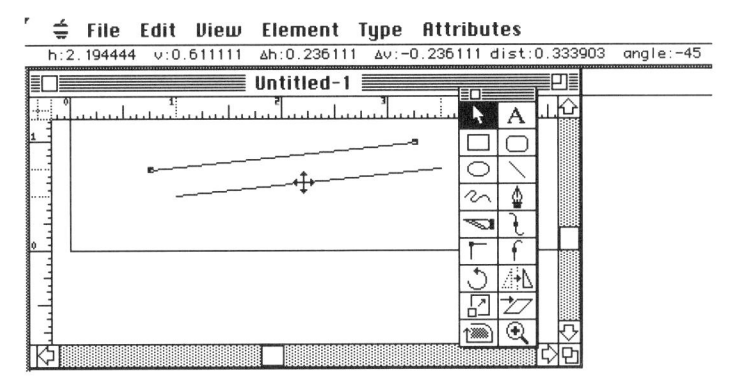

Figure 12.6 Information bar displays position of mouse pointer and horizontal distance, vertical distance, diagonal distance, and angle of the movement

Symbols displayed in the information bar are listed in the following table.

Abbreviation	Information
	Locked element selected
h: or v:	The horizontal or vertical location of the mouse pointer
Δh: or Δv:	The change in horizontal or vertical location of the moved element
angle:	With the Pointer tool, the angle of movement for the selected element
	With the Rotating tool, the angle of rotation or reflection of the selected element
width:	The width of the selected basic shape
height:	The height of the selected basic shape
dist:	The distance from the fixed point to the mouse pointer
ch:	The horizontal location of the fixed point
cv:	The vertical location of the fixed point
sh:	The percent of horizontal scaling or skewing of the selected element
sv:	The percent of vertical scaling or skewing of the selected element

Δletter space:	The change in spacing between characters in a text block
Δword space:	The change in spacing between words in a text block
Δleading:	The change in spacing between lines of text
kerning:	The sum of the em-space fractions added or deleted between characters in the Text dialog box

Tool and task	Information displayed
Pointer tool when resizing	Δletter space:, Δleading:
With Option Key	sh:, sv:, Δword space:, Δleading:
Pointer tool when moving an element	h:, v:, Δh:, Δv:, dist:, angle:
Text tool	h:, v:
Text I-beam in Text dialog box	kerning: (in ems)
Line tool	h:, v:, Δh:, Δv:, dist:, angle:
Rectangle, Rounded-rectangle, and Ellipse tools	h:, v:, width:, height:
Freehand tool	h:, v:
Corner, Curve, Connector, and Pen tools	h:, v:, Δh:, Δv:, dist:, angle:
Rotating and Reflecting tools	ch:, cv:, angle:
Scaling and Skewing tools	ch:, cv:, sh:, sv:
Knife tool	h:, v:

Introduction to the Toolbox

FreeHand's Toolbox is much like a conventional artist's assortment of drawing tools. But pens, rulers, protractors, and knives are replaced by icons that you select to perform the artist's work. The Toolbox includes a Pointer tool, a Text tool, four basic shape tools, four freeform drawing tools, four transformation tools, a Tracing tool, a Knife tool, and a Magnifying tool.

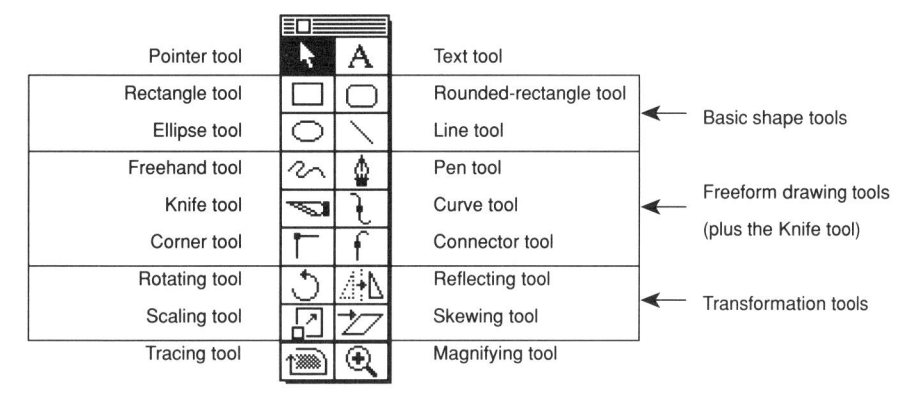

Pointer tool		Text tool	
Rectangle tool		Rounded-rectangle tool	← Basic shape tools
Ellipse tool		Line tool	
Freehand tool		Pen tool	
Knife tool		Curve tool	← Freeform drawing tools (plus the Knife tool)
Corner tool		Connector tool	
Rotating tool		Reflecting tool	
Scaling tool		Skewing tool	← Transformation tools
Tracing tool		Magnifying tool	

Figure 12.7 The Toolbox

The Toolbox is a separate palette on the screen. You can drag the palette by its title bar to any position on the screen. You can also close it by clicking the close box or by choosing Toolbox from the Windows command submenu in the View menu. To re-display the Toolbox after you have closed it, choose Toolbox from the Windows command submenu when it is not checked.

Selecting a Tool

To select any tool in the Toolbox, position the mouse pointer on the tool and click. You can also select nine of the tools using a keyboard shortcut—you simply type a number (from 0 through 9) to change tools. The number associated with each tool is shown in Figure 12.8. You cannot select a tool when a dialog box is displayed.

318 Using Aldus FreeHand 3.0

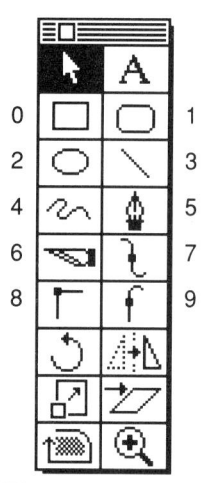

Figure 12.8 Keyboard shortcuts for selecting tools

A tool remains active until you deselect it by selecting another tool, but two tools can be temporarily activated from the keyboard:

- Temporarily activate the Pointer tool (▶) by holding down the Command key.
- Temporarily activate the Magnifying tool (⊕) by holding down the Command key and the Space bar; activate the Reducing tool (⊖) by holding down the Option key as well.
- Holding down the Space bar temporarily changes the current tool to the Grabber hand (✋) for moving the page view in the window. (The Grabber hand is not shown in the Toolbox—it can only be activated from the keyboard.)

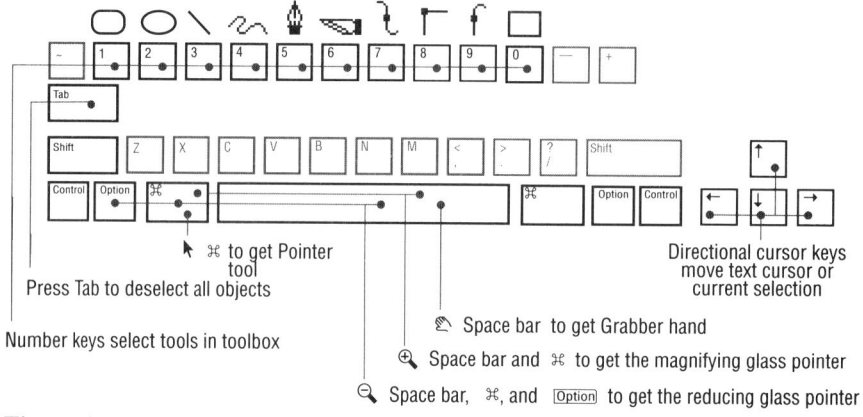

Figure 12.9 Keyboard shortcuts to temporarily activate tools

When using the keyboard to change tools, hold down the key(s) *before* pressing the mouse button. These keystrokes are considered shortcuts because many times you will be performing an action with one tool (for example, the Pen tool) and you will need to use another tool (for example, the Pointer tool) to modify the action. In such cases, you do not have to divert your attention away from the drawing area of your screen to access the Toolbox, select a new tool, and complete your activity. You simply hold down the appropriate key(s).

The currently active tool affects the appearance of the mouse pointer on the screen, as described for each tool in the following sections.

Grabber Hand Tool

The Grabber hand (🖑) is a tool that does not appear in the Toolbox. You choose the Grabber hand by holding down the Space bar. When you release the Space bar, the previously selected tool will once again be active. When the Grabber hand is active, the cursor changes to a hand.

You use the Grabber hand as an alternative to the scroll bars. To scroll with the Grabber hand, position the hand on the active window, hold down the mouse button, and drag in the direction you wish to scroll. The Grabber hand can move the image of your artwork in the active window vertically, horizontally, and diagonally. It moves the whole page, not the selected objects on the page.

Think of the Grabber hand as your own hand and the image in the active window as a piece of paper sitting on your desk. Just as you place your hand on top of the paper and move it across your desk, so does the Grabber hand move the image across the screen. By using the Grabber hand, you can scroll diagonally with one movement instead of needing to click two scroll bars to accomplish the same movement.

Pointer Tool

The Pointer tool (▶) is the most commonly used tool, since you use it to select, move, and scale objects. You can select the Pointer tool from the Toolbox to activate it, or you can hold down the Command key to temporarily activate the Pointer tool at any time—when you release the Command key, the previously selected tool becomes active. When the Pointer tool is selected, the pointer becomes an arrow (▶).

TIP
Since the Pointer tool is used so frequently, always use the Command key to access the Pointer tool temporarily while using another tool. For example, draw a curve with the Pen tool, then hold down the Command key and use the Pointer tool to adjust it.

There are three basic methods for selecting objects on the screen: click once to select one object; drag a selection marquee to select a group of objects; or Shift-click to select a group of objects. These methods are described in the next sections.

Selecting One Object

Objects that you create and manipulate in FreeHand include text objects, anchor points, line segments, curve handles, paths, and grouped objects. When you first create an object, it is automatically selected. The two basic methods for selecting objects after they are drawn are to click on the object, or to drag a selection marquee around the object.

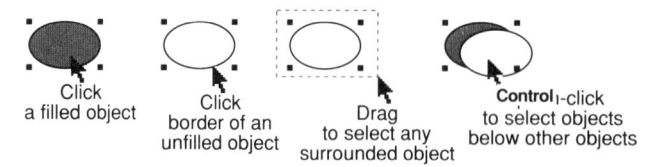

Click a filled object   Click border of an unfilled object   Drag to select any surrounded object   Control₁-click to select objects below other objects

Figure 12.10 Methods of selecting objects

Both of these methods are standard in many graphics applications and on the Macintosh desktop. Figure 12.10 shows both methods of selecting objects. If two or more objects overlap, clicking will select the topmost one, and dragging the selection marquee around the objects selects both (see "Selecting Multiple Objects" later in this chapter). (The selection marquee is a rectangle of dashed lines that appears when you drag the mouse on-screen without first selecting any objects.)

The most common method of selecting one object is to click it once with the arrow pointer. To select a shape that has no fill, you must click on the border of the object. To select an object that falls below other objects in stacking order on the current layer, hold down the Control key and keep clicking until the desired object is selected. (The Control key is not available on the older keyboards that came with the Macintosh 512K and the Macintosh Plus.)

In Preview mode, you can select an object that is a closed shape with a fill pattern by clicking anywhere on the object—either the border or the fill area. To select a line or an open path or a closed shape that has no fill pattern, you must click on the line or border to select the object. When Preview mode is off, no fill patterns are shown so you must click on lines to select objects. (Note too that you cannot select a rectangle or ellipse by its center mark; you must click on the border to select these objects.)

When you click on a grouped object, it is framed by four handles. When you click on an ungrouped line or a path, the path displays anchor points. You can subselect an item within a group by first selecting the group, then Option-clicking an object within the group.

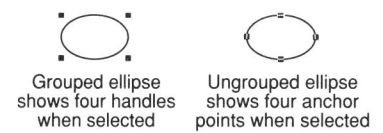

Grouped ellipse shows four handles when selected   Ungrouped ellipse shows four anchor points when selected

Figure 12.11 Selected grouped objects show four handles; ungrouped objects show anchor points

When you click text using the Pointer tool, the text becomes framed in a box with eight sizing handles, and any commands you choose will apply to all of the selected text. Methods of selecting a *range* of text (i.e., not the whole text block) are described in the "Text Tool" section later in this chapter.

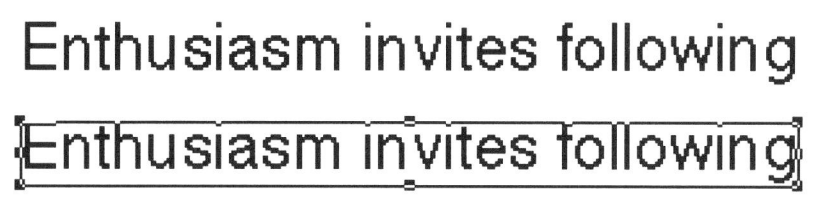

Enthusiasm invites following

Enthusiasm invites following

Figure 12.12 Selected text is framed in a box on the screen

Selecting One Object that is Part of a Group

When you use the Pointer tool to click on an element that has been made part of a group (via the Group command), you select the whole group. To select one element in the group, hold down the Option key when you click the arrow pointer on the element you wish to select. This works in selecting one object in a grouped set, or selecting one point in a path that has been grouped, but this does not work with rectangles or ellipses that have been created with the basic shape tools. You must ungroup those elements with the Ungroup command to select a point.

Selecting an Anchor Point

To select an anchor point on an ungrouped path, first select the path to display all of the anchor points, then click the arrow pointer on the anchor point you wish to select. A selected anchor point displays as a hollow square, and might also show curve handles. (Paths, anchor points, and curve handles are described in the "Pen Tool" section later in this chapter.)

To select an anchor point on an object that is part of a group, first select the group, then Option-click with the Pointer tool on one object to display its anchor points, then Option-click the anchor point you wish to select.

Ungrouped ellipse shows four anchor points when selected

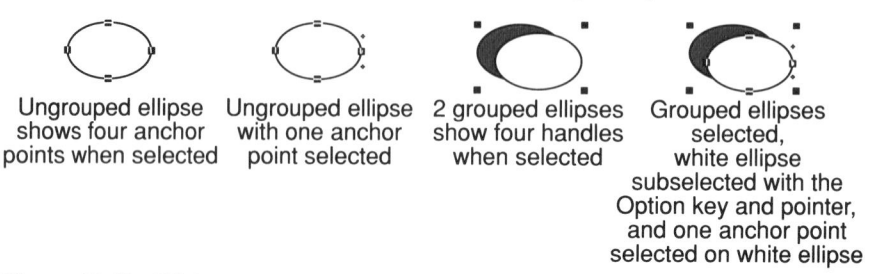

Ungrouped ellipse with one anchor point selected

2 grouped ellipses show four handles when selected

Grouped ellipses selected, white ellipse subselected with the Option key and pointer, and one anchor point selected on white ellipse

Figure 12.13 Click to select a group (framed in four handles). Option-click to select one element in the group

Selecting Multiple Objects

You can select more than one object at a time by dragging a selection marquee around all of the objects or by Shift-clicking objects. When dragging a selection marquee around objects, only those objects that are completely encompassed by the marquee will be selected.

Drag the pointer to select several objects at once

Shift-click to add to a selection

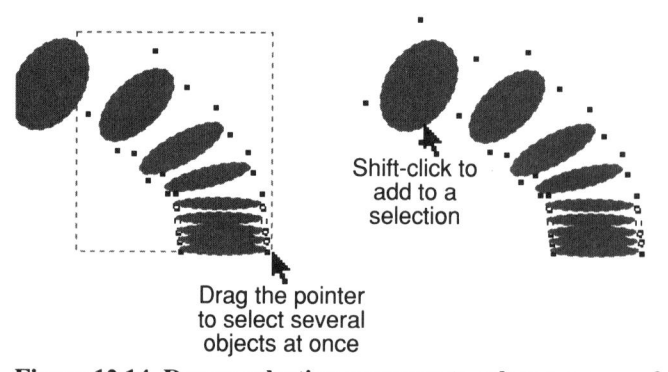

Figure 12.14 Drag a selection marquee to select a group of objects or Shift-click to add objects to a selection

To select...	Action
An unfilled path	Click the path's outline.
A filled path	Click any part of the object.
More than one object	Shift-click each object, or drag the pointer to create a selection marquee.
All elements	Choose Select all from the Edit menu (⌘A).
One object behind others	Control-click until the desired object is selected.
One object in a grouped set	Click to select the group, then Option-click the desired object.
One object below others in a grouped set	Click to select the group, then Control-Option-click until the desired object is selected.
Stacked, ungrouped objects	Shift-Control-click the area above each object until the desired object is selected.

To Deselect...	Action
One selected object	Press Tab; or click an empty area; or Shift-click the object; or click another object to select it (and simultaneously deselect other objects).
All selected objects	Press Tab; or click an empty area; or click another object to select it (and simultaneously deselect other objects).
One object of several selected objects	Shift-click the object. Use the additional key combinations listed above for deselecting objects that are buried under other objects.

Figure 12.15 Table of selection methods

To extend a selection to include a second object (after one object is selected) or to include additional objects that could not be encompassed by the selection marquee, Shift-click the desired objects, or hold down the Shift key and drag a selection marquee around the desired objects.

The same action applies to deselecting individual objects in a group selection: you can select any number of objects, then Shift-click to deselect one or more.

Selecting Objects on Different Layers

You can use any of the selection techniques described above to select objects on any *visible* layer if Multilayer is chosen from the Layers palette pop-up menu. You can select objects on the *active* layer only if Multilayer is turned off.

See the description of the Layers palette in Chapter 13 for information about displaying and activating different layers.

Deselecting All Objects

To deselect all objects, click with the Pointer tool on any blank area of the page or pasteboard. Pressing the Tab key also deselects all objects. The Undo command sometimes deselects the current selection.

TIP

It's a good practice to deselect objects as soon as you know you are finished working with the current selection. Otherwise, you might inadvertently send objects to another layer or apply a style when you had intended only to change layers or styles for the next action.

Moving Objects

To move an object or a group of selected objects, first position the arrow pointer on the object to select it—positioning the pointer on a line or the fill but not on an anchor point. Hold down the mouse button and wait for the pointer to change from a single-pointed arrow to a four-pointed moving arrow, and then continue holding down the mouse button as you drag. As you move any object, the information bar shows the current position and the distance and direction of the movement.

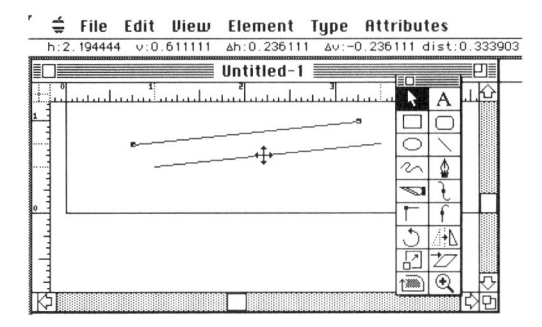

Figure 12.16 Information bar shows the horizontal, vertical, and diagonal distance plus the angle of the movement

Note that if the pointer does not change to a four-pointed arrow, either you have not positioned the pointer on the line or border or visible fill, or you have positioned the pointer over an anchor point or handle. If you select an anchor point or handle, you will be moving that point only, and not the whole object.

Figure 12.17 Four-pointed arrow appears when you are moving the entire object; one-pointed arrow remains when you are moving an anchor point only

In moving any object, you can constrain the movement to 45-degree angles only by holding down the Shift key as you drag. In other words, while holding down the Shift key, you will be able to move the object along only one of eight angles: 0°, 45°, 90°, 135°, 180°, 225°, 270°, or 315°.

You can also move selected objects by pressing the Arrow keys (available on most keyboards). The increment of movement per keystroke can be set in the Preferences dialog box. You can also move a selected object or group of objects using the Move command from the Edit menu. (The Preferences command and the Move command are described in detail in Chapter 14.)

Scaling Objects

To scale text or a grouped graphic, first select it and then hold down the mouse button as you drag one of the handles. In scaling a rectangle or ellipse, holding down the Shift key as you drag forces the object to become a perfect square or circle. In scaling any other grouped graphic object or text, holding down the Shift key preserves the object's or the text's proportions. As you scale a rectangle or ellipse, the information bar shows the new height and width; for any other object, the information bar shows the current position and the distance and direction of the movement.

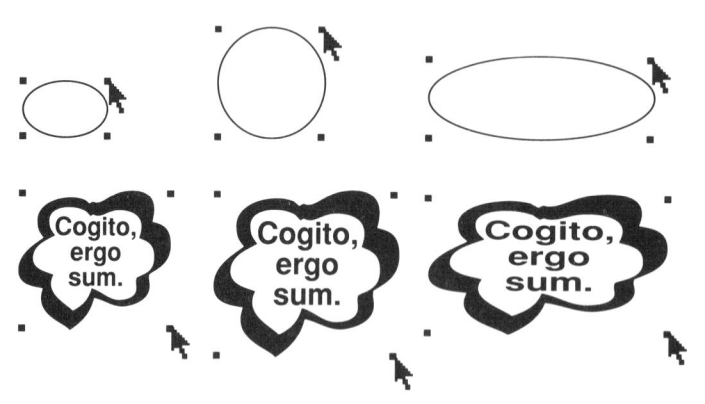

Figure 12.18 Scaling grouped objects with the Pointer tool: original object (left), scaled with the Shift key (center), and without the Shift key (right)

In scaling imported bitmapped images, you might introduce unwanted moiré patterns (a mottled effect) unless you use FreeHand's "magic stretch" feature. Hold down the Option key as you scale imported bitmaps, and the graphic jumps to sizes that are exact multiples of the resolution of your target printer. Hold down the Shift and Option keys to scale a bitmapped graphic proportionally.

Figure 12.19 Scaling bitmaps: scaled using Option key for "magic stretch" (left), and scaled without the Option key (right)

In using the magic stretch feature, FreeHand determines increments of the scale based on the printer resolution specified in the Document setup dialog box. Lower resolutions yield fewer incremental sizes than high resolutions.

CAUTION

When you use the magic stretch feature, be sure to choose your target printer first before you scale the object (see the discussion of the Document setup command in Chapter 14). If you later choose a target printer with a different resolution, you may need to re-scale the bitmaps to get the best results.

In scaling text, you can change the size, letter spacing, and line spacing as described in the "Text Tool" section later in this chapter. You can scale ungrouped graphics and selections that include more than one object by using the Scaling tool, discussed later in this chapter. You can also change the size of a rectangle or an ellipse by Option-double-clicking it, as described next.

Double-clicking Objects for Element Information

If you double-click certain objects, you get dialog boxes for editing the object. These are the same dialog boxes that are displayed when you select an object and choose the Element info command from the Element menu. These dialog boxes are mentioned elsewhere in this chapter, and are discussed in detail in the Element info command description in Chapter 14, but we summarize them here as a function of the Pointer tool.

Double-click a single text element to display the Text dialog box for editing the text or formatting different parts of the text (as described in the section on the Text tool later in this chapter).

Hold down the Option key and double-click a rectangle or ellipse to get the Rectangle or Ellipse dialog box that lets you view and numerically modify the object's position, size, corner radius, and flatness.

Hold down the Option key and double-click a collection of grouped objects to get the Group dialog box that lets you view and numerically modify the object's position and specify whether transformations (rotations, skews, scaling, and mirroring) will affect the group as a unit.

Hold down the Option key and double-click an ungrouped path to display the Path dialog box in which you can view the number of points in the path and the flatness. You can also check whether the path is open or closed, and change the Even/odd fill option. This dialog box is described in the section on the Element info command in Chapter 14.

Hold down the Option key and double-click an imported bitmap to get the Image dialog box that lets you manipulate the contrast and brightness as well as change the position or scale of the image.

Text Tool

To type new text on the page, click the Text tool (**A**) in the Toolbox, then position the I-beam pointer (I) on the page and click or drag with the mouse to display the Text dialog box. If you simply click the I-beam pointer, the width of the text block will be determined by line breaks you create when typing the text. If you drag the I-beam pointer, you can pre-define a text block width that will force automatic text wrap when lines are longer than the width of the block.

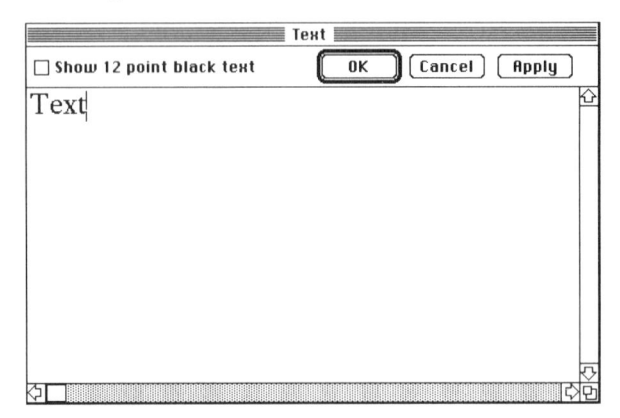

Figure 12.20 The Text dialog box is displayed when you select the Text tool and click on the page

When you type in this dialog box, you can force a new line by pressing the Return key. Otherwise, text wraps automatically to fit the width of the text block you created by dragging the I-beam pointer on the page, but you will not see the line breaks in the Text dialog box. You will see how the text wraps on the page after you close the Text dialog box.

TIP

If you do not want two words to be separated by a line break when automatic text wrap occurs, you can type a non-breaking space between them by holding down the Option key as you press the Space bar.

The text in the Text dialog box is normally displayed in the font size and style defined through the commands in the Type menu, if you choose sizes between 4 and 72 points. Very small and very large font sizes and some other type styles are not displayed as accurately in the dialog box as they are in the FreeHand document window or when the document is printed. Leading, special effects, alignment, and other formatting is shown on the artwork only—not in the Text dialog box. If you check the **Show 12 point black text** option, the text in the Text dialog box displays more quickly on the screen and shows more of the text in the window when you are creating text in a large font.

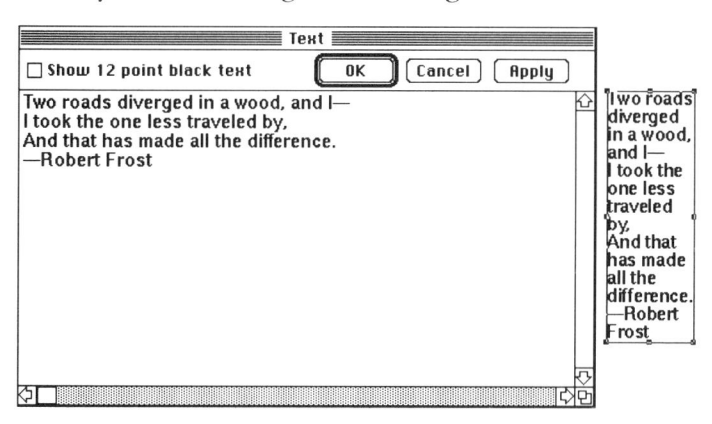

Figure 12.21 Text typed in the Text dialog box (left) shows lines breaks created with the Return key, but not the text wrap forced by the width of the text block on the page (right)

You can use any of the commands in the Type menu to change the appearance of the text. If you make the menu selections before you type text, the choices will apply to the next text you type. If there is already text in the dialog box, you must select the text first to apply formatting commands, as described in the section "Selecting and Editing Portions of Text" later in this chapter.

TIP
The Undo command is not available when you are working in the Text dialog box, but you can undo all the changes you have made once you close the dialog box.

You must click OK or press Enter to close the Text dialog box. (This is the only dialog box in which pressing Return does *not* close the box. Pressing Return adds a carriage return and moves the text cursor to a new line.) When you close the Text dialog box, the text appears on the page framed in a box with eight handles, indicating that the text is selected. This box disappears when the text is deselected.

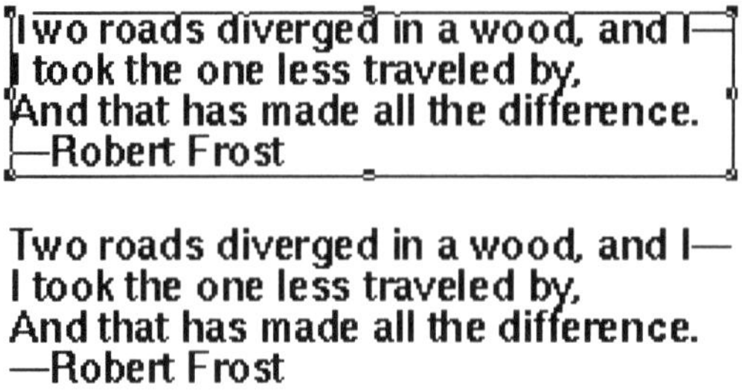

```
┌─────────────────────────────────────┐
│Two roads diverged in a wood, and I─┤
│I took the one less traveled by,    │
│And that has made all the difference.│
│─Robert Frost                       │
└─────────────────────────────────────┘
```

Two roads diverged in a wood, and I—
I took the one less traveled by,
And that has made all the difference.
—Robert Frost

Figure 12.22 Text displayed on the page when selected (top) and not selected (bottom)

You can specify text in decimal point sizes as small as one-tenth of a point, but only whole number sizes are displayed on the screen—you won't see the actual size until the text is printed.

Selecting and Formatting a Text Block

When you first close the Text dialog box, the text is selected on the page, i.e., it is framed in a box with eight handles. Otherwise, to select text on the page you must activate the Pointer tool—either by holding down the Command key or by clicking the Text tool in the Toolbox.

CAUTION
You cannot select the text on the artwork with the I-beam pointer (that is, when the Text tool is active). If you try to click the text in the artwork, a blank Text dialog box will again be displayed for you to type new text. If you open this dialog box by mistake, simply click Cancel to close the dialog box, then select the text with the Pointer tool.

When you click the Pointer tool once on the text to select it, you can use any of the Type menu commands to format the entire text block; you can use available commands in the Element and Attributes menus to change the stroke and fill of the text; and you can use the transformation tools to rotate, reflect, enlarge, or skew the text. You can also use the Convert to paths command to convert the text to graphic elements that you can then modify with the freeform tools.

You can also change the color of the text through the Colors palette. Normally in this palette, the Line of text is set to None. You cannot change this through the Colors palette unless you specify a visible stroke for the text using the Fill and stroke command from the Effect command submenu in the Type menu.

Dragging Text Block Handles to Change Size or Spacing

You can drag the handles of selected text to change the size of the text block and simultaneously change the size of the text or change the letter spacing or line spacing (to make it fit the new text block size):

- Drag a corner handle to change the size of the text block and the text wrap. Line breaks that were created by using the Return key in the Text dialog box do not change.
- Drag a top or bottom handle to change the leading (space between lines).
- Drag a side handle to change the letter spacing.
- Option-drag a side handle to change word spacing.
- Scale type proportionally by Shift-Option-dragging a corner handle.
- Stretch or compress the *characters* of text by Option-dragging a corner handle.

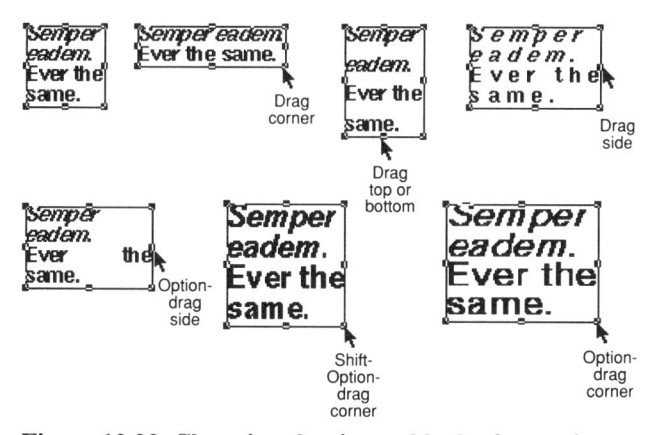

Figure 12.23 Changing the size and look of text with the Pointer tool

Selecting and Editing Portions of Text

Click with the Pointer tool twice on the text (or click once and then choose the Element info command from the Element menu) to display the Text dialog box. In this dialog box, you can edit the content of the text or use commands from the Type menu to format selected parts of the text without affecting the whole text block.

332   Using Aldus FreeHand 3.0

You select text in the Text dialog box the same way you select text on the desktop (such as file names and folder names) and in most Macintosh applications:

- Position the I-beam pointer within a line of text and click once to position the pointer for inserting text.
- Double-click a word to select the whole word, or drag the I-beam pointer over a range of characters to select them. You can also double-click to select a word and then drag to select adjacent words.
- Click once to position the pointer and then move the pointer to another location and Shift-click to select all characters between the two positions.
- Choose Select all from the Edit menu (⌘A) to select all of the text in the Text dialog box.

You see, but you do not observe.—*Sir Arthur Conan Doyle*
Click I-beam pointer
to position cursor

You see, but you do not observe.—*Sir Arthur Conan Doyle*
Double-click the I-beam pointer
on a word to select it

You see, but you do not observe.—*Sir Arthur Conan Doyle*
Drag the I-beam pointer to select a range,
or click to position the cursor at the beginning of the range
then Shift-click at the end of the range

You see, but you do not observe.—*Sir Arthur Conan Doyle*
Choose Select all (Command-A) to select all of the text in the Text dialog box

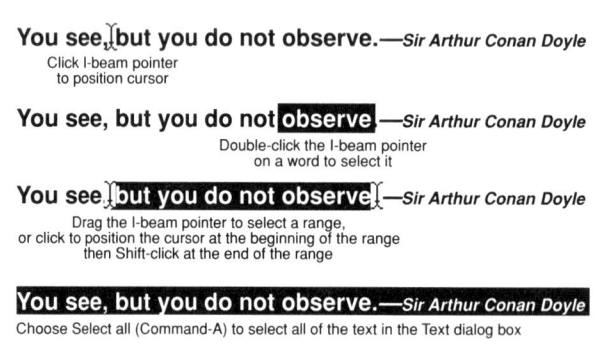

Figure 12.24 Methods of selecting text

When you type you replace the selected characters. You can also use the Colors palette or the Colors command from the Attributes menu to color selected portions of the text. Other Attributes menu commands, most Element menu commands, and the transformation tools cannot be applied from the Text dialog box.

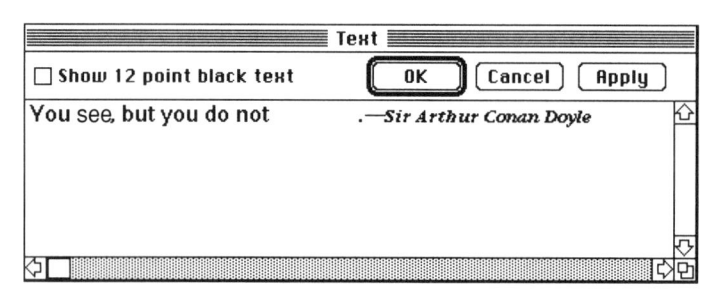

Figure 12.25 Text formatted in the Text dialog box

You can kern (i.e. reduce or increase) the space between individual letters in the Text dialog box. Click the I-beam pointer between two letters and then press the key combinations listed below to increase or decrease the space between the letters in percentages of an em space. (An em space is approximately the width of the capital letter M in the current font and size.) Kerning information is displayed in the information bar.

- Press ⌘Delete (Backspace) or ⌘(←) to decrease space in .01-em increments.
- Press ⌘Shift-Delete (Backspace) or ⌘(→) to increase space in .01-em increments.
- Press ⌘Shift-(←) to decrease space in .1-em increments.
- Press ⌘Shift-(→) to increase space in .1-em increments.

NEW WAVE
NEW WAVE

Figure 12.26. Example of text before (above) and after (below) kerning to decrease space between the pairs E-W, W-A, and A-V. The space between E and W in the word NEW has been kerned so tightly that the characters actually touch

The results of the kerning cannot be seen in the Text dialog box, but you can see the effects on the page by clicking the Apply button without closing the dialog box. (You might need to move the dialog box to see the text on the page.)

Basic Shape Tools

The Rectangle tool (□), the Rounded-rectangle tool (◻), the Ellipse tool (○), and the Line tool (\ ) are used to create four basic shapes: boxes with square corners, boxes with rounded corners, circles and ovals, and straight lines, respectively. All of these tools work in similar ways, so we will describe their common characteristics before describing any unique features.

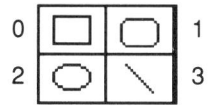

Figure 12.27 The four basic shape tools in the Toolbox and their keyboard shortcuts

When any of these tools is selected, the pointer becomes a crossbar (⌘). To draw an object, first select the tool and then position the crossbar pointer on the page or pasteboard, hold down the mouse button, and drag in any direction to create a line, or diagonally to create a rectangle or ellipse. You can see the line or shape change as you drag. In creating an ellipse, you define the opposite corners of the imaginary rectangle that contains the ellipse. Click the mouse button to define one corner of the bounding rectangle, then drag and release the mouse button at the diagonally opposite corner.

Holding down the Shift key as you drag constrains rectangles to perfect squares, ellipses to perfect circles, and lines to 45-degree angles (0°, 45°, 90°, 135°, 180°, 225°, 270°, or 315°).

Release the mouse button when you have the shape you want. The object remains selected, as indicated by visible handles.

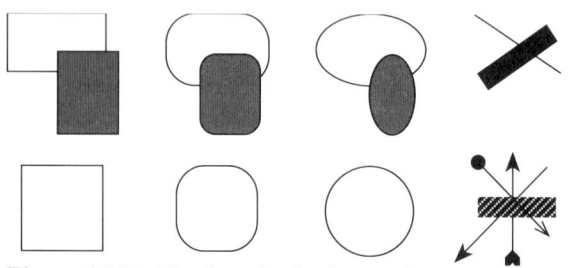

Figure 12.28 The four basic shapes drawn without holding down the Shift key (above) and with the Shift key (below)

When you release the mouse button after drawing a shape or line, the pointer remains a crossbar, indicating that the next mouse action will create another object of the same type. To select and then move or modify an object that is already drawn, you must use the Pointer tool as described earlier in this chapter.

Rectangle, Rounded-rectangle, and Ellipse Tools

Besides the basic operations described above, several additional features apply to these three objects that do not apply to lines.

To construct rectangles and ellipses from center to edge (rather than corner to corner), hold down the Option key while you drag.

You can adjust the position or size of a rectangle or ellipse in the Rectangle dialog box or the Ellipse dialog box. You display this dialog box by selecting the object and choosing Element info from the Element menu, or by Option-double-clicking the object with the Pointer tool.

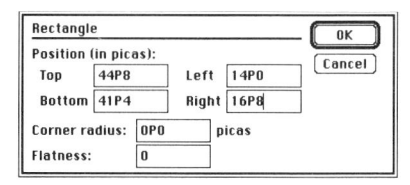

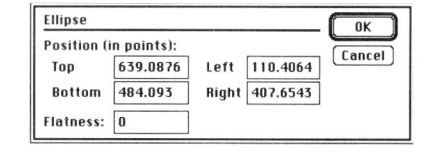

Figure 12.29 Rectangle and Ellipse dialog boxes

You can also adjust the corner radius of any rectangle—whether it was first drawn with the Rectangle tool or with the Rounded-rectangle tool—through the Rectangle dialog box. The corner radius cannot exceed half the length of the short sides of the rectangle. If you enter a larger value, FreeHand will draw the largest ellipse or circle that can fit into the rectangle. The value you enter for the corner radius will apply to all objects subsequently drawn with the Rounded-rectangle tool if you have selected "Changing elements changes defaults" in the Preferences dialog box (see description of the Preferences command in Chapter 14).

Figure 12.30 Rectangles drawn with different degrees of roundness

You can also adjust the flatness through these dialog boxes. (See the description of the Preferences command in Chapter 14 for a definition of flatness.)

Objects drawn with the Rectangle tools or the Ellipse tool are automatically closed and grouped when you draw them. This means that you can select the whole object and move it or scale it with the Pointer tool or modify it using the Scaling, Rotating, Reflecting, and Skewing tools but you cannot select individual points on the object.

To select individual points, you must first select the object(s) and choose the Ungroup command from the Element menu. You can then select and move individual points on the object. In keyline view (i.e., when Preview mode is off), the grouped objects show a small X in the center—a helpful feature for aligning objects—but when the paths are ungrouped, the center mark disappears.

336   Using Aldus FreeHand 3.0

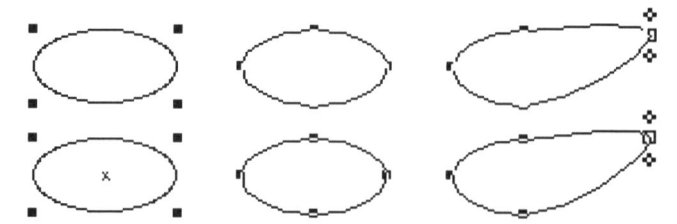

Figure 12.31 Grouped (left) and ungrouped (center) ellipses in Preview (top) and keyline view (bottom). You must ungroup rectangles and ellipses to move individual points (right)

Line Tool

Lines drawn with the Line tool are ungrouped, open paths with two points. You can modify them using the Pointer tool, as described earlier, or connect them to other open, ungrouped paths and edit them with the Pen tool (as described later in this chapter).

Freeform Drawing Tools

The five freeform tools are the Freehand tool ( ), for drawing as you drag the mouse; the Pen tool ( ), for placing curve points and corner points; the Corner tool ( ), for placing corner points only; the Curve tool ( ), for placing curve points only; and the Connector tool ( ) for placing connector points that join straight line segments to curves. They are called freeform tools because they let you draw any path or shape—creating *Bezier curves*, named after Pierre Bezier, the mathematician who defined them. The Knife tool ( ) is included with these tools in the Toolbox, and under this heading in the book, because you can use it either to edit a path you have already drawn or to break a path into segments while you are still drawing.

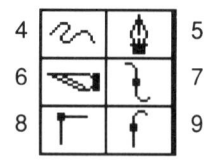

Figure 12.32 The five freeform tools plus the Knife tool and their keyboard shortcuts

While some artists will choose to use the Freehand tool for all curves, others will use the Pen tool most frequently, and still others will use keyboard shortcuts to switch between the freeform tools.

About Paths, or Bezier Curves

All of the drawing tools in FreeHand create *Bezier curves*—paths composed of dots (anchor points) connected by lines (segments). (The four basic shape tools described in the previous sections—Rectangle, Rounded-rectangle, Ellipse, and Line tools—also create Bezier curves that can be modified with the techniques described here and in this chapter's "Pen Tool" section if you first use the Ungroup command.)

Paths may be composed of both curved and straight line segments, and may be open (lines) or closed (shapes). An *open* path has two endpoints; a *closed* path or solid shape has no endpoints—all points are connected to each other. The anchor points along curves usually have *curve handles*. Each of these elements is shown in Figure 12.33 below, and you will learn how to create and modify them in the following tool descriptions.

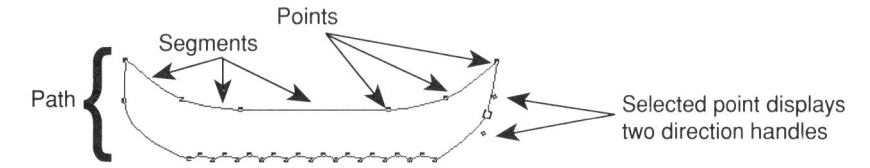

Figure 12.33 In PostScript, Bezier curves are paths composed of points that are joined by straight lines or curves defined by direction handles

To understand the difference between the Pen tool and the related Curve tool, Corner tool, and Connector tool, you need to understand the differences between the three types of points that can occur on a path:

- Curve points create a smooth curve between two other points. They display as hollow circles with two handles when selected.

- Corner points cause an abrupt change in the direction of the curve or line. They display as hollow squares with no visible handles when selected.

- Connector points make a smooth connection between a straight line segment and a curve. They display as hollow triangles with one visible handle when selected.

Selected curve point
displays as a hollow circle
with two handles

Selected corner point
displays as a hollow square
with no handles

Selected connector point
displays as a hollow triangle
with one handle

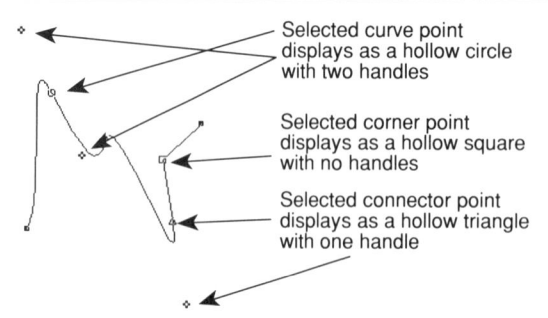

Figure 12.34 Examples of the three types of points

TIP

You can use the Pen tool to draw paths composed of curve and corner points. This is more efficient than switching from the Pen tool to the other freeform tools while you are drawing a path, though you might want to select one of the other tools to draw a path composed of all one type of point. The Curve, Corner, and Connector tools are most useful for adding points to a curve you have already drawn, as described in the sections for those tools.

Freehand Tool

Use the Freehand tool to draw a continuous line of any shape freehand—that is, without the restrictions on shapes imposed by the other drawing tools.

Choose the Freehand tool( ) by clicking its icon in the Toolbox. The mouse pointer changes to a + in the active window. Hold down the mouse button and begin drawing your object by dragging along the path you wish to draw. You can erase anchor points while you are drawing by holding down the Command key and backing up along the line you have just traced with the Freehand tool.

Option and Shift keys held down
while dragging between these
two points to create horizontal
straight line

Option key held while
dragging the Freehand tool
between these two points
to create straight line
then released

Option and Shift keys held down while
dragging between these
two points, to create 45-degree
straight line

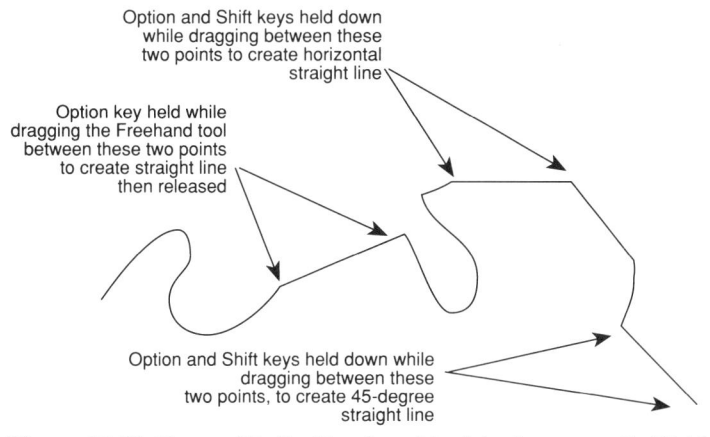

Figure 12.35 Drag with the Freehand tool to draw a path. Hold down the Option key for a straight line. Hold down the Option and Shift keys while dragging to constrain the straight line to a 45-degree angle

Hold down the Option key while dragging with the Freehand tool to draw a straight line. Hold down the Option and Shift keys while dragging to constrain the straight line to a 45-degree angle.

Double-clicking on the tool brings up the Freehand dialog box, where the usual defaults are **Tight** and **Connect the dots**. Deselect Tight if you want fewer anchor points created along the path. The Connect the dots option affects how FreeHand displays the path as you draw: with the option on, you see a continuous line as you draw; with the option off, you see a dotted line as you draw. In either case, the resulting path will still be a solid line (or whatever the current settings are in the Fill and line dialog box).

TIP

When using the Freehand tool to manually trace the outline of some other object, turning the Connect the dots off option will let you more easily "see through" the path you are tracing to the object(s) below.

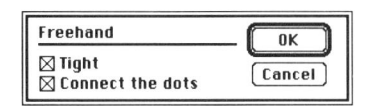

Figure 12.36 The Freehand dialog box

After you have drawn a path with the Freehand tool, you can:

- Adjust the line segments and anchor points as described under the Pen tool (described next),
- Scale or move the object with the Pointer tool (described earlier),
- Transform the object using the transformation tools (described later in this chapter), and
- Change the object using commands in the Element and Attributes menus (as described in Chapter 14).

Pen Tool

Choose the Pen tool ( ) by clicking the icon in the Toolbox. The pointer changes to a crossbar (+) in the active window. To use the Pen tool, position the crossbar pointer on the screen and either click or drag the mouse. As you drag the crossbar pointer around the screen while holding down the mouse, the curve shape between the anchor points changes. When you release the mouse button, the anchor point and curve handles are set and the pointer is ready to position the next anchor point along the path. You have the option of continuing the current path with another line segment by either clicking or dragging the third point, or you can end the path by pressing the Tab key to deselect all points.

The shape and direction of the line segment you create will depend on:

- Whether you clicked or dragged the first or previous point, and
- Where and how you position the next point.

The variety of curve shapes that you can create is limitless, but the shape of a curve between two points can be classified in four basic categories: straight lines, lines that are straight at one end but curved at the other, smooth curves or arcs, and S-shaped curves. Figure 12.37 shows how these four basic segments are created.

Clicking two points creates a straight line segment between them.

Clicking the first point and dragging the second point creates a line segment that begins a straight line but curves smoothly into the second point. The second point has two handles, equidistant apart.

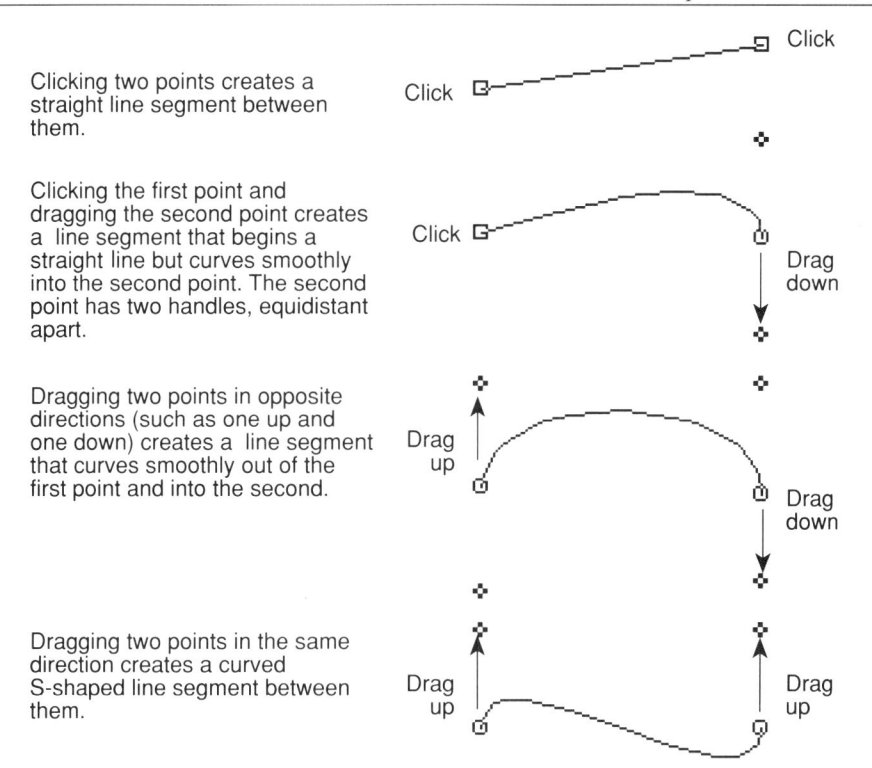

Dragging two points in opposite directions (such as one up and one down) creates a line segment that curves smoothly out of the first point and into the second.

Dragging two points in the same direction creates a curved S-shaped line segment between them.

Figure 12.37 Click or drag the mouse to position each point along a path. The direction and length of the drag are shown by arrows in this figure

Curve handles are tangent to the curve they define, and the depth of the curve is related to the distance of the handle from the point. These two characteristics are described under the next headings.

DETERMINING THE DIRECTION OF THE CURVE

The direction of a curve is determined by the direction in which you drag as you position an anchor point. In dragging a curve handle after positioning an anchor point, drag in a direction that is tangent to the curve you intend to draw. A tangent is a straight line that touches a curve at only one point, as illustrated in the next figure.

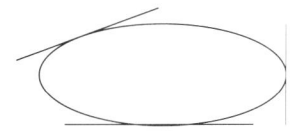

Figure 12.38 A tangent is a straight line that touches a curve at only one point

Once you have positioned a point, the point is selected and you can see the curve handles. You can display any point's curve handles by selecting the point: click on the path to select it, then click on the point. Figure 12.39 shows a variety of curves created by dragging the mouse in a different direction when positioning the middle point. (The endpoints on each curve have vertical handles.)

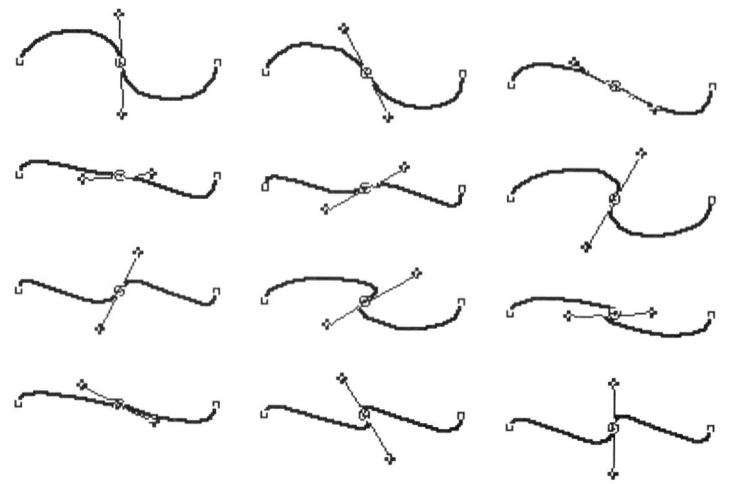

Figure 12.39 The curve handles are always tangent to the curve

TIP

Normally, handles are displayed as clover-shaped indicators when a curve or connector point is selected. (The handles of corner points are usually contracted to the point itself, and are therefore not visible until you drag them out as described below.) You have the option of displaying the *curve levers*—lines from the point to the handle—by choosing the Display curve levers option in the Preferences dialog box (described in the section on the Preferences command in Chapter 14). When curve handles are displayed, it is easier to see that handles are tangent to the curve they define, and that the depth of the curve is related to the distance of the handle from the point (as described next).

DETERMINING THE DEPTH OF A CURVE

The depth of a curve—the size of the hump—is determined by the length of the curve levers. When you first create a curve point, the distance you drag affects both the incoming and the outgoing line segment. One rule of thumb is to drag the curve handle a distance that is about one-third of the length of the curve between the current and the next anchor points. Later, you can select a point and drag individual curve handles to change the incoming and outgoing line segments separately.

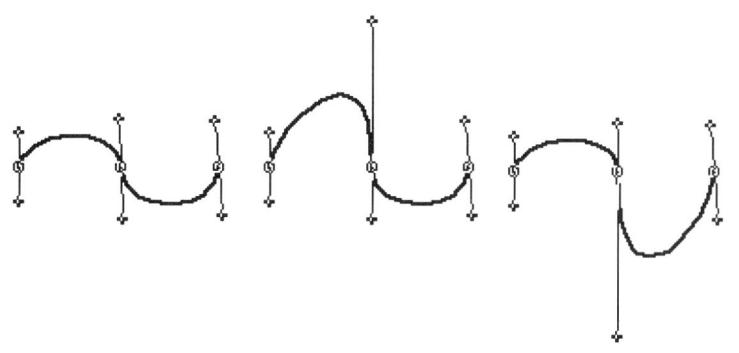

Figure 12.40 The length of the curve levers determines the size of the curve

CONVERTING A CURVE POINT TO A CONNECTOR POINT AS YOU DRAW

If you *drag* to position an anchor point, you can continue drawing a smooth curved line (by clicking or dragging the next point). Alternatively, you can prepare to add a straight line segment by holding down the Option key after you have created the curve you want (but before releasing the mouse button on the second point) and then by dragging the *handle* onto the point itself. Holding down the Option key before you release the mouse button converts a curve point to a corner point.

Drag down to
create 1st
curve segment

Hold Option key down and
drag outgoing line segment
handle into the point to set
up 2nd segment as a
straight line

Dragging third point
creates curve handle
for third segment
only—2nd segment
remains a straight line

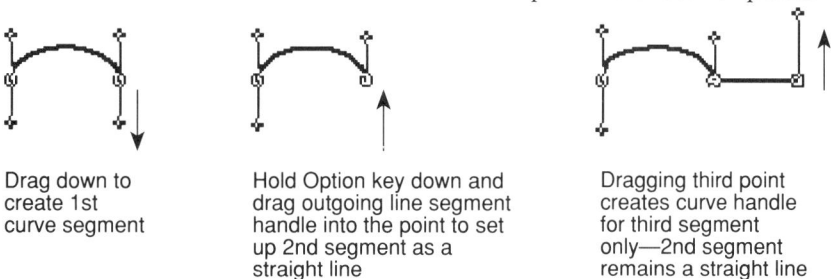

Figure 12.41 Converting a point from a curve point to a corner point

HOLDING DOWN THE SHIFT KEY WHILE YOU DRAW WITH THE PEN TOOL

Holding down the Shift key *before* positioning on an anchor point constrains the position of the point to 45-degree angles relative to the previously positioned point. Holding down the Shift key *as you drag* to create a new curve point constrains the direction of the curve handle to 45-degree angles.

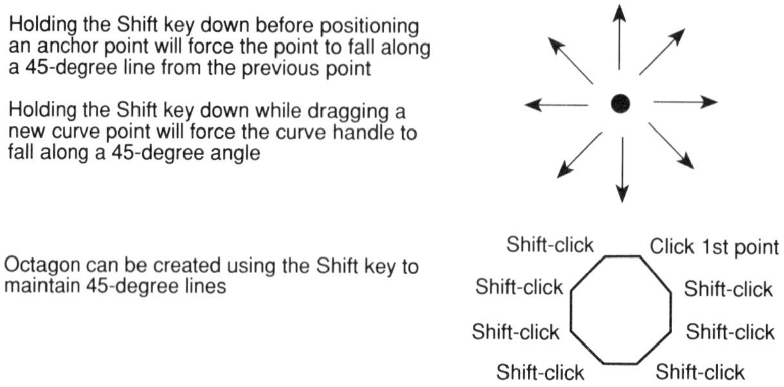

Holding the Shift key down before positioning an anchor point will force the point to fall along a 45-degree line from the previous point

Holding the Shift key down while dragging a new curve point will force the curve handle to fall along a 45-degree angle

Octagon can be created using the Shift key to maintain 45-degree lines

Shift-click   Click 1st point
Shift-click   Shift-click
Shift-click   Shift-click
Shift-click   Shift-click

Figure 12.42 Effects of the Shift key

CLOSING A PATH

To close a path and thereby create a solid shape while you are drawing, click the last anchor point position on top of the first anchor point of the path. You can also close an open path by selecting the two endpoints and using the Join elements command (described in Chapter 14) or by selecting the whole object and then choosing the Element info command and clicking Closed (as described in "Opening and Closing Paths" later in this chapter). Alternatively, you can close a path by selecting one of the endpoints with the Pointer tool and then using the freeform tools to continue the path and close it by clicking the last endpoint on top of the first endpoint.

TIP

You might find it easier to work in magnified views when drawing or editing a path.

COMPLETING AN OPEN PATH

To complete an open path (that is, end one path without closing it), press the Tilde key (~) to deselect the last point without deselecting the path. You can also end an open path by holding down the Command key to change the pointer to the Pointer tool, then click anywhere on the page to deselect the last-placed point *and* the path.

CAUTION

If you forget to deselect the last point of a new path after completing an open path, you will end up with a line joining the last anchor point in the previous path to the first anchor point on your new path. If this happens, simply press Delete (Backspace) once to remove the new anchor point. Then click the Pen tool icon, or hold down the Command key to change the pointer to the Pointer tool, and click anywhere on the page to start a new path.

Use combinations of the techniques that have been described to create paths composed of curved and straight line segments.

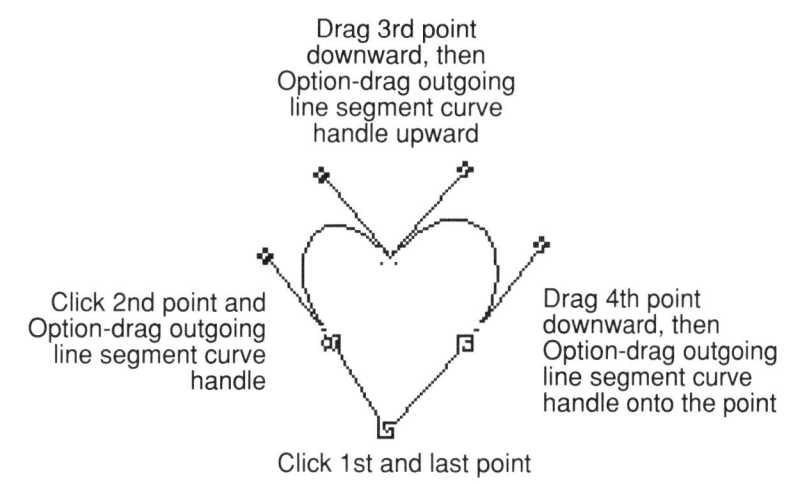

Figure 12.43 Heart composed of curved lines and straight lines

DRAWING PATHS EFFICIENTLY

The more efficiently you build your paths, the easier they will be to edit and the less editing they are likely to need. The goal is to build paths as efficiently as possible using the minimum number of anchor points. You will need to practice with the Pen tool to learn where anchor points are best placed and how to drag curve handles, but here's a tip about how efficient curves are constructed:

Anchor points along a curved path are best placed where the direction of the curve changes. Another way of saying this is that anchor points usually are not required in the middle of continuous curves, such as the peak of a hill or the bottom of a valley. This is sometimes called the "bump" rule—points should be positioned at either side of a bump, rather than at the peak.

You can think of the anchor points as the places along a winding mountain road where you would turn the wheels of the car from pointing right to pointing left, or vice versa. Remember that when you are driving around the hump of a curve you are holding the wheels in one direction, and an anchor point is not required. As you come out of the turn you let the steering wheel return to center, and you turn it in the opposite direction when you come to the next curve. It's at the moment that the steering wheel passes the center point that you position an anchor point.

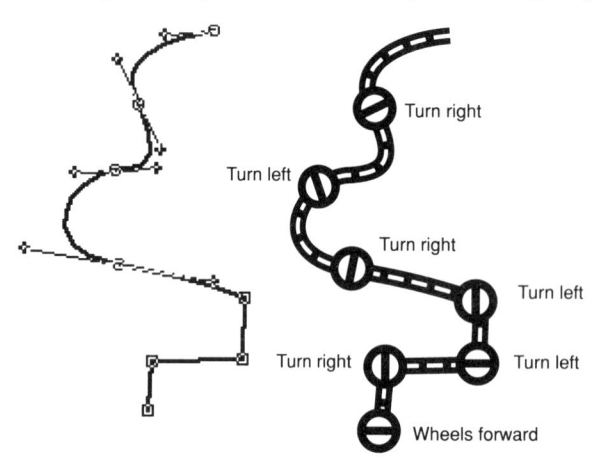

Figure 12.44 Anchor points placed where the direction of the wheels would change in driving around curves in a road

By following this guide, you can create curves that are easy to control, and that can be edited with a minimum number of anchor points—two goals for efficiency and economy of disk space.

EDITING A PATH

Once a path is created—or while you are creating it—you can switch to the Pointer tool to adjust the path by moving points or the handles at curve or connector points. You can also add or delete points, change a point from one type to another, open or close paths, and join paths. Each of these editing methods is described in the next sections.

TIP

You will find that using the Command key shortcut to switch to the Pointer tool makes it easier to adjust curves while you draw. This way you do not need to end the path by going to the Toolbox to select the Pointer tool, and you can resume adding points to the same path after adjusting part of the path.

ADJUSTING THE PATH WITH THE POINTER TOOL

You can use the Pointer tool to move an anchor point or to adjust curve handles. Figure 12.45 shows editing a path in each of these ways.

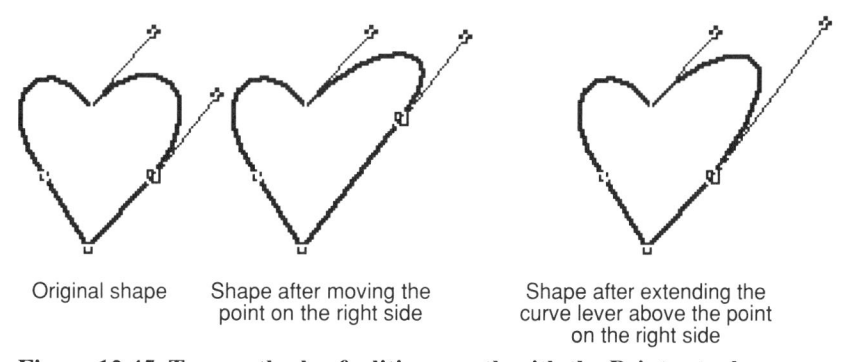

Original shape   Shape after moving the point on the right side   Shape after extending the curve lever above the point on the right side

Figure 12.45 Two methods of editing a path with the Pointer tool

In adjusting curve handles, handles on a curve point move in unison—when you move one, the other one moves as well. Handles on corner points and connector points move independently. You can adjust one handle and the curve it controls without affecting the handle and curve on the other side of the point.

You can change the shapes of the line segments that are joined by corner points by dragging the handles away from the corner point. To do this, you first select the curve and then the point with the Pointer tool, then hold down the Option key as you position the pointer in the center of the corner point and drag away from the point. As you drag, you will see the incoming line segment change (the segment joined to the point you created before this point originally, or the last segment joined to this point to close the path). The second handle you drag out with the Option key will affect the outgoing line segment (that is, the segment joined to the point you added after creating this point originally).

Original shape

Shape after Option-dragging the first handle from the bottom point.

Shape after Option-dragging the second handle from the bottom point.

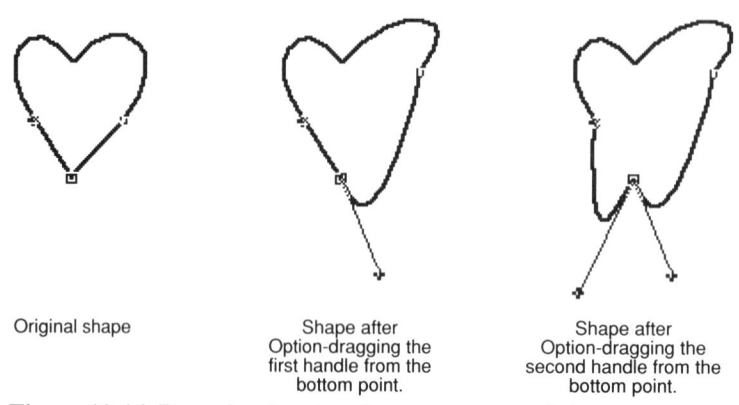

Figure 12.46 Dragging handles from a corner point

You can drag curve handles out of connector points the same way you drag them out of corner points—by using the Option key. As you drag the first handle, the incoming line segment changes. The second handle you drag out with the Option key will affect the outgoing line segment.

TIP

If you have trouble selecting the handle inside a corner or connector point—and you end up moving the point instead—choose the Undo command to reposition the point and then use the Magnifying tool to enlarge your view of the area until the handle can be clearly identified.

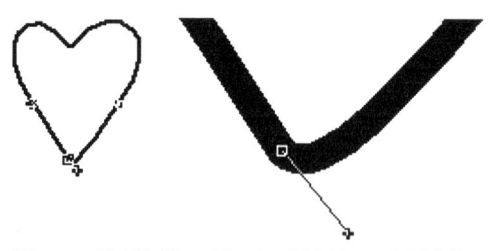

Figure 12.47 Handles in 100% and 800% magnifications

To delete a point from a path, use the Pointer tool to select the path, then select the point, then press Delete (Backspace), or choose Remove point from the Points command submenu in the Element menu. Free-Hand draws a straight line between the two points that were previously connected to the deleted point.

ADDING POINTS WITH THE CURVE, CORNER, OR CONNECTOR TOOL

To add a point to a path, first select the path with the Pointer tool, then select the Curve tool, the Corner tool, or the Connector tool and click on the location along the path where you wish to add a point. Remember that the Curve tool adds curve points, the Corner tool adds corner points, and the Connector tool adds connector points.

CHANGING A POINT FROM ONE TYPE TO ANOTHER

All points look like solid black squares when the whole path is selected, but if you select individual points by clicking them with the Pointer tool, you can tell what type of point it is:

- Curve points look like hollow circles.
- Corner points look like hollow squares.
- Connector points look like hollow triangles.

Selected curve point displays as a hollow circle with two handles

Selected corner point displays as a hollow square with no handles

Selected connector point displays as a hollow triangle with one handle

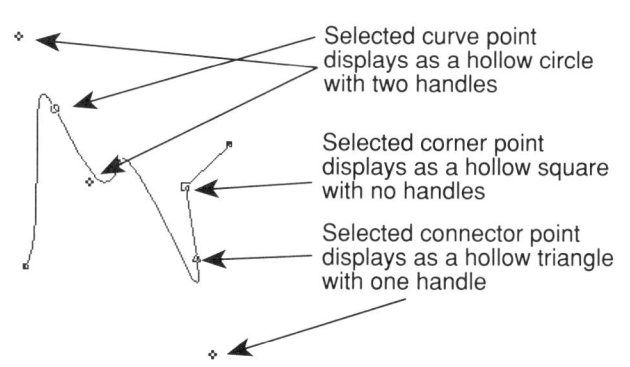

Figure 12.48 Curve points, corner points, and connector points look different when selected

You can also change a point or any number of selected points from one type to another by selecting the point and then choosing from the Points command submenu in the Element menu.

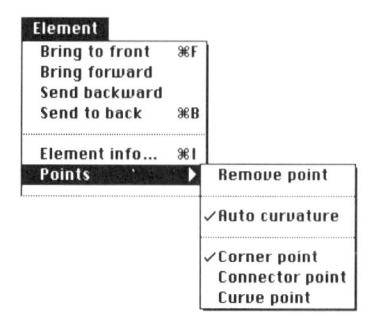

Figure 12.49 The Points command submenu

You can also edit a point by selecting it and then choosing Element info from the Element menu, or by Option-double-clicking on the point with the Pointer tool. Either of these actions displays the Path/point dialog box, similar to the Path dialog box, with additional fields for viewing and changing the point type and position and the handle positions.

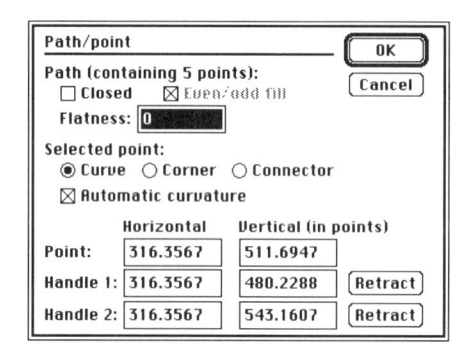

Figure 12.50 The Path/point dialog box

You can click Retract to retract a handle on a curve point and make the adjoining curve a straight line. Handle 1 affects the incoming path, and Handle 2 affects the outgoing path. This is the same order in which you drag handles from a connector point or a corner point.

Figure 12.51 Curve point before (left) and after (right) retracting the second handle

OPENING AND CLOSING PATHS

You can use the Knife tool (described in detail later in this chapter) to open a closed path, or to split an open path into two paths. You can also close an open path by either selecting the two endpoints and using the Join elements command in the Element menu (described in Chapter 14), or by selecting one of the endpoints with the Pointer tool and then using the freeform tools to continue the path and close it by clicking the last endpoint on top of the first endpoint.

You can also open or close a path through the Path dialog box. This dialog box is displayed when you select an ungrouped object and choose Element info from the Element menu, or—a quicker method—hold down the Option key and double-click with the Pointer tool on the object. The Path dialog box lets you view the number of points in the path and the path's flatness. You can also see whether the path is open or closed, and how Even/odd fill is set (see the section on the Element info command in Chapter 14).

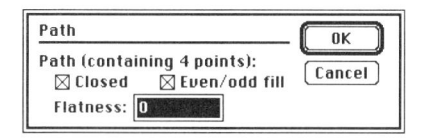

Figure 12.52 The Path dialog box

You can close an open path or open a closed path by clicking the Closed check box. If the path is open and you click Closed, FreeHand will close the path by joining the two endpoints. If the path is closed and you click the Closed check box to open it, FreeHand removes the last line segment that you added to close the path.

JOINING TWO OPEN PATHS

You can join two open paths by positioning the endpoint of one path on top of the endpoint of the other path, selecting the two overlapping endpoints, and then using the Join elements command from the Element menu.

CAUTION

The two endpoints must be touching for the Join elements command to work.

Knife Tool

You use the Knife tool ( ) to break a path into two or more separate objects. Splitting a closed path produces one open path. Splitting an open path produces two open paths. (See "Pen Tool" earlier in this chapter for definitions of open and closed paths.)

First click anywhere on the path you wish to split or add anchor points to. If the object is grouped (i.e., shows four black handles instead of anchor points along the path) choose Ungroup from the Element menu. Then choose the Knife tool by clicking its icon in the Toolbox. The cursor changes to a crossbar (+) in the active window.

You can split a path anywhere except the endpoints of an open path. Wherever you click on the path, the Knife tool splits the path, producing two new endpoints, as shown in Figure 12.53 below.

Figure 12.53 First click anywhere on a path to select it (left), then select the Knife tool and click on a line segment to cut the line (middle). You can separate the points to see that they are two endpoints (right)

After splitting a path, you can use the Pointer tool to separate the new endpoints of the two paths. Click the Pointer tool in any open space in the drawing window to deselect all objects. Click on the location of the two new endpoints. This selects one of the endpoints, which you can then drag to separate the ends of the path(s).

CAUTION

Cuts made with the Knife tool will snap to points, grids, and ruler guides if these options are activated in the View menu. It is a good idea to turn all snap-to options off when you use the Knife tool—unless you are intentionally using ruler guides to line up cuts or you want to cut objects at their anchor points. Otherwise, the cut points might not appear where you intend.

Curve Tool

Use the Curve tool ( ) to draw paths that are composed entirely of curve points, or to add curve points along a path that has already been drawn. The latter use is most common, since the Pen tool creates curve points as well. You can also switch to the Curve tool while drawing a path with another freeform tool.

To draw a path with the Curve tool, first select the tool, then click to position points along the path. The difference between the Curve tool and the Pen tool is that the Curve tool *always* creates curve points, whether you click or drag in placing the point, whereas the Pen tool creates corner points if you click and curve points if you drag. Dragging the pointer when the Curve tool is active changes the point location, not the handles that determine the shape of the curve.

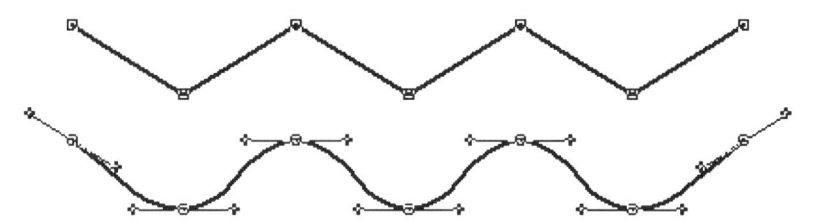

Figure 12.54 Effects of clicking the Curve tool (bottom) vs. clicking the Pen tool (top) in creating paths with the same number of segments and point locations

To add a curve point as the next point after an endpoint of an open path, first select the path and then select the point (unless the point is already selected). Next, select the Curve tool and click to position the next curve point. This is an alternative to positioning and dragging the Pen tool to create a curve point.

To add a point along a path that has already been drawn, select the path with the Pointer tool and then click the Curve tool on the path, as described earlier in "Adding Points with the Curve, Corner, or Connector Tool."

Corner Tool

Use the Corner tool ( ) to draw paths that are composed entirely of corner points, or to add corner points along a path that has already been drawn. The latter use is most common, since the Pen tool creates corner points easily. You can also switch to the Corner tool while drawing a path with another freeform tool.

To draw a path with the Corner tool, first select the tool, then click to position points along the path. The difference between the Corner tool and the Pen tool is that the Corner tool *always* creates corner points, whether you click or drag in placing the point, whereas the Pen tool creates corner points if you click and curve points if you drag.

To add a corner point as the next point after an endpoint of an open path, select the path and then select the point (unless the point is already selected), then choose the Corner tool and click to position the next corner point. This is an alternative to clicking the Pen tool to create a corner point.

To add a corner point along a path that has already been drawn, select the path with the Pointer tool and then click the Corner tool on the path, as described earlier in "Editing a Path." When you add a corner point along a curved line segment, it does not automatically force a pointed corner along the segment. Instead, it creates a point with two curve handles that can be moved *independently*, so you can create the corner or abrupt change of direction along the path by selecting the point and dragging one or both curve handles.

Figure 12.55 Simple curve (left) with corner point added (middle) and handles moved on the corner point (right)

Connector Tool

You must use the Connector tool ( ) when you want to add connector points to a path you are creating with the Pen tool or to insert connector points along a path that has already been drawn. The Pen tool cannot create connector points. If you use the Connector tool on its own to draw paths that are composed entirely of connector points, they are all joined by straight line segments.

The difference between the Connector tool and the Corner tool is that the Corner tool *always* creates corner points, whereas the Connector tool creates connector points that behave the same as corner points when they join two straight line segments. They also behave like curve points when they join a straight line segment and a curve or two curved segments.

To add a connector point as the next point after an endpoint of an open path, select the path and then select the point (unless the point is already selected), then choose the Connector tool and click to position the next point.

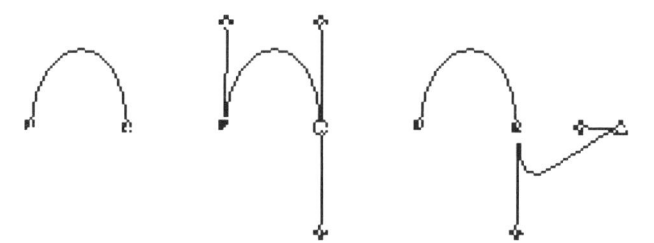

Figure 12.56 Using the Connector tool to create a connector point

To add a connector point along a path that has already been drawn, select the path with the Pointer tool and then click the Connector tool on the path, as described earlier in "Adding Points with the Curve, Corner, or Connector Tool."

Transformation Tools

FreeHand provides four *transformation* tools—the Rotating tool, the Reflecting tool, the Scaling tool, and the Skewing tool. They are called transformation tools because they transform—that is, change the form or shape of—objects. Actions performed with these tools are "remembered" by FreeHand and they can be repeated using the Duplicate and Transform again commands (see the descriptions of those commands in Chapter 14).

Rotating Tool

The Rotating tool (☉) lets you rotate selected objects on a page.

First select the object(s) to be rotated, then choose the Rotating tool by clicking its icon in the Toolbox. The mouse pointer changes to a starburst pointer (✻) in the active window. You can rotate objects visually on the screen, or by an amount you specify in the Rotate dialog box.

ROTATING VISUALLY ON THE SCREEN

To rotate an object visually on the screen, first select the object(s), then select the Rotating tool, then position the starburst pointer at the point you want to be the origin for the rotation and hold down the mouse button. To make the object rotate, keep holding down the mouse button, and drag in the direction of the desired rotation. An X on the screen indicates the focal point around which the rotation occurs. The first position of the starburst pointer is marked by a small X on the screen; this is the "center" around which you rotate the object. Release the mouse button when you have rotated the object(s) as much as you want.

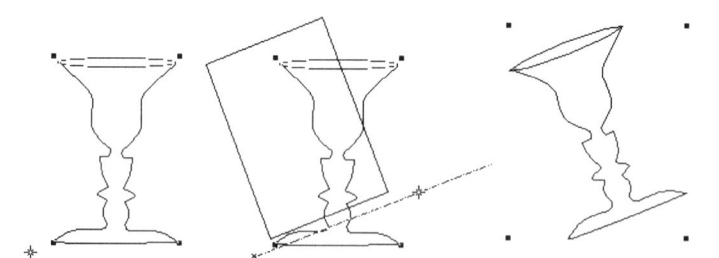

Figure 12.57 Rotating objects visually on the screen: (1) position the starburst pointer over an origin point (bottom left corner in this example), then (2) drag to rotate the object relative to the origin. An X marks the origin at the end of an axis line that marks the angle of rotation as you drag the mouse; a box outlines the new position of the rotated object (center figure). (3) Release the mouse button. The rotated object remains selected (right)

Shift-dragging the starburst pointer (pressing the Shift key as you drag the mouse) constrains the rotation to multiples of 45-degree angles.

ROTATING BY A SPECIFIED AMOUNT

To rotate an object numerically instead of visually, hold down the Option key when you click to set a point of origin for the rotation. The Rotate dialog box appears, allowing you to specify the angle of rotation (in degrees) and the origin around which to rotate.

You can also specify whether or not to rotate the contents (if the object was filled by using the Paste inside command) or the fill pattern tiles (if the object is filled with a custom tile pattern). (See the section on the Fill and line command in Chapter 14, and the descriptions of pattern techniques in Chapter 6.)

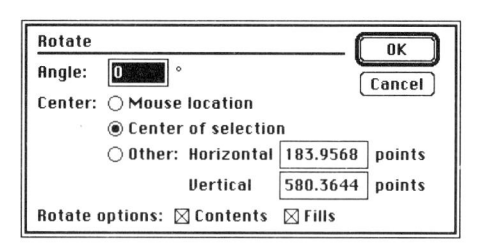

Figure 12.58 The Rotate dialog box

Angles are measured *counterclockwise*, with zero at twelve o'clock. You can rotate objects in a *clockwise* direction by entering a negative number. You can specify the point of origin as the mouse location, the center of the selected object(s), or any horizontal/vertical position you define (measured from the zero point on the ruler). When you have set the parameters you want, click OK.

See Chapter 4 for examples of using the Rotating tool to create symmetrical objects such as those shown in Figure 12.59.

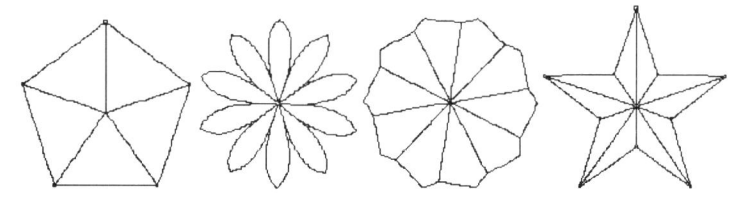

Figure 12.59 Symmetrical objects created with the Rotating tool in Chapter 4

Reflecting Tool

You use the Reflecting tool ( ) to transform an object into a mirror image of itself. First select the object(s) to be transformed, then choose the Reflecting tool by clicking its icon in the Toolbox. The mouse pointer changes to a starburst pointer ✳ in the active window. When you first position the starburst pointer on the page, an X indicates the focal point around which the reflection occurs. You can reflect objects visually on the screen, or at an angle you specify in the Reflect dialog box.

REFLECTING A MIRROR IMAGE VISUALLY ON THE SCREEN

To reflect an object visually on the screen, first select the object and then choose the Reflecting tool. Next, position the starburst pointer at the point you want to be the origin for the reflection and hold down the mouse button. To reflect the object, keep holding down the mouse button, and drag in the direction of the desired reflection. The first position of the starburst pointer is marked by a small X on the screen; this marks a point on the axis of the reflection. As you drag the mouse, the position of the starburst pointer is a second point on the axis across which you reflect the object. Release the mouse button when you have reflected as much as you want.

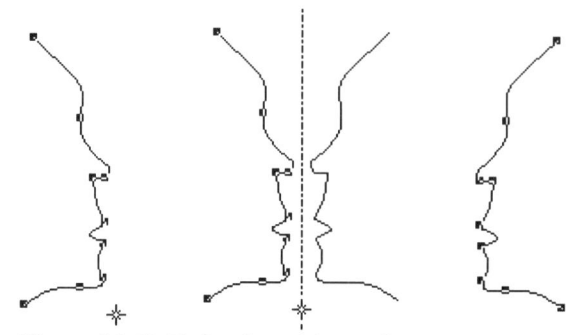

Figure 12.60 Reflecting objects visually on the screen: **(1) position the mouse pointer over an origin point (bottom right corner of a silhouette in this case), then (2) hold down the mouse button to display the vertical axis—drag to pivot the axis across which the object is reflected. The position of the reflected object is shown as you work. (3) Release the mouse button. The reflected object remains selected (right)**

Shift-dragging the pointer (holding down the Shift key and dragging with the mouse) constrains the axis of reflection to multiples of 45-degree angles.

REFLECTING BY A SPECIFIED AMOUNT

To reflect an object numerically instead of visually, hold down the Option key when you click to set a point of origin for the reflection transformation. The Reflect dialog box appears, allowing you to specify which axis to reflect across (horizontal, vertical, or angled), the origin around which to reflect, and whether or not to reflect the contents or the fill pattern tiles.

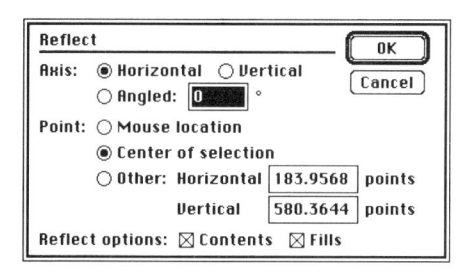

Figure 12.61 The Reflect dialog box

The angles for reflection are measured *counterclockwise*, with zero at twelve o'clock. You can reflect over an axis in a *clockwise* direction from twelve o'clock by entering a negative number. You can specify the point of origin as the mouse location, the center of the selected object(s), or any horizontal/vertical position you name (measured from the zero point on the ruler).

You can also specify whether or not to reflect the contents (if the object was filled by using the Paste inside command) or the fill pattern tiles (if the object is filled with a custom tile pattern). (See the section on the Fill and line command in Chapter 14, and the discussion of pattern techniques in Chapter 6).

When parameters are set as you wish, click OK.

TIP

The Reflecting tool is one of the most difficult tools to control at first. To avoid unwanted effects, always group the objects (if you are reflecting more than one at a time), then choose the Clone command from the Edit menu (⌘=) to make a copy before you use the Reflecting tool. If the copy is reflected correctly, delete the original. Or, if the effect is not what you want, delete the copy and repeat.

Scaling Tool

You use the Scaling tool ( ) to change the size of selected objects. Scaling an object stretches or compresses it horizontally, vertically, or both, relative to some fixed point you choose. First select the object(s) to be scaled. Then choose the Scaling tool by clicking the icon in the Toolbox. The mouse pointer changes to a starburst pointer ( ) in the active window. You can scale objects visually on the screen or by an amount specified in the Scale dialog box.

SCALING OBJECTS VISUALLY ON THE SCREEN

To scale an object visually on the screen, first select the object, select the Scaling tool, then position the starburst pointer at the point you want to be the origin for the scaling transformation. To scale the object, keep holding down the mouse button and drag. When you first position the starburst pointer on the page, an X indicates the focal point of the scaling. Release the mouse button when you have achieved the effect you want.

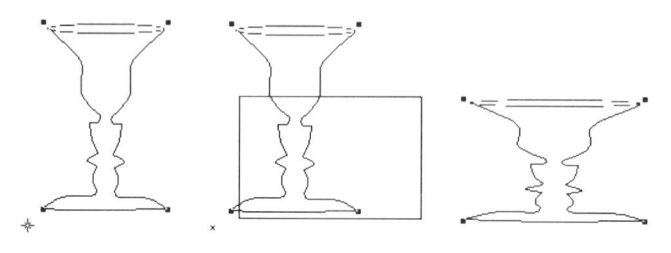

Figure 12.62 Scaling objects visually on the screen: (1) position the mouse pointer over an origin point (bottom left corner in this case), then (2) drag to scale the object relative to the origin. An X marks the origin as you drag the mouse; a box outlines the new size of the scaled object (center figure). (3) Release the mouse button. The scaled object remains selected (right)

Shift-drag the starburst pointer to constrain the transformation to proportional scaling.

SCALING OBJECTS BY A SPECIFIED PERCENTAGE

To scale an object numerically instead of visually, hold down the Option key when you click to set a point of origin for the scaling transformation. The Scale dialog box appears (as shown in Figure 12.63 below), allowing you to specify whether to scale uniformly or not, the origin around which to scale, and whether or not to scale the contents, the fill pattern tiles, or the line weights.

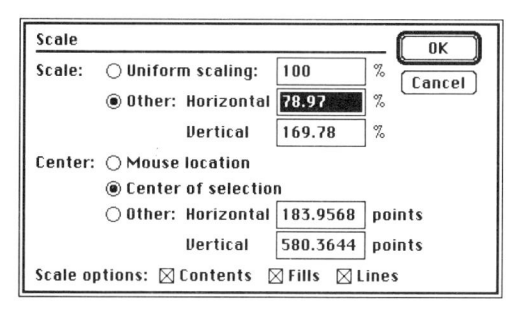

Figure 12.63 The Scale dialog box

If you choose Uniform scale, the object will be scaled horizontally and vertically by the same percentage, or you can specify different values for the horizontal and vertical scaling. You can specify the point of origin as the mouse location, the center of the selected object(s), or any horizontal/vertical position you define (measured from the zero point on the ruler line).

You can also choose whether or not to scale the line weights, the contents (if the object was filled using the Paste inside command), or the fill pattern tiles (if the object is filled with a custom tile pattern). (See the description of the Fill and line command in Chapter 14 and the discussion of pattern techniques in Chapter 6).

When you have set the parameters you want, click OK.

See Chapters 4, 6, and 10 for examples of using the Scaling tool to create a series of concentric shapes.

See also: The Blend command and Print command sections in Chapter 14. The Blend command can be used to create a series of concentric shapes and the Print command can be used to scale whole illustrations during printing.

Skewing Tool

You can use the Skewing tool to change the angle between the axes of selected objects. (Normally the x and y axes are set at 90-degree angles.) Skewing can be visualized as the action of the blades of scissors, as shown in Figure 12.64 below.

Figure 12.64 In skewing, the change of the angle between the axes is similar to the movement of the blades on scissors

First select the object(s) to be skewed, then select the Skewing tool by clicking its icon in the Toolbox. The mouse pointer changes to a starburst pointer ✣ in the active window. You can skew objects visually on the screen, or at an angle specified in the Skew dialog box.

SKEWING OBJECTS VISUALLY ON THE SCREEN

To skew an object visually on the screen, first select the object to skew, select the Skewing tool, then position the starburst pointer at the point you wish to be the origin for the skewing transformation. To skew the object, keep holding down the mouse button and drag. When you first position the transformation pointer on the page, an X indicates the intersection of the horizontal and vertical axes. The direction in which you drag defines the axis of skew: if you drag left or right you change the angle of the vertical axis; if you drag up or down you change the angle of the horizontal axis. The distance you drag defines the angle of skew.

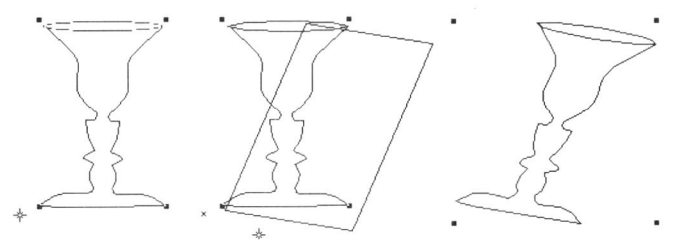

Figure 12.65 Skewing objects visually on the screen: (1) position the starburst pointer over an origin point (bottom left corner in this case), then (2) drag horizontally to change the angle of the x axis, vertically to change the angle of the y axis. An X marks the origin (intersection of axes) as you drag the mouse; a box outlines the new position of the skewed object (center figure). (3) Release the mouse button. The skewed object remains selected (right)

If you Shift-drag the starburst pointer, the axis of skew will be constrained to multiples of 45-degree angles.

SKEWING BY A SPECIFIED AMOUNT

To skew an object numerically instead of visually, hold down the Option key when you click to set a point of origin for the skewing transformation. The Skew dialog box appears, allowing you to specify the angles of skew, the origin around which to skew, and whether or not to skew the contents or the fill pattern tiles.

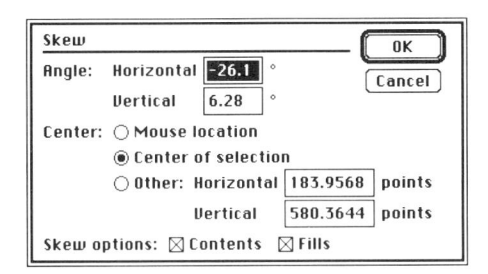

Figure 12.66 The Skew dialog box

You can specify the point of origin as the mouse location, the center of the selected object(s), or any horizontal/vertical position you define (measured from the zero point on the ruler).

You can also specify whether or not to skew the contents (if the object was filled using the Paste inside command) or the fill pattern tiles (if the object is filled with a custom tile pattern). (See the discussion of the Fill and line command in Chapter 14, and the descriptions of pattern techniques in Chapter 6).

When the parameters are set as you wish, click OK.

Tracing Tool

You use the Tracing tool (🖳) to trace automatically the path around any solid object that is created in FreeHand or imported. This is especially useful in converting imported bitmaps and TIFF images into paths. Using the Tracing tool can be faster and easier than tracing over the object manually with the Freehand tool or the Pen tool.

Choose the Tracing tool by clicking its icon in the Toolbox. The mouse pointer changes to a crossbar (+). Position the crossbar pointer at one edge of the object(s) to be traced and drag a selection marquee around the objects or areas that you want traced. The Tracing tool creates separate paths for each different shaded area of the object. For example, in tracing a circle with no fill, the Tracing tool creates two circles: one around the outer edge of the circle and one around the inside edge. You can see in Figure 12.67 that solid-filled objects yield single outlines, while white-filled objects yield double outlines around each object.

Figure 12.67 Areas selected with the Tracing tool (top) and the resulting paths (bottom)

TIP

The paths created by the Tracing tool take on the line attributes currently set in the Fill and line dialog box. Always check these settings before using the Tracing tool.

TIP

Give objects a black fill before tracing them unless you want double outlines, or trace the objects with white fill and delete one of the double lines around the edge.

CAUTION

Objects filled with custom or PostScript fills cannot be traced. You can remove the fill before tracing and then reapply it later.

Double-clicking on the tool brings up the Trace dialog box, where the usual defaults are **Tight**, **Trace background elements,** and **Trace foreground elements**.

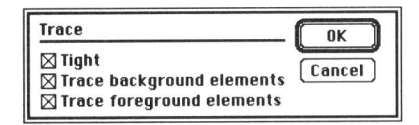

Figure 12.68 The Trace dialog box

When Tight is selected, FreeHand places more points on the traced path so it more closely matches the original object, and TIFF images are traced at the resolution of the image. (If the items to be traced use different resolutions, FreeHand will display the prompt: "The items to trace are not all the same resolution. Trace anyway?") Deselect Tight if you want fewer anchor points created along the path, and if you want TIFF images to trace at 72 dpi resolution—thus using less memory and tracing faster.

Deselect Trace background elements if you do not want to trace elements on layers that fall on or below the background layer. Deselect Trace foreground elements if you do not want to trace elements on the layers that fall above the background (see the description of the Layers palette in the next chapter).

TIP

It's a good idea to convert color TIFF images to grayscale, and grayscale images to black-and-white, before tracing them with the Tracing tool. See the description of how to convert TIFF images in the section on the Element info command in Chapter 14.

TIP

For better results in tracing low-contrast bitmapped images, use the Element info command to increase the contrast.

TIP

If you want to create line art from a halftone photograph, you can save scanning time, disk space, and screen redraw time by quickly tracing the significant lines of the photo by hand—using a pen or pencil on paper—and then scanning only the traced lines. You can then import the scan into FreeHand and use the Tracing tool.

Figure 12.69 Scan and resulting autotrace (top) vs. hand-traced scan and resulting autotrace (bottom)

After you have drawn a path with the Tracing tool, you can adjust the line segments and anchor points, scale or move the object using the Pointer tool, transform the object using the transformation tools, and change the object using commands in the Element and Attributes menus. (The Pen tool, Pointer tool, and transformation tools are described earlier in this chapter, and the Element and Attributes menu commands are detailed in Chapter 14.)

Magnifying Tool

The Magnifying tool (Q) lets you change the scale in which you are viewing the page. When this tool is selected, the pointer becomes a magnifying glass with a plus sign inside (⊕), or a minus sign (⊖) when the Reducing tool is activated by holding down the Option key. FreeHand provides seven levels of magnification, each increased or decreased by a factor of two. From actual size (100%), you can zoom in (magnify) to 200%, 400%, and 800%, and zoom out (reduce) to 50%, 25%, and 12.5% of actual size.

The Magnifying tool is particularly useful when you need to magnify an area to see the anchor points for fine, detailed adjustment, or when you are working with several points or paths lying close together. Figure 12.70 on the next page illustrates the benefit of using the Magnifying tool to magnify a section of your image that you want to modify.

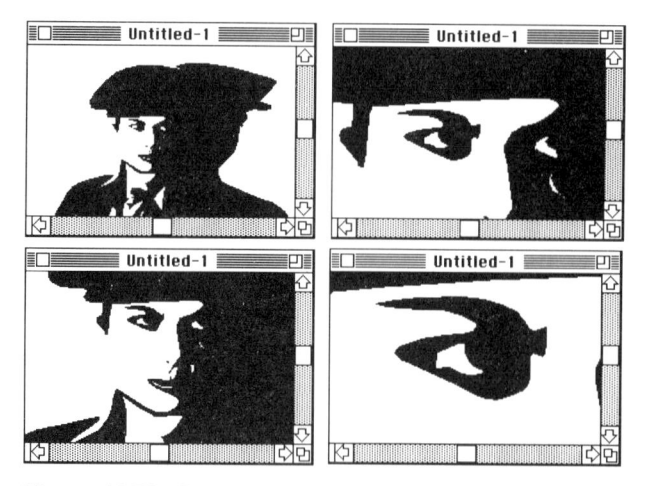

Figure 12.70 Close-up and reduced views of the same detail

You can choose the Magnifying tool by clicking its icon in the Toolbox, or hold down the Command key and the Space bar to select the Magnifying tool temporarily while another tool is selected. The mouse pointer changes to a magnifying glass with a plus sign (+) in the center. When you release the Command key and the Space bar, the previously selected tool will once again be selected.

Activate the Reducing tool by clicking the Magnifying tool in the Toolbox and then holding down the Option key, or by pressing ⌘Option-Space bar to temporarily select the Reducing tool while another tool is selected. The mouse pointer changes to a magnifying glass with a minus sign (-) in the center. When you release the Command and Option keys and the Space bar, the previously selected tool will once again be selected.

Figure 12.71 below shows the various pointer shapes for the Magnifying and Reducing tools: a plus sign enlarges the view, a minus sign reduces the view, and an empty magnifying glass icon indicates that you have enlarged or reduced to the limit.

Figure 12.71 The appearances of the Magnifying tool: A plus sign enlarges the view, a minus sign reduces the view, an empty magnifying glass indicates that you have enlarged (or reduced) to the limit

The position of the pointer on the screen when you are using the Magnifying tool or the Reducing tool determines the center of the screen in the next view. For example, you position the magnifying glass at the top left of the artwork to zoom in to the top left, position the magnifying glass in the center to zoom in to the center, and so on.

You can also change magnifications by choosing percentages from the Magnification command submenu in the View menu (see the discussion of the Magnification command in Chapter 14). When you use the commands, the current selection becomes the center of the screen.

TIP

Always use the Command key and Space bar to magnify a detail of your drawing, or use the keyboard shortcuts shown in the Magnification command submenu. These methods are much faster than clicking the icon in the Toolbox (to select the tool) or opening a menu and a submenu (to choose a command).

TIP

The Magnifying tool aligns to the invisible grid when Snap to grid is chosen from the View menu. Turn Snap to grid off if the grid is large and you have trouble zooming in to the details you want to work on.

13

The Colors, Layers, and Styles Palettes

The opening screen in FreeHand displays the Colors palette if you are working with the initial defaults that are built into FreeHand. You can also display a Layers palette and a Styles palette. These palettes are tremendous productivity tools. You can create any illustration in FreeHand without using the palettes at all, but once you see how they can be used, you will find them convenient aids in creating any illustration, and indispensable in producing complex artwork. This chapter describes these three palettes in detail.

The Colors palette is a quick alternative to menu commands in applying or defining colors. The Layers palette lets you create and manage layers of artwork. The Styles palette allows you to create sets of attributes (color, fill, line, and screen definitions) for one-step application of a series of commands or steps.

372   Using Aldus FreeHand 3.0

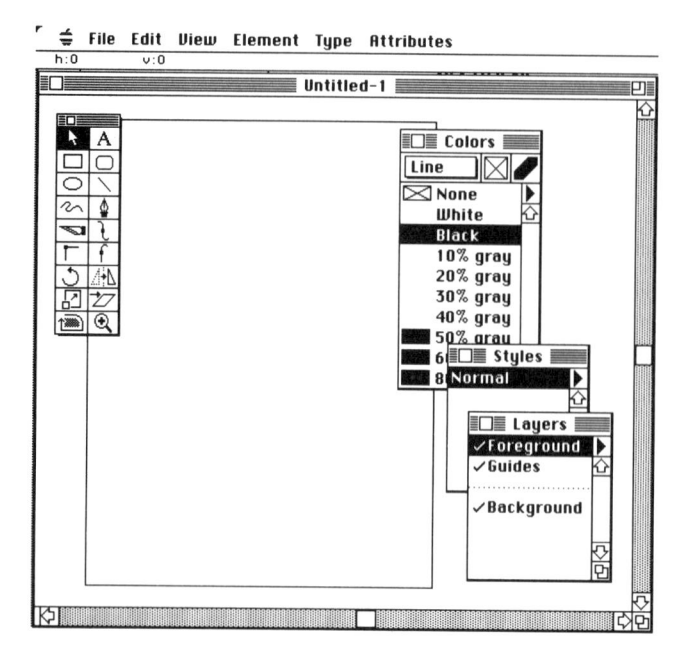

Figure 13.1 Screen displaying a new document window with the palettes

You can display the palettes by choosing commands from the submenu of the Windows command in the View menu, or by using the commands' keyboard shortcuts: ⌘9 to display the Colors palette, ⌘6 to display the Layers palette, and ⌘3 to display the Styles palette. (Notice that 9, 6, and 3 appear one above the other in the last column of numbers on the keypad, reflecting the normal default for the physical placement of the palettes on the screen.)

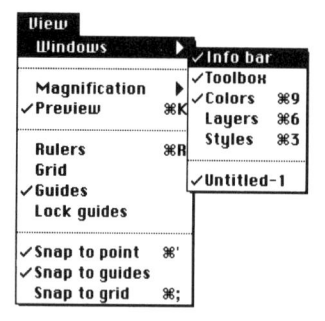

Figure 13.2 The View menu's Windows command submenu

You can close any of the palettes by clicking the close box in the upper left corner of the palette. You can move any of the palettes by dragging the palette's title bar. You can size the palettes by dragging the size box in the lower right corner.

When you first start FreeHand or open a FreeHand document, the palettes are displayed as they were when you last used FreeHand *if* you have chosen the Save palette positions option (through the Preferences command, as described in Chapter 14). If you have chosen *not* to save palette positions, FreeHand displays only the Info bar, the Toolbox, and the Colors palette (i.e., the original palette positions set up by Aldus).

Colors Palette

FreeHand's Colors palette is an easy-access alternative to using the Type specs command to apply color to text, using the Fill and line command to apply color to text and paths, or using the Colors command to create or edit a color.

The default Colors palette that comes with FreeHand lists Black, White, None, and eight shades of gray (percentages of black). New colors and tints that you create are added automatically to the Colors palette.

TIP

You can change the default color template by opening a new document and creating all your colors through the Colors dialog box, then saving the document as a template file with the name *Aldus FreeHand Defaults* and storing it in the *Aldus FreeHand 3.0* application folder.

The top of the palette provides icons, called the Fill indicator and the Line indicator, that you can click to color the line or the fill of a selected object. Alternatively, you can choose from a pop-up menu to color both the line and fill. A second pop-up menu lets you add, edit, copy, or remove a color, or add a predefined color from a library. The Fill and Line indicators at the top of the Colors palette show the default color selections for fill and line if nothing is selected, or the fill and line colors of the current selection.

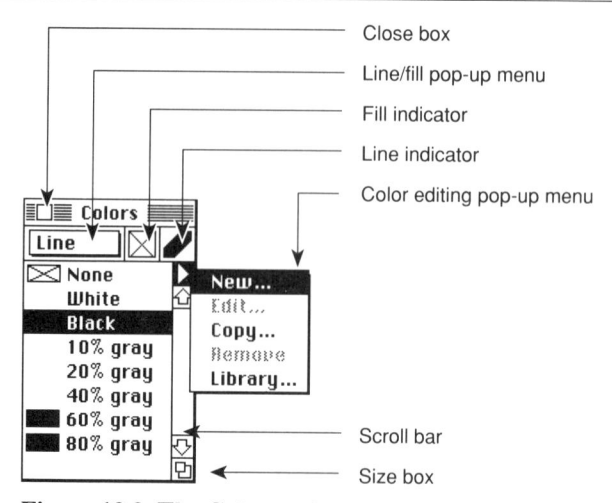

Figure 13.3 The Colors palette

TIP

When working with Preview turned off, you can quickly see the fill and line colors of an object by selecting it and viewing the top line in the Colors palette.

Note that the shades of gray and tints of other colors may appear grainy in the palette and in the preview of the artwork, but they will improve when printed at higher resolutions.

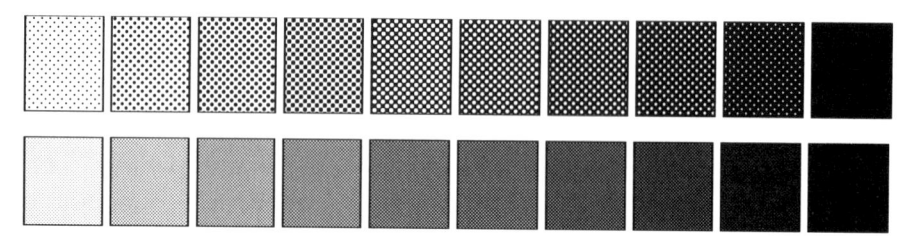

Figure 13.4 Gray shades as displayed on-screen and as printed on a high resolution printer

TIP

Colors display most accurately on the screen and in dialog boxes when the monitor is set to 256 or millions of colors (through the Control Panel in the Apple menu). If your monitor is set to 16 colors, the colors on the screen and in the Colors palette will not be as accurate as the colors displayed in the Colors dialog box (when you are editing a color or creating a new color).

Patterns, line widths, and special line fills do not appear in the Colors palette, but they can be added to the Styles palette, described later in this chapter.

Applying Colors

PostScript views everything in terms of Bezier curves with lines (strokes) and fills. The normal FreeHand defaults give graphic objects black lines with no fill, and text objects black fill with no line color. To apply a color to an object through the Colors palette, first select the object. Next, click the Fill indicator or the Line indicator in the Colors palette, or hold down the Shift key and click either the Line or Fill indicator to choose both, then click the color or tint you wish to apply. (You can instead choose Line, Fill, or both from the pop-up menu to the left of the Fill indicator and the Line indicator.)

If all of the colors are not visible in the window, you can use the scroll bars to scroll down the list, or you can drag the size box in the lower right corner of the palette to enlarge the palette.

In applying colors to closed paths, you can color the fill and the line separately. You can apply a fill to an open path, but FreeHand will not display or print the fill unless you close the path. The color or tint you apply to text automatically affects the fill only—the line or stroke around text is always set to None (unless you choose Fill and stroke from the Effect command submenu in the Type menu and change the settings). You can use the Fill and line command in the Attributes menu to change the appearance of text that has been converted to paths. See the section on the Convert to paths command in Chapter 14.

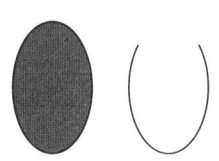

Normal Text   **Text with Fill/Stroke Specified**   **Text converted to Paths**

Figure 13.5 Objects with 40% gray fill and black line settings: a closed path (top left), an open path (top right), normal text (with white stroke), text with fill and stroke specified through the Effect submenu, and text converted to paths

TIP

If you select a fill and nothing happens, either the path is not selected or it is not closed. Option-double-click the object to display the Element info dialog box, and check the Closed box if it is not already checked. FreeHand will close the path for you.

TIP

If you set both Fill and Line to None or White, the object might disappear in Preview mode. You can select the object by dragging a selection marquee around it (if you already know where it is), or by choosing Select all from the Edit menu to find handles or points on invisible objects, or by switching Preview off to view all paths in keyline view.

Changing the Default Color

Each new object you create will automatically take on the default colors for Fill and Line. Each time you specify a new color Fill or Line for a selected object, the new selections automatically become the new defaults for objects that you add to the artwork. To change the defaults without affecting the artwork, simply press Tab to deselect all objects and then make Fill and Line color selections from the Colors palette.

Adding, Editing, Moving, and Removing Colors

Choosing New, Edit, or Copy from the pop-up menu results in the Colors dialog box. This dialog box is described in detail in the section on the Colors command in Chapter 14, but we summarize the uses of this dialog box here.

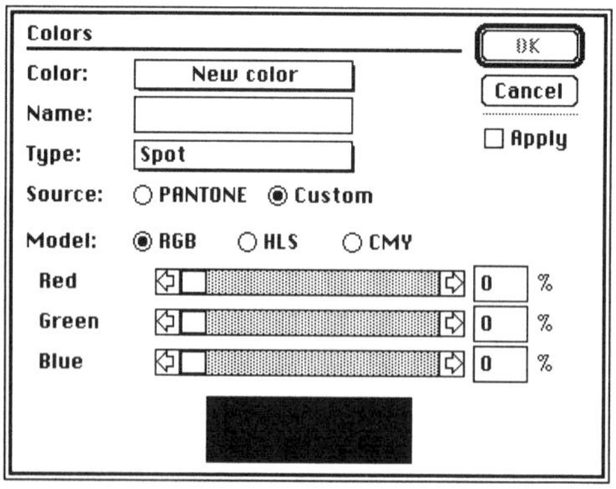

Figure 13.6 The Colors dialog box

CAUTION

Always press Tab to deselect all items on the artwork before clicking or double-clicking colors in the palette as you use the commands described here—otherwise, you might apply the colors to selected objects.

CREATING A NEW COLOR

To create a new color that is not based on any other color, choose New from the pop-up menu to display the Colors dialog box. Make entries in the dialog box (as described in the section on the Colors command in Chapter 14). The new color will be added to the bottom of the list in the palette, but you can change the sequence as described later in "Rearranging Colors on the Palette."

EDITING AN EXISTING COLOR

You can edit any color listed in the palette except None, White, and Black. To edit an existing color, you can simply double-click the color name in the palette to display the Colors dialog box. Double-clicking is the quicker alternative to choosing the color and then choosing Edit from the palette pop-up menu.

Changes you make to a color are automatically applied to all elements in the artwork that were previously assigned that color. If you want to change a color without changing the artwork, you can copy the color as described next.

COPYING A COLOR

You can create a new color based on an existing color by first clicking the color you wish to copy and then choosing Copy from the palette pop-up menu. Alternatively, you can double-click the color name you want to copy in the palette to display the Colors dialog box, then choose New color from the pop-up list of colors at the top of the dialog box.

GETTING A COLOR FROM A LIBRARY

FreeHand comes with a color library, named CrayonLibrary.clib, that contains process-color formulas for the colors that are often part of a box of 64 crayons. You can also create your own color libraries as described in "Creating a Color Library" in Chapter 6.

To add colors from a library to your palette, choose Library from the Colors palette pop-up menu. A dialog box displays a list of libraries.

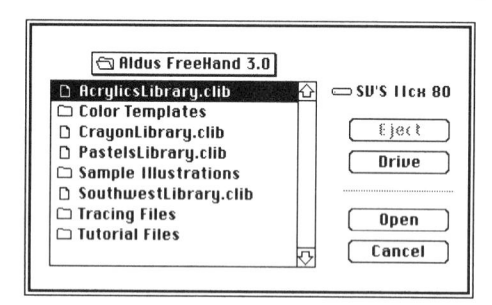

Figure 13.7 Dialog box listing color libraries

Techniques for viewing the contents of different disks or folders are described in the section on the Open command in Chapter 14. Double-click a library name to open it and display the list of colors in the Select library color(s) dialog box.

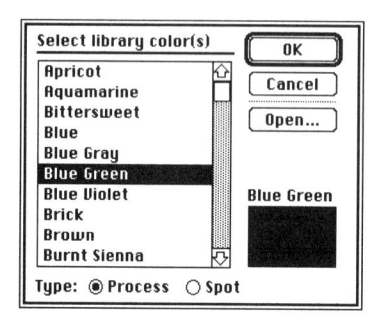

Figure 13.8 The Select library color(s) dialog box

If this is not the library you intended to open, click Open to return to the list of libraries. To select colors, first click Process or Spot at the bottom of the Select library color(s) dialog box to choose the model you wish to use—colors set up with the opposite model will become grayed in the list.

Click a color name to select it, or Shift-click to select more than one color from the list, then click OK to close the dialog box and add the selected colors to your Colors palette.

To add colors from a different color model, choose Library again from the Colors palette's pop-up menu and go back to the Select library color(s) dialog box.

REARRANGING COLORS ON THE PALETTE

FreeHand always adds new colors to the bottom of the list in the palette, but you can arrange the colors in any order you wish by clicking the color you wish to move and dragging it to a new location on the palette.

REMOVING COLORS FROM THE PALETTE

You can remove a color from the list in the Colors palette by selecting the color and then choosing Remove from the Colors palette pop-up menu. Make sure no objects are selected when you click the color in the palette, or you might inadvertently color the selection before deleting the color. You cannot delete colors that are currently applied to objects in the artwork or colors that are part of a style listed in the Styles palette.

Layers Palette

The Layers palette introduced in Aldus FreeHand 3.0 is a tremendously useful feature for managing complex illustrations. You open the Layers palette by choosing Layers from the Windows command submenu in the View menu, or by typing the keyboard shortcut ⌘6. The default Layers palette shows three named layers—Foreground, Guides, and Background—plus a dotted line that divides visible layers (above the line) and invisible layers (below the line).

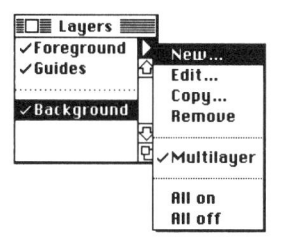

Figure 13.9 The Layers palette

Imagine a FreeHand 3.0 illustration as a series of transparent overlays—like the "cels" used in creating early cartoons and Warner Brothers animations. The bottom layer might show the sky behind a second layer of landscape elements. A third layer might show buildings, and a fourth layer might show text. *Each layer* contains a number of different elements, each with different fill and line settings.

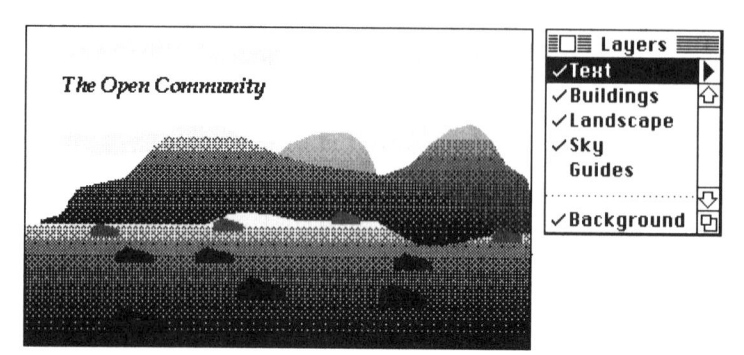

Figure 13.10 An illustration composed of four layers for artwork (plus Guides and Background)

The layers reflected in the Layers palette, therefore, are not the same as the stacking sequence that you might already be accustomed to from other object-oriented drawing programs. In that type of sequence, the first object you draw is on one level, the second object you draw is on the level above the first, the third object is on another level, and so on. In FreeHand 3.0, elements within each layer are stacked in the order you create them, and within the layer they can be shuffled using the Bring to front, Bring forward, Send backward, and Send to back commands. These commands change the stacking order of elements within the current layer only.

You can use the Layers palette to create, copy, and remove layers, move elements from one layer to another, control the stacking sequence of layers, and make some layers invisible on-screen and in printing.

The next sections describe how to work with the Layers palette, and Chapter 9 offers more suggestions for using this incredible productivity aid.

The Default Palette

Even if you do not add any layers to your work, FreeHand automatically creates three layers: the Foreground layer, the Guides layer, and the Background layer. The Foreground layer is the layer in which all of your artwork is created if you never open the Layers palette or add other layers. The Guides layer is where FreeHand automatically positions any ruler guides or grid marks. The Background layer never prints (unless you move it above the dotted line in the palette). Additional layer numbers might also be displayed when you open artwork created with earlier versions of FreeHand.

Selecting the Active Layer

The currently selected layer is highlighted in the Layers palette; this is the only active layer unless Multilayer is checked. You can make another layer active by clicking the layer name or by selecting an object on that layer (when Multilayer is on). Whatever you add to the artwork is automatically added to the active layer (except guides, which are always added to the Guides layer by FreeHand).

When Multilayer is checked in the Layers palette pop-up menu, all visible layers are active—i.e., you can select and edit elements on any layer that shows a check mark at the left in the Layers palette. You can also group-select elements on different layers (by using the selection marquee or Shift-clicking) and edit them as a group selection. With Multilayer unchecked, you will only be able to select elements on the active layer—the layer that is highlighted in the Layers palette.

The same select-through technique that is used on objects stacked within one layer can be used to select objects stacked on multiple layers when Multilayer is on. Hold down the Control key and click the Pointer tool to select the element below the currently selected element. Each click of the mouse while holding down the Control key takes you down another layer. The Control key also works in conjunction with the Shift key (to select more than one object), and/or the Option key (to subselect elements in a group).

CAUTION

It is possible to make an invisible layer the active layer. If this is the case when you create a new object, that object will not be visible on the screen. If you create or import an object when an invisible layer is active, the object will disappear as soon as it is drawn or imported—showing only the handles or points that indicate it is selected. You can immediately click a visible layer to move the object to that layer, or click to the left of the current, unchecked layer name to make that layer visible.

CAUTION (AGAIN)

Make it a habit to always press the Tab key to deselect all objects before clicking a name in the Layers palette—otherwise, the selected elements will be moved to the layer that you next select.

Moving Elements from One Layer to Another

You can move elements from one layer to another by first selecting the elements, then clicking the name of the layer to which you want them moved. If Multilayer is chosen in the Layers palette pop-up menu, you can select elements from several different layers at once and move them to another layer.

Moving Layers

You can rearrange layers by dragging a layer name from one position to another. This moves all of the elements on the layer to a new position with respect to the elements on other layers. If you move a name below the dotted line on the Layers palette, it becomes a non-printing layer. (You can also drag the dotted line to move it in the palette.)

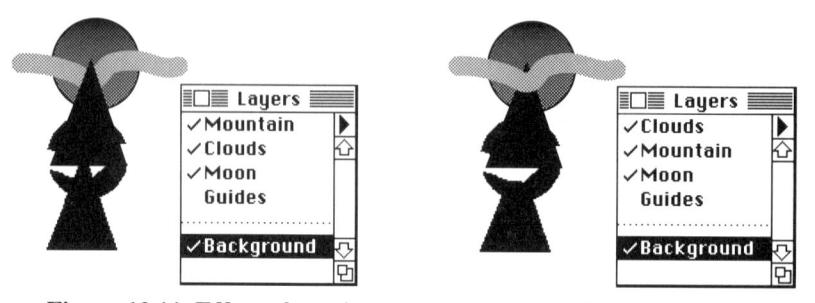

Figure 13.11 Effect of moving layers on the palette

Besides moving layers to the non-printing area below the dotted line on the palette, you can control which layers are printed by making them invisible, as described next.

Making Layers Visible or Invisible

All layers are listed in the Layers palette, but only layers that show a check mark at the left are visible on the screen. You make a layer visible (or invisible) by clicking on the check mark or on the space at the left of the layer name—you do not click the name itself. You can also make a layer visible or invisible by checking Visible in the Layer dialog box that is displayed when you create or edit a layer, or whenever you double-click a layer name in the Layers palette. You can make all layers visible or invisible by choosing All on or All off from the Layers palette pop-up menu.

CAUTION

Make it a habit to always press the Tab key to deselect all objects before clicking a name in the Layers palette—otherwise, the selected elements will be moved to the next layer that you select. (You may notice that this important warning is repeated several times throughout this book.)

TIP

You can print selected layers without rearranging them above and below the background line by making only the layers you wish to print visible, and then choosing Print visible layers only in the Print options dialog box (see the section on the Print command in Chapter 14).

Adding and Editing Layers

Choosing New, Edit, or Copy from the Layers palette pop-up menu results in the Layer dialog box. This dialog box lets you name or rename a layer and set it to visible or invisible. You can add as many layers to your artwork as you like—subject to limitations imposed by your computer's memory.

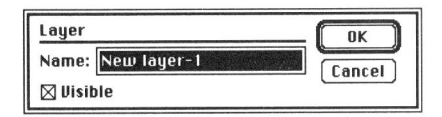

Figure 13.12 The Layer dialog box

When you choose New, a new layer is added to the top of the list—and therefore to the top of all other layers—in the Layers palette. You can move the layer to another location as described later in this section. The new layer becomes the active layer, ready for the next addition to the artwork.

When you choose Edit, all you can do is change the name of the layer or make it visible or invisible.

When you choose Copy, a new layer is added on top of all other layers—*including all of the contents of the layer that was copied*. This can be useful when you want to experiment with a set of elements without changing the originals—you can copy the layer and make one layer invisible while you experiment with the visible set. After the experiment, delete the layer you don't want to keep.

Removing Layers

To remove a layer, click the layer name in the Layers palette and then choose Remove from the palette pop-up menu. The layer *and all objects on it* will be deleted. Because this affects the artwork, FreeHand displays a warning message before deleting the layer. You can also undo the removal by choosing Undo from the Edit menu.

Styles Palette

If your artwork is composed of a large number of objects that fall into a few categories that share the same attributes for fill, line, and halftone screen, you can simplify the process of defining each object by assigning styles. A style is a complete set of attributes that you can define, name, and save as part of the Styles palette for that document. The attributes that can be defined as part of a style are all of the variables that can be specified in the Fill and line dialog box and in the Halftone screen dialog box.

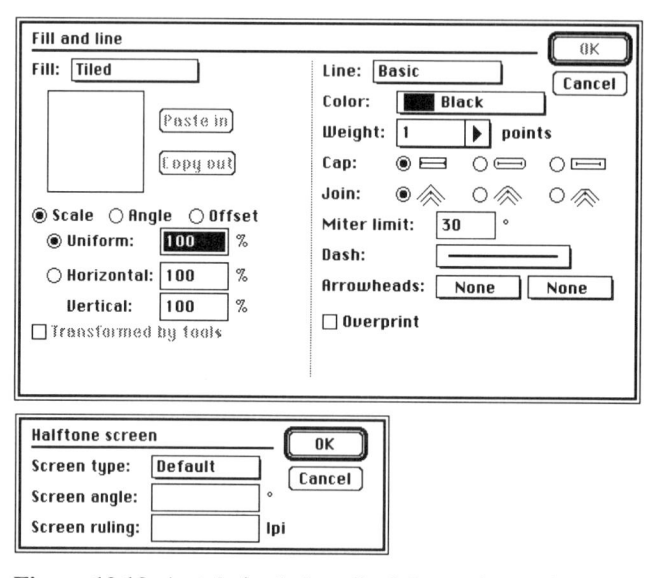

Figure 13.13 A style includes all of the variables in the Fill and line and Halftone screen dialog boxes

Once you set up a style system for a document, you can define a selected object by making selections from the Styles palette instead of using several commands to format each element. If you edit the style later, all elements to which that style was applied will change automatically. This feature makes changing a design idea relatively quick and painless. The next section eulogizes this and several other benefits of using a Styles palette in your work.

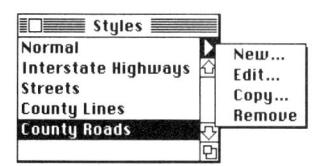

Figure 13.14 A simple style system

Advantages of Using Styles

The Styles palette is a tremendous productivity tool in at least four respects: (1) it reduces the number of steps required to define an object, (2) it simplifies the drawing process by reducing the amount of information you have to remember—letting you focus on the content and the global issues related to design rather than the specific boring details, (3) it embodies "design" and enforces consistency, and (4) it lets you change your design easily.

SAVES TIME

The process of defining an object or creating a style the first time might require opening two dialog boxes, whereas the process of applying the style requires only one step—clicking in the Styles palette. This savings is one of the first benefits of using a style system. You can save hours or days over the life of a project by using a style system for complex illustrations.

A Styles palette also makes it easy to copy a set of attributes from one FreeHand document to another. For example, let's say you want a rectangle in a new document to have the same attributes as a rectangle you have created in another document. Let's say the rectangle has some really eccentric attributes that are hard to recall—like a 2.35-point line weight and a 37% black fill, with a custom dash pattern (or custom miter joints and end caps). Without a Styles palette, you might have to open the first document, select the rectangle, open the Fill and line dialog box and make notes of the specifications, then exit that document, go to the new document, create a new rectangle, and open the Fill and line dialog box to enter the specifications. With a Styles palette, you simply copy the rectangle from the first document into the second document and the style name appears automatically on the Styles palette of the new document.

LIBERATES BRAIN CELLS

If an illustration has many different graphic elements, or if you are creating a series of illustrations that share elements, then a style system can simplify the drawing process by reducing the number of variables that you have to remember or look up. ("Was the line width 1 or 1.25?") This can be especially important when the work on a series of illustrations is shared by different people. Even if the specifications are already clearly written out on paper, when "captured" in the Styles palette, the list of specifications is reduced to a simple list of styles.

SERVES AS DESIGN POLICE

The Styles palette can serve the functions of preserving a design on an aesthetic level, and of enforcing consistency within an illustration and between illustrations—especially if more than one artist is involved in a group project. By incorporating as many of the design specifications as possible into a Styles palette, the production group is aided in preserving the "look" intended.

INCREASES FLEXIBILITY

Styles palettes can serve as "design police," but they actually offer a tremendous amount of flexibility in changing the design of an illustration. Have you ever gone through a complex illustration meticulously setting elements with line widths of .5, 1, and 2 points, and later decided that you wished you had made them 1, 2, and 4 points wide? The change would be a nightmare without a style system, but if a Styles palette was used in the first place you could globally change the line widths for each element simply by changing the settings for each style.

This is especially handy during the initial design stages for a new document. You can test different design ideas by changing the specifications for each style, and quickly print the variations for review by your team or your client.

Applying Styles

As described in the beginning of this chapter, you display the Styles palette by choosing Styles from the Windows command submenu in the View menu. The style of the current selection is highlighted on the palette. A + symbol to the left of the style name indicates that the style has been applied to the object but that subsequent modifications to the object were made directly through the Colors palette, through the Fill and line command, or through the Halftone screen command. (An F or an L at the left of a style name indicates that the styles were created by an earlier version of Aldus FreeHand.)

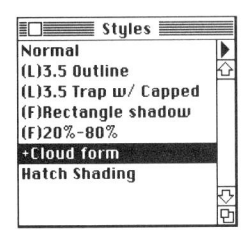

Figure 13.15 Style name is preceded by a + symbol if the object was modified after the style was applied

To apply a style that you have already created to an object through the Styles palette, first select the object, then click the name of the style you want to apply in the Styles palette.

If all of the styles are not visible in the window, you can use the scroll bars to scroll down the list, or drag the size box in the lower right corner of the palette to enlarge the palette. FreeHand always adds new styles to the bottom of the list in the palette, but you can arrange the styles in any order you wish by clicking the style you want to move and dragging it to a new location on the palette.

To re-apply a style to an element that was modified directly through the Colors palette, the Fill and line command, or the Halftone screen command after the style was first applied, first select the object and then click the style name in the Styles palette. The plus sign disappears from the style name, and the element reverts to the original style's attributes.

An F or an L at the left of a style name indicates that the styles were created by an earlier version of Aldus FreeHand. You can apply an F style to assign fill only, an L style to assign line style only, or a +F style to apply both. You can also edit the styles to make them version 3.0 styles.

TIP
When working with Preview turned off, you can quickly see the style of an object by selecting it and viewing the selection in the Styles palette.

Creating Styles

One way to define a style is to first select an element that has already been set up with the attributes that you want to use in the style. Next, choose New from the Styles palette pop-up menu, type the name of the new style in the Styles dialog box, click Apply (if it is not already checked), then click OK to close the dialog box and apply the style to the selected element. Do not click Apply if you do not want the selected element to be affected by changes you make to that style later. In either case, the appearance of the element does not change when you first create the style (unless you make additional adjustments by clicking the Fill and line button or the Halftone button in the Styles dialog box), but the style name is added to the Styles palette.

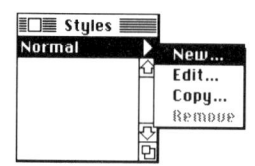

Figure 13.16 The Styles palette with pop-up menu

To create a new style before creating any elements with the desired style attributes, press Tab to make sure that no elements are selected on the artwork, then choose New from the Styles palette pop-up menu, or choose Styles from the Attributes menu. In the Styles dialog box, type the new style name. If you have already defined other styles, you can base the new style on an existing style by choosing from the Based on pop-up menu. (See the following discussion about based-on styles.)

Figure 13.17 The Styles dialog box

Click Fill and line to display the Fill and line dialog box and make changes. Click Halftone to display the Halftone screen dialog box and make changes. These dialog boxes are described in the sections on the Fill and line and Halftone screens commands in Chapter 14.

If you want to create a new style based on an existing style, you simply double-click a style name in the Styles palette to display the Styles dialog box, then choose New style from the Styles pop-up menu and continue as described for creating a new style.

ABOUT BASED-ON STYLES

As discussed above, you can create a new style *based on* another style. This automatically sets up the Fill and line and Halftone screen dialog boxes for the new style exactly as they are set up for the style on which the new style is based. You can then change only those attributes that differ between the two styles.

Besides saving a few clicks and drags in a dialog box, basing a style on another brings another advantage: whenever you change the *parent* style on which other styles are based, the changed attributes will automatically change for the *descendant* styles—unless those attributes were modified in creating the descendant.

A specific example will help you visualize this: Let's say you set up a style named Gray Fill 1 with a 50% gray fill and a 1-point black line. Next, you create a style named Gray Fill 4—*based on* Gray Fill 1—with the same 50% fill but a 4-point line. The next figure shows two rectangles set with these styles.

Figure 13.18 Gray Fill 1 style (left) and Gray Fill 4 style (right)

Next, you edit the Gray Fill 1 style to have an 80% gray fill and an 8-point patterned line. The fill and line of all objects to which Gray Fill 1 is applied will change automatically. The fill percentage for Gray Fill 4, and all objects to which that style was applied, will automatically change to 80% because Gray Fill 4 was based on Gray Fill 1. The line weight for Gray Fill 4 will not change, however, because that attribute was not shared by the two styles.

Figure 13.19 After fill and line weight were changed for the parent style

CAUTION

This relationship between parents and descendants can be a disadvantage when you don't want changes to the original style to be reflected in the newer style that was based on the old one. Build relationships between your styles carefully to avoid unexpected results.

If you want to create a new style that is similar to an existing style but not *based on* that style, use the Copy command as described next.

Copying a Style in the Palette

You can create a new style that is similar to an existing style, but not based on any style, by first clicking the name of the style you want to copy and then choosing Copy from the palette pop-up menu.

Copying Styles from One Illustration to Another

You can copy styles from one illustration to another. Simply select elements from the illustration that have been formatted with the style(s) you wish to copy and use the Copy command from the Edit menu to copy them to the Clipboard. Next, open the document into which you want to copy the styles and choose Paste from the Edit menu. The pasted elements bring their styles with them. The style names are added to the Styles palette automatically, and you can then delete the copied elements from the second document.

Chapter 6 includes a technique for creating a style template.

CAUTION
If styles already exist in the second document that use the same names as the copied styles, the second document's style attributes will remain unchanged.

Editing Styles

You can edit any style listed in the Styles palette, including Normal. To edit an existing style, you can simply double-click the style name in the palette to display the Styles dialog box. Double-clicking is the quicker alternative to choosing the style and then choosing Edit from the palette pop-up menu, or choosing Styles from the Attributes menu.

When you change a style, all of the elements in the artwork to which that style applies will be changed automatically to match the new style specifications. Any elements assigned styles that were based on the changed style might also change, as described earlier in "About Based-on Styles." If you want to change a color without changing the artwork, you can create a new color based on the existing color.

Removing Styles from the Palette

You can remove a style from the list in the Styles palette by selecting the style and then choosing Remove from the Styles palette pop-up menu. Make sure no objects are selected when you click the style in the palette, or you might inadvertently apply the style to the selection before deleting the style. When you delete styles that are currently applied to objects in the artwork, the objects retain their attributes but they become associated with Normal style. They are identified as "modified" Normal (i.e., a + symbol appears to the left of the Normal style name in the Styles palette when the object is selected).

14

Menu Commands

This chapter explains how to choose commands and make dialog box entries, and describes all of the menus in FreeHand and the commands they contain.

Choosing a Command

FreeHand, like all applications that run on a Macintosh, displays a menu bar at the top of the screen, listing the names of the menus of available commands. Commands are displayed below each menu title. To choose a command, position the mouse pointer over the menu title, hold down the mouse button, drag down the menu until the desired item is highlighted, then release the mouse button.

You can select some commands using keyboard shortcuts instead of the mouse. The shortcuts are listed on the menus next to those commands that have them. A ⌘ symbol represents the Command key, an up arrow symbol (⇧) indicates the Shift key, and a ⌥ symbol represents the Option key.

Some of the command names displayed on the menus are followed by an ellipsis (. . .). Whenever you use one of these commands, a dialog box will be displayed, letting you select from various options, enter information required by the command, or cancel the command. Note that commands that are not followed by an ellipsis have an immediate result that can only be canceled by using the Undo command. Some operations cannot be undone.

Some commands, such as the Font, Size, Leading, Type style, Effect, and Alignment commands displayed in the Type menu, are followed by a right-facing triangle. When you hold down the mouse button on one of these commands, a hierarchical submenu appears beside the menu command. To select a command from the submenu, drag across to the submenu, then drag down the submenu until the item you want is highlighted, and release the mouse button.

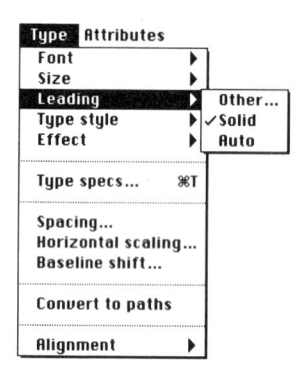

Figure 14.1 The Type menu and the Leading submenu

Dialog Box Entries

Commands followed by an ellipsis in a menu result in the display of a dialog box on the screen. Most dialog boxes can be moved around by dragging the title bar, just as any other window can be moved. A dialog box may contain any or all of the following:

- Warnings or messages
- Edit boxes for typing text or numbers
- Pop-up menus that let you choose from a list of alternatives
- Scrolling lists of fonts or file names
- Check boxes that let you choose one or more options from a list
- Radio buttons, small circular buttons that are used to select one option from a list of several mutually exclusive choices
- Larger rectangular option buttons that close the dialog box, offering options such as OK and Cancel, or that open additional dialog boxes

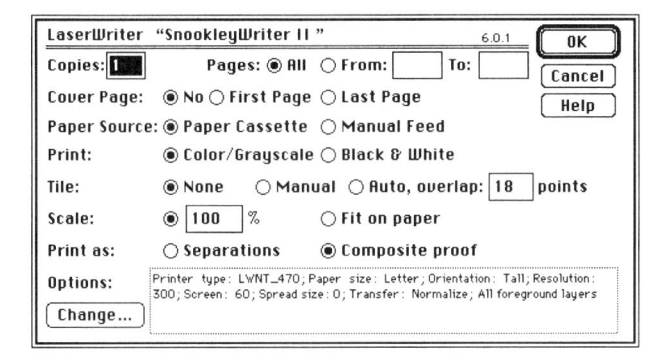

```
LaserWriter  "SnookleyWriter II"                    6.0.1    [  OK  ]
Copies: [1]         Pages: ⦿ All  ○ From: [   ] To: [   ]   [Cancel]
Cover Page:    ⦿ No ○ First Page  ○ Last Page              [ Help ]
Paper Source: ⦿ Paper Cassette  ○ Manual Feed
Print:         ⦿ Color/Grayscale  ○ Black & White
Tile:          ⦿ None    ○ Manual   ○ Auto, overlap: [18] points
Scale:         ⦿ [100] %   ○ Fit on paper
Print as:      ○ Separations   ⦿ Composite proof
Options:       Printer type: LWNT_470; Paper size: Letter; Orientation: Tall; Resolution:
               300; Screen: 60; Spread size: 0; Transfer: Normalize; All foreground layers
[Change...]
```

Figure 14.2 The Print dialog box for PostScript printers

Some of the general procedures that apply to all dialog boxes are described here. Specific dialog box entries are described in detail in the sections on their specific commands later in this chapter.

WARNINGS OR MESSAGES

If the dialog box displays only the text of a warning or message, you can either click OK (to indicate that you have read the message) or Cancel (to indicate that you have read the warning and wish to cancel the current command).

EDIT BOXES

If there are edit boxes for typing text or numbers in the dialog box, the cursor will normally be positioned in the first such box when the dialog box opens. You can move the cursor from one edit box to another by clicking the text label that describes the entry; or using the mouse to position the pointer inside the edit box and clicking to position the cursor; or by pressing the Tab key. You can select text inside an edit box by clicking the text label that describes the entry to select all of the text; using the mouse to drag the cursor over the text; double-clicking to select a word; or tabbing into the edit box to select all of the text.

POP-UP MENUS

Some edit boxes are framed by a drop-shadow, indicating that you can choose from a list of alternatives by holding down the mouse button as you click the edit box to display the pop-up menu, then dragging the mouse to make your selection.

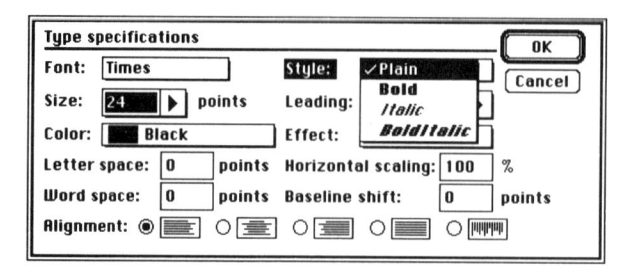

Figure 14.3 The Style pop-up menu from the Type specifications dialog box

SCROLLING LISTS

Lists of file names or Pantone colors are often displayed in a small window within the dialog box, with scroll bars on the right for moving up or down the list. You select from a scrolling list by using the scroll bar (if necessary) to find the name you wish to select, then clicking on the name to highlight it. In most cases, you can jump ahead in a long alphabetical list by typing the first letter of the name you wish to choose.

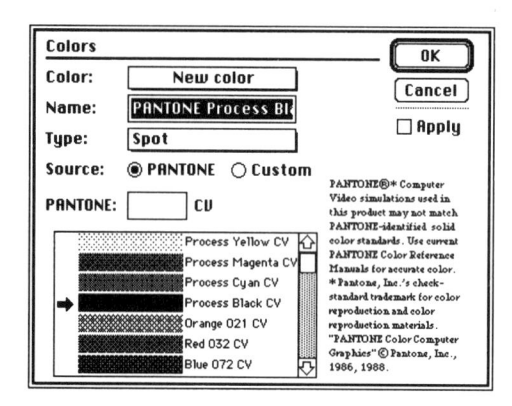

Figure 14.4 The PANTONE colors list in the Colors dialog box

CHECK BOXES

You can choose one or more options from a list that displays check boxes. Options that are selected show an x inside the box. Otherwise, an empty check box indicates that the option is not selected. Check boxes are toggles: clicking an empty box selects the option, clicking a box with an x deselects the option. You can also select or deselect these options by clicking the text label that describes the entry.

RADIO BUTTONS

Small circular buttons are used to select one option from a list of several mutually exclusive choices. The current selection is indicated by a dark circle inside the button. You can change the selection by clicking another button in the list, or by clicking anywhere on the text label that describes that option.

OPTION BUTTONS

Larger rectangular buttons are used to close the dialog box, offering options such as OK and Cancel, or to open additional dialog boxes. Often, one option button is framed in a double-rule border, indicating that pressing the Return key will have the same effect as clicking that button.

ENTERING MEASUREMENTS

FreeHand offers unique flexibility in entering measurements in any dialog box. Regardless of the unit of measure that is currently displayed, you can enter a new value in inches, millimeters, or picas and points. To enter a measure in units other than the current default unit of measure, simply indicate the measurement system using the following abbreviations.

Units	Abbreviation	Example
Inches	i	1i
Millimeters	m	1m
Picas	p	1p
Points		1p3
		(one pica, three points)

You can enter most measurements in increments as fine as 0.0001 of a point, and you can enter font sizes from 0.1 to 3,000 points.

398 Using Aldus FreeHand 3.0

The Apple Menu

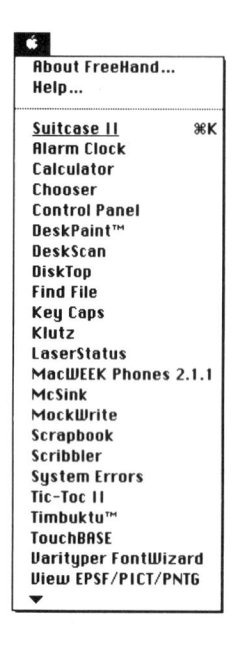

```
About FreeHand...
Help...

Suitcase II          ⌘K
Alarm Clock
Calculator
Chooser
Control Panel
DeskPaint™
DeskScan
DiskTop
Find File
Key Caps
Klutz
LaserStatus
MacWEEK Phones 2.1.1
McSink
MockWrite
Scrapbook
Scribbler
System Errors
Tic-Toc II
Timbuktu™
TouchBASE
Varityper FontWizard
View EPSF/PICT/PNTG
▼
```

Figure 14.5 The Apple menu under System 6.0.5

The Apple menu is always displayed at the top left corner of the screen. It lists all of the Macintosh desk accessories that you have installed in your System Folder, along with two commands specific to FreeHand: About FreeHand and Help.

This section describes the About FreeHand and Help commands and other Apple menu desk accessories that are especially useful with Free-Hand, including the Control Panel (for setting up color display on a Macintosh II), and the Chooser.

Under Macintosh System 6.0.x, you can add desk accessories to the Apple menu using the Font/DA Mover application program that is supplied by Apple on the Macintosh system disk, or on the desk accessory's installation program. You can also add fonts to the System using the Font/DA Mover application. If you use MultiFinder, the titles of any open applications also appear in the Apple Menu.

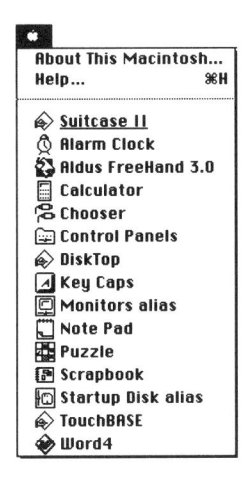

```
┌─────────────────────────┐
│ ■                       │
│ About This Macintosh... │
│ Help...            ⌘H   │
│─────────────────────────│
│ ◈ Suitcase II           │
│ ⏰ Alarm Clock          │
│ 🔷 Aldus FreeHand 3.0   │
│ 🖩 Calculator           │
│ 👤 Chooser              │
│ 📋 Control Panels       │
│ ◈ DiskTop               │
│ 🅰 Key Caps             │
│ 🖥 Monitors alias       │
│ 📝 Note Pad             │
│ 🧩 Puzzle               │
│ 📖 Scrapbook            │
│ 💾 Startup Disk alias   │
│ ◈ TouchBASE             │
│ ◆ Word4                 │
└─────────────────────────┘
```

Figure 14.6 The Apple menu under System 7.0

Under Macintosh System 7.0, you install desk accessories by dragging them into the Apple Menu Items folder inside the System Folder, and you install fonts by simply dragging them into the System File inside the System Folder. Similarly, you can add applications, documents, or folders to the Apple menu by placing them in the Apple Menu Items Folder, or you can make an alias and place the alias in the Apple Menu Items folder.

Refer to your Macintosh user manual for more information on how to configure the Apple menu.

About FreeHand...

Choosing About FreeHand from the Apple menu displays a dialog box that shows the version of FreeHand you are using, the version of the System software you are using, the authors of FreeHand, a copyright notice, and the amount of free memory available (in bytes). As your artwork becomes larger, the free memory will decrease. The dialog box also has a control button that lets you go to the Help screens.

PROCEDURE

Choose About FreeHand from the Apple menu after you have started FreeHand by double-clicking the program icon on the desktop.

Help...

Choosing Help from the Apple menu displays a dialog box that lets you read help text for commands or topics.

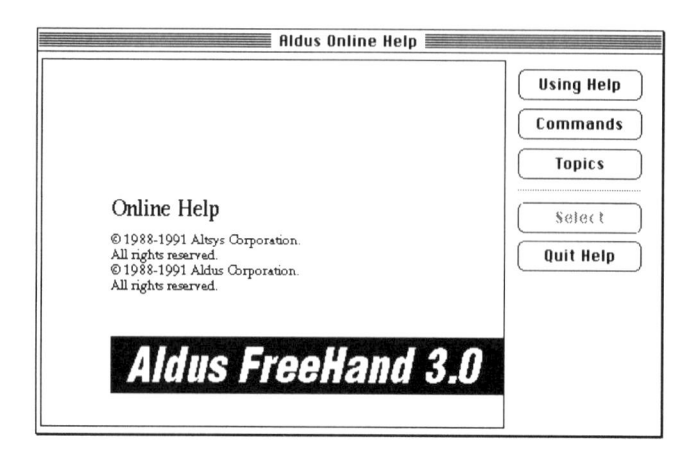

Figure 14.7 The Help dialog box

PROCEDURE

Choose Help from the Apple menu to display the Help dialog box. Click **Using Help** for an explanation of how to use the Help system.

Click **Commands** to display a list of the commands available in FreeHand. You can select the help text for a command by highlighting the command name in the scrolling list and clicking **Select**, or by double-clicking the command name in the scrolling list. The help text for the selected command appears. When the help text is too long to fit in the window, a scroll bar to the right of the text lets you scroll through the text. A pop-up menu entitled **More Help** contains the names of related commands and topics. Choosing one of these opens the help text for that command or topic.

Click **Topics** to display a list of topics for which online help is available. Help topics are divided into groups: topic group names appear in all caps, with a bullet at the start of the name. The subtopics appear in normal text below the group headings. You can select the help text for a topic or subtopic by highlighting its name in the scrolling list and clicking Select, or by double-clicking its name in the scrolling list. The help text for the selected topic or subtopic appears. A pop-up menu entitled More Help contains the names of related topics, subtopics, or commands. Choosing one of these opens the relevant help text.

Click **Select** to open the help text for a selected Command or Topic name. When no Command or Topic name is selected, this button is dimmed, indicating that it is inactive. Click **Quit Help** to close the Help dialog box.

Chooser

The AppleTalk network and AppleShare software allows Macintosh computers to share printers and file servers. The Chooser lets you select which printer you will use to print your artwork, or select a file server that you wish to access.

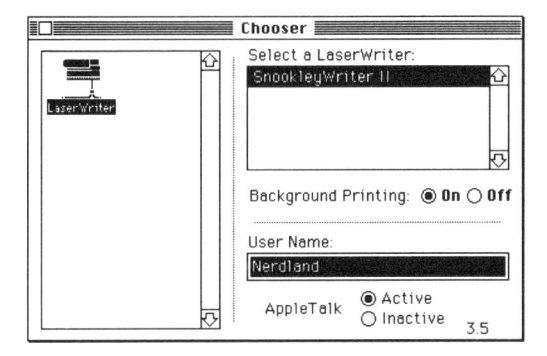

Figure 14.8   The Chooser dialog box

PROCEDURE

Select the Chooser from the Apple menu. Click a printer driver icon or the AppleShare icon. A list of all available devices will appear. Then click the appropriate device name. If you are running MultiFinder or System 7.0, you can turn on background printing by clicking the Background Printing On radio button. Click the close box when you are done.

CAUTION

The dialog box displays only those devices for which the power switch is on. If the full list of printers on your network is not displayed, it may be due to a loose cable connection between your machine and the printer.

Background printing lets you work while a document is printing, but it can severely degrade the performance of the foreground application.

Control Panel

Choosing Control Panel from the Apple menu displays the Control Panel, which is standard with Macintosh System software version 4.1 through 6.0.x. A scrolling list of icons in the left part of the General Control Panel provides access to different system functions. Under System 7.0, the Control Panel is a normal Finder window, and can display individual control icons in icon or list view. Using the Control Panel, you can change some of the configuration settings of your Macintosh, including the desktop pattern, the blinking rate of the text insertion point, the blinking rate of pull-down menus, the system time, the system date, the date format (a 12-hour or 24-hour clock), the speaker volume, the amount of RAM cache in use, and whether the RAM cache is on or off.

The icons represent different parts of your Macintosh System configuration. Two of these are of particular interest to FreeHand users: the General Control Panel (or the Memory Control Panel under System 7.0) and the Monitors Control Panel (for setting color display on the Macintosh II).

PROCEDURE

Choose Control Panel from the Apple menu. The Control Panel window appears, as shown in the next figure. When you have made the desired adjustments, click the close box to close the window. Under System 7.0, you must double-click a Control Panel icon to activate it. Under earlier versions of the System software, a single click activates Control Panel icons.

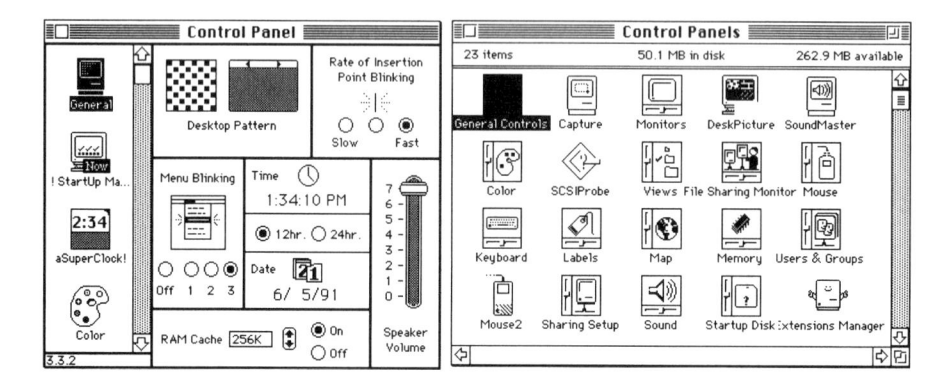

Figure 14.9 The General Control Panel (System 6.0.x). The Control Panel Window (System 7.0)

SETTING THE RAM CACHE

Click the **General** icon in the Control Panel (under System 6.0.x) or the Memory Control Panel (under System 7.0) to gain access to the RAM cache controls. If you are running FreeHand on a Macintosh equipped with only 2 MB of RAM, you should turn the RAM cache off. If you have more RAM available, you can use the RAM cache to boost system performance.

SETTING THE NUMBER OF COLORS THE MONITOR DISPLAYS

If you are using a Macintosh II equipped with a color monitor and you want to display your artwork in color, you can set the monitor to 4, 16, 256, or to millions of colors, depending on the video card you have installed. To do this, click the **Monitors** icon in the left column of the Control Panel and make the appropriate selections by scrolling through the Colors scroll box and then clicking the desired number of colors, as shown in the next figure.

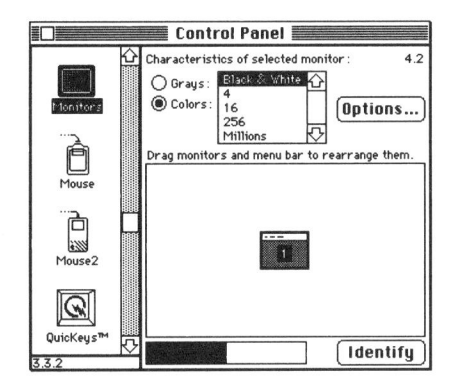

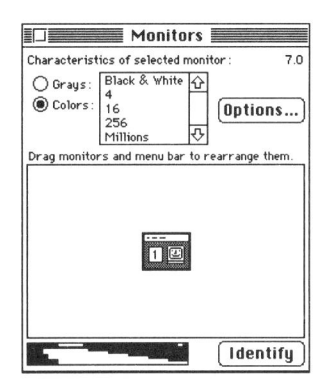

Figure 14.10 The Monitors Control Panel (System 6.0.x and System 7.0)

TIP

If you do not need color, you can speed up screen response and save memory by selecting black-and-white in the Monitors Control Panel. Displaying millions of colors can slow screen redrawing. If you need to work with millions of colors on a regular basis, you may want to install an accelerated video card. Working in 256-color mode is a good compromise for most situations.

CAUTION

FreeHand does not display all colors accurately in 4- or 16-color modes.

404   Using Aldus FreeHand 3.0

The File Menu

Figure 14.11 The File menu

The File menu contains commands that apply to entire FreeHand documents, or to documents created in another application that you want to either convert to FreeHand documents or import into a FreeHand file. When you start a FreeHand session, the File menu will usually be the first menu you use. You use File menu commands to open new or existing FreeHand files; to convert other files into FreeHand format; to import other files into your illustration; to export FreeHand files in another format; to close and save FreeHand files you are working on; to discard changes you have made to a FreeHand document and revert to the last version you saved; to prepare files for printing and to print FreeHand artwork; and to quit a FreeHand session.

New...

The New command creates a new FreeHand document. The keyboard shortcut is ⌘N. Choosing the New command first opens the Document setup dialog box, where you specify the size and orientation of your document, the unit of measurement used, the frequency of the visible and invisible alignment grids, and the resolution of the target printer. When you have made these settings and closed the dialog box, FreeHand opens a new, untitled artwork window.

PROCEDURE

Choose New from the File menu, or press ⌘N. The Document setup dialog box appears, where you set specifications for your document.

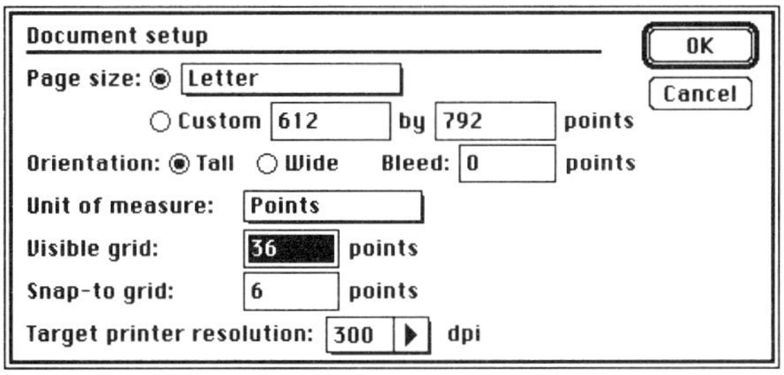

```
Document setup                              [  OK  ]
Page size: ⦿ [Letter    ]
                                            [ Cancel ]
           ○ Custom [612  ] by [792 ] points
Orientation: ⦿ Tall  ○ Wide  Bleed: [0] points
Unit of measure:    [Points]
Visible grid:       [ 36  ] points
Snap-to grid:       [  6  ] points
Target printer resolution: [300 ▶] dpi
```

Figure 14.12 The Document setup dialog box

Page size determines the size of the page that will appear in the document window. You can draw anywhere in the window, but only those elements placed on the page, or within the specified bleed area, will print. Hence the page size you enter in the Document setup dialog box determines the area that will print. It is not necessarily the same as the size of the paper on which the artwork will be printed. You can define a page size that is smaller than the paper you will use, or you can tile a larger illustration onto several sheets of paper. (See the discussion of tiling in the section on the Print command below.) You can choose one of the default page sizes from the Page size pop-up menu, or you can enter dimensions for a custom page size by clicking the Custom radio button and entering the dimensions in the adjacent edit boxes.

Choose **Tall Orientation** if you want the page to be taller than it is wide, and **Wide Orientation** if you want it to be wider than it is tall.

If you want to create an illustration that bleeds, or prints to the very edge of the final printed and trimmed page, you can specify a bleed area that extends beyond the edges of the page by entering a value in the **Bleed** edit box. The bleed area is represented in the artwork window by a non-printing dotted line around the page. Elements that extend beyond the page boundary into the bleed area print to the outer edge of the bleed area.

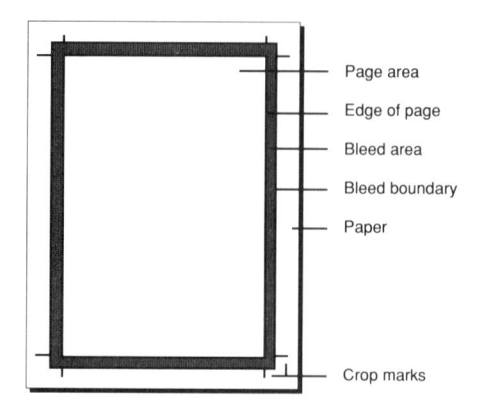

Figure 14.13 The bleed area

Choose your preferred unit of measurement from the **Unit of measure** pop-up menu. The choices are Points, Picas, Inches, Decimal Inches, and Millimeters. The unit of measurement you choose here will apply to all measurements shown in the rulers, in the information bar, and in all of FreeHand's dialog boxes.

Enter spacing values for the **Visible grid** and the **Snap-to grid** in the Visible grid and Snap-to grid edit boxes. The visible grid appears when you choose Grid from the View menu, while the invisible snap-to grid is activated by choosing Snap to grid from the View menu. You can set the grids independently of each other, but you will probably want to make sure that the snap-to grid falls on the intersections of the visible grid. To do so, make sure that the number you enter for the snap-to grid is either equal to, or divides evenly into, the number you enter for the visible grid. The default is 36 points for the visible grid and 6 points for the snap-to grid. At these settings, every sixth snap-to point falls on a visible grid intersection. (See the sections on the View menu's Grid command and Snap to grid command later in this chapter.) The minimum size you can specify for either grid is 1 point, and the maximum size is 864 points (or their equivalent in the chosen unit of measure).

Under **Target printer resolution**, enter the resolution (in dots per inch) of the printer you will use for the *final* output of your artwork. For example, if you use a 300 dpi laser printer for proofing, and a 2450 dpi imagesetter for final output, you should enter the imagesetter's resolution, 2450, in the Target printer resolution edit box. FreeHand uses the value entered here for resizing imported TIFF and bitmap images to get the best resolution possible, and for avoiding printer memory problems in complex illustrations. Printer resolution is always measured in dots per inch, so the number you enter is not affected by the unit of measure you choose under Unit of measure. FreeHand supports printer resolutions from 72 dpi to 5080 dpi. You can choose one of the available resolutions from the pop-up menu, or you can specify a target resolution by typing a number into the edit box.

TIP
When you enter measurements in dialog boxes, you can always override the unit of measure chosen in Document setup.

- To enter a value in points, type "p" *before* the number, as in p6 for 6 points.
- To enter a value in picas, type "p" *after* the number, as in 18p for 18 picas.
- To enter a value in picas and points, type "p" *between* the number of picas and the number of points, as in 9p6 for 9 picas and 6 points.
- To enter a value in inches, type "i" after the number, as in 4i for 4 inches.
- To enter a value in millimeters, type "m" after the number, as in 24m for 24 millimeters.

Open...

The Open command opens an existing document. The keyboard shortcut is ⌘O. You can use it to open existing FreeHand 3.0 documents, or to convert documents in FreeHand 1.0, FreeHand 2.0, FreeHand 2.02, Adobe Illustrator 1.1, or PICT format documents to FreeHand 3.0 format. When you open a document other than a FreeHand 3.0 document, FreeHand converts it and opens a new untitled document, leaving the original document unchanged on disk.

You can have more than one document open at a time. The actual number of documents you can open simultaneously depends on the amount of RAM you have available, and the complexity of the documents.

PROCEDURE
Choose Open from the File menu, or press ⌘O. The Open dialog box appears, containing a scrolling list of documents in the current folder or disk that FreeHand 3.0 can open. The folder or disk name is displayed in a pop-up menu above the files list. You can navigate up through the

hierarchy of folders by choosing a higher folder from the pop-up menu, or switch to a different disk by clicking the Drive button (or the Desktop button under System 7.0).

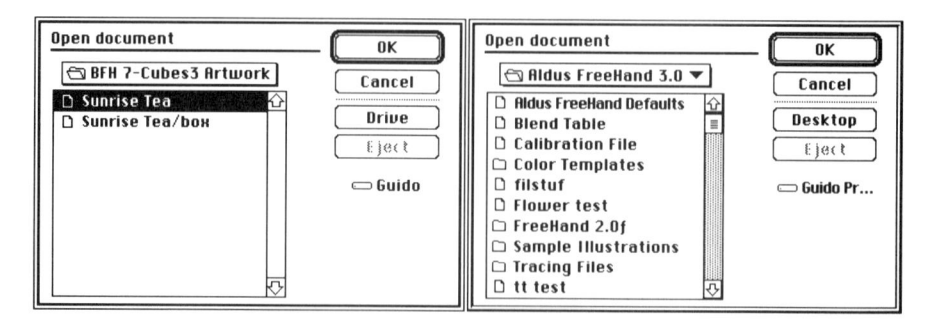

```
Open document                          OK
  BFH 7-Cubes3 Artwork              Cancel
  Sunrise Tea
  Sunrise Tea/box                    Drive
                                     Eject
                                    Guido
```

```
Open document                          OK
  Aldus FreeHand 3.0 ▼              Cancel
  Aldus FreeHand Defaults
  Blend Table                        Desktop
  Calibration File                    Eject
  Color Templates
  filstuf                           Guido Pr...
  Flower test
  FreeHand 2.0f
  Sample Illustrations
  Tracing Files
  tt test
```

Figure 14.14 **The Open dialog box (System 6.0.x). The Open dialog box (System 7.0)**

Once you have found the document you want to open, you can open it by selecting the document's name in the scrolling list and clicking the OK button, or by double-clicking the document name in the list. If the document is a FreeHand 3.0 illustration, it will open. If it is a FreeHand template, a copy of the illustration will appear in a new, untitled window. (See "Save as" below.) If the document is in one of the other formats FreeHand 3.0 can open, a message will appear telling you that FreeHand is converting the document. When the conversion is complete, FreeHand will open a new, untitled document with the artwork converted to FreeHand 3.0 format, leaving the original document unchanged.

Click the Cancel button to cancel the command. Click the Eject button to eject a floppy disk. (The Eject button is dimmed unless the current disk is a floppy disk or a removable cartridge.)

TIP

You can use the keyboard to navigate in the Open dialog box. Press the Up Arrow and Down Arrow keys to move up and down through the scrolling list, and press ⌘Up Arrow to move up through the hierarchy of folders. You can also type the first few letters of a document's name to move quickly to that document in the scrolling list.

Close

The Close command closes the current document. Its effect is the same as clicking the active window's close box.

PROCEDURE

Choose Close from the File menu. The current document closes. If you close a document containing unsaved changes, a message box appears giving you the opportunity to save the changes to the document before closing. Clicking Yes saves the changes to the document. Clicking No closes the document without saving the changes. Clicking Cancel returns you to the current document and cancels the Close command.

Save

The Save command saves changes to an open document, overwriting the previous version. The keyboard shortcut is ⌘S.

PROCEDURE

Choose Save from the File menu, or press ⌘S. FreeHand saves the changes you have made to the document since the last time you saved, overwriting the previous version. Unlike many other commands in FreeHand, the effects of the Save command cannot be reversed by using the Undo command. If you want to keep the original document, you should use the Save as command to save the changed artwork under a different name or in a different location. When you first save a new, untitled document, the Save document as dialog box appears, allowing you to name the document and save it in the desired location. (See "Save as" below.)

Save as...

The Save as command lets you save an illustration under a different name, save an illustration in a different folder or disk, or save an illustration as a template. When you use the Save command for the first time with a new, untitled document, it acts like the Save as command.

PROCEDURE

Choose Save as from the File menu. The Save document as dialog box appears, containing a scrolling list of files and folders. The file names are grayed, indicating that you cannot take any action on them, while the folder names are black, indicating that you can open them. The name of the current folder or disk appears in a pop-up menu above the scrolling list.

You can navigate up through the hierarchy of folders by choosing a higher folder from the pop-up menu, or switch to a different disk by clicking the Drive button (or the Desktop button under System 7.0). When you click OK to save the document, it will be saved in the folder or disk whose name appears in the pop-up menu.

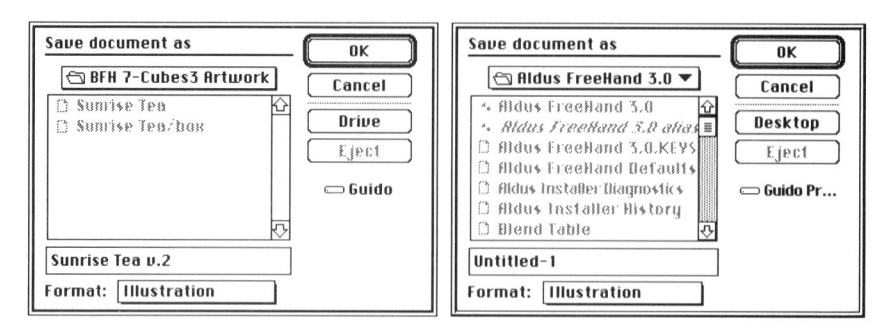

Figure 14.15 The Save document as dialog box (System 6.0.x). The Save document as dialog box (System 7.0)

An edit box below the scrolling list contains the current name of the document, and the name is highlighted, ready for you to type a new one. (If you are saving a new document for the first time, the document name appears as Untitled-1.)

The Format pop-up menu lets you save the document as an illustration or as a template. A template contains all the same elements as an illustration, but it cannot be modified. When you open a template, FreeHand opens a copy of the template as a new, untitled illustration, leaving the original unchanged. To modify a template, make the desired changes to the untitled copy, then save it as a template. You can replace the original template by saving the new one in the same place with the same name. A message box will appear asking you to confirm that you want to replace the template.

Click the Cancel button to cancel the Save as command. Click the Eject button to eject a floppy disk. (The Eject button is dimmed unless the current disk is a floppy disk or a removable cartridge.)

- To save a document for the first time, or under a different name, choose Save as from the File menu, type a name for the document, then click OK.
- To save a document in a different location, choose Save as from the File menu, use the Drive button (the Desktop button in System 7.0) to switch

disks if desired, select the folder into which you want to save the file, then click OK.

- To save a document as a template, choose Save as from the File menu, choose Template from the Format pop-up menu, type a new name if desired, then click OK.

Revert

The Revert command returns a document to the state it was in when it was last saved, discarding any changes that have since been made.

PROCEDURE

Choose Revert from the File menu. A message appears asking you to confirm that you want to revert to the last version you saved. Click OK to revert to the last saved version, discarding any changes you have made since you last saved the document. Click Cancel to cancel the Revert command, keeping intact any changes you have made since you last saved the document.

CAUTION

Unlike most operations in FreeHand, you cannot reverse the effects of the Revert command by choosing Undo from the Edit menu.

Document setup...

The Document setup command opens the Document setup dialog box, where you can set specifications that apply to the whole document. This is the same dialog box that appears when you first create a new illustration. You can use the Document setup command to change any or all of the specifications you set when you first created the document.

Changing the document setup does not change any of the illustration elements. It may, however, move the entire illustration relative to the page. For example, if you change a large page size to a much smaller one, some of the elements in the illustration may be moved off the page, hence they will no longer print.

PROCEDURE

Choose Document setup from the File menu. The Document setup dialog box appears, where you can change the page size and orientation, specify a bleed area, choose a different unit of measure, change the spacing of the visible and invisible grids, and specify a new target printer resolution.

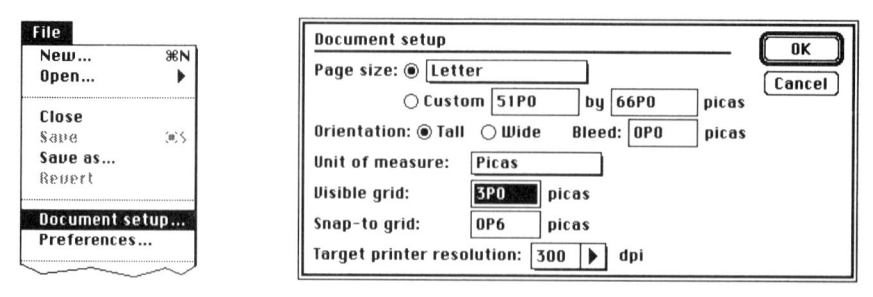

Figure 14.16 The Document setup dialog box

Page size determines the size of the page that will appear in the document window. You can draw anywhere in the window, but only those elements placed on the page will print. Hence the page size you enter in the Document setup dialog box determines the area that will print. It is not necessarily the same as the size of the paper on which the artwork will be printed. You can define a page size that is smaller than the paper you will use, or you can tile a larger illustration onto several sheets of paper. (See the description of tiling in "The Print dialog box" below.) You can choose one of the default page sizes from the Page size pop-up menu, or you can enter dimensions for a custom page size by clicking the Custom radio button and entering the dimensions in the adjacent edit boxes.

Choose **Tall Orientation** if you want the page to be taller than it is wide, and **Wide Orientation** if you want it to be wider than it is tall.

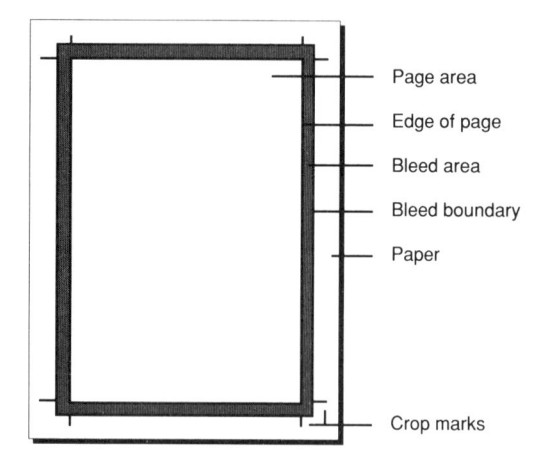

Figure 14.17 The bleed area

If you want to create an illustration that bleeds, or prints to the very edge of the final printed and trimmed page, you can specify a bleed area that extends beyond the edges of the page by entering a value in the **Bleed** edit box. The bleed area is represented in the artwork window by a non-printing dotted line around the page. Elements that extend beyond the page boundary into the bleed area will print to the outer edge of the bleed area.

Choose your preferred unit of measurement from the **Unit of measure** pop-up menu. The choices are Points, Picas, Inches, Decimal Inches, and Millimeters. The unit of measurement you choose here will apply to all measurements shown in the rulers, in the information bar, and in dialog boxes.

Enter spacing values for the **Visible grid** and the **Snap-to grid** in the Visible grid and Snap-to grid edit boxes. The visible grid appears when you choose Grid from the View menu, while the invisible snap-to grid is activated by choosing Snap to grid from the View menu. You can set the grids independently of each other, but you will probably want to make sure that the snap-to grid falls on the intersections of the visible grid. To do so, make sure that the number you enter for the snap-to grid is either equal to, or divides evenly into, the number you enter for the visible grid. The default is 36 points for the visible grid and 6 points for the snap-to grid. At these settings, every sixth snap-to point falls on a visible grid intersection. (See the descriptions of the View menu's Grid command and Snap to grid command later in this chapter.) The minimum size you can specify for either grid is 1 point, and the maximum size is 864 points (or their equivalent in the chosen unit of measure).

Under **Target printer resolution**, enter the resolution (in dots per inch) of the printer you will use for the *final* output of your artwork. For example, if you use a 300 dpi laser printer for proofing, and a 2450 dpi imagesetter for final output, you should enter the imagesetter's resolution, 2450, in the Target printer resolution edit box. FreeHand uses the value entered here for resizing imported TIFF and bitmap images to get the best resolution possible, and for avoiding printer memory problems in complex illustrations. Printer resolution is always measured in dots per inch, so the number you enter is not affected by the unit of measure you choose under Unit of measure. FreeHand supports printer resolutions from 72 dpi to 5080 dpi.

TIP

When you enter measurements in dialog boxes, you can always override the unit of measure chosen in Document setup.

- To enter a value in points, type "p" *before* the number, as in p6 for 6 points.
- To enter a value in picas, type "p" *after* the number, as in 18p for 18 picas.
- To enter a value in picas and points, type "p" *between* the number of picas and the number of points, as in 9p6 for 9 picas and 6 points.
- To enter a value in inches, type "i" after the number, as in 4i for 4 inches.
- To enter a value in millimeters, type "m" after the number, as in 24m for 24 millimeters.

CAUTION

If you change the page size, any existing artwork maintains its position relative to the bottom left corner of the page. Changing a large page size to a small one may force part of the artwork off the pasteboard area, and could result in changes to the top and right edges of the artwork.

Preferences...

The Preferences command lets you select options that affect the FreeHand drawing environment in all illustrations. Changes you make using the Preferences command stay in effect until you change them again. You can change Preference options at any time.

PROCEDURE

Choose Preferences from the File menu. The Preferences dialog box appears, where you can select various options that affect the FreeHand drawing environment.

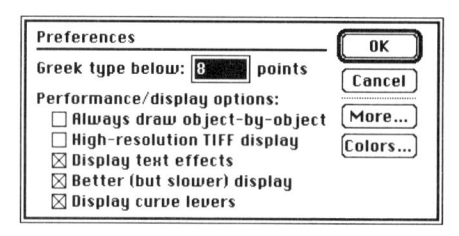

Figure 14.18 The Preferences dialog box

THE PREFERENCES DIALOG BOX

Enter a value in **Greek type below** to control the minimum size at which text is displayed as type. Type that is smaller than the size you enter appears on the screen as gray bars that show the line length and spacing. This is known as "greeked" type. Greeking type speeds up screen redrawing. For example, if you enter a value of 10 in the Greek type below box, 12-point text will display normally when viewed at actual size. If you change the view to 50% size, 12-point text appears as 6-point text, hence it will appear greeked. Greeking only affects screen display. The type will print normally at all sizes.

The **Performance/display options** check boxes let you choose five options that affect the way the illustration is displayed on the screen. Screen redrawing is faster when these options are left unchecked. Checking **Always draw object-by-object** makes FreeHand draw one object at a time on the screen. If you leave it unchecked, FreeHand redraws the entire illustration off-screen, then sends the whole illustration to the screen at once, resulting in a faster screen redraw. Drawing object-by-object is slower, but it requires less memory than drawing the entire image off-screen. When available memory is limited, FreeHand automatically redraws object-by-object.

Checking **High-resolution TIFF display** makes FreeHand display imported grayscale and color TIFF images at the highest resolution possible with the current screen magnification. If the option is left unchecked, FreeHand displays a lower-resolution image.

Checking **Display text effects** makes FreeHand display text effects like Fill and stroke, Outline, Inline, Shadow, and Zoom text as they will appear when printed. If the option is left unchecked, the text displays, but the effect does not.

Checking **Better (but slower) display** makes FreeHand display stroked lines and graduated and radial fills as accurately as possible, at the expense of speed.

When you select a point on a path, FreeHand displays the handles that you can use to adjust the curves of the path segments on either side of the point. Checking **Display curve levers** makes FreeHand display both the handles for the selected point and the handles at the other end of the path segments adjacent to the point.

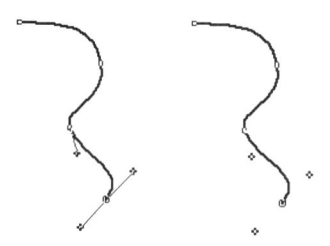

Figure 14.19 Display curve levers checked and Display curve levers unchecked

If you have a color monitor using either 256 or millions of colors, you can use the **Colors** button in conjunction with the *Color Monitor Adjustment Card* supplied in the FreeHand package to adjust the colors displayed on your screen so that they provide a closer match to the appearance they will have when printed. FreeHand's color display is much less accurate using 4 or 16 colors. Click the **Colors** button to open the Display color setup dialog box. The dialog box contains seven color swatches that match the ones printed on the *Color Monitor Adjustment Card*. Hold the card near the screen to compare the colors.

To adjust a color, click the color swatch in the dialog box. The Color Picker appears. A swatch at the upper left of the Color Picker is divided into two halves. The bottom half shows the color as it is currently set, and the top half changes to show you the new color you select. You can change the color by clicking the mouse on the color wheel, and adjust the brightness of the color using the vertical scroll bar. You can also adjust colors using the scroll arrows next to the Hue, Saturation, Brightness, and Red, Green, Blue boxes. When you have adjusted a color to your satisfaction, click OK to close the Color Picker. Repeat the process for any other colors you want to adjust. When all the colors have been adjusted to your satisfaction, click OK to close the Display color setup dialog box.

THE MORE PREFERENCES DIALOG BOX

Click the **More** button to open the More preferences dialog box, which contains more options. You can specify from 1 to 99 levels of Undo by entering a number in the **Number of undo's** edit box. The larger number of Undos specified, the more memory FreeHand will require. The default setting is 8, which is suitable for a Macintosh that can devote 1.8 MB of memory to FreeHand.

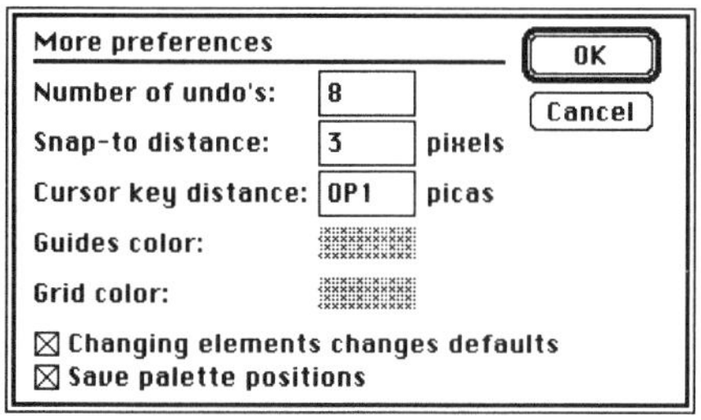

Figure 14.20 The More preferences dialog box

The number of pixels entered in the **Snap-to distance** edit box determines:

- The distance at which points on an element snap to points on another element
- The distance at which endpoints on a freeform path will snap together to join
- The distance at which the cursor will select handles and points
- The distance at which elements will snap to grids and guides

You can specify a distance from 1 to 5 pixels. For example, if you set the Snap-to distance at 3 pixels and then draw an element only 2 pixels from a guide, the element will snap to the guide.

You can move selected elements up, down, left, and right using the arrow keys on the Macintosh keyboard. The number entered in the **Cursor key distance** edit box controls how far the element moves when you press one of the arrow keys. You can enter whole or fractional numbers using any of FreeHand's units of measure.

If you are using a color monitor, you can set colors for the visible grid and for ruler guides by clicking the color swatches next to **Guides color** and **Grid color**, respectively. Clicking one of the color swatches opens the Color Picker, described in the description of the Colors button on page 416.

When **Changing elements changes defaults** is checked, each time you assign attributes such as type specifications, fill, line, or color to an element, FreeHand treats those attributes as the new defaults, and applies them to each element you subsequently create. For example, if you draw a box and apply a blue fill, the next closed path you create will automatically be given a blue fill too. When this box is unchecked, you change default attributes by choosing new attributes with no elements selected.

Checking the **Save palette positions** option makes FreeHand remember the positions of the Toolbox and the Colors, Styles, and Layers palettes each time you quit FreeHand. If you leave this option unchecked, only the Toolbox and the Colors palette appear when you start FreeHand.

Page Setup...

The Page Setup command opens the Page Setup dialog box, where you can specify options that affect the way your document is printed. For non-PostScript printers, the Page Setup dialog box is specific to the particular printer being used. With PostScript printers, most of the options in the Page Setup dialog box are overridden by the options you select in the Print dialog box. Only two options, Font Substitution and Unlimited Downloadable Fonts in a Document, affect printing in FreeHand.

PROCEDURE

Choose Page Setup from the File menu. The Page Setup dialog box appears. If you check **Font Substitution**, FreeHand will substitute Times for New York, Helvetica for Geneva, and Courier for Monaco. If you uncheck this option, FreeHand creates a 72-dot-per-inch bitmap representation of the font in question. Font substitution affects only New York, Geneva, and Monaco bitmap fonts. If you use any other font for which the PostScript printer font is not available, FreeHand will create a bitmap representation of the font, whether or not Font Substitution is checked.

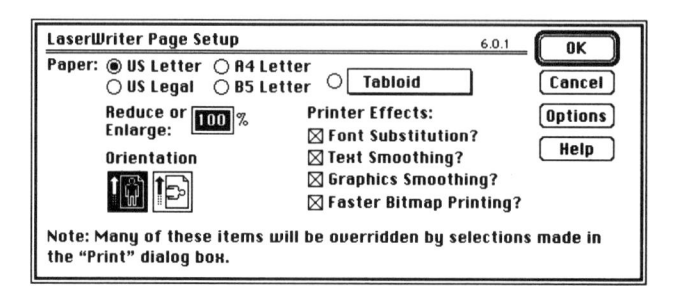

Figure 14.21 The Page Setup dialog box for PostScript printers

Click the **Options** button to open the Page Setup Options dialog box. The option relevant to FreeHand documents is Unlimited Downloadable Fonts in a Document. If you attempt to print a FreeHand document that contains several downloadable fonts, and the printer returns a "VM_error" message, check this option and try to print the document again. In most cases the document will print without further problems. A VM_error message indicates that the printer has run out of memory—"VM" stands for Virtual Memory. Checking this option makes the printer purge each downloadable font from memory after it has been used. Moving fonts in and out of printer memory increases printing time, but all the fonts specified in your document should print. Because this option slows printing, we recommend leaving it unchecked unless you get a VM_error message while printing.

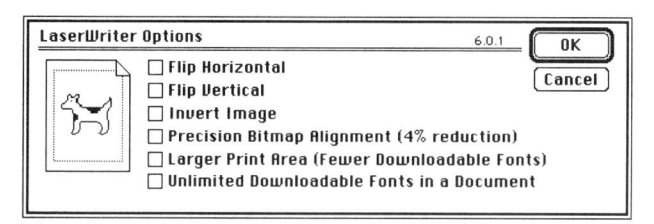

Figure 14.22 The Page Setup Options dialog box for PostScript printers

Print...

The Print command opens the Print dialog box, where you can choose options that control the way your illustration will print, and initiate printing. The keyboard shortcut is ⌘P. You use the Print command to print both composite proofs (in black and white or in color if you have a color printer) and to print color separations.

PROCEDURE

Choose Print from the File menu, or press ⌘P. The Print dialog box appears. The name of the printer currently selected in the Chooser appears at the top left of the dialog box. The Print dialog box contains many options.

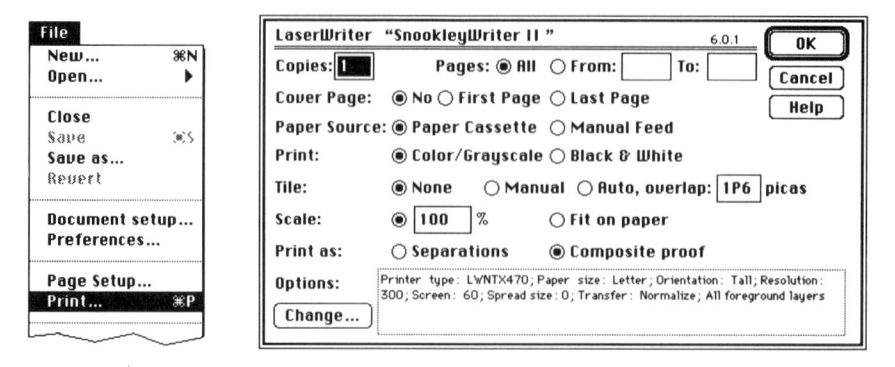

Figure 14.23 The Print dialog box for PostScript printers

THE PRINT DIALOG BOX

Enter a number in the **Copies** edit box to specify the number of copies you want printed. FreeHand illustrations are contained on one page, so leave All selected under the **Pages** option. The **Cover Page** option lets you print a cover page containing the illustration name, the user name entered in the Chooser, the printer's network name, the date, and the time. Select No if you do not want a cover page. Select First Page if you want the cover page printed before the illustration, and select Last Page if you want the cover page printed after the illustration.

Under **Paper Source**, select Paper Cassette if you want to feed paper automatically from the printer's paper tray, and Manual Feed if you want to feed paper manually into the printer.

The options under **Print**, which appear in versions of the LaserWriter driver later than 6.0, have no effect on FreeHand, which can always print colors and grayscales to PostScript printers. You can ignore these options.

You use the **Tile** options to print an illustration that is larger than the paper in your printer. When you tile an illustration, FreeHand divides the illustration into sections and prints each section on a separate sheet of paper. You can then trim and paste the separate sheets, or tiles, together to create a complete illustration. You can tile an illustration manually, or let FreeHand do it for you automatically. When you choose Auto tiling, FreeHand starts tiling from the lower-left corner of the page, using the amount of overlap you specify in the Auto, overlap edit box. With manual tiling, you control the tiling by moving the zero point on the rulers to the lower-left corner of the tile you want printed.

In the **Scale** edit box, you can specify a scaling percentage from 10% to 1,000%. If you choose Fit on paper, FreeHand will reduce the illustration so it fits on a single sheet of paper. If you do not choose Fit on paper or one of the tiling options, and your illustration is too large to fit the paper, FreeHand will warn you that the illustration is too large to fit the paper. If you click OK to close the warning box, FreeHand will print as much of the illustration as fits the paper, starting at the lower-left corner.

Under the **Print as** options, you have the choice of printing color separations, or printing a composite proof. Composite proof is the default. Leave it checked if you want FreeHand to print all colors in blacks and grays on a black-and-white printer, or in color on a color printer. Click Separations if your illustration contains color and you want to print a separate page for each color ink used. If you are using process color, FreeHand will print four sheets, one for each process color (cyan, magenta, yellow, and black). If you use spot color, FreeHand will print one sheet for each spot color used. Tints are printed on the same page as their base color. You can mix spot and process colors within an illustration, although this can result in an expensive final print job.

Under **Options**, the printer type, paper size, orientation, resolution, screen frequency, spread size, transfer function, and layers to be printed are listed. To change any of these, click the Change button to open the Print options dialog box.

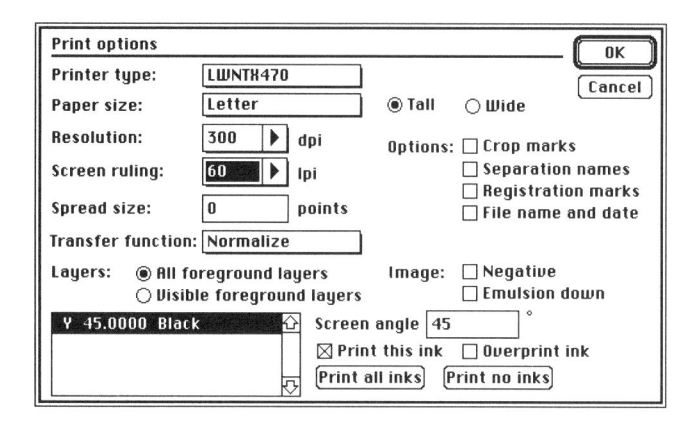

Figure 14.24 The Print options dialog box for PostScript printers

THE PRINT OPTIONS DIALOG BOX

From the **Printer type** pop-up menu, select the PPD/PDX files for the printer you are using. The menu displays all printer types for which PostScript Printer Description (PPD) or Printer Description Extension (PDX) files have been installed. You should select the Printer type option before selecting other options, because the printer type you choose determines the options that are available for paper size, screen ruling, resolution, and default screen angles. The names displayed in the Printer type menu are somewhat cryptic, usually consisting of some letters followed by some numbers. Generally, the letters refer to the printer type, and the numbers to the version of PostScript that the printer uses. Thus the PPD for the Apple LaserWriter IINT is displayed as LWNT_470, because that printer uses version 47.0 of PostScript, while the PPD for earlier Apple printers is displayed as Apple380.

From the **Paper size** pop-up menu, select the size of paper that is loaded in your printer. This may be different from the page size specified in Document setup. The available paper sizes vary according to the printer type selected.

The number of dots per inch specified in **Resolution** is the same as that specified for Target printer resolution under Document setup. If you change the setting in the Print options dialog box, the change is reflected in Document setup as well. You should always select the resolution you will use for the final printed version. The Resolution setting does not control the resolution of the printer, but it does tell FreeHand how to size black-and-white bitmaps and how to handle long paths to avoid running out of printer memory. For example, if you intend to print your final artwork on a 2450 dpi imagesetter but want to print a proof on a 300 dpi laser printer, you should choose the laser printer under Printer type, but leave the resolution set at 2450 dpi.

The **Screen ruling** pop-up menu lists screen rulings (in lines per inch) that are optimized for the printer you have chosen. You can choose one of these screen rulings, or type a number in the Screen ruling edit box.

When you print separations, FreeHand automatically enlarges the boundaries of basic fills and lines by the number of points specified for **Spread size**. (Spread size is always specified in points, no matter what unit of measure is chosen under Document setup.) The spread compensates for registration variations on the press, preventing paper from showing between elements that touch. This option does not apply to type, or to any element or ink that you have set to overprint. To turn off auto-spread, enter a spread value of 0 (zero) points.

The **Transfer function** pop-up menu offers three options that control how FreeHand matches the densities of color on the printed page to those specified in your artwork. The **Default** option uses the default densities built into your printer, bypassing density calibrations set in the PDX (Printer Description Extension) file. Use the **Normalize** option for most printing jobs, especially if you have calibrated color density settings in the PDX file. This will result in more accurate color densities and smoother radial and graduated fills. Use the **Posterize** option for a high-contrast effect. Posterize converts tints of 0% to 25% to white, 26% to 50% to a 33% tint, 51% to 75% to a 67% tint, and tints darker than 76% to black.

In the **Layers** options, check **All foreground layers** to print all the foreground layers. If you want to print only certain layers, make the layers you do not want to print invisible by unchecking their names in the Layers palette, then click **Visible foreground layers** to print only the visible foreground layers.

The **Options** section lets you add standard printer's marks to your illustration. Check **Crop marks** to add crop marks at the boundary of the illustration. These indicate where the final printed page should be trimmed. Check **Separation names** if you are printing color separations and want FreeHand to print the name of each color at the bottom of its separation. Check **Registration marks** to add registration marks to each separation. The commercial printer uses the registration marks to make sure that the different separations are properly lined up. Check **File name and date** to print the file name and date of your illustration in the upper-left corner.

All the printer's marks specified under Options will print only when the page size of your illustration (specified in Document setup) is smaller than the paper size used in your printer, when you tile your illustration, or when you check **Fit on paper** under the Scale option described above. To calculate the room required for printer's marks and bleeds, add the value for Page size (in Document setup), and twice the value set for Bleed (also in Document setup) to the following values:

- Crop marks and/or registration marks: Add 36 points to height and width
- Separation names: Add 9 points to height
- File names: Add 9 points to height

Remember that the portion of the paper on which the printer can print is often smaller than the paper size, so your paper size must be larger than the total area needed to print the illustration with the specified printer's marks. Otherwise, a message will appear when you try to print, reading "The entire image will not fit on the selected paper. Do you want to print just a portion of the image?" If you click OK to dismiss the message, FreeHand will print as much of the illustration as fits the selected paper, starting at the lower-left corner. If you want to print the entire illustration on the selected paper, you can use the Fit on paper option under Scale, described above in this section.

Use the options under **Image** when you are printing color separations on a high-resolution imagesetter. You should check with your commercial printer which options you should use. Check **Negative** to make a negative image of the illustration. Leave this option unchecked to create a positive image. Check **Emulsion down** to print the illustration on film, emulsion side down, right reading. Leave the option unchecked to print emulsion side up, right reading.

The lower part of the Print options dialog box lets you control how color separations are printed. For each ink listed in the inks list box, you can specify the screen angle for the separation, whether or not to print the separation, and whether or not an ink should overprint. The letter before the ink name indicates whether or not the ink is set to print, and whether or not it is set to overprint. A capital "Y" indicates that the ink will print, but knocks out in separations; a lowercase "y" indicates that the ink will overprint; a capital "N" indicates that the ink is set to knock out but is turned off; and a lowercase "n" indicates that the ink is set to overprint, but is turned off. When you print spot color separations, and two or more colors overlap, FreeHand normally knocks out the bottom color so the top color will print as expected. If you select an ink and check **Overprint ink**, the underlying colors are no longer knocked out. By default, all elements except 100% black text knock out, unless you check Overprint in the Fill and line dialog box for selected elements. (See "Fill and line command" below). 100% black text normally overprints, unless you change this setting through the Fill and stroke command in the Effect command submenu in the Type menu.

To print an ink, select the ink name in the inks list, then check **Print this ink**. To print all inks, click the **Print all inks** button. If you want to print only certain inks, first click the **Print no inks** button, then select each ink you want to print and check Print this ink.

The number before the ink name is the screen angle that will be used in the separation for that ink, according to the value set in the Screen angle edit box. To change the screen angle, click to select the ink name, then type a new screen angle in the Screen angle edit box. For spot colors, the default angle is 45 degrees. For process colors, FreeHand uses the screen angle and frequency you have specified to determine the best screen angles for the target printer you have chosen, and applies the screen angles globally to each separation. These angles are optimized to avoid moiré patterns in the printed artwork. Elements with halftone screens applied to them directly and imported EPS files containing screen angles override the global screen angle settings.

CAUTION

Unlike text created in FreeHand, text in artwork imported from Adobe Illustrator is not automatically set to overprint.

Place...

The Place command opens the Place document dialog box, containing a scrolling list of documents that you can import into a FreeHand illustration. You can import documents in TIFF (Tag Image File Format), EPS (Encapsulated PostScript), PICT, or MacPaint formats.

PROCEDURE

Choose Place from the File menu. The Place document dialog box appears, containing a scrolling list of documents in the current folder or disk that FreeHand 3.0 can import. The folder or disk name is displayed in a pop-up menu above the files list. You can navigate up through the hierarchy of folders by choosing a higher folder from the pop-up menu, or switch to a different disk by clicking the Drive button (or the Desktop button under System 7.0).

Once you have found the document you want to import, you can open it by selecting the document's name in the scrolling list and clicking the OK button, or by double-clicking the document name in the list. Click the Cancel button to cancel the command. Click the Eject button to eject a floppy disk. (The Eject button is dimmed unless the current disk is a floppy disk or a removable cartridge.)

426   Using Aldus FreeHand 3.0

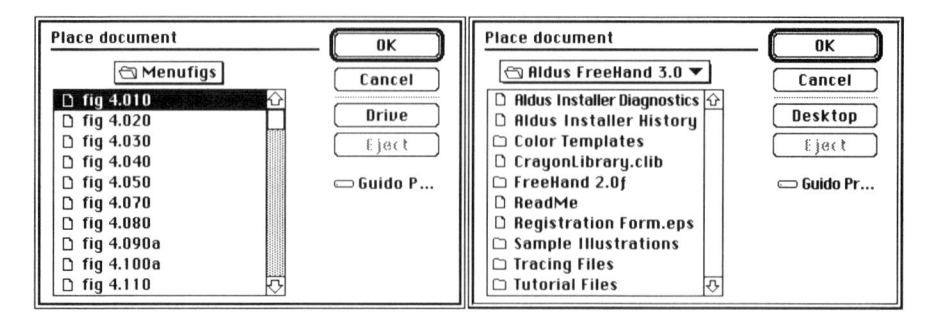

Place document		Place document	
📁 Menufigs	OK	📁 Aldus FreeHand 3.0 ▼	OK
🗋 fig 4.010	Cancel	🗋 Aldus Installer Diagnostics	Cancel
🗋 fig 4.020	Drive	🗋 Aldus Installer History	Desktop
🗋 fig 4.030	Eject	📁 Color Templates	Eject
🗋 fig 4.040		🗋 CrayonLibrary.clib	
🗋 fig 4.050	💾 Guido P...	🗋 FreeHand 2.0f	💾 Guido Pr...
🗋 fig 4.070		🗋 ReadMe	
🗋 fig 4.080		🗋 Registration Form.eps	
🗋 fig 4.090a		📁 Sample Illustrations	
🗋 fig 4.100a		📁 Tracing Files	
🗋 fig 4.110		📁 Tutorial Files	

Figure 14.25 The Place document dialog box (System 6.0.x). The Place document dialog box (System 7.0)

TIPS

You can use the keyboard to navigate in the Place document dialog box. Press the Up Arrow and Down Arrow keys to move up and down through the scrolling list, and press ⌘Up Arrow to move up through the hierarchy of folders. You can also type the first few letters of a document's name to move quickly to that document in the scrolling list.

Avoid importing scanned images in PICT or PICT2 formats. Importing scanned PICTs requires much more memory than importing the same images in TIFF or EPS formats, and will often cause FreeHand to run out of memory.

Export...

The Export command lets you export your FreeHand illustration in EPS (Encapsulated PostScript) format for use with other software. Use the Export command when you want to place your illustration in a document created by another program, such as a page layout program.

PROCEDURE

Choose Export from the File menu. The Export dialog box appears, containing a scrolling list of files and folders. The file names are grayed, indicating that you cannot take any action on them, while folder names are black, indicating that you can open them. The name of the current folder or disk appears in a pop-up menu above the scrolling list. You can navigate up through the hierarchy of folders by choosing a higher folder from the pop-up menu, or switch to a different disk by clicking the Drive button (or the Desktop button under System 7.0). When you click OK the document is exported to the folder or disk whose name appears in the pop-up menu.

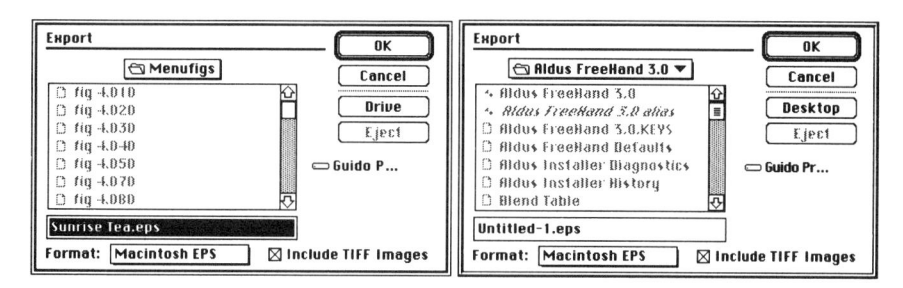

Figure 14.26 The Export dialog box (System 6.0.x). The Export dialog box (System 7.0)

An edit box below the scrolling list contains the current name of the document with the suffix ".eps" appended, and the name is highlighted, ready for you to type a new one if you so desire. (If you are exporting an unsaved, new document, the document name appears as Untitled-1.eps.)

The Format pop-up menu lets you choose one of three available formats. **Macintosh EPS** exports the illustration in EPS format with a PICT screen representation of the artwork. When the document is placed in other Macintosh applications, the artwork will be visible on the screen. You should use this format when you intend to place the artwork in another Macintosh application.

MS-DOS EPS exports the illustration in EPS format with a TIFF screen representation of the artwork. You should use this format when you intend to place the artwork in a PC program. Graphics exported in this format cannot be imported back into FreeHand.

Generic EPS exports the illustration in EPS format with no screen representation. When the document is placed in a Macintosh or PC application, it appears on the screen as a gray box, but will print correctly.

Checking the **Include TIFF Images** check box includes a copy of any TIFF images contained in the illustration. If this option is left unchecked and the illustration contains TIFF images, the exported EPS file contains OPI (Open Prepress Interface) comments about the size and placement of the TIFF. You will need to supply your service bureau or prepress system with a copy of the original TIFF image. Unless you are sure that the program you or your service bureau will use to print the EPS file can link to the original TIFF, you should check Include TIFF images to include the TIFF image in the exported EPS document.

TIP

If you want to include a FreeHand illustration in a document created by a program that does not support EPS format, such as Microsoft Word, you can create a PICT format copy of the illustration with embedded PostScript by selecting the entire illustration, holding down the Option key and choosing Copy from the Edit menu. You can then paste this graphic into applications that do not support EPS format. The embedded PostScript will make the graphic print at the resolution of the printer rather than at the 72 dot-per-inch resolution of the screen image. If you do not want to paste the image immediately, you can store it for later use by pasting it into the Scrapbook. See your Macintosh documentation for more information about using the Scrapbook.

Quit

The Quit command closes all open documents and quits the FreeHand application. The keyboard shortcut is ⌘Q. If any of the open documents contain unsaved changes, a message box appears allowing you to save the changes, close without saving, or cancel the Quit command.

PROCEDURE

Choose Quit from the File menu, or press ⌘Q. FreeHand closes any open documents and quits. If any of the open documents contain unsaved changes, a message box appears, asking if you want to save changes to the specified document. Clicking Yes saves the changes to the document. Clicking No closes the document without saving the changes. Clicking Cancel returns you to the current document and cancels the Quit command. The message box appears once for each document that contains unsaved changes.

The Edit Menu

The Edit menu contains commands for editing your FreeHand illustration, including undoing or redoing an operation; managing the Macintosh Clipboard (a "storage area" in the computer's memory from which the contents can be retrieved using the Paste command) by cutting, or copying to it, and pasting from it; selecting all the objects in an illustration; deleting selected objects; pasting objects inside other objects; duplicating or cloning objects; and repeating a transformation.

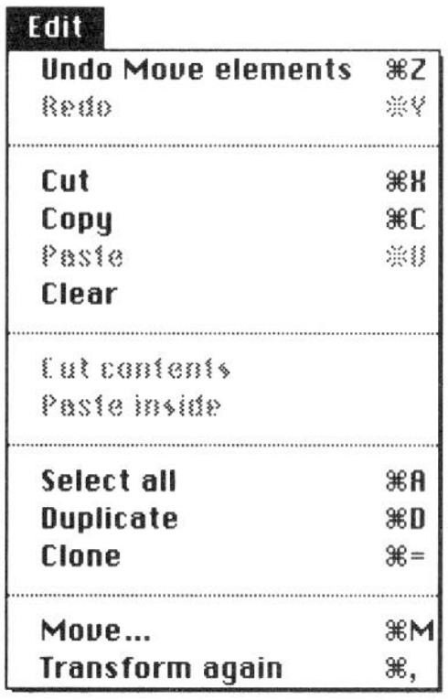

Figure 14.27 The Edit menu

Although different applications have different menu commands, and hence different keyboard shortcuts, the Command-key (⌘) equivalents for Undo, Cut, Copy, and Paste are constant throughout all Macintosh applications. Knowledge and use of these keyboard shortcuts is basic to Macintosh literacy—if you learn only four Command-key menu equivalents, they should be Undo, Cut, Copy, and Paste. These Command-key menu equivalents use the four keys located closest to the Command key (the left-hand Command key on extended keyboards): ⌘Z is Undo, ⌘X is Cut, ⌘C is Copy, and ⌘V is Paste.

Undo

The Undo command reverses the effect of the previous operation. The keyboard shortcut is ⌘Z. The command changes to reflect the last operation. For example, if you add text, the command changes to read Undo Add Text. You can set the number of operations that can be undone using the Preferences command in the File menu. (See "Preferences" earlier in this chapter.)

PROCEDURE

Choose Undo from the Edit menu, or press ⌘Z. The last operation you took is reversed. The Redo command will change to reflect the operation that has just been undone. You can undo multiple actions, up to the number you specify in Preferences.

Note that if you use the Undo command to reverse the effect of an action prior to the last action, you will not be able to selectively redo the later actions. For example, if you create a text block, move it, scale it, and duplicate it, you can use the Undo command to reverse any of these actions (assuming that you have allowed at least four levels of Undo in Preferences). The first Undo command will read Undo Duplicate, and the Redo command will change to read Redo Duplicate. The second Undo command will read Undo Scale. If you choose it, the Redo command will change to read Redo Scale, and the Undo command will change to read Undo Move elements. If you choose Undo Move elements, the move will be undone. You will not, however, be able to use the Redo command to redo the scaling and duplicating operations unless you also use it to redo the move.

CAUTION
You cannot undo the following operations:

- Changing views
- Scrolling the drawing window
- Selecting elements
- Using Save or Save as
- Reverting to the last-saved version of your illustration

Redo

The Redo command reverses the effect of the last Undo operation. The keyboard shortcut is ⌘Y. The command changes to reflect the last Undo operation. For example, if the last Undo command that you chose was Undo Add text, the Redo command will read Redo Add text. The number of operations that can be redone is the same as the number that can be undone. You set this number using the Preferences command in the File menu. (See "Preferences" earlier in this chapter.)

PROCEDURE
Choose Redo from the Edit menu, or press ⌘Y. The effect of the last Undo operation is reversed.

TIP
If you want to use Redo, make sure that you choose it immediately after using Undo. If you use Undo and then take some other action, such as drawing, the Redo command will be dimmed, and you will no longer be able to use it to reverse the effect of the Undo operation.

Cut

The Cut command deletes the selected element or elements from your artwork and stores it on the Clipboard (a "storage area" in the computer's memory), replacing whatever was previously on the Clipboard. The keyboard shortcut is ⌘X. You can paste the cut element or elements back into the current file, or another FreeHand file, using the Paste command.

PROCEDURE

Select the element or elements you wish to cut, then choose Cut from the Edit menu, or press ⌘X. The selected elements are deleted from your artwork and stored on the Clipboard, replacing whatever was previously stored on the Clipboard.

TIP

Use the Cut command whenever you wish to remove selected objects from the artwork and temporarily store them on the Clipboard. If you want to remove objects from the artwork but do not want to lose the contents of the Clipboard, select one of these alternatives to the Cut command:

- Press the Delete (Backspace) key, or choose the Clear command from the Edit menu. This action removes the selected objects from the artwork but it does not store them on the Clipboard. (See also "Clear" below.)
- Before using the Cut command, move the contents of the Clipboard back to the artwork by choosing Paste (see "Paste" below).
- Drag the selected objects off to the side of the illustration for storage as part of the artwork until you delete them.

Copy

The Copy command copies the selected element or elements to the Clipboard (a "storage area" in the computer's memory from which the contents can be retrieved using the Paste command), leaving the elements in place as artwork, and replacing whatever was previously on the Clipboard. The keyboard shortcut is ⌘C.

PROCEDURE

Select the element or elements you want to copy, then choose Copy from the Edit menu, or press ⌘C.

You can copy FreeHand elements into a PICT format which can then be pasted into Microsoft Word, PowerPoint, and some other (but not all) Macintosh applications that do not support PostScript formats. To do this, hold down the Option key and choose Copy from the Edit menu, or press Option-⌘C. A message appears briefly telling you that FreeHand is converting the Clipboard. This action copies not only the PostScript information in the FreeHand elements, but the screen image as well, making it possible to paste the artwork into the other applications that support bitmapped or PICT formats. The PostScript information contained in the copy makes the copied element print at the maximum resolution of the printer when you print to a PostScript printer. You can paste the copied elements immediately into a document created by another application, or you can store them for later use in the Scrapbook.

TIP

The Copy command is most useful when you want to store selected objects on the Clipboard for repeated use (over a short period), when you need to paste the copies between layers (not onto the top layer), and when you need to copy selected elements from one document to another.

Otherwise, copy objects using the Duplicate or Clone command from the Edit menu. This is a more efficient method of copying objects when you want to align the copies, or when you want to combine the copy procedure with a movement or a transformation before using the Transform again command from the Edit menu to repeat the procedures. (See "Transform again" on page 439.)

The Copy command does not delete objects from the artwork. To delete objects, use the Cut or Clear command or the Delete (Backspace) key. (See "Cut" and "Clear" sections later in this chapter.)

As with the Cut command, the Copy command replaces the contents of the Clipboard.

Paste

The Paste command pastes the contents of the Clipboard to the center of the active window and to the current drawing layer, in front of all the other objects in the current layer. The keyboard shortcut is ⌘V.

PROCEDURE

After storing the desired elements on the Clipboard using the Copy or Cut command, choose Paste from the Edit menu or press ⌘V. The pasted elements appear in the center of the screen on the current drawing layer, and become selected. All other objects are deselected. A copy of the pasted elements remains on the Clipboard until you replace it by using the Cut or Copy command again.

You can paste an element immediately behind another element by selecting the element you want to paste behind, then pressing ⌘-Shift-V.

TIP

Since all the pasted elements are selected when they appear on the screen, it is a good idea to immediately carry out any further operations you want to apply to all the pasted elements, such as moving or grouping them.

Clear

The Clear command deletes all selected elements from the artwork. This command is the equivalent of pressing the Delete (Backspace) key. Cleared objects are not stored on the Clipboard, and using the Clear command does not affect the contents of the Clipboard.

PROCEDURE

Select the element or elements to be cleared, then choose Clear from the Edit menu or press the Delete (Backspace) key. The selected elements are deleted from the illustration.

CAUTION

Since elements deleted with the Clear command or the Delete (Backspace) key are *not* copied to the Clipboard (a "storage area" in the computer's memory from which the contents can be retrieved using the Paste command), you must use the Undo command immediately if you wish to reverse the command and retrieve the elements (see "Undo" earlier in this chapter).

TIP

The fastest way to clear elements is to select them and press the Delete (Backspace) key.

Cut contents

This command removes the contents of a clipping path created using the Paste inside command, and places the path's contents in the illustration window at the location the element occupied before it was pasted inside the clipping path. It also makes the path's contents the selected object. When the contents are cut, the clipping path reverts to its previous state as either a normal path or a compound object, and becomes deselected. Cutting the contents of a clipping path is the only way to convert it to its previous state. This command is dimmed and unavailable unless a clipping path is selected. (See "Paste inside" and "Join elements" below.)

PROCEDURE

Select a clipping path from which you want to cut the contents, then choose Cut contents from the Edit menu. The clipped element is removed and placed in the illustration window at the location it occupied before it was pasted inside the clipping path. The clipped element becomes selected, and all other objects are deselected.

Figure 14.28 Clipping path before and after using the Cut contents command

Paste inside

The Paste inside command pastes the contents of the Clipboard into a selected path, converting the selected path into a clipping path. A clipping path is one of the two ways FreeHand provides to achieve a traditional graphic design technique called masking. The other masking method, the composite path, is described in the section on the Join elements command in the Element menu later in this chapter.

A clipping path is like a sheet of paper with a hole in it: If you lay the paper over a patterned background, the background shows through the hole. If you changed the shape of the hole, you would see a different part of the background. When you use the Paste inside command, the path you have selected is the equivalent of the hole, and the element or elements you are pasting are the equivalent of the background.

You can use a freeform path, a composite path, or a basic element (a rectangle, rounded rectangle, or oval) as a clipping path. The background can be text, fills, bitmap images (TIFF or EPS), other freeform paths, basic elements, or several of these elements combined.

PROCEDURE

First create the path you want to use as a clipping path. Place the clipping path over the background element, and position it so the part of the background that you want to show is inside the clipping path. Next, select the background and choose Cut from the Edit menu, or press ⌘X. This removes the background from the illustration and places it on the Clipboard. Finally, select the path you want to use as a clipping path, and choose Paste inside from the Edit menu. The background element is pasted inside the clipping path.

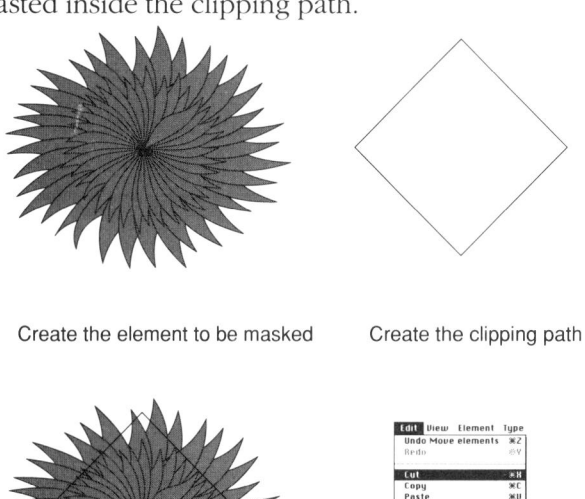

Create the element to be masked   Create the clipping path

Position the element over the clipping path    Cut the element

Select the clipping path
and choose Paste inside

The element is pasted
inside the clipping path

Figure 14.29 Creating a clipping path

TIPS

If you want to use several freeform paths, composite paths, or basic elements to mask the same background element, you can use the Join elements command from the Element menu to convert all the clipping paths into a single composite path. You can then use the Paste inside command once to paste the background into the composite path. Otherwise, you would have to separately paste the background into each clipping path.

You can use type as a clipping path by first converting it to a composite path using the Convert to paths command from the Type menu. (See "Convert to paths" below.)

CAUTION

Basic elements (circles, rectangles, rounded rectangles, and ovals) are the only grouped objects that can be used as clipping paths. To use any other grouped object as a clipping path, you must first ungroup it, then make it a composite path using the Join elements command from the Element menu. (See "Join elements" on page 471 of this chapter.)

Wherever possible, use a composite path instead of a clipping path to mask an object, because composite paths print more efficiently. Use a clipping path when it is the best or the only way to achieve the effect you want.

Select all

The Select all command selects all the elements in the current document. The keyboard shortcut is ⌘A. If Multilayer in the Layers palette is turned on, Select all selects all elements on visible layers. If Multilayer is turned off, Select all selects all elements in the active layer, whether the layer is visible or not.

PROCEDURE

Choose Select all from the Edit menu, or press ⌘A. If Multilayer in the Layers palette is turned on, all elements on visible layers are selected. If Multilayer is turned off, all elements in the active layer are selected, whether the layer is visible or not.

Duplicate

The Duplicate command copies a selected element or elements, and places the copy in front of the original and slightly offset down and to the right, or moves it the same distance as a previous move following the Clone command. The keyboard shortcut is ⌘D. The Duplicate command will also repeat any transformations applied to a selected element since the last Duplicate or Clone command. The Duplicate command does not change the contents of the Clipboard.

PROCEDURE

Select the element you want to duplicate, then choose Duplicate from the Edit menu, or press ⌘D. A duplicate of the selected element is placed in front of, and slightly below and to the right of, the original, and the duplicate becomes selected.

TIPS

The real power of the Duplicate command is shown when you use it in conjunction with transformations like moving, scaling, or rotating. If you duplicate or clone an element, then transform the duplicate by moving, scaling, skewing, reflecting or rotating it, the Duplicate command will "remember" that transformation and apply it to subsequent duplicates. The only constraint is that you must keep the duplicated element selected until you choose Duplicate again. If you deselect the element, the transformation information is lost. You can achieve the same effect by using the Clone command, transforming the clone, using the Clone command again, then using the Transform again command, but "power-duplicating" with the Duplicate command requires fewer steps.

Figure 14.30 Some uses of the Duplicate command (See Chapter 4)

When you want to copy an element within a single FreeHand illustration, the Duplicate and Clone commands are more efficient than the Copy command. Copying to the Clipboard takes a small but noticeable amount of time, and also destroys the Clipboard's previous contents. In contrast, the Duplicate and Clone commands leave the Clipboard undisturbed. Use the Copy command only when you need to copy elements from one document to another, or from FreeHand to another application.

Clone

The Clone command copies a selected element and places the copy directly on top of the original. The original is deselected, and the clone becomes selected. The keyboard shortcut is ⌘= (Command-equals).

PROCEDURE

Select the element you want to clone, then choose Clone from the Edit menu, or press ⌘=. A copy of the selected element is placed directly on top of the original, the original becomes deselected, and the clone is selected.

TIP

You can use the Clone command in conjunction with the Move command when you need to move a copy of an element by a specified distance. First clone the element using the Clone command, then choose Move from the Edit menu (⌘M) and enter the distance by which you want to move the clone. (See also "Duplicate" earlier in this chapter.)

Move...

The Move command opens the Move elements dialog box. In the dialog box you can specify a horizontal and vertical distance by which to move the selected element. The keyboard shortcut is ⌘M. You can select and move any selection from a single point to an entire illustration with the Move command.

PROCEDURE

Select the element or elements you want to move, then choose Move from the Edit menu, or press ⌘M. The Move elements dialog box appears, containing edit boxes where you can type distances for horizontal and vertical movement.

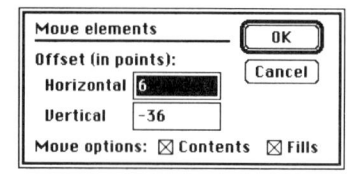

Figure 14.31 The Move elements dialog box

In **Horizontal**, type positive numbers to move the element to the right, and negative numbers to move it to the left. In **Vertical**, type positive numbers to move the element up, and negative numbers to move it down.

The **Move options** apply only to entire paths. If the path is a clipping path, check Contents if you want the contents to move with the path. Leave this option unchecked if you want to move the path but leave the contents stationary. If the path contains a tiled fill, check Fills if you want the tiled fill to move with the path. Leave this option unchecked if you want to move the path but leave the tiled fill stationary.

TIP

Changing the way a clipping path masks an image can be done quickly with the Move command if you leave the Contents option unchecked. The alternative is to use the Cut contents command to remove the contents from the path, reposition them, cut them using the Cut command, then use the Paste inside command to paste the image back into the clipping path. Using the Move command requires many fewer steps.

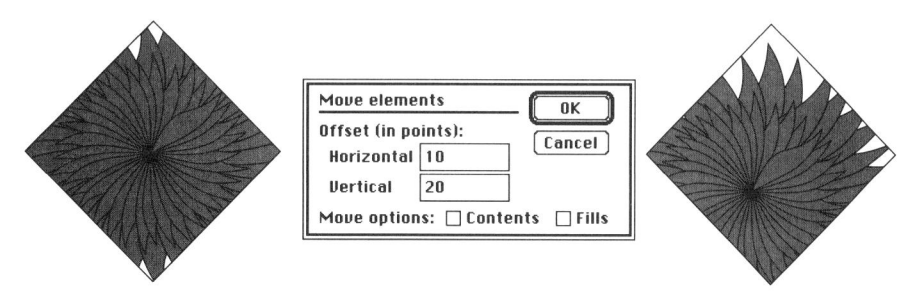

Figure 14.32 Moving a clipping path to change the way the contents are masked

Transform again

The Transform again command repeats the previous transformation, regardless of how many actions you have taken since the last transformation. (A transformation is any move, rotate, reflect, skew, or scale operation.) The keyboard shortcut is ⌘, (Command-comma).

PROCEDURE

Select the element you want to transform, then choose Transform again from the Edit menu, or press ⌘, (Command-comma). The previous transformation is applied to the selected element.

CAUTION

Note that the Transform again command only remembers the last transformation, not a series of transformations. This is unlike the Duplicate command, which is capable of remembering a series of transformations.

The View Menu

The View menu contains commands that control the way your artwork is displayed on the screen. The commands on this menu let you display or hide the various palettes and the Toolbox, and switch between different open documents. The View menu also contains commands to let you view a document at several levels of magnification, to fit an entire file into a window, or to display the file in its actual size. See also the description of the Magnifying tool in Chapter 12 for methods of changing magnifications of artwork.

Figure 14.33 The View menu

Other commands on this menu let you switch between Preview and keyline view, show or hide the rulers, visible grid, and guides, lock the guides in place, and turn the various snap-to options on or off.

Windows

The Windows command displays a submenu containing commands that let you show or hide the information bar, the Toolbox, and the various palettes. The name of each open document appears at the bottom of the menu. You can make a different open document the current document by choosing its name from the submenu.

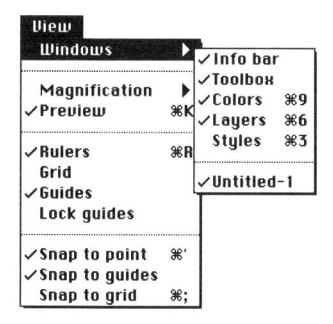

Figure 14.34 The Windows submenu

PROCEDURE

Choose Windows from the View menu, then drag across to the right into the submenu. The commands in the upper portion of the submenu are toggles: if the item on the submenu is currently visible, a check mark is displayed by the item's name on the submenu. Choosing the item's name on the menu hides the item, and the check mark is no longer displayed. Conversely, if the item is not currently visible, choosing its name from the submenu makes it visible, and displays the check mark by the item's name.

INFO BAR

The Info bar command shows or hides the information bar immediately below the main menu bar. If the information bar is visible, a check mark appears before the command.

TOOLBOX

The Toolbox command shows or hides the Toolbox palette. If the Toolbox palette is visible, a check mark appears before the command.

COLORS

The Colors command shows or hides the Colors palette. If the Colors palette is visible, a check mark appears before the command. The keyboard shortcut is ⌘9. You can use the 9 key on the numeric keypad or on the regular alphanumeric keyboard.

LAYERS

The Layers command shows or hides the Layers palette. If the Layers palette is visible, a check mark appears before the command. The keyboard shortcut is ⌘6. You can use the 6 key on the numeric keypad or on the regular alphanumeric keyboard.

442   Using Aldus FreeHand 3.0

STYLES

The Styles command shows or hides the Styles palette. If the Styles palette is visible, a check mark appears before the command. The keyboard shortcut is ⌘3. You can use the 3 key on the numeric keypad or on the regular alphanumeric keyboard.

DOCUMENT NAMES IN THE WINDOWS SUBMENU

The lower portion of the submenu contains the names of all currently open FreeHand documents. You can open several documents at once, limited by the amount of RAM available, but only one document at a time can be active. To make any open document the active document, choose its name from the Windows command submenu.

TIP

Using the keyboard shortcuts for displaying and hiding the palettes is much faster and more efficient than using the submenu commands.

Magnification

The Magnification command displays a submenu containing commands that let you view your artwork at any of seven different levels of magnification or reduction, or zoom out to fit the entire illustration in the active drawing window.

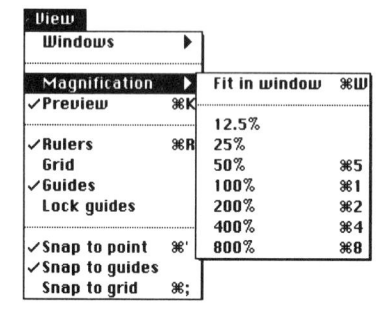

Figure 14.35 The Magnification submenu

PROCEDURE

Choose Magnification from the View menu, then drag across to the right into the submenu. The submenu commands are as follows:

FIT IN WINDOW

Fit in window zooms out as far as necessary to fit the entire page into the active window. It does not change the size of the artwork itself, only the level of magnification or reduction at which it is viewed. The actual level of magnification or reduction that results depends on both the size of the window and the size of the page. The keyboard shortcut is ⌘W.

PRESET LEVELS OF MAGNIFICATION

The seven remaining commands on the submenu provide different fixed levels of magnification or reduction. When you choose a different level of magnification and an element is selected, the view changes so that the selected element is in the center of the window. If no element is selected, the center of the page is in the center of the window.

The levels of magnification or reduction offered are **12.5%**, **25%**, **50%**, **100%**, **200%**, **400%**, and **800%**, respectively. The latter five also have keyboard shortcuts: ⌘5 for 50%, ⌘1 for 100% (actual size), ⌘2 for 200%, ⌘4 for 400%, and ⌘8 for 800%.

For information on using the Magnifying tool to change views, see "Magnifying Tool" in Chapter 12.

Preview

The Preview command lets you toggle between Preview and keyline views. In Preview mode, the screen display resembles the printed page as closely as possible. In keyline view, paths are represented as "wire-frame" outlines, text is displayed as solid black, and line weights and fills are not shown. The keyboard shortcut is ⌘K. In Preview mode, a check mark is displayed beside the Preview command. In keyline mode, the check mark is absent.

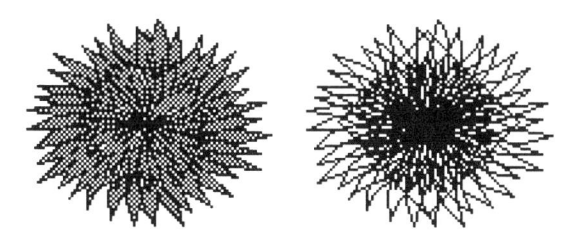

Figure 14.36 Preview and keyline views

444 Using Aldus FreeHand 3.0

PROCEDURE

Choose Preview from the View menu, or press ⌘K. FreeHand switches from Preview to keyline mode, or vice versa.

TIP

Use keyline view when you want to speed up screen redrawing, see or select elements that are hidden behind other elements, find elements that seem invisible because they are the same color as surrounding elements, or find the center point of a basic shape. (Basic shapes are those created with the Rectangle, Rounded-rectangle, and Ellipse tools. In keyline view, the center point of a basic shape is indicated by an X unless the shape has been ungrouped.)

Rulers

The Rulers command displays or hides the on-screen rulers at the top and left edges of the window. The keyboard shortcut is ⌘R. A check mark appears beside the Rulers command when the rulers are visible.

Dotted lines in the rulers track the horizontal and vertical position of the cursor, to help you position or resize elements. The rulers are marked in the unit of measure specified for the illustration in Document setup. (See "Document setup" earlier in this chapter.)

You can move the zero point of either or both rulers to control the way an illustration is tiled on multiple sheets of paper, or to help you measure distances. By default, the zero point is set at the lower-left corner of the page. (See tiling in the discussion of the Print command earlier in this chapter.)

You can drag non-printing guides from the rulers to help position elements precisely on the page. (See "Guides," later in this chapter.)

PROCEDURE

Choose Rulers from the View menu to display or hide the rulers, or press ⌘R. To change the unit of measure used in the rulers, use the Document setup command from the File menu.

To move the zero point on the rulers, position the cursor on the zero point marker, shown below, then press the mouse button and drag the marker to the desired location. If Snap to grid in the View menu is turned on, the zero point marker moves by grid increments as you drag. If it is turned off, you can move the zero point freely.

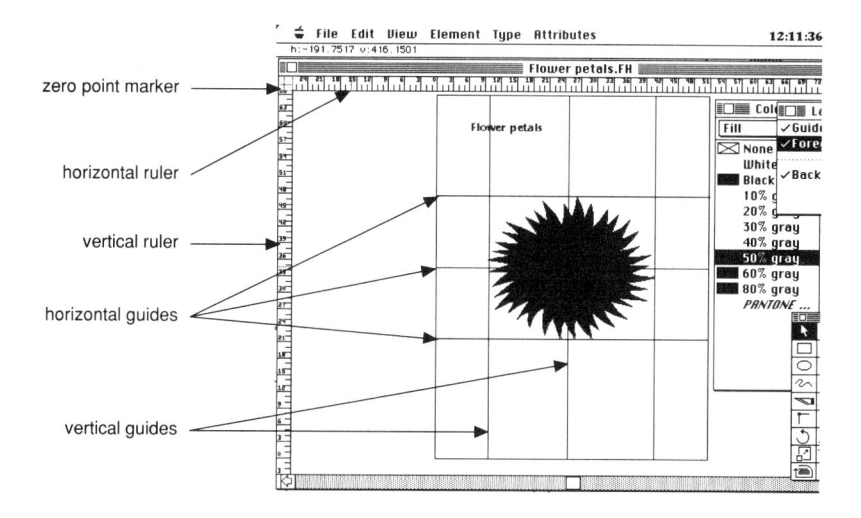

Figure 14.37 Rulers and guides

To create a non-printing guide, first make sure that the Guides layer is visible. (If the Guides layer is visible, a check mark is displayed beside the Guides command in the View menu, and beside the Guides layer name in the Layers palette.) Then, press the mouse button on the horizontal or vertical ruler and drag to the guide's desired location. The guide appears as a dashed line as you drag. When you release the mouse button, the guide appears as a solid line in the color specified in the Preferences dialog box. (See "Preferences," earlier in this chapter.)

TIP
You do not need to change tools to create a guide, because the cursor automatically switches to the pointer when you position it on the ruler. Once you release the mouse button, it reverts to the tool you were using. However, to move an existing guide, you do need to use the Pointer tool. You can temporarily switch any tool to the pointer by holding down the Command key (⌘).

Grid

The Grid command displays or hides the visible grid, which you can use as an aid in placing or aligning elements. When the grid is displayed, a check mark appears beside the command. You can specify the distance between grid dots (and their color on color monitors) in the Preferences dialog box, obtained by choosing the Preferences command from the File menu. (See "Preferences," earlier in this chapter.)

PROCEDURE

Choose Grid from the View menu to display or hide the visible grid. If the grid is displayed, choosing the command hides it, and if it is hidden, choosing the command displays it. When the grid is displayed, it continues to be displayed if you make the Guides layer invisible.

(See also the section on the View menu's Snap to grid command later in this chapter.)

Guides

The Guides command makes the Guides layer, and hence any non-printing guides, visible or invisible. When the Guides layer is visible, a check mark is displayed beside the Guides command in the View menu, and beside the Guides layer's name in the Layers palette. Non-printing ruler guides can only be placed on the Guides layer, so you can only place, move, or see the guides when the Guides layer is visible.

PROCEDURE

Choose Guides from the View menu to display or hide the Guides layer. If the Guides layer is displayed, choosing the command hides it, and if it is hidden, choosing the command displays it.

(See also the section on the View menu's Snap to guides command later in this section.)

TIP

It is generally faster and more efficient to turn the Guides layer on or off by clicking next to its name in the Layers palette.

Lock guides

The Lock guides command locks any non-printing guides in place, preventing you from accidentally moving them. You can continue to place new guides, but any new guides are locked in place as soon as you release the mouse button.

PROCEDURE

Choose Lock guides from the View menu to lock or unlock all non-printing guides. When the guides are locked, a check mark is displayed next to the Lock guides command. When the Guides layer is invisible, this command is dimmed and unavailable.

Snap to point

The Snap to point command turns Snap to point on and off. The keyboard shortcut is ⌘'. When Snap to point is turned on, a check mark appears next to the Snap to point command. When active, Snap to point automatically pulls any point that you are moving into alignment with a stationary point when the moving point comes within the snap-to distance of the stationary point. You set the snap-to distance using the Preferences command from the File menu.

PROCEDURE

Choose Snap to point from the View menu to turn Snap to point on and off, or press ⌘'. When Snap to point is turned on, a check mark appears next to the Snap to point command.

TIP

Use Snap to point when you want to position a point or an element at precisely the same place as another point. You can use Snap to point to snap a single selected point to a point on another element, to snap a selected point on an element to a stationary point on the same element (to close a path), or to snap an entire selected element to a point on another stationary element. Snap to point has no effect on elements that were drawn or moved before you turned Snap to point on.

Snap to guides

The Snap to guides command turns Snap to guides on and off. When Snap to guides is turned on, a check mark appears next to the Snap to guides command. When active, Snap to guides automatically pulls any element that you are moving into alignment with a non-printing guide when the moving element comes within the snap-to distance of the non-printing guide. You set the snap-to distance using the Preferences command from the File menu. When the Guides layer is invisible, this command is dimmed and unavailable.

PROCEDURE

Choose Snap to guides from the View menu to turn Snap to guides on and off. When Snap to guides is turned on, a check mark appears next to the Snap to guides command. Snap to guides has no effect on elements that were drawn or moved before you turned Snap to guides on.

Snap to grid

The Snap to grid command turns Snap to grid on and off. The keyboard shortcut is ⌘;. When Snap to grid is turned on, a check mark appears next to the Snap to grid command. When active, Snap to grid automatically pulls any element that you are moving into alignment with the invisible grid when the moving element comes within the snap-to distance of an invisible grid coordinate. You set the snap-to distance and the spacing of the invisible grid using the Preferences command from the File menu. This command is unrelated to the visible grid, which is purely a visual aid.

PROCEDURE

Choose Snap to grid from the View menu to turn Snap to grid on and off, or press ⌘;. When Snap to grid is turned on, a check mark appears next to the Snap to grid command. Snap to grid has no effect on elements that were drawn or moved before you turned Snap to grid on.

The Element Menu

The Element menu contains commands that let you manipulate elements of your artwork in various ways. The commands on this menu let you control the stacking order of elements within a single layer, get information about an element, convert a point from one kind to another, lock and unlock elements, group and ungroup elements, align elements, blend elements, change the angle at which basic shapes are drawn, and create composite paths.

Chapter 14. Menus   449

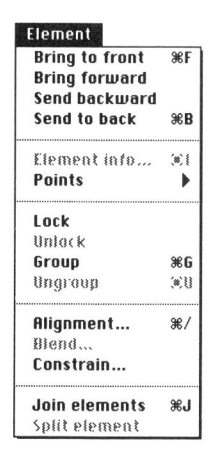

Figure 14.38 The Element menu

Bring to front

The Bring to front command changes the stacking order of elements so that the selected element is placed at the front of its layer. The keyboard shortcut is ⌘F.

PROCEDURE

Select the element or elements you want to bring to the front, then choose Bring to front from the Element menu, or press ⌘F. If you selected a single element, it is placed at the front of its layer. If you selected several elements, they retain their relative stacking order and are placed in front of all other elements on their layer.

If you select elements on different layers, each element moves to the front of its layer, but each element stays on its own layer.

Bring forward

The Bring forward command moves a selected element in front of an element that is positioned in front of it on the same layer. If you select several elements, they retain their relative stacking order, but each element moves in front of the element that was formerly immediately in front of it.

PROCEDURE

Select the element or elements you want to bring forward, then choose Bring forward from the Element menu. If you selected a single element, it moves in front of the element that was formerly immediately in front of it. If you selected several elements, each element moves in front of the element that was formerly immediately in front of it. If the selected elements were on different layers, each element stays on its own layer, but moves in front of the element that was formerly immediately in front of it.

TIP

The Bring forward command offers a finer degree of control than does Bring to front. Use Bring forward when you have multiple elements stacked on a single layer and want to adjust the stacking order of objects in the middle of the stack.

Send backward

The Send backward command moves a selected element behind an element that is positioned behind it on the same layer. If you select several elements, they retain their relative stacking order, but each element moves behind the element that was formerly immediately behind it.

PROCEDURE

Select the element or elements you want to send backward, then choose Send backward from the Element menu. If you selected a single element, it moves behind the element that was formerly immediately behind it. If you selected several elements, each element moves behind the element that was formerly immediately behind it. If the selected elements were on different layers, each element stays on its own layer, but moves behind the element that was formerly immediately behind it.

TIP

The Send backward command offers a finer degree of control than does Send to back. Use Send backward when you have multiple elements stacked on a single layer and want to adjust the stacking order of objects in the middle of the stack.

Send to back

The Send to back command changes the stacking order of elements so that the selected element is placed at the back of its layer. The keyboard shortcut is ⌘B.

PROCEDURE

Select the element or elements you want to send to the back, then choose Send to back from the Element menu, or press ⌘B. If you selected a single element, it is placed at the back of its layer. If you selected several elements, they retain their relative stacking order and are placed behind all other elements on their layer.

If you select elements on different layers, each element moves to the back of its layer, but each element stays on its own layer.

Element info...

The Element info command opens different dialog boxes, depending on the kind of element you selected. The dialog boxes generally contain information about the selected element, and also contain options that you can use to change the selected element. The keyboard shortcut is ⌘I. You can also Option-double-click an element to get element info, or in the case of a text object, simply double-click it.

PROCEDURE

Select the element about which you want to get information, then choose Element info from the Element menu, press ⌘I, or Option-double-click the object. A dialog box appears containing information about the selected element, and also contains some options that you can change. The dialog box you get varies according to the kind of element you selected.

THE PATH DIALOG BOX

When you choose Element info with a freeform path selected, the Path dialog box appears. It tells you how many points the path contains, and lets you change the following options:

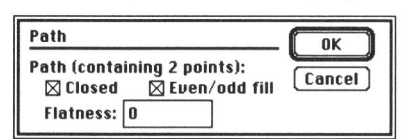

Figure 14.39 The Path dialog box

Closed is checked if the path is a closed path, and unchecked if the path is an open path. You can convert a closed path to an open path or vice versa by checking or unchecking this option. If you convert an open path to a closed path, FreeHand does so by joining the endpoints. If you convert a closed path to an open path, FreeHand does so by deleting the last line segment drawn.

The **Even/odd fill** option is checked by default. When a path intersects itself, FreeHand normally alternates filled and unfilled areas, as in the example of the five-pointed star below. If you want to fill the entire path, you should uncheck this option.

Figure 14.40 A five-pointed star with Even/odd fill checked and unchecked

The **Flatness** setting controls how FreeHand prints curves. PostScript treats curves as a series of very short straight-line segments. A path that requires more line segments than your printer can handle can cause a "limitcheck" error, which causes the printer to stop printing. You can control the number of segments in a path using a flatness setting from 0 to 100. A flatness setting of 0 attempts to reproduce the curve as faithfully as possible: increasing the flatness setting makes FreeHand use progressively fewer line segments to create the curve.

The flatness required to print a complex path will depend on the resolution of your printer. A high-resolution imagesetter produces a much smoother image at a given flatness value than does a desktop laser printer. For example, a flatness setting of 3 will generally produce excellent results on an imagesetter. Reducing the flatness setting may not improve the results noticeably, and increasing the flatness setting may still produce acceptable results and lessen the time required to print the illustration.

Unless you get a limitcheck error, or the illustration takes an unacceptably long time to print, you can leave the flatness value alone. You may want to experiment with it to arrive at an acceptable trade-off between image quality and printing speed.

Figure 14.41 Path flatness set at 0, 3, and 100, respectively

Click **OK** to put any changes you have made into effect and close the dialog box. Click **Cancel** to discard any changes and close the dialog box.

THE PATH/POINT DIALOG BOX

If you select a point on a freeform path and choose Element info, the Path/point dialog box appears. This contains the same options as does the Path dialog box, and adds options that apply to the selected point.

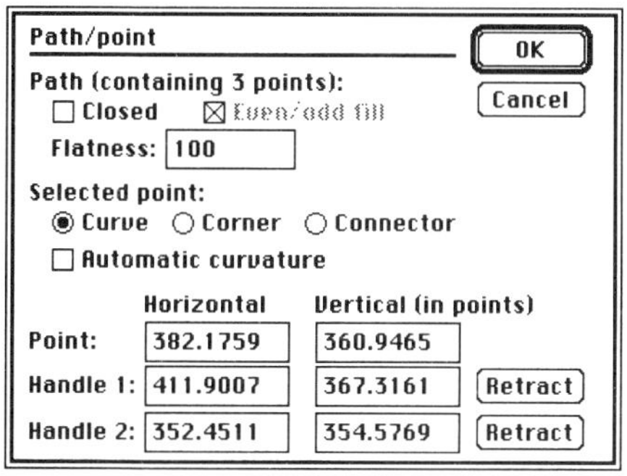

Figure 14.42 The Path/point dialog box

Under **Selected point**, you can use the radio buttons to change the point to another kind of point. The options are Curve point, Corner point, or Connector point.

When you create a point using the Curve, Corner, or Connector tool, FreeHand automatically places the point handles for you. This feature is called **Automatic curvature**. If you move a point handle, Automatic curvature is automatically turned off. You can check Automatic curvature to restore the path to its original shape.

The edit boxes at the bottom of the dialog box show the position of the selected point and both of its handles, using the unit of measure specified in the Document setup dialog box. You can type in new positions for the point and for either or both handles, or you can use the Retract buttons to retract either of the handles into the point.

Click **OK** to put any changes you have made into effect and close the dialog box. Click **Cancel** to discard any changes and close the dialog box.

THE ELLIPSE DIALOG BOX

If you select an ellipse (a basic shape created with the Ellipse tool) and choose Element info, the Ellipse dialog box appears. The dialog box contains edit boxes that show the position of the Top, Left, Bottom, and Right edges of the ellipse, using the unit of measure specified in the Document setup dialog box. (The coordinates are those of the smallest rectangle that would completely surround the ellipse.) You can type new positions in any of the edit boxes. The remaining option, **Flatness**, works identically to the Flatness option described under the Path dialog box above.

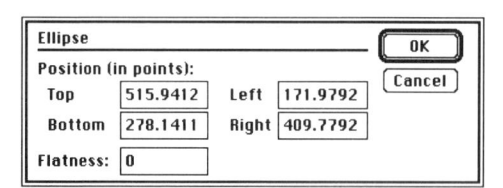

```
┌─────────────────────────────────────────┐
│ Ellipse                      ┌────OK────┐│
│ Position (in points):        │ Cancel  ││
│  Top    [515.9412]  Left [171.9792]    │
│  Bottom [278.1411]  Right [409.7792]   │
│  Flatness: [0]                          │
└─────────────────────────────────────────┘
```

Figure 14.43 The Ellipse dialog box

Click **OK** to put any changes you have made into effect and close the dialog box. Click **Cancel** to discard any changes and close the dialog box.

THE RECTANGLE DIALOG BOX

If you select a rectangle (a basic shape created with the Rectangle or Rounded-rectangle tool) and choose Element info, the Rectangle dialog box appears. This contains the same options as the Ellipse dialog box, plus one additional option, **Corner radius**. Corner radius shows the corner radius of the rectangle, using the unit of measure specified in the Document setup dialog box. You can change the corner radius by typing in a new value. A corner radius of 0 results in square corners.

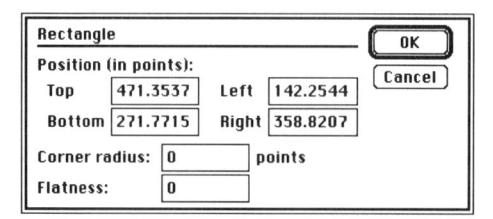

```
┌─────────────────────────────────────────┐
│ Rectangle                    ┌────OK────┐│
│ Position (in points):        │ Cancel  ││
│  Top    [471.3537]  Left [142.2544]    │
│  Bottom [271.7715]  Right [358.8207]   │
│  Corner radius: [0]    points           │
│  Flatness:      [0]                     │
└─────────────────────────────────────────┘
```

Figure 14.44 The Rectangle dialog box

Click **OK** to put any changes you have made into effect and close the dialog box. Click **Cancel** to discard any changes and close the dialog box.

THE GROUP DIALOG BOX

If you select a grouped object other than a basic shape and choose Element info, the Group dialog box appears. The edit boxes under **Position** give the vertical and horizontal coordinates of the lower-left corner of the imported image, using the unit of measure specified in the Document setup dialog box. Leave **Group transforms as a unit** unchecked if you want line weights and fill patterns in the group to remain undistorted during transformations. Check this option if you want to distort the line weights and fills during transformations. If you transform a group as a unit, you can return the distorted line weights and fills to an undistorted (but transformed) state by ungrouping the group.

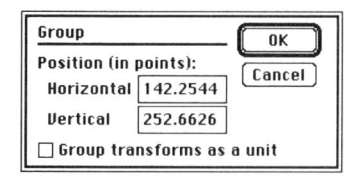

Figure 14.45 The Group dialog box

THE BLEND DIALOG BOX

If you select a blended object created using the Blend command and choose Element info, the Blend dialog box appears. You can change the **Number of steps** in the blend, or change the percentages for **First blend** and **Last blend**. When you click OK to close the dialog box, FreeHand recalculates the blend according to your specifications. (See the description of the Blend command on page 468.)

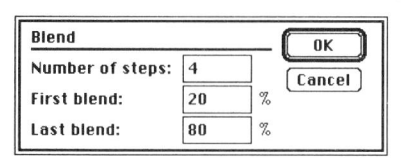

Figure 14.46 The Blend dialog box

THE COMPOSITE PATH DIALOG BOX

If you select a composite path created using the Join elements command and choose Element info, the Composite path dialog box appears. The options it contains are **Even/odd fill** and **Flatness**. These options work as described under the Path dialog box on page 451.

456 Using Aldus FreeHand 3.0

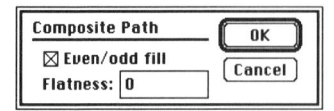

Figure 14.47 The Composite path dialog box

THE TEXT DIALOG BOX

If you select a text object and choose Element info, the Text dialog box appears. See "Text Tool" in Chapter 12 for a full description of the options in the Text dialog box.

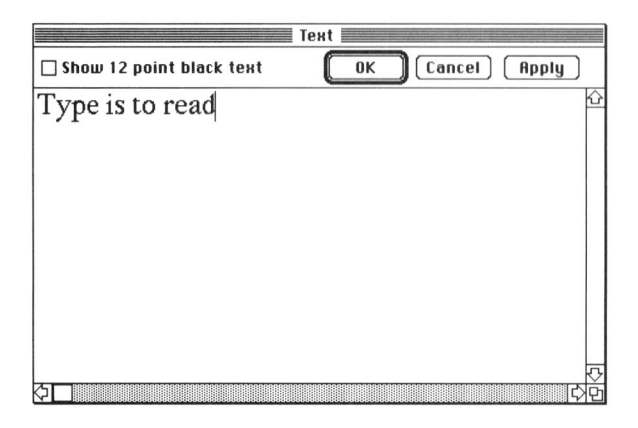

Figure 14.48 The Text dialog box

THE TEXT ALONG A PATH DIALOG BOX

If you select text that is bound to a path using the Join elements command and choose Element info, the Text along a path dialog box appears. Under **Align text to path using**, three options are offered. **Baseline** aligns the baseline of the text to the path, **Ascent** aligns the tops of the ascenders to the path, and **Descent** aligns the bottoms of the descenders to the path.

Figure 14.49 The Text along a path dialog box

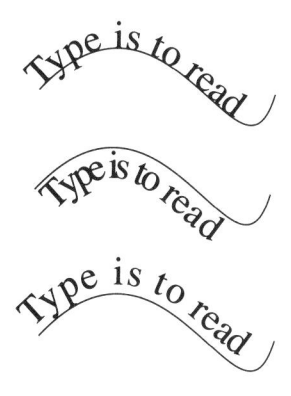

Figure 14.50 Text aligned to a path using Baseline, Ascent, and Descent

Under **Orientation of text**, four options are offered. **Rotate around path** rotates each character so that its baseline is parallel to the path. **Vertical** keeps each character vertical, but moves the baseline to follow the path. **Skew horizontally** skews each character horizontally by the angle between the baseline and the path, while **Skew vertically** skews each character vertically by the angle between the baseline and the path.

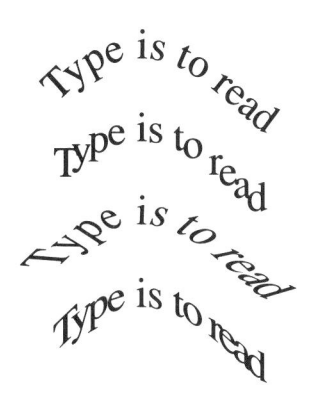

Figure 14.51 Text oriented to a path using Rotate around path, Vertical, Skew horizontally, and Skew vertically

When the **Show path** option is turned off, fill colors selected from the Colors palette apply to the text only. When Show path is turned on, fill colors selected from the Colors palette apply to the path only. You can still apply color to the text using the Text dialog box. Click **OK** to put any changes you have made into effect and close the dialog box. Click **Cancel** to discard any changes and close the dialog box. Click **Edit text** to open the Text dialog box, where you can edit the text.

THE TEXT ON AN ELLIPSE DIALOG BOX

If you select text that is bound to an ellipse using the Join elements command and choose Element info, the Text on an ellipse dialog box appears. Text on an ellipse behaves like a special case of text on a path. When you bind text to a freeform path and the text contains a Return character, any text after the Return is ignored. When you bind text to an ellipse, text before the Return is bound to the top of the ellipse, and text after the Return is bound to the bottom of the ellipse. The Text on an ellipse dialog box thus offers separate options for aligning text to the top and the bottom of the ellipse. The options, Baseline, Ascent, and Descent, work identically to those described under the Text along a path dialog box.

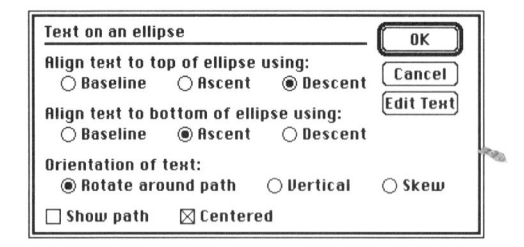

Figure 14.52 The Text on an ellipse dialog box

Under **Orientation of text**, the options work as they do for text along a path, except that there is no Skew horizontally option. The **Skew** option works the same as Skew vertically in the Text along a path dialog box.

When the **Show path** option is turned off, fill colors selected from the Colors palette apply to the text only. When Show path is turned on, fill colors selected from the Colors palette apply to the path only. You can still apply color to the text using the Text dialog box. Click the **Centered** option if you want text center-aligned and bound to the top and bottom of the ellipse. If you leave this option unchecked, the text will take on the alignment you specified in the Text dialog box, and will be bound to the top of the ellipse only. Click **OK** to put any changes you have made into effect and close the dialog box. Click **Cancel** to discard any changes and close the dialog box. Click **Edit text** to open the Text dialog box, where you can edit the text.

THE EPS ELEMENT AND COLOR IMAGE DIALOG BOXES

If you select an imported EPS or color TIFF image and choose Element info, the EPS element or Color image dialog box, respectively, appears. The options in these dialog boxes are identical. **Position** gives the vertical and horizontal coordinates of the lower-left corner of the imported image, using the unit of measure specified in the Document setup dialog box. **Scale** shows the horizontal and vertical scaling percentage. You can scale an imported image by typing a new scaling percentage in either of the Scale edit boxes. To scale proportionally, type the same percentage in both the Horizontal and Vertical scale edit boxes.

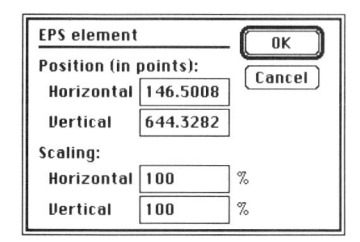

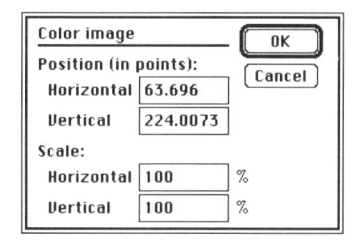

Figure 14.53 The EPS element and Color image dialog boxes

Click **OK** to put any changes you have made into effect and close the dialog box. Click **Cancel** to discard any changes and close the dialog box.

THE IMAGE DIALOG BOX

If you select an imported grayscale TIFF or a MacPaint format image and choose Element info, the Image dialog box appears. Four radio buttons at the upper left control how the image is displayed and printed. **Black and white** converts a grayscale image to black-and-white. You can use the Gray-level bars to control which levels of gray are converted to black and which to white. Black and white is automatically selected if the image is a MacPaint-format (black and white) bitmap. See the discussion of Gray-level bars, below. **Transparent** makes the white pixels in a black-and-white image transparent. **Screened** makes grayscale images display as screened black-and-white images for faster screen redrawing. It has no effect on the way the image prints. **Gray** displays grayscale images with true gray levels when you have a monitor capable of doing so. If your monitor cannot display true gray levels, this option is dimmed and grayscale images appear in black and white.

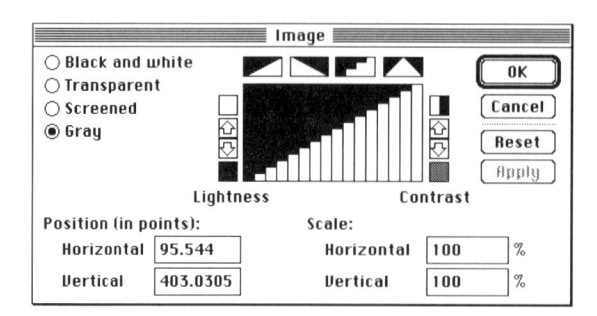

Figure 14.54 The Image dialog box

The **Gray-level bars** let you control the levels of gray in a grayscale image, or control how a grayscale image is converted to black and white. The bars show 16 levels of gray, from black at the left to white at the right. You can drag the individual gray bars to modify the gray levels. Although only 16 levels are shown, FreeHand will adjust levels across all 256 shades of gray available in a grayscale TIFF image. When you convert a grayscale image to black and white, the default is to convert all pixels lighter than 50% gray to white and all pixels darker than 50% gray to black. You can adjust the way pixels are converted by dragging the Gray-level bars to make different gray levels black or white.

The **Lightness** control adjusts the overall brightness of the image. Click the up or down arrow to increase or decrease the brightness of the image. The Gray-level bars move interactively as you adjust the Lightness control. You cannot apply this option to an unscreened black-and-white image.

The **Contrast** control adjusts the ratio of dark to light areas in the image. Click the up or down arrow to increase or decrease the contrast of the image. The Gray-level bars move interactively as you adjust the Lightness control. You cannot apply this option to an unscreened black-and-white image.

The **Special effects icons** apply special effects to gray-level images. ◾ resets the image to normal after you have adjusted the gray levels. ◾ converts the image to a negative. ◾ posterizes the image to four shades of gray. ◾ solarizes the image, converting half of the gray levels in the image to negative.

The horizontal and vertical **Position** edit boxes show the current position of the lower-left corner of the image. You can move the image by typing in new position coordinates. The unit of measure used is the one you specified in the Document setup dialog box. (See "Document setup," earlier in this chapter.)

The Horizontal and Vertical **Scale** edit boxes let you scale the image by typing in scaling percentages. To scale the image proportionally, enter the same scaling percentage for horizontal and vertical scaling.

Points

The Points command displays a submenu containing commands that apply to one or more selected points. You can remove a selected point or points, apply automatic curvature to a selected point or points, or change the point or points from one type to another. If no points are selected, all commands on the submenu are dimmed and unavailable.

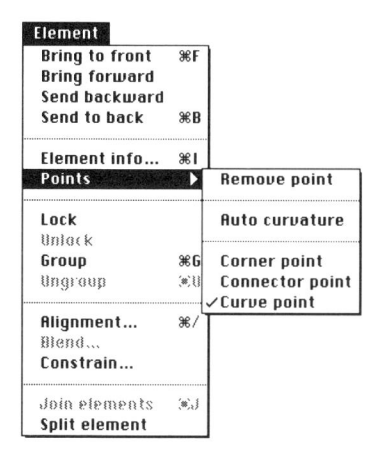

Figure 14.55 The Points submenu

PROCEDURE

First select the point or points you want to modify. Then, choose Points from the Element menu and drag across to the right into the submenu to the command you want to choose.

REMOVE POINT

The Remove point command removes the selected point or points. The selected points can be on different paths. If you remove a point from a closed path, FreeHand closes the path by joining the points adjacent to the one you removed. If you remove a point from an open path, FreeHand joins the adjacent points unless the point you removed was an endpoint. In that case, the point adjacent to the one you removed becomes the new endpoint of the open path.

AUTOMATIC CURVATURE

When you create a point using the Curve, Corner, or Connector tool, FreeHand automatically places the point handles for you. This feature is called Automatic curvature. If you move a point handle, Automatic curvature is automatically turned off. You can choose Automatic curvature to turn Automatic curvature on for the selected points, and thereby restore the path to its original shape. The selected points can be on different paths. If Automatic curvature is on, a check mark is displayed in front of the command. You can also use the command to turn Automatic curvature off, but since it is automatically turned off when you move a point handle, it makes little sense to use the menu command to do so.

CORNER POINT

Choose Corner point to convert all selected points to corner points. The handles of a corner point can be adjusted completely independently of one another.

CONNECTOR POINT

Choose Connector point to convert all selected points to connector points. The handles of a connector point are constrained to move in a straight line formed by the connector point and the previous point for the first handle, the connector point, and the following point for the second handle.

CURVE POINT

Choose Curve point to convert all selected points to curve points. The handles of a curve point move in unison, and always fall along a straight line that passes through the center of the point.

Lock

The Lock command lets you lock an element or elements. You can select a locked element and apply attributes like color and line weight, but you cannot delete, move, or transform it.

PROCEDURE

Select the element or elements you want to lock, then choose Lock from the Element menu. The element remains selected, but is locked in position. A small padlock symbol appears in the information bar, indicating that the element is locked. Note that you can only lock an entire element, not points. You cannot for example, lock only the endpoints of a path.

TIP

If you want to align an element or elements to another element, but you do not want that element to move, lock it. You can then use the Alignment command to align the unlocked elements with the locked one.

Unlock

The Unlock command unlocks a selected element that has been locked in place using the Lock command. If no selected elements are locked, the command is dimmed and unavailable.

PROCEDURE

Select a locked element that you want to unlock, then choose Unlock from the Element menu. The selected element remains selected but is no longer locked in place.

Group

The Group command combines selected elements into a single grouped object, freezing them in relation to each other. The keyboard shortcut is ⌘G. You can move, resize, or transform the group as a single object. When you group elements, they all move to the current drawing layer, but they retain their relative stacking order. You can group any combination of single paths, basic shapes (which are grouped when you create them), composite paths, and text blocks. You can also group grouped objects: you can use the Group command up to eight times, creating groups within groups. When you want to work with individual elements in a group, you can either ungroup the object or subselect the individual elements by Option-clicking with the Pointer tool.

PROCEDURE

Select two or more elements that you want to group, then choose Group from the Element menu, or press ⌘G. The selected elements are combined into a single grouped object, and the group displays four handles at the corners of the imaginary box that surrounds it, indicating that it is selected. You can resize a grouped object by dragging one of the corner handles. To resize the group proportionally, hold down the Shift key as you drag.

You can control how grouped elements transform using the Element info command from the Element menu. (See the description of the Element info command on page 451.)

TIP

The Group command is invaluable when working with complex illustrations. By grouping related elements in an illustration, you minimize the chance of accidentally selecting or moving a component of an illustration. Whenever you have a component of an illustration that you want to treat as a single unit, use the Group command to combine the elements into a single entity. You can still work with the individual components of the group using the subselection techniques discussed in the description of the Pointer tool in Chapter 12.

You can nest groups within other groups. To subselect a nested group, first Option-click the Pointer tool on an element in the nested group to select that element. Then press the Tilde (~) key. This selects the subgroup that contains the subselected element. Each subsequent press of the Tilde key selects the next subgroup added to the group.

CAUTION

When you create a group, all elements move to the same layer. While the relative stacking order among the elements in the group is preserved, this can change the stacking order relative to elements that are not part of the group. Think carefully before grouping a large number of elements in a multi-layer document.

Ungroup

The Ungroup command reverses the effect of the Group command, turning a grouped object back into independent elements. The keyboard shortcut is ⌘U.

PROCEDURE

Select the grouped object you want to ungroup, then choose Ungroup from the Element menu, or press ⌘U. The grouped object reverts to its independent components, which remain selected.

If a grouped object is itself composed of groups, the subgroups remain as grouped objects. Choose Ungroup again to ungroup the subgroups.

Basic shapes (ellipses and rectangles) are created as grouped objects. If you want to adjust individual points on a basic shape, you must first ungroup it.

Alignment...

The Alignment command opens the Alignment dialog box, where you can align two or more elements, distribute (average) three or more elements, or align a single element to the snap-to grid. The keyboard shortcut is ⌘/.

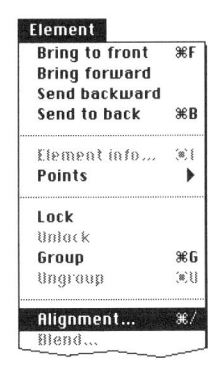

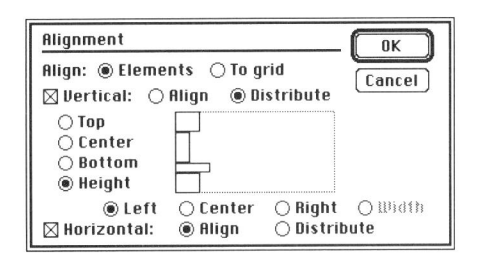

Figure 14.56 The Alignment dialog box

ALIGNING ELEMENTS TO THE GRID

To align an element to the snap-to grid, make sure that Snap to grid is turned on, then select the element you want to align, and choose Alignment from the Element menu, or press ⌘/. The Alignment dialog box appears.

Under **Align**, click To grid. To align the element vertically to the grid, check **Vertical** and select Top, Center, or Bottom. To align the element horizontally to the grid, check **Horizontal** and select Left, Center, or Right, then click OK to close the dialog box. FreeHand aligns the element to the grid using the imaginary bounding box that encloses it. For example, if you specified Top under Vertical and Left under Horizontal, FreeHand aligns the top left corner of the bounding box to the nearest grid point.

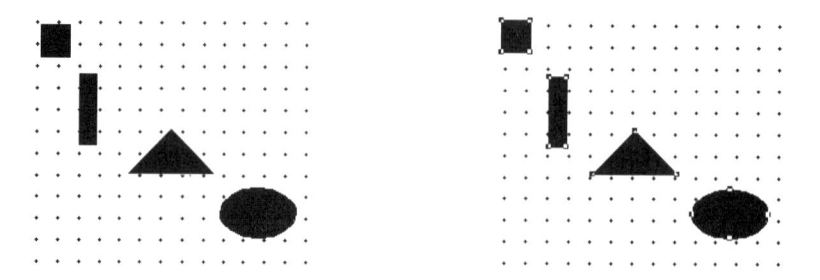

Figure 14.57 Elements not aligned to grid. Elements aligned to grid

ALIGNING ELEMENTS TO EACH OTHER

You can also use the Alignment command to align elements to each other. You can align paths, grouped elements, composite paths, and a combination of locked and unlocked elements to each other. If one or more of the elements is locked, the locked elements will not move, and the other elements will align to them. If all selected elements are locked, the Alignment command is dimmed and unavailable. If none of the elements are locked, FreeHand will align them all according to the specifications you set in the dialog box.

You can set specifications for aligning or distributing vertically and/or horizontally, in any combination. The shapes in the center of the dialog box move to reflect the settings you have chosen. The settings are as follows:

Vertical align. Top aligns the topmost handle or point of each selected element, or aligns all elements to the topmost locked element. Center aligns the elements at the average vertical distance between the centers of the elements. Bottom aligns the lowest handle or point of each selected element, or aligns all elements to the lowest locked element.

Figure 14.58 Elements' centers aligned vertically

Vertical distribute. Top places the tops of the selected elements at an equal vertical distance. Center places the centers of the selected elements at an equal vertical distance. Bottom places the bottoms of the selected elements at an equal vertical distance. Height places the elements so there is an equal amount of vertical space between each element.

Figure 14.59 Elements distributed vertically by height

Horizontal align. Left aligns the leftmost handle or point of each selected element, or aligns all elements to the leftmost locked element. Center aligns the elements at the average horizontal distance between the centers of the elements. Right aligns the rightmost handle or point of each selected element, or aligns all elements to the rightmost locked element.

Figure 14.60 Elements' centers aligned horizontally

Horizontal distribute. Left places the left sides of the selected elements at an equal vertical distance. Center places the centers of the selected elements at an equal horizontal distance. Right places the right sides of the selected elements at an equal horizontal distance. Width places the elements so there is an equal amount of horizontal space between each element.

Figure 14.61 Elements distributed horizontally by width

Blend...

The Blend command creates a series of intermediate shapes or colors between two selected paths. The two elements must be freeform paths. You cannot blend grouped objects, composite paths, basic shapes (unless you first ungroup them), text, or imported TIFF, EPS, or MacPaint-type images. Furthermore, both paths must be the same type, either both open or both closed. You cannot blend an open path with a closed one. Finally, lines, fills, and colors must be the same type on both paths. You cannot blend a process color with a spot color, or a patterned fill with a basic fill. You can blend two paths with patterned fills or basic dashed lines, but the fills and lines themselves will not blend. They will switch from one to the other at the halfway point. You can, however, blend a radial fill into another radial fill, or a graduated fill into another graduated fill as long as both are logarithmic or both are linear.

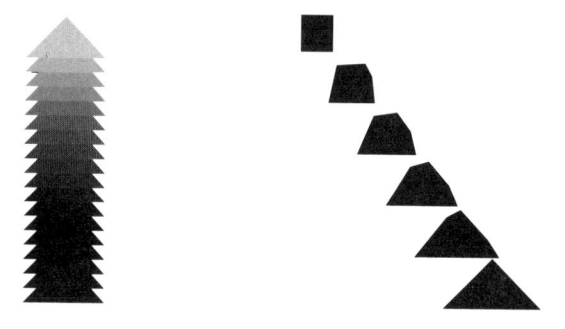

Figure 14.62 1. A blend between two shades 2. A blend between two shapes

PROCEDURE

First select the two paths that you want to blend. If both are closed paths, you must select a point on each path to act as a reference point before the Blend command becomes available. FreeHand connects one reference point to the other when it blends the shapes, so the reference points you choose affect the intermediate shapes produced. If both are open paths, you can choose the Blend command from the Element menu immediately, because FreeHand automatically uses the endpoints as reference points. Once you choose the Blend command, the Blend dialog box appears.

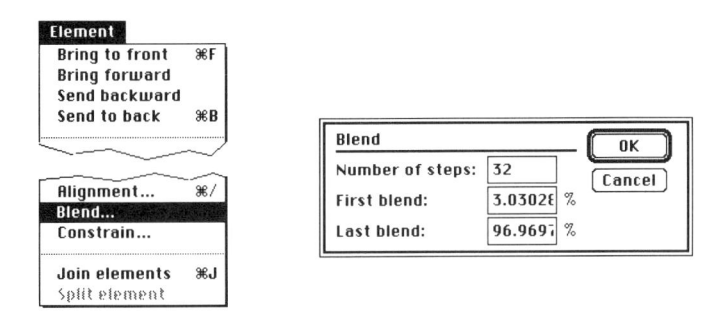

Figure 14.63 The Blend dialog box

In the **Number of steps** edit box, type the number of intermediate shapes and/or colors that you want FreeHand to create. For information on the number of steps required to produce smooth color gradients, see Chapter 6.

If you leave the **First blend** and **Last blend** values unchanged, FreeHand automatically calculates the percentage required to space the intermediate elements evenly between the two original paths.

First blend is the percentage of the distance between the two paths where the first intermediate shape will be placed. **Last blend** is the percentage of the distance between the two paths where the last intermediate shape will be placed. The allowable range of values for First blend and Last blend is from -100 to 200. If you use a value of less than 0% or more than 100%, the blend created will extend beyond the original paths.

Click OK to close the dialog box and create the blend. FreeHand creates the blend as a single grouped object that includes the two original paths. The new blended element remembers the number of steps and the first and last blend percentages. If you subsequently edit one of the original paths, FreeHand will automatically reblend the blended element. You can edit the blended element in any of three ways.

- You can select the blended object, then choose Element info from the Element menu or press CI. The Blend dialog box appears, where you can change the number of steps, or the percentage for First blend and Last blend.

- You can subselect one of the original paths by Option-clicking with the Pointer tool, then change the line, the fill, the color, the position, or the shape of the path.

- You can use the Ungroup command to ungroup the blended element, then edit the individual shapes. In this case, only the shape you edit changes. The blended element does not reblend.

TIP

If the blended element appears to cross over itself, and that is not the effect you intended, the original paths may have been drawn in opposite directions. If this problem occurs, you can fix it in one of two ways. If the path is symmetrical, you can flip it with the Reflecting tool. If the path is asymmetrical, you can redraw the path, or trace it with the Tracing tool. (The Tracing tool always draws clockwise.)

Constrain...

The Constrain command opens the Constrain dialog box, where you can change the constrain angle. The constrain angle applies to basic shapes, and also to the drawing tools when the Shift key is held down. By default, the constrain angle is set at 0 degrees. When you draw a basic shape, the sides are oriented to the horizontal and vertical axis. Likewise, if you hold down the Shift key while using one of the drawing tools, their movement is constrained to the horizontal and vertical. If you want to draw basic shapes at a different angle, or constrain the drawing tools to a different angle, you can do so using the Constrain command.

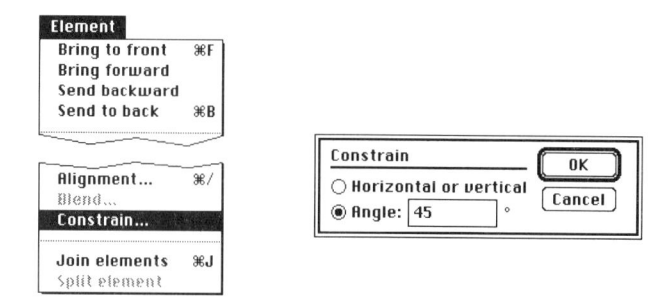

Figure 14.64 The Constrain dialog box

PROCEDURE

Choose Constrain from the Element menu. The Constrain dialog box appears. Type the constrain angle you want in the Angle edit box. To restore the constrain angle to the horizontal and vertical axes, type 0 in the Angle edit box, or click the Horizontal or Vertical radio button.

Figure 14.65 A rectangle drawn with a constrain angle of 0 (left), 45% (center), and 72% (right)

Join elements

The Join elements command has three functions. You can use it to join two open paths, you can use it to combine two or more unlocked, ungrouped, closed paths to form a composite path, or you can use it to bind text to a path. The keyboard shortcut is ⌘J.

The main use of composite paths is to create objects that have transparent holes through which you can see the elements that lie behind the composite path. When you join two or more paths to create a composite path, the parts of the paths that overlap become holes, and the rest of the composite takes on the fill and line attributes of the rearmost path.

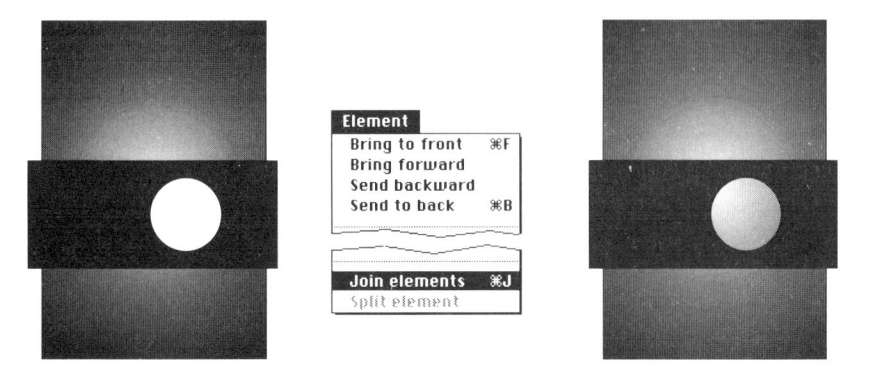

Figure 14.66 A composite path composed of a black rectangle and a circle yields a rectangle with a transparent hole

You can also join closed paths that do not overlap, allowing some interesting special effects. For example, if you apply a graduated fill, it graduates across the entire composite path, rather than within each individual path.

You can join any number of closed paths (including other composite paths) to make a composite path, either by selecting and joining them all simultaneously, or by successively adding more closed paths to an existing composite path. If you do the latter, FreeHand nests them, remembering the order in which the paths were joined. If you later split them apart, FreeHand splits them in the reverse order.

Figure 14.67 A composite path (three rectangles) with a graduated fill

You can also use the Join elements command to join text to freeform paths or to basic shapes. You can place text along curves, within circles, around squares, or along vertical or diagonal lines. If you join text to an ellipse, you can divide it so part of the text appears at the top of the ellipse, and the remainder appears right side up along the bottom of the ellipse. When you join text to a path, the type specifications remain intact. You can change these specifications without splitting the text from the path. The path itself can be visible or invisible.

Figure 14.68 Text along a path

JOINING TWO OR MORE OPEN PATHS

To join two or more open paths to make a single path, first make sure that the paths are open, ungrouped, and unlocked. Next, position an endpoint of one path on top of an endpoint of the path you want it to join. You can simultaneously join several open paths as long as one endpoint on each path is positioned on top of an endpoint of one of the other paths to be joined, and all the paths are selected.

Once the paths are positioned, select each path to be joined, then choose Join elements from the Element menu, or press ⌘J. The paths join to create a single path. If the selected paths were on different layers, FreeHand moves them to the current drawing layer when they are joined.

CREATING COMPOSITE PATHS

To create a composite path, select two or more ungrouped, unlocked, closed paths. Position the paths on top of each other to create transparent holes. Position them separately to create special effects. Then choose Join elements from the Element menu, or press ⌘J. FreeHand joins the elements into a single composite path. Once the paths are joined, handles appear at the four corners of the invisible bounding box that encloses the composite path. You can resize the composite path by dragging one of the handles. To resize it proportionally, hold down the Shift key as you drag.

Each of the paths you joined is a subpath of the composite path. You can subselect individual subpaths by Option-clicking with the Pointer tool. You can move, transform, resize, split, duplicate, or delete a selected subpath. If you duplicate a subpath, the duplicate is not part of the composite path. If you split a subpath of a composite path, the entire path is treated as open, and cannot be filled until the open subpath is either closed or removed from the composite path.

When you apply a fill to a composite path, FreeHand fills the path but leaves areas where subpaths intersect unfilled, creating transparent holes. If you want to fill the entire path uniformly, choose Element info from the Element menu, and uncheck Even/odd fill in the Composite path dialog box. (See the section on the Element info command, above.) If the paths you have joined were drawn in opposite directions, however, FreeHand continues to alternate filled and unfilled areas. To fill this kind of composite path uniformly, you must either redraw the subpath that was drawn in the wrong direction, or subselect it and reflect it using the Reflecting tool.

JOINING TEXT TO A PATH

To join text to a path or a basic shape, select the path or basic shape and the text object you want to join to it, then choose Join elements from the Element menu, or press ⌘J. FreeHand joins the text to the path, and the path itself becomes invisible.

If the text object contains a Return character, only the text before the Return appears on the path, unless the path is an ellipse or circle. In that case, the text before the Return appears at the top of the circle or ellipse, and the text after the Return appears right side up at the bottom of the ellipse. Text is aligned on the path according to the alignment you choose from the Alignment command submenu in the Type menu.

If the text is shorter than the path, all the text appears on the path. If the text is longer than the path, the remaining text is hidden. If the text is aligned left or vertically, overflow text disappears from the right end. If it is centered, the overflow disappears from both ends. If it is aligned right, the overflow disappears from the left end, and if it is justified, the space between words and letters disappears and the letters overlap.

To edit text joined to a path, or to control how the characters conform to the shape of the path, use the Element info command from the Element menu. (See "Text Along a Path" and "Text on an Ellipse" under the Element info command, above. See also Chapter 7.)

TIPS

Composite paths can become complex and difficult to print when the subpaths together contain many points. If you just want to keep a set of elements together, and are not using any of the attributes that are unique to composite paths, group the elements using the Group command instead. (See "Group" earlier in this chapter.)

Composite paths provide a more efficient way of masking objects than do clipping paths created using the Paste inside command. Unless you need to use a clipping path, use a composite path instead. (See "Paste inside," above.)

Text that has been converted to paths using the Convert to paths command from the Type menu is also a composite path. You can obtain interesting special text effects by using the Join elements command to join composite paths converted from text to other paths. (See "Convert to paths" later in this chapter.)

Split element

The Split element command splits elements that were joined using the Join elements command. It can also be used to split an ungrouped path at a selected point. If you split an open path, it becomes two open paths. If you split a closed path, it becomes an open path.

PROCEDURE

To split a path, select the point at which you want the path to split, then choose Split element from the Element menu. If the path was an open path, it becomes two open paths, both of which are selected. If the path was a closed path, it becomes an open path and remains selected.

To split a composite path, select the composite path and choose Split element from the Element menu. The subpaths of the composite path become separate paths, and all are selected. The paths retain the stacking order they had before they were joined to make the composite, but keep the fill and line attributes of the composite path, rather than the attributes they had before they were joined to make the composite path.

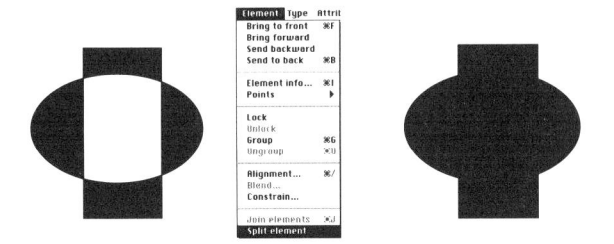

Figure 14.69 Splitting a composite path

To split text along a path from the path, select the text's path with the Pointer tool and choose Split element from the Element menu. The text block returns to its original position in the illustration window, and the path remains in place. If the path was invisible, it becomes visible, and both the path and the text block are selected.

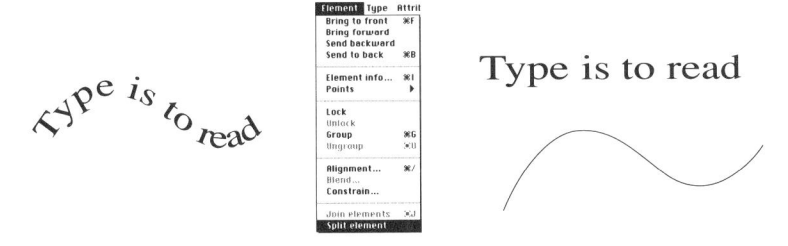

Figure 14.70 Splitting text from a path

The Type Menu

The Type menu contains commands for formatting text. In addition to basic text formatting options such as font, size, style, leading, and alignment, the Type menu contains commands that let you control word spacing and letter spacing, scale type horizontally, shift the baseline of selected characters or an entire text block up or down, apply special effects to text in PostScript Type 1 or Type 3 fonts, and convert text in PostScript Type 1 or Type 3 fonts to editable composite paths. For information on installing and working with fonts, see Appendix B: Using Fonts with Aldus FreeHand.

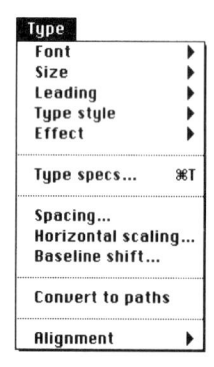

Figure 14.71 The Type menu

You can apply the commands in the Type menu to an entire text object by selecting it with the Pointer tool and choosing the command you want. You can apply most of the commands to individual characters or a range of characters in a text object by opening the Text dialog box for that text object and selecting the characters to which you want the commands to apply. The Alignment commands and the Convert to paths command apply to entire text blocks.

To open the Text dialog box for a text object, you can select the text object with the Pointer tool and choose Element info (⌘I) from the Element menu, or double-click the text object with the Pointer tool. When you create a new text object by clicking or dragging the Text tool in the illustration window, the Text dialog box appears automatically.

Font

The Font command displays a submenu that lists all the fonts available on your system. For information on how to install fonts, consult the documentation that came with your Macintosh system software.

PROCEDURE

First select the text object or the characters whose font you want to change. Then choose Font from the Type menu, drag across to the right into the submenu, drag to the font you want, then release the mouse button. The selected text is displayed in the font you chose.

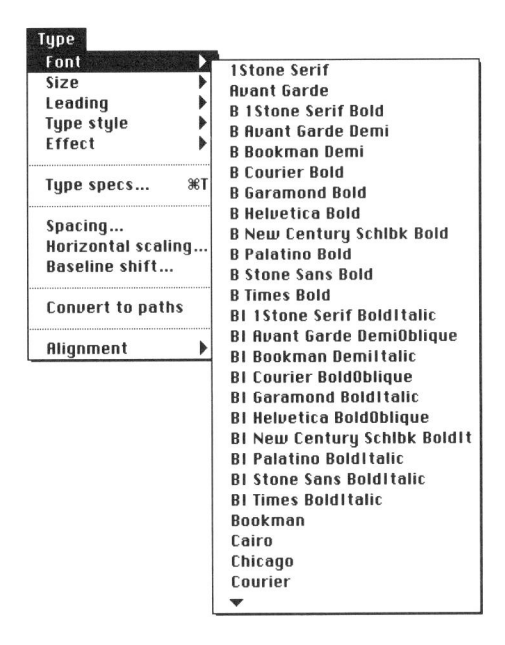

Figure 14.72 The Font submenu

TIP

In general, PostScript and TrueType fonts print more legibly and offer much more flexibility than do bitmapped fonts. You can transform PostScript fonts and apply special effects to them that are unavailable for TrueType or bitmapped fonts. Unless you are deliberately aiming for a bitmapped appearance as a special effect, you should always use PostScript or TrueType fonts for text in FreeHand. (See Appendix B: Using Fonts with Aldus FreeHand.)

Size

The Size command displays a submenu that lists eleven commonly used type sizes from 8 to 72 points, plus the Other command. The Other command lets you specify any type size from 0.1 points to 3000 points. Only whole point sizes can be displayed on the screen. When you enter a fractional point size, the size is rounded to the nearest whole number for display, but prints exactly as you specified. Sizes smaller than 4 points or larger than 72 points are not displayed at actual size in the Text dialog box, but appear at the specified size in the illustration window. Text is never greeked in the Text dialog box.

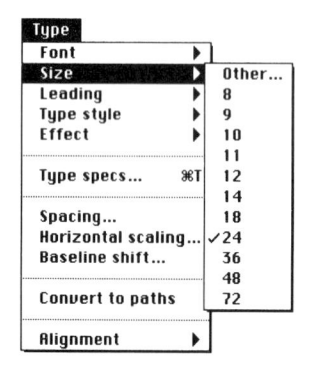

Figure 14.73 The Size submenu

PROCEDURE

First select the text object or the characters whose size you want to change. Then choose Size from the Type menu, drag across to the right into the submenu, drag to the size you want, then release the mouse button. The selected text is displayed at the size you chose. If you want to use a size other than those in the list, choose Other. The Type size dialog box appears. Type the size you want in the Size edit box, then click OK. The selected text is assigned the size you chose. If you choose a size smaller than 4 points or larger than 72 points, the type will not be displayed at actual size in the Text dialog box, but will appear at the specified size in the illustration window.

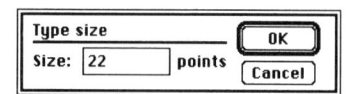

Figure 14.74 The Type size dialog box

Leading

The Leading command displays a submenu that offers a choice of Auto leading, Solid leading, or Other, where you can specify a value for leading in 0.1-point increments. Leading (pronounced to rhyme with "heading") is the amount of vertical space between lines of type, measured in points from baseline to baseline. In the printing and design industry, type is usually described by its type size in relation to its leading. For example, the term "10 on 12" (written 10/12) indicates 10-point type on 12-point leading.

PROCEDURE

First select the text object or the characters whose leading you want to change. Then choose Leading from the Type menu, drag across to the right into the submenu, and choose the command you want.

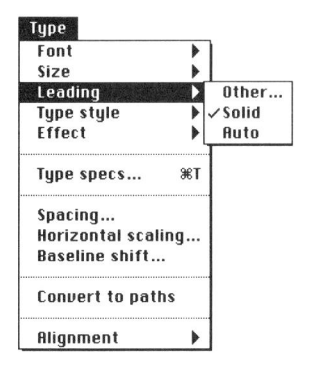

Figure 14.75 The Leading submenu

SOLID

Choose Solid to apply leading that equals the point size of the type, as in 10-point type on 10-point leading.

AUTO

Choose Auto to apply leading that is 120% of the type size, as in 10-point type on 12-point leading.

OTHER

Choose Other to open the Leading dialog box, where you can type a leading value in 0.01-point increments.

480 Using Aldus FreeHand 3.0

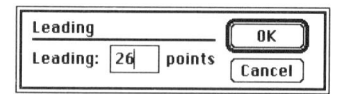

Figure 14.76 The Leading dialog box

If you apply different leading values to characters on the same line, the line takes on the largest leading value applied to any of the characters it contains.

TIP
Large type, type in all caps, and type with no descenders generally look best when you specify negative leading, that is, leading that is smaller than the type size. Conversely, type in small sizes is often made more readable by adding extra leading.

Type style

The Type style command displays a submenu that offers a choice of Plain, Bold, Italic, and Bold italic styles. Whether or not these styles are available for a particular font depends on whether the styles are included in the font file. If a font lacks these styles, the styles that it lacks will be dimmed and unavailable. However, you can simulate them using commands from the Effect submenu. (See "Effect," below.)

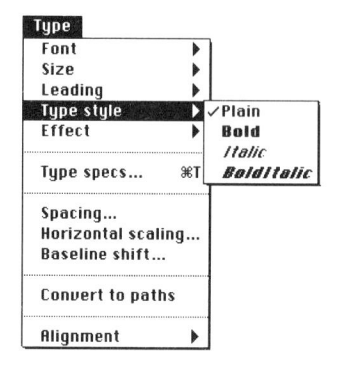

Figure 14.77 The Type style submenu

If you use *unharmonized* fonts (that is, if the Helvetica family appears on your font menu as BHelvetica Bold, BIHelvetica Bold Italic, IHelvetica Italic, and Helvetica, rather than Helvetica alone), you should choose the styled font directly from the Font menu, and ignore the Type style command.

PROCEDURE

First select the text object or the characters whose type style you want to change. Then choose Type style from the Type menu, drag across to the right into the submenu, and choose the style you want.

The Type style submenu offers four styles: Plain, Bold, Italic, and Bold italic, as shown in Figure 14.78.

plain, **bold**
italic, ***bold italic***

Figure 14.78 Plain, Bold, Italic, and Bold italic type

Effect

The Effect command displays a submenu that offers a choice of special effects that you can apply to PostScript fonts. If the font you are using is not a PostScript Type 1 or Type 3 font, these effects cannot be used and the commands are dimmed and unavailable. Some of the effects simulate type styles that are missing from the font, while others let you design distinctive special type effects. You cannot apply more than one command from the Effect submenu to the same character, but you can apply multiple effects within a text object.

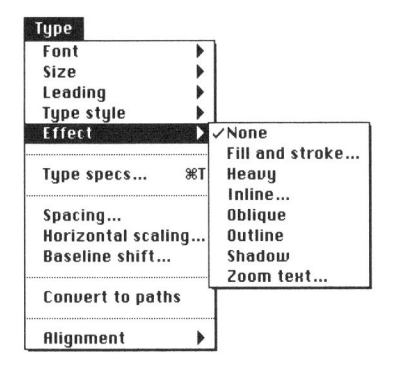

Figure 14.79 The Effect submenu

Text effects are not displayed in the Text dialog box, but they display on the screen if the Display text effects option is checked in the Preferences dialog box. (See the description of the File menu's Preferences command earlier in this chapter.)

PROCEDURE

First select the text object or the characters to which you want to apply an effect. Then choose Effect from the Type menu, drag across to the right into the submenu, and choose the effect you want. The Effect submenu offers the following commands:

NONE

None is the default and applies no special effect.

FILL AND STROKE

The Fill and stroke command opens the Fill and stroke dialog box, where you can apply a different color to the interior of a character than to the outline. You can also control the width of the outline, and whether or not the fill or the stroke (outline) overprints. PostScript text is drawn by default as a filled path with no line, so adding a stroke to type usually makes it appear somewhat heavier than normal.

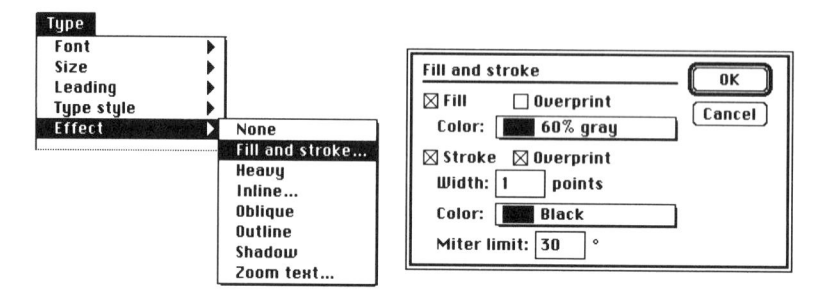

Figure 14.80 The Fill and stroke dialog box

Check **Fill** to fill the text. You can choose any of the colors you have defined for your illustration from the **Color** pop-up menu. When you are printing spot color separations and two or more elements (including text) overlap, FreeHand normally knocks out the background color. If you check **Overprint**, the background color will not be knocked out. Text in 100% black automatically overprints.

Check **Stroke** to apply an outline to the text. You can specify the width of the outline in points by typing a value in the Width edit box, and you can choose a color from the **Color** pop-up menu. In the **Miter limit** edit box, you can set the angle at which corners are converted to mitered angles, preventing spikes from appearing on sharp corners. **Overprint** works the same as for the Fill settings. You can compensate for slight misregistration problems in spot color separations by setting the stroke of a character to overprint.

When you have applied a fill and stroke to text, you can use the Colors palette to change both the fill and stroke colors. To change the fill color, click the Fill indicator in the palette, then click the color you want. To change the stroke, click the Line indicator and choose a color.

filled and stroked type

Figure 14.81 Filled and stroked type

HEAVY

The Heavy command simulates bold type for fonts that lack a bold style, or makes a bold font even bolder.

INLINE

The Inline command opens the Inline dialog box. Inline text is a solid character surrounded by a background space and one or more outlines. When several characters are grouped together in a word, overlapping sections of the individual outlines disappear so the adjoining characters share the same background area.

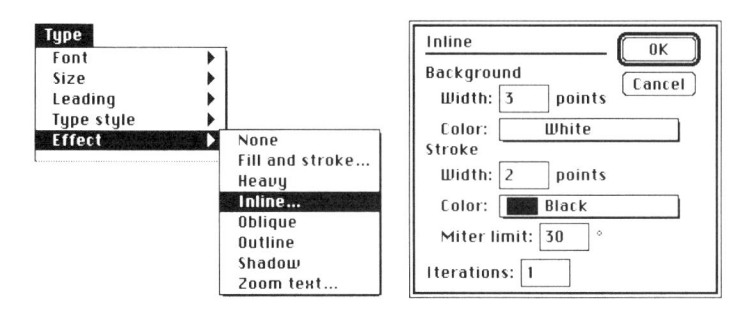

Figure 14.82 The Inline dialog box

Under **Background**, you can specify the width (in points) and the color (from any of the colors defined for the illustration) of the background. Since the background surrounds the inline character, twice the width you specify is actually added to the character. For example, if a character is in a 10-point size and you specify 1 iteration of a 6-point inline, the overall size of the final inline character will be 22 points—10 points for the character, 6 points for the background above, and 6 points for the background below.

Under **Stroke**, you can specify the width (in points) and the color (from any of the colors defined for the illustration) of the inline characters and of the outline enclosing the background.

Under **Iterations**, type the number of outlines that you want. Each outline is separated from the previous one by the amount you specified for Width in Background. If you specify more than 3 iterations, printing time will increase significantly and the effect may not display accurately on the screen. **Miter limit** sets the angle at which corners are converted to mitered angles, preventing spikes from appearing on sharp corners.

Figure 14.83 Inline type

OBLIQUE

The Oblique command simulates italic type for faces that lack an italic style by slanting the characters. You can also use it to slant italic type even more.

OUTLINE

The Outline command removes the interior fill of a character, leaving only the outline.

SHADOW

The Shadow command applies a 50% gray drop shadow below and to the right of the text. You cannot edit the color or the angle of the drop shadow.

oblique type

outline type

shadow type

Figure 14.84 Oblique, outline, and shadow type

ZOOM TEXT

The Zoom text command opens the Zoom text dialog box. The Zoom text effect lets you project the text by a specific percentage and at a specific angle to give perspective effect. It also lets you blend the color from the foreground to the background text.

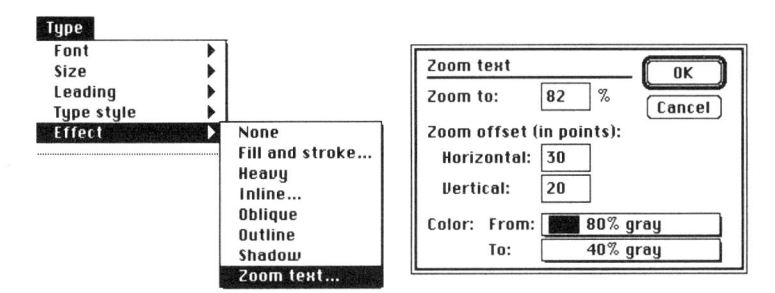

Figure 14.85 The Zoom text dialog box

Type a percentage in the **Zoom to** edit box to determine the size of the background character that zooms forward to the foreground character. For example, if the text is 24-point and you enter a zoom percentage of 60%, FreeHand creates a 14.4-point background character. The smaller you make the zoom percentage, the more pronounced the perspective illusion becomes as the text seems to zoom forward sharply from a vanishing point.

Zoom offset values (in points) determine the direction and distance of the zoom. Horizontal offset is measured relative to the center of the text, and Vertical offset is measured relative to the baseline.

From the **Color** pop-up menus, choose a color for the background from the **From** pop-up menu, and a color for the foreground from the **To** pop-up menu. The intermediate colors blend from the background to the foreground color.

Figure 14.86 Zoomed text

CAUTION

Because zoomed text is relatively complex, you should use it sparingly to avoid excessively long screen redrawing and printing times.

Type specs...

The Type specs command opens the Type specifications dialog box, where you can set all the options from the Type menu at once. When you need to change more than one attribute of selected text, you should use the Type specs command. The keyboard shortcut is ⌘T.

PROCEDURE

First select the text object or characters whose attributes you want to change, then choose Type specs from the Type menu, or press ⌘T. The Type specifications dialog box appears, offering all the options in the Type menu in one dialog box. All the options work as they do if you choose the individual commands from the Type menu.

Figure 14.87 The Type specifications dialog box

When one or more text blocks contain type with more than one variation of an attribute, the Type specifications dialog box displays all the attributes that are shared by all the type, and leaves blank those that differ. You can use the Type specifications dialog box to change these attributes. For example, you can select type in several different colors and change it all to the same color.

Spacing...

The Spacing command opens the Spacing dialog box, where you can increase or decrease the amount of space between words and between characters. Default letter space and word space values are built into all PostScript fonts. The Spacing command lets you override these default values. Entering values of 0 points restores spacing to its default values.

PROCEDURE

First select the text object or characters whose spacing you want to change, then choose Spacing from the Type menu. The Spacing dialog box appears.

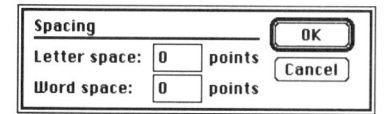

Figure 14.88 The Spacing dialog box

In the **Letter space** edit box, you can type a value from -288 points to 288 points for the space between letters. If you use a large negative value compared with the type size, the text will reverse itself and read from right to left.

In the **Word space** edit box, you can type a value from -288 points to 288 points for the space between words. If you use a large negative value compared with the type size, the word order will change. An extremely large negative value will make each word wrap to the next line.

14 points with default spacing

14 points with 2 points letter spacing

14 points with 2 points letter spacing, 2 points word spacing

Figure 14.89 Examples of type with different spacing values

Horizontal scaling...

The Horizontal scaling command opens the Horizontal scaling dialog box, where you can type a percentage for horizontal scaling. A percentage of less than 100% makes the characters narrower, and a percentage greater than 100% makes them wider. The point size of the text remains the same.

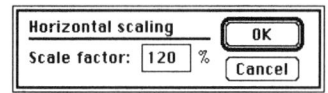

Figure 14.90 The Horizontal scaling dialog box

PROCEDURE

First select the text object or characters whose horizontal scaling you want to change, then choose Horizontal scaling from the Type menu. The Horizontal scaling dialog box appears. In the **Scale factor** edit box, you can type a percentage between 0.1% and 10,000%. Scale factors of less than 100% make the characters narrower, and Scale factors greater than 100% make them wider. The point size of the text remains the same.

Type scaled horizontally 100%

Type scaled horizontally 120%

Type scaled horizontally 130%

Type scaled horizontally 90%

Type scaled horizontally 80%

Figure 14.91 Examples of horizontally scaled type

Baseline shift...

The Baseline shift command opens the Baseline shift dialog box, where you can type a value to shift selected text above or below its normal baseline, the invisible line on which characters rest.

You can use baseline shift to superscript or subscript certain characters or words, or you can join text to a curved path and use baseline shift to control the distance between the text and the path.

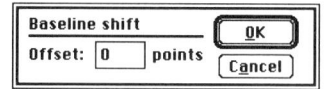

Figure 14.92 The Baseline shift dialog box

PROCEDURE

First select the text object or characters whose baseline shift you want to change, then choose Baseline shift from the Type menu. The Baseline shift dialog box appears. In the **Offset** edit box, you can type a value from -10000 points to 10000 points. Positive values raise the type above the baseline, while negative values lower it below the baseline.

positive values of baseline shift create ^{superscript}, negative values create $_{subscript}$

Figure 14.93 Type shifted above and below the baseline

Convert to paths

The Convert to paths command lets you convert a selected text object formatted with a PostScript Type 1 or Type 3 font into a composite path. You can then edit the character shapes, or use the composite path to mask other objects. The outline font file for the PostScript font must be available on your system. For information on installing and using fonts, see Appendix B: Using Fonts with Aldus FreeHand.

Once a text object has been converted to a composite path, it becomes a graphic object, and can no longer be formatted or edited as text. The conversion process is one-way. You cannot convert the composite path back to text. You can only convert entire text objects. You cannot convert a single character or range of characters within a text object.

PROCEDURE

Select the text object you want to convert to a composite path, then choose Convert to paths from the Type menu. The selected text object is converted to a composite path, and it becomes selected. If you converted a text object containing more than one character, each character is also a composite path. If you want to manipulate individual characters, you can subselect them by Option-clicking with the Pointer tool, or you can choose Split element from the Element menu to turn the characters into independent composite paths. For more information on composite paths, see the description of the Element menu's Join elements command earlier in this chapter. See Chapter 7 for examples of text converted to paths.

text

text converted to paths

Figure 14.94 A text object and a text object converted to paths

CAUTION

To convert type to paths, the printer fonts must be installed and available. For information on installing and using fonts, see Appendix B: Using Fonts with Aldus FreeHand.

Alignment

The Alignment command displays a hierarchical submenu that offers a choice of five different alignment options: Align left, Align center, Align right, Justify, and Vertical. These options, which control how type aligns to the margins of text objects, apply only to entire text objects, not to ranges of text within a text object.

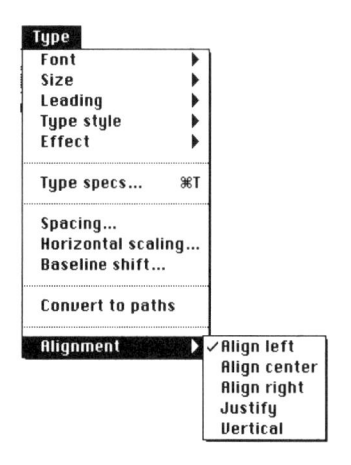

Figure 14.95 The Alignment submenu

A check mark on the Alignment submenu indicates the current alignment of selected text. If several text blocks with different alignments are selected, no check mark is displayed. If no text is selected, the check mark displays the current default setting.

PROCEDURE

Select the text object whose alignment you want to change. Then choose Alignment from the Type menu, drag across to the right into the submenu, and choose the command you want.

The Alignment submenu offers the following commands:

ALIGN LEFT

The Align left command aligns the beginning of each line of type to the point where the Text tool was clicked to create the text object.

these three lines of
sample text are
aligned left

Figure 14.96 Text aligned left

ALIGN CENTER

The Align center command aligns the center of each line of type to the point where the Text tool was clicked to create the text object.

these three lines of
sample text are
aligned center

Figure 14.97 Text aligned center

ALIGN RIGHT

The Align right command aligns the end of each line of type to the point where the Text tool was clicked to create the text object.

these three lines of
sample text are
aligned right

Figure 14.98 Text aligned right

JUSTIFY

The Justify command aligns the beginning of each line of type to the left margin of the text object, and the end of each line of type with the right margin of the text object, adding space between words as necessary.

**three   lines   of
sample   text   with
justified   alignment**

Figure 14.99 Justified text

VERTICAL

The Vertical command positions characters vertically one above the other, so the text reads from top to bottom.

```
t    s    a
h    a    l
r    m    i
e    p    g
e    l    n
     e    e
l    t    d
i    e
n    x    v
e    t    e
s         r
               t
o         i
f         c
          a
          l
```

Figure 14.100 Vertical text

The Attributes Menu

The Attributes menu contains commands that let you define and apply fill and line attributes; create spot colors, process colors, and tints of a spot color that appear on the Colors palette; specify a halftone screen angle and frequency; define a collection of line, fill, and halftone screen specifications as a style that appears on the Styles palette; attach a non-printing note to an element; and choose from a variety of line weights.

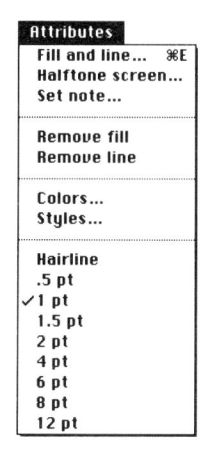

Figure 14.101 The Attributes menu

Fill and line...

The Fill and line command opens the Fill and line dialog box, where you can define and apply a wide variety of fills and lines to a selected element or elements. The keyboard shortcut is ⌘E.

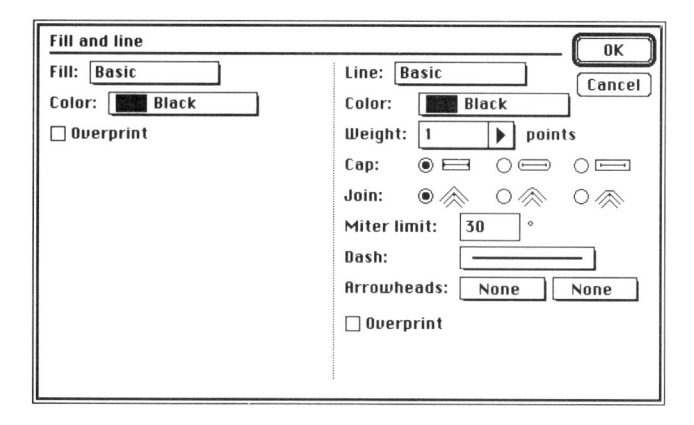

Figure 14.102 The Fill and line dialog box

Only a closed path or a composite path with all of its subpaths closed can display or print a fill. You can apply a fill to an open path, but it will neither display nor print until you close the path. (You can close an open path using the Element info command from the Element menu. See "Element info" earlier in this chapter.)

The kinds of fill available in FreeHand are:

- No fill at all (None)
- A solid color or tint (Basic)
- A smooth linear or radial color gradient (Graduated or Radial)
- One of many patterns supplied with FreeHand (Patterned or Custom)
- A pattern you create using PostScript code (PostScript)
- Repeat patterns composed of a design that you have created in FreeHand (Tiled)

A line follows the outline of a path. You can define a line's width (in points), its pattern, color, and the type of cap and join at corners. The kinds of line available in FreeHand are:

- No line (None)
- A line in a solid color or tint, which can be a solid line or a dashed line, with or without arrowheads at one or both ends (Basic)
- A line using one of many patterns supplied with FreeHand (Patterned or Custom)
- A patterned line you create using PostScript code (PostScript)

If you want to apply a basic fill or line, it is usually faster and easier to do so using the Colors palette. (See the description of the Colors palette in Chapter 13.)

PROCEDURE

Select the element or elements to which you want to apply a fill, a line, or both, then choose Fill and line from the Attributes menu, or press ⌘E. The Fill and line dialog box appears, where you can specify the kind of fill and/or line you want.

From the **Fill** pop-up menu, choose the kind of fill you want. The other options available depend on the kind of fill you choose.

The **None** command applies a fill of None. If you choose None, there are no other options to be set.

BASIC FILLS

The Basic fill command applies a fill in a solid color or tint. If you choose Basic, you can choose any of the colors or tints you have defined for the illustration from the Color pop-up menu. When you are printing spot color separations and two or more elements (including text) overlap, FreeHand normally knocks out the background color. If you check **Overprint**, the background color will not be knocked out.

Fill and line
Fill: Basic
Color: ■ Black
☐ Overprint

Figure 14.103 Basic fill dialog box options

GRADUATED FILLS

The Graduated fill command fills an element with a smooth variation in color from one side of the object to the other. You can specify the starting and ending colors, and the direction of the fill. When you select an element with a graduated fill, the Colors palette shows the starting color.

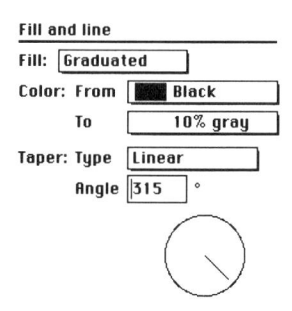

Fill and line
Fill: Graduated
Color: From ■ Black
        To   10% gray
Taper: Type Linear
       Angle 315 °

Figure 14.104 Graduated fill dialog box options

You can use a variety of color combinations in a graduated fill:

- Two process colors
- White and a spot color
- White and a process color
- A spot color and a tint based on that spot color
- Two tints based on the same spot color

You cannot use two different spot colors, a spot color and a process color, or black and another spot or process color.

In the **Color** options, choose the starting color from the **From** pop-up menu, and the ending color from the **To** pop-up menu.

In the **Taper** options, the **Type** pop-up menu lets you choose either a linear or a logarithmic gradation. A **Linear** gradation has equal increments of color change throughout. A **Logarithmic** gradation starts with a narrow band of the starting color and progresses in increasingly wider increments to the ending color. You can type a number of degrees in the **Angle** edit box, or you can drag the dial arm in the circle to set the angle. The arm points toward the edge of the circle in the direction of the ending color. FreeHand measures angles clockwise, with 0 degrees at the three-o'clock position.

PATTERNED FILLS

The Patterned fill command fills the element with one of the 64 designs provided by FreeHand. These are designed primarily for printing on non-PostScript printers, and provide support for imported PICT images that use these patterns. You can use the scroll bars to scroll through the patterns, and select one by clicking it. You can use the patterns as supplied, or edit them, pixel by pixel, to create your own using the enlarged view of the pattern immediately below the Color menu.

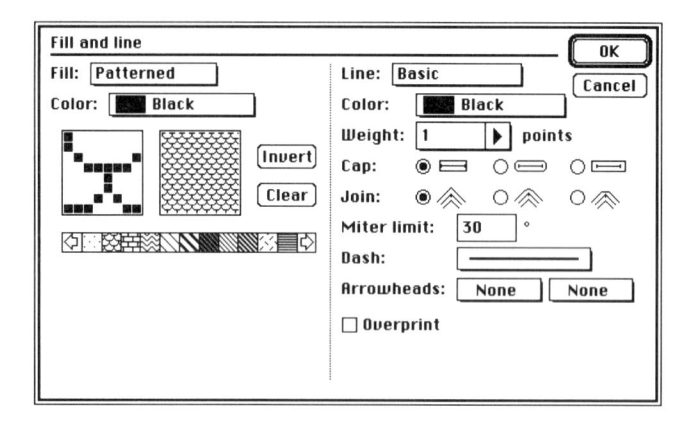

Figure 14.105 Patterned fill dialog box options

Patterns are opaque, and print at a fixed resolution of 72 dots per inch. They contain two colors, white and the color you select from the **Color** pop-up menu. Patterns print accurately only with spot colors that are not tints and with the primary colors derived from combining process colors (cyan, magenta, yellow, cyan+yellow=green, cyan+magenta=blue, magenta+yellow=red), plus black. Click **Invert** to change the selected color to white, and white to the selected color. Click **Clear** to remove a pattern from the display box and create another pattern.

POSTSCRIPT FILLS

The PostScript fill command lets you create your own fills by typing up to 255 characters of PostScript code in the edit box. On the screen, PostScript fills display as a series of small PSs, but print accurately on a PostScript printer providing the code conforms to PostScript-language standards.

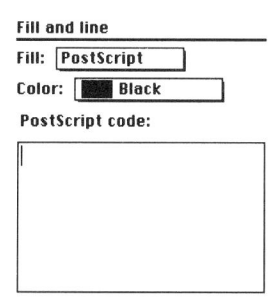

Figure 14.106 PostScript fill dialog box options

RADIAL FILLS

The Radial fill command fills the element with smooth gradations of color in concentric circles. Choose a color from the **From** pop-up menu for the center color, and another from the **To** pop-up menu for the color that appears at the edge of the element. The constraints on the kinds of colors you can use are the same as for Graduated fills.

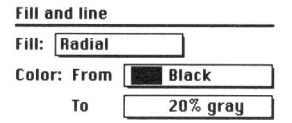

Figure 14.107 Radial fill dialog box options

TILED FILLS

The Tiled fill command fills a path with repetitions of a tile that you have created yourself. The tile repeats in all directions as a fill. You can use any combination of basic shapes, open or closed paths, composite paths, and text objects in a tile. You cannot use imported TIFF, EPS, or MacPaint-type images, or another element containing a tiled fill.

To create a tiled fill, first create an element to use as the tile, and give it a line, fill, and color. If you want space between each tile in your fill, draw a square larger than the tile, position it over the tile, give it a fill and line of None, then choose Send to back from the Edit menu. Select the element (and the square, if you want space between the tiles), then choose Cut from the Edit menu to cut the element from the illustration and place it on the Clipboard.

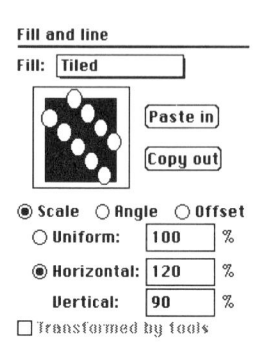

Figure 14.108 Tiled fill dialog box options

Next, select the path to be filled with the tiles and choose Fill and line from the Attributes menu. Then choose Tiled from the Fill pop-up menu. Click **Paste in** to paste the tile from the Clipboard into the dialog box. The element then appears in the dialog box. The remaining options affect the way the tile fills the element. The **Copy out** button copies a tile from a fill onto the Clipboard, so that you can paste it back into the illustration for editing. When you have edited to your satisfaction, you can cut it once more and paste it into the dialog box to recreate the tiled fill.

Click the **Scale** button if you want to change the size of the tile. **Uniform** scale lets you type in a single percentage to scale the tile proportionally. Or you can click the **Horizontal** button to enter different horizontal and vertical scaling percentages.

Click **Angle** to rotate the tile. You can type a number of degrees in the edit box, or drag the dial arm in the circle. FreeHand measures angles clockwise, with 0 degrees at the three-o'clock position.

Click **Offset** to change the way the path frames the tile. You can type horizontal and vertical offset values in the **H** and **V** edit boxes. By default, tiles are placed starting at the lower left corner of the illustration page, which is the location of the Offset value of 0,0.

When you transform an element containing a tiled fill, the tiles are transformed with the element, and the **Transformed by tools** option becomes active. If you select the transformed element, choose Fill and line, and uncheck this option, the path remains transformed but the tiled fill reverts to its previous untransformed state.

CUSTOM FILLS

The Custom fill command lets you choose one of FreeHand's 19 built-in Custom fills for a wide variety of special effects. For a complete description and sample of each Custom fill, see Chapter 6.

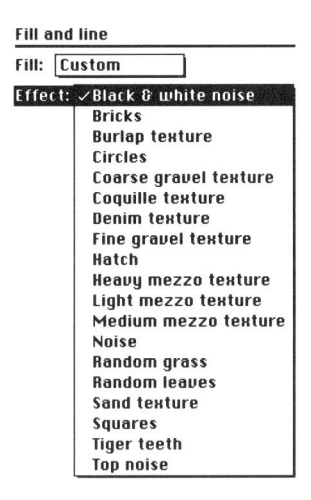

```
Fill and line
Fill: [Custom    ]
Effect: ✓Black & white noise
        Bricks
        Burlap texture
        Circles
        Coarse gravel texture
        Coquille texture
        Denim texture
        Fine gravel texture
        Hatch
        Heavy mezzo texture
        Light mezzo texture
        Medium mezzo texture
        Noise
        Random grass
        Random leaves
        Sand texture
        Squares
        Tiger teeth
        Top noise
```

Figure 14.109 Custom fill dialog box options

LINE OPTIONS

From the Line pop-up menu, choose the kind of line you want. The other options available depend on the kind of line you choose.

The **None** command applies a line of None. If you choose None, there are no other options to be set.

BASIC LINES

The Basic command applies a basic line, which may be solid or dashed. You can choose a color for the line from the Color pop-up menu, which lists all the colors you have defined for the illustration. In the Weight edit box, you can specify a line weight from 0 to 288 points. A line of zero weight will make the printer print the thinnest line of which it is capable. Bear in mind that a 1-pixel line printed on a 2,540 dpi imagesetter will be very difficult, if not impossible, to reproduce on a printing press. In general, you should choose Hairline from the pop-up menu beside the edit box when you want a fine line.

Figure 14.110 Basic line dialog box options

The **Cap** option gives you three choices for the shape of the end of the line. Butt caps (the default) are squared off perpendicular to the path; the cap does not extend beyond the path. Round caps end the line in a semicircular cap with a diameter equal to the line weight. Projecting caps have square ends that project half the line weight beyond the end of the path.

The **Join** option gives you three choices for the shape of corners formed by the line. Miter joins (the default) extend the edges of two converging lines until they meet. (The description of Miter limit appears next in this section.) Round joins connect corners with a circular arc whose diameter is equal to the line weight. Bevel joins finish the converging lines with butt caps and fill the resulting notch with a triangle, giving the corner a squared-off appearance.

Miter joins at very small angles result in a long spike that projects from the corner. To avoid this, the **Miter limit** edit box lets you specify the minimum angle for miter joins. Corners with a smaller angle than the limit you specify are converted to bevel joins instead.

Figure 14.111 Cap style and miter examples

You can choose a solid or dashed line from the **Dash** pop-up menu. To change the length of the dashes within a line, hold down the Option key while you select the kind of line you want. The Line pattern dialog box opens, where you can specify how many points should be on (black) and how many should be off (white). The line you create is saved in the Dash pop-up menu for subsequent use in the illustration.

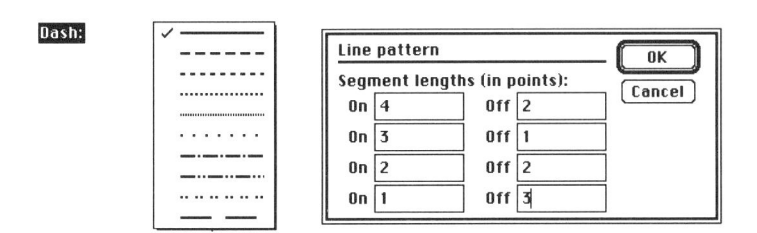

Figure 14.112 The Dash pop-up menu

You can choose a variety of arrowhead styles from the **Arrowheads** pop-up menus. The menu on the left applies the arrowhead you select to the first point on the path, and the menu on the right applies the selected arrowhead to the last point on the path. FreeHand applies the arrowhead to the end of the path, which extends the path's length. You can then resize the path as necessary. To make arrowheads visible in keyline view, hold down the Option key as you move or resize a line containing an arrowhead.

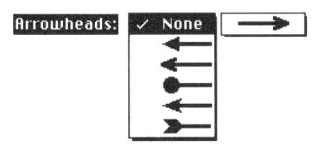

Figure 14.113 The Arrowheads pop-up menus

When you are printing spot color separations and two or more elements (including text) overlap, FreeHand normally knocks out the background color. If you check **Overprint**, the background color will not be knocked out.

PATTERNED LINES

The **Patterned** command lets you apply the same set of patterns that are available for fills to lines. These work best with thick lines, because the pattern remains the same size, regardless of line width. See "Patterned Fills," above, for details on how to choose and edit the patterns. The **Weight**, **Cap**, **Join**, and **Miter limit** options are the same as for a basic line.

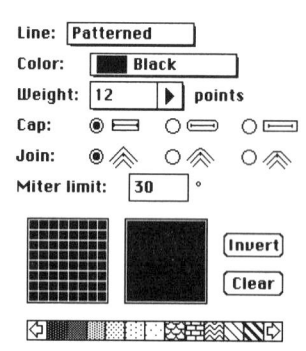

Figure 14.114 Patterned line options

POSTSCRIPT LINES

The PostScript command lets you create your own custom lines by typing up to 255 characters of PostScript code in the edit box. On the screen, PostScript lines display as solid lines of the weight and color you specify, but print accurately on a PostScript printer providing the code conforms to PostScript-language standards.

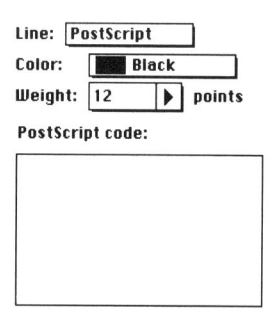

Figure 14.115 PostScript line options

CUSTOM LINES

The Custom command lets you choose one of FreeHand's 23 built-in custom lines for a wide variety of special effects. For a complete description and sample of each custom line, see Chapter 3.

Halftone screen...

The Halftone screen command opens the Halftone screen dialog box, where you can specify a screen type, angle, and frequency for a selected element. If you apply a halftone screen to an element using the Halftone screen command, the specifications will override those you set in the Print options dialog box, but only for the selected element. If an element uses process colors, you should avoid applying halftone screens using the Halftone screen command, because process color rotates the screen to a different angle for each of the four process colors (cyan, magenta, yellow, and black).

You can use the Halftone screen command to apply different screens to different parts of your illustration for special effects, such as screening an imported grayscale image with a low-frequency screen using a line pattern instead of the usual dot pattern.

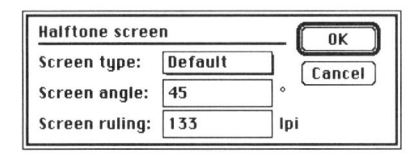

Figure 14.116 The Halftone screen dialog box

PROCEDURE

Select the element or elements to which you want to apply a halftone screen, then choose Halftone screen from the Attributes menu. The Halftone screen dialog box appears, where you can choose the screen type, angle, and ruling (frequency).

The **Screen type** pop-up menu offers three choices:

Default uses the screen pattern built into your PostScript printer. In most cases the default is set to produce black dots on a white background for light shades and white dots on a black background for dark shades.

Line produces a screen composed of parallel lines, usually used for special effects. The lines narrow to produce light shades and widen to produce dark shades.

Round dot produces a pattern of black dots that increase in size as the shade gets darker.

In the **Screen angle** edit box, type a number to represent the direction of the screen pattern. FreeHand measures the screen angles clockwise, with 0 degrees at the three-o'clock position. Note that if you print to an imagesetter and choose a transverse paper size from the Paper size option in the Print options dialog box, the entire illustration is rotated 90 degrees to save film. However, the halftone screens do not rotate with the illustration, so if you want to preserve the orientation of the halftone screens, you should add 90 degrees to the screen value when you use one of the transverse paper sizes.

In the **Screen ruling** edit box, type a number to represent the number of lines per inch (lpi) that the screen should use. In general, if you are printing to a 300-dots-per-inch (dpi) laser printer, you should use a screen ruling of 65 lpi or less, or a screen ruling of 150 lpi or less if you are printing to a 2,540 dpi imagesetter. Screen rulings of less than 9 lpi for a laser printer or 20 lpi for an imagesetter are not recommended. They will print very slowly and may make the printer run out of memory, causing a failure to print.

default screen at 133 lpi, 45°

round dot screen at 85 lpi, 45°

line screen at 30 lpi, 0°

Figure 14.117 Halftone screen types

Set note...

The Set note command opens the Set note dialog box, where you can type a short, non-printing note that you can attach to an element. For example, if you are creating a color illustration on a black-and-white screen, you can attach a note reminding you of the color you have applied to the element.

PROCEDURE

Select the element or elements to which you want to attach a note, then choose Set note from the Attributes menu. The Set note dialog box appears. You can type up to 255 characters, including spaces. When you type the note, do not press Return to move to the next line or you will close the dialog box. FreeHand wraps the lines automatically.

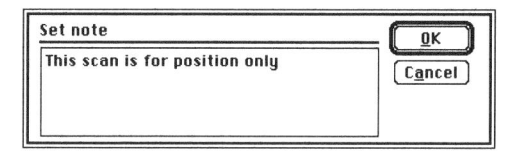

Figure 14.118 The Set note dialog box

You can review or edit an existing note by selecting the element to which the note is attached and choosing the Set note command. The Set note dialog box appears, containing the note. Review or edit the note, then click OK to save the changes to the note and close the dialog box.

CAUTION

You can inadvertently overwrite an existing note by attaching a note to several elements. If you select more than one element and choose Set note, the Set note dialog box that appears is blank even though one of the elements may have a note attached to it. If you type a note and click OK, you will overwrite any existing notes attached to any of the currently selected elements.

Remove fill

The Remove fill command removes the fill from a selected element or elements, replacing it with a fill of None.

PROCEDURE

Select the element or elements from which you want to remove the fill, then choose Remove fill from the Attributes menu. All selected elements take on a fill attribute of None.

Remove line

The Remove line command removes the line from a selected element or elements, replacing it with a line of None.

PROCEDURE

Select the element or elements from which you want to remove the line, then choose Remove line from the Attributes menu. All selected elements take on a line attribute of None.

Colors...

The Colors command opens the Colors dialog box, where you can define and name process and spot colors, or tints based on a spot or process color. You can also use the Colors command to edit an existing color, and apply the new color to all elements that contain that color. The same dialog box appears when you choose New or Edit from the pop-up menu on the Colors palette, when you double-click a color in the Colors palette, or when you hold down the Option key while choosing a color from the Colors pop-up menu in any dialog box that contains one. Note that you cannot edit either black or white.

You can define custom spot colors using any of three color models: RGB (red, green, blue); HLS (Hue, Lightness, Saturation); or CMY (cyan, magenta, yellow); or you can choose one of over 700 PANTONE® colors. For process colors, you can define custom colors by specifying percentages of cyan, magenta, yellow, and black, or you can choose a PANTONE color as the source color and let FreeHand calculate the percentages of cyan, magenta, yellow, and black necessary to reproduce it. You define a tint as a percentage of a base color, which can be a spot color, a process color, or another tint.

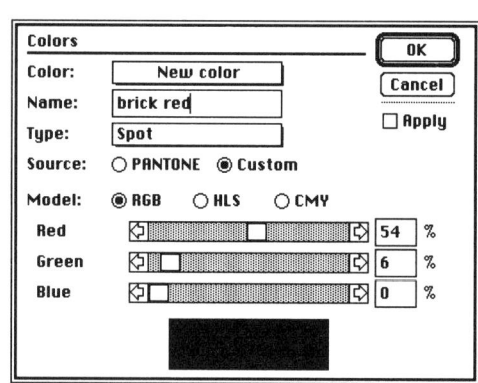

Figure 14.119 The Colors dialog box

PROCEDURE

Choose Colors from the Attributes menu. The Colors dialog box appears. From the **Color** pop-up menu, choose **New color** to define a new color, or choose an existing color to edit. In the **Name** edit box, enter a unique name for a new color, up to 32 characters. This is optional for process colors, but you must name spot colors before FreeHand will let you click OK to close the dialog box and define the color.

From the **Type** pop-up menu, choose the type of color you want to define. The choices are Process, Spot, or Tint.

PROCESS COLOR

For Process color, you can create a Custom color or select a simulated PANTONE color from FreeHand's built-in library of PANTONE colors. Bear in mind that process color simulations of PANTONE colors may not match the PANTONE ink exactly.

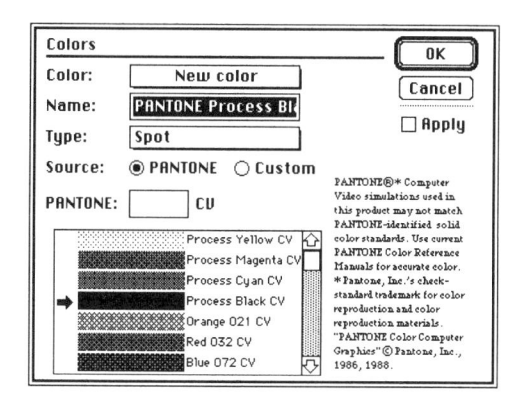

Figure 14.120 The PANTONE colors list

In the **Source** options, click PANTONE to display a scrolling list of PANTONE colors, from which you can choose a color by clicking it, or click Custom to display a set of scroll bars and edit boxes for cyan, magenta, yellow, and black. When you define a new custom process color, the starting point is by default 100% black. You can change this either by operating the scroll bars to obtain varying percentages of the four process colors, or by typing percentages directly into the edit boxes. A color swatch is displayed at the bottom of the dialog box. The left half of the swatch changes to reflect the changes you make to the color's definition.

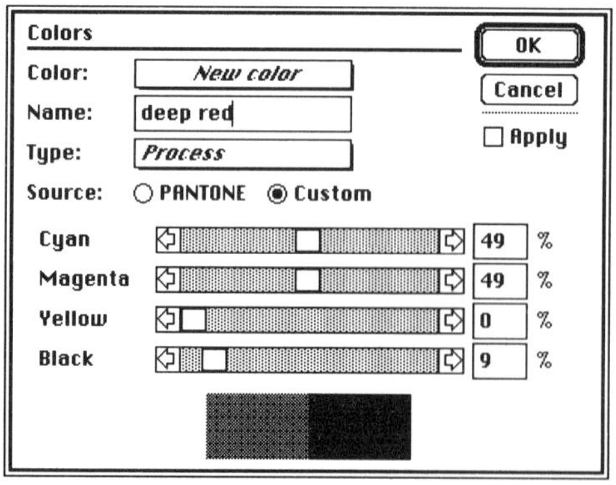

Figure 14.121 The Custom process color options

If you check the **Apply** option, FreeHand applies the new color to the fill, the line, or the fill and line of any selected elements, depending on what you have chosen from the pop-up menu in the Colors palette. If you leave this option unchecked, the new color is stored on the Colors palette, but the selected elements do not change. The names of process colors and tints of process colors always appear in Italics to remind you that you are working with process color.

SPOT COLORS

For Spot color, you have the same choices of Source, that is, PANTONE and Custom. You choose PANTONE spot colors as you do PANTONE process color simulations, but spot colors print their own separation when you print color separations. You must enter a unique name in the **Name** edit box for spot colors, because FreeHand places the color name on the separation. For Custom spot colors, you have a choice of three color models: RGB (red, green, blue), HLS (Hue, Lightness, Saturation), or CMY (cyan, magenta, yellow). You can choose whichever model you prefer, and switch freely between models. The way you define colors is the same no matter which model you use: you can change the percentages of the color components by operating the scroll bars, or you can type percentages directly into the edit boxes. As with process color, a color swatch is displayed at the bottom of the dialog box. The left half of the swatch changes to reflect the changes you make to the color's definition.

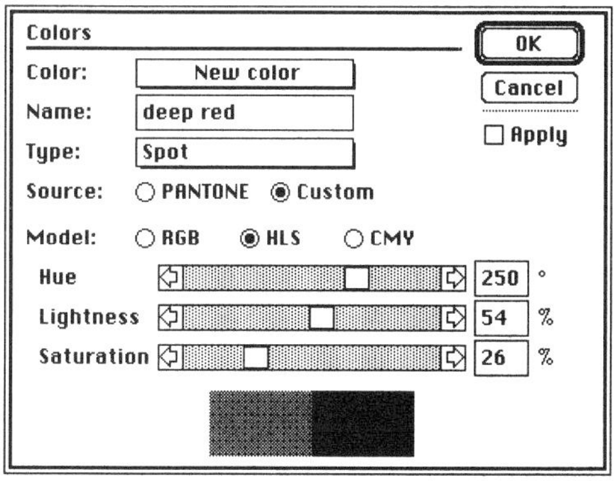

Figure 14.122 The Custom spot color options

If you check the **Apply** option, FreeHand applies the new color to the fill, the line, or the fill and line of any selected elements, depending on what you have chosen from the pop-up menu in the Colors palette. If you leave this option unchecked, the new color is stored on the Colors palette, but the selected elements do not change.

A **Tint** is a lighter shade of an existing color. To create a Tint, choose New color from the **Color** pop-up menu, then choose Tint from the Type pop-up menu. Choose a base color or tint from the **Based on** pop-up menu, which displays all the colors and tints you have defined for your illustration, then specify a percentage by scrolling the **Tint** scroll bar or typing a percentage in the edit box.

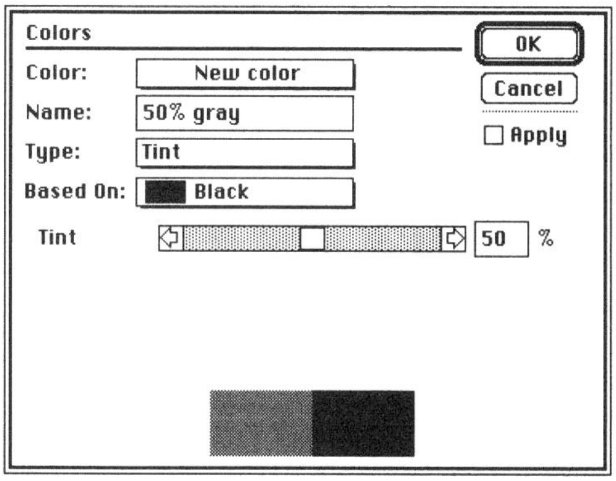

Figure 14.123 The Tint options

Check the **Apply** option to apply the new color to the fill, the line, or the fill and line of any selected elements, depending on what you have chosen from the pop-up menu in the Colors palette. Leave this option unchecked to store the new color on the Colors palette without changing any currently selected elements.

If you edit an existing color, the new color replaces the old one in both the Colors palette and the illustration. Any tint based on that color also changes, but the percentage of the tint remains the same.

TIP

You can open the Colors dialog box from any dialog box containing a Color pop-up menu by holding down the Option key while you choose a color from the menu. If you edit the selected color, it is replaced in the palette and in the illustration by the redefined color.

CAUTION

To use PANTONE colors, the PANTONE Colors file must be installed in the Aldus Folder, inside the current System Folder.

Styles...

The Styles command opens the Styles dialog box, where you can create new styles and edit existing ones. A style is a complete set of graphic attributes, comprising information about color, fill, line, and halftone screen specifications, that you define, name, and save. Then, when you want to apply those attributes to a selected element or elements, you can do so by simply clicking the style's name in the Styles palette. You can also base a style on an existing style. If you subsequently change the parent style, any styles based on it will inherit the changes.

PROCEDURE

Choose Styles from the Attributes menu. The Styles dialog box appears. To define a new style, choose New style from the **Style** pop-up menu. If you have already created an element that has the attributes that you want for the style, select the element before you choose the Styles command. FreeHand loads the attributes of the selected element into the Styles dialog box. Then, type a name (up to 32 characters) in the **Name** edit box, and click **OK** to save the style and close the dialog box. The new style appears on the Styles palette.

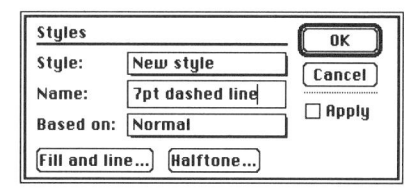

Figure 14.124 The Styles dialog box

If you want to specify new attributes for the style, click the **Fill and line** button to open the Fill and line dialog box, where you can specify fill and line specifications, and click the **Halftone** button to open the Halftone screen dialog box if you want to specify a halftone screen. (See "Fill and line" and "Halftone screen" earlier in this chapter.)

To base a style on an existing style, choose the base style from the **Based on** pop-up menu, then use the Fill and line and Halftone buttons to make any changes you want, type a name for the new style in the Name edit box, and click OK to save the new style. If you subsequently change the base style, any style based on it will inherit changes to attributes that it shares with the base style. If you just want to clone a set of attributes without basing a style on another, you should open the Styles dialog box by selecting the style you want to clone from the Styles palette, then choose Copy from the palette's pop-up menu. Change the attributes you want to change, then rename the copy and click OK to save it.

To edit an existing style, choose the Styles command, then choose the style you want to edit from the Style pop-up menu in the Styles dialog box. Use the Fill and line and Halftone buttons to make any changes you want, then click OK to save the changes to the style. FreeHand applies the new attributes to all elements in the illustration that use that style, and to any elements that use styles based on that style, whether they are selected or not.

Check **Apply** if you want to apply a newly-created or edited style to currently selected elements.

TIPS

You can override style specifications by applying attributes directly to a selected element using the Fill and line and/or Halftone screen commands from the Attributes menu. The style definition remains unchanged, but the element takes on the attributes you apply. When you select the element, a plus sign appears in front of the style's name in the Styles palette, indicating that the style has been overridden. You can remove the overrides from the element by clicking the style's name in the Styles palette. The plus sign disappears, and the selected element takes on the attributes defined in the style once more.

Styles are particularly useful for handling complex attributes like graduated, radial, or tiled fills. See Chapter 6 for more uses of styles.

Hairline, .5pt, 1 pt, 1.5 pt, 2 pt, 4 pt, 6 pt, 8 pt, and 12 pt

The remaining commands on the Attributes menu let you choose a variety of line weights to apply to selected elements. If you want to use a line weight other than one of the ones listed in the menu, you can specify it using the Fill and line command from the Attributes menu. (See the description of the Attributes menu's Fill and line command, above.)

PROCEDURE

Select the element or elements to which you want to apply one of the line weights listed on the menu, then choose the line weight you want from the Attributes menu.

Appendixes

A

Macintosh Basics

If you have never used a Macintosh, this appendix will introduce you to some basic operations. You may still need to refer to Apple Computer's manuals for the Macintosh operating environment to find information not presented in this book, and you should go through the tutorials that come with every Macintosh system.

Summary of Basic Macintosh Operations

Aldus FreeHand implements the basic Macintosh interface features and commands common to most applications on the Macintosh. Throughout this book, we have assumed that you are already familiar with the Macintosh basics, and we used common terms like "point," "click," and "drag" without explaining what they mean. Basic Macintosh procedures are summarized here.

The Macintosh uses a single-button mouse. You achieve different results by moving the mouse to move the pointer on the screen and then either clicking the mouse button once, clicking it twice, clicking it three times, or dragging it (i.e., holding down the mouse button as you move the mouse, then releasing the button). You introduce additional variations in the use of the mouse by holding down the Shift key, Option key, and/or Command key as you click or drag.

The terms used in this book to define these actions are summarized below.

ACTION	DESCRIPTION
Click	First move the mouse without holding down any keys or the mouse button to position the pointer over an object, then press the mouse button once and release it immediately.
Double-click	First move the mouse without holding down any keys or the mouse button to position the pointer over an object, then press the mouse button twice, quickly.
Drag	First move the mouse without holding down any keys or the mouse button to position the pointer over an object, then hold down the mouse button and move the mouse to a new position, then release the mouse button.
Shift-click	Click the mouse button while holding down the Shift key.
Option-click	Click the mouse button while holding down the Option key.
Control-click	Click the mouse button while holding down the Control key (if your keyboard has a Control key).
Shift-Option-click	Click the mouse button while holding down both the Shift key and the Option key.
Shift-Control-click	Click the mouse button while holding down both the Shift key and the Control key (if your keyboard has a Control key).
Shift-drag	Drag with the mouse while holding down the Shift key.
Option-drag	Drag with the mouse while holding down the Option key.
Shift-Option-drag	Drag with the mouse while holding down both the Shift key and the Option key.

More specific uses of the mouse in FreeHand and on the Macintosh desktop are described in this appendix and in the rest of the book.

The Desktop

The Macintosh desktop is the normal screen display when no applications are running, or when the Finder is active under MultiFinder while other applications are running. The desktop includes menu titles at the top of the screen, icons representing the contents of the current disks (plus the Trash icon), and windows (if any have been opened).

Icons can represent:

- Disks, including floppy disks, the internal hard disk, external hard disks, removable hard disks, and CD-ROMs
- Application programs (such as Aldus FreeHand)
- Documents (such as FreeHand artwork)
- Fonts, desk accessories, and other elements related to the system
- Folders that can contain any of the above elements, plus other folders

Icons are displayed in a window when by Icon is chosen from the View menu. You can select an icon by clicking it once. You can then drag the icon to move it or use File menu commands such as Open, Get Info, Duplicate, or Print. If you have chosen by Name, by Date, or by Kind from the View menu, you can still click an item to select it and use commands from the File menu, and you can drag an item from one window to another. However, you will not be able to drag that item to a new location within the same window.

If you double-click an icon, the result depends on the type of icon:

- Double-click a disk icon or folder icon to open it and view the contents of the disk or folder in a window.
- Double-click an application icon to start the program.
- Double-click a document icon to start the application that created the document and simultaneously opened the document in a window.

518 Using Aldus FreeHand 3.0

Opening, Closing, Moving, and Sizing Windows on the Desktop

The Macintosh desktop and all applications on the Macintosh display documents and other elements in windows. Most windows can be opened, closed, moved, sized, or rearranged using the same basic operations, summarized in the figure below.

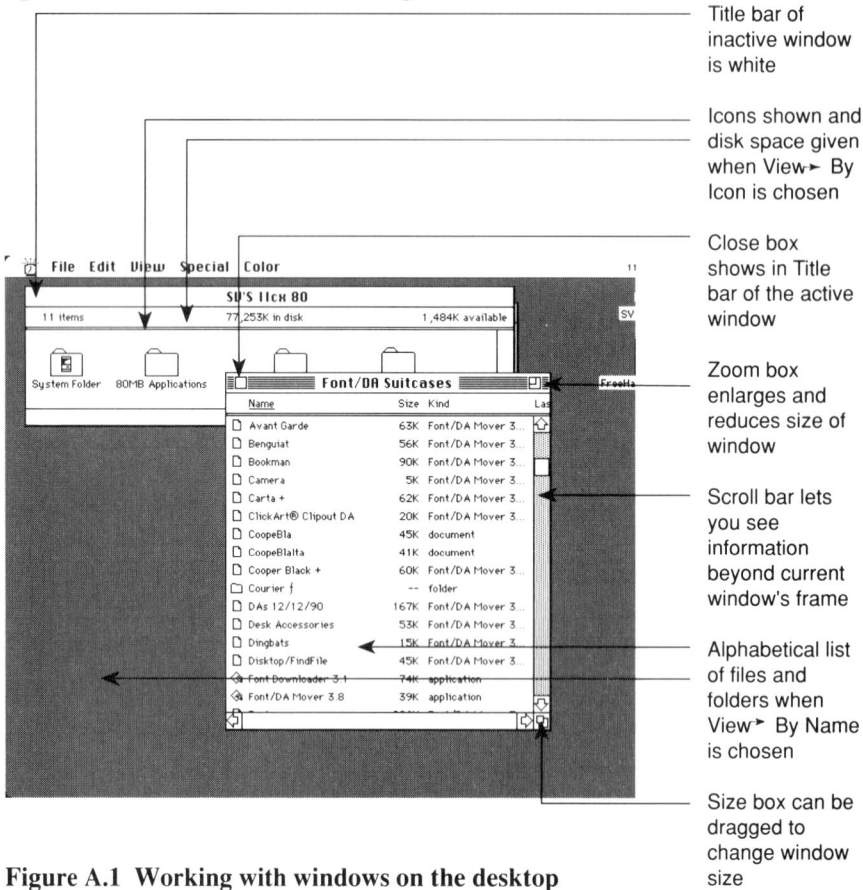

Figure A.1 Working with windows on the desktop

Title bar of inactive window is white

Icons shown and disk space given when View► By Icon is chosen

Close box shows in Title bar of the active window

Zoom box enlarges and reduces size of window

Scroll bar lets you see information beyond current window's frame

Alphabetical list of files and folders when View► By Name is chosen

Size box can be dragged to change window size

The most common operations on the Macintosh that result in the display of a window are:

- Double-clicking an icon on the desktop, or

- Clicking an icon to select it and then choosing the **Open** command from the File menu from the desktop or choosing Open or New from within Aldus FreeHand, or

- Choosing one of the commands in the Windows command submenu in the View menu to display a palette (another type of window) in Aldus FreeHand (described in Chapter 13).

Once you have opened a window, you can:

- Drag the title bar to move the window.
- Click the zoom box in the upper right corner to quickly enlarge or reduce the window—toggling between the two most recent sizes of the window.
- Drag the size box in the lower right corner to change the window to any size.

If there are more contents than will fit in the window, you can use the **scroll bars** to change your view of the contents:

- Click an **arrow** to scroll up, down, or sideways in small increments.
- Drag the **elevator** (white box on the gray scroll bar) to scroll in variable increments. The position of the white box on the scroll bar indicates the position in the list relative to the whole list or the screen image relative to the page and the pasteboard.
- Click the **gray area** above or below the elevator to scroll up, down, or sideways in large increments.
- Click the **close box** in the upper left corner to close a window. You can also close the active window by choosing the Close command from the File menu (from the desktop or from within Aldus FreeHand). When you use this command, Aldus FreeHand prompts you to save the file if you have not already done so.

Some applications, including Aldus FreeHand, offer a menu through which you can make a window active when more than one window is open (see the description of the Windows command in Chapter 14).

Choosing a Command from a Menu

The Macintosh desktop and all applications on the Macintosh display menu titles along the top of the screen. When you position the mouse pointer (↖) over a menu title and hold down the mouse button, the menu drops down on the screen to show all commands in that menu. You choose a command by positioning the mouse pointer over a menu title and holding down the mouse button as you drag the mouse to highlight a command. Release the mouse button when the command you want is highlighted.

Menus make it easy to find a command, but using a mouse and a menu is usually slower than entering a keyboard command. For this reason, most commonly-used commands in Aldus FreeHand (and in other Macintosh applications) have keyboard alternatives. These are shown in the menus, next to the command name. The ⌘ represents the Command key—to execute the command, hold down the Command key while you type the letter shown. For example, the keyboard alternative to choosing New from the File menu is ⌘N. You will find that it is easy to remember the keyboard shortcuts for the commands you use most often.

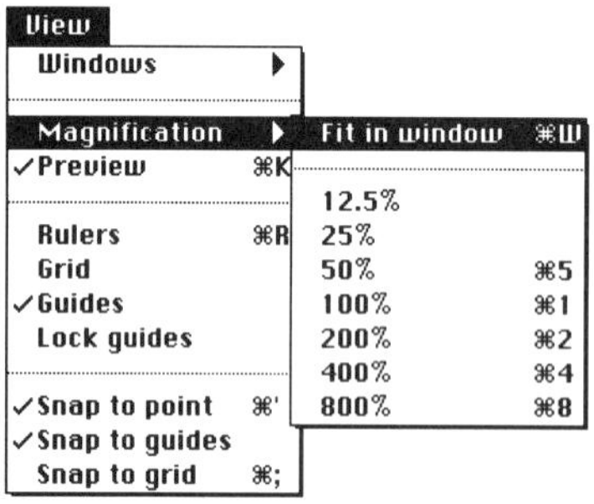

Figure A.2 The View menu shows keyboard shortcuts and a submenu

A check mark (✓) in front of a command indicates a toggle switch (an on/off option). The feature is on if it is checked; you can turn off the feature by choosing the command. The feature is off if it is not checked; you activate the feature by choosing the command.

Commands that are followed by a right-pointing triangle or arrow (▶) display additional commands in a submenu, and you drag the mouse to highlight the desired selection and then release the mouse button.

Commands that are followed by an ellipsis (…) always result in a dialog box, described next.

Making Entries in Dialog Boxes

Commands that display an ellipsis after the command name on the menu always result in the display of a dialog box—a type of window that lets you select from alternatives for various options.

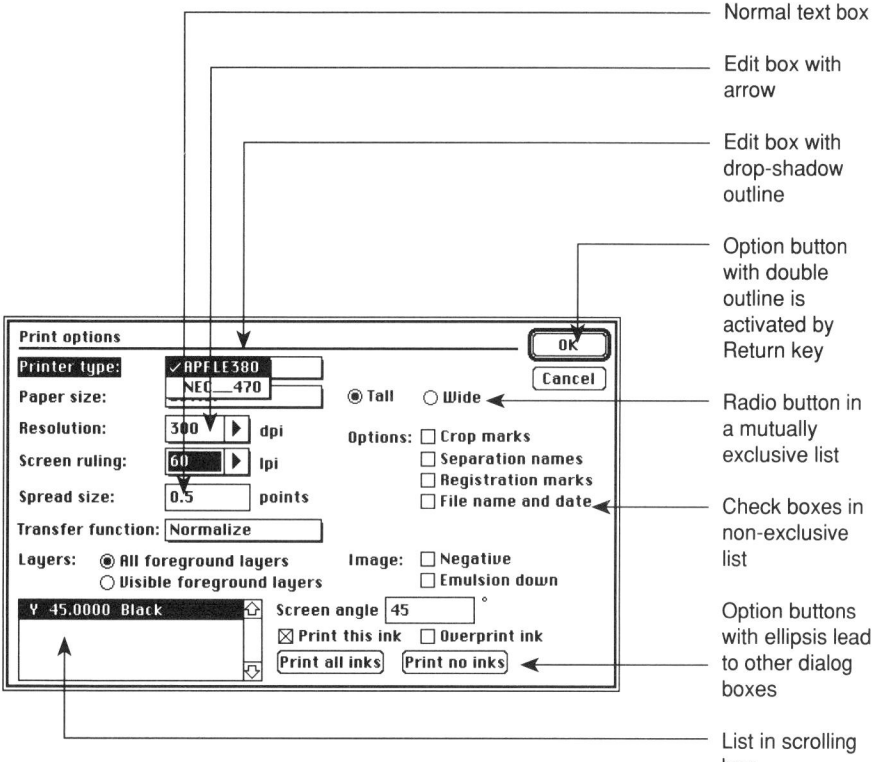

Figure A.3 A dialog box with a variety of edit boxes

There are a variety of methods for making entries in a dialog box:

- Click an **option button**, or press Return to choose the option button that is surrounded by a double border.

For instance, most dialog boxes include an OK button that closes the dialog box and implements the choices you have made. Most dialog boxes also include a **Cancel** button, so you can close the dialog box without implementing any of the choices you may have entered. Some dialog boxes include additional buttons that show the button name followed by an ellipsis (...); these buttons result in additional dialog boxes.

- Some dialog boxes are really windows that can be moved on the screen. These usually have a **close box** that you can click to close the dialog box. Usually—*but not always*—this has the same effect as clicking **Cancel**. Exceptions to this rule are noted where appropriate in the descriptions of tools and commands earlier in this book.

- Click a **radio button** or its label to choose one item from a list of mutually exclusive alternatives.

- Click a **check box** or its label to select items in a series of non-exclusive options.

- Press the Tab key to move from one **edit box** to another—or drag the pointer over an edit box to select it—and type new text in the box. You can also click once in an edit box to position the cursor and insert or delete characters from the current entry.

- If the edit box shows a **drop-shadow border and a right-pointing arrow** next to the text entry, you can edit the text as described above, or you can position the pointer over the arrow and hold down the mouse button to display a pop-up list of choices, then drag to highlight the selection you wish to make and release the mouse button.

- Position the pointer over an **edit box with a drop-shadow border (but no arrow)** and hold down the mouse button to display a pop-up list of choices, then drag to highlight the selection you wish to make and release the mouse button. (Edit boxes with a drop-shadow border but no arrow cannot be edited through the keyboard.)

- Click once on a name in a **scrolling list** to select it. In some dialog boxes, double-clicking a name in a scrolling list selects the name and closes the dialog box at the same time. The scroll bars work the same way as described earlier in this chapter for any Macintosh window.

Methods of making entries in specific dialog boxes and palettes are described in Chapters 12–14 of this book.

Managing Files from the Desktop

To manage the files you create with FreeHand, you should be familiar with the essential desktop operations summarized here.

Copying

To copy a file on the desktop, first find the file by opening folders or disk icons as needed, then choose the Duplicate command from the File menu (⌘D) on the desktop. To copy a file from one disk to another, either drag the file onto the other disk's icon or into the open window representing the other disk. If you drag the file into a different folder on the same disk, you do not make a copy of the file—you simply move it as described next.

Moving

To move a file from one folder to another, first find the file by opening folders or disk icons as needed, then drag the file onto the folder icon or into the open window representing a different folder on the same disk. If you drag the file into a folder on a different disk, you actually make a copy of the file—you can remove the original by dragging it into the Trash icon.

Renaming

To change the name of a file, first select the file by clicking it once with the pointer, then position the pointer over the name of the file. The pointer changes to an I-beam pointer which you can use to edit text the same way you edit text in FreeHand and in most Macintosh applications:

- Position the I-beam pointer within a line of text and click once to position the pointer for inserting text, or
- Double-click a word to select the whole word and then type to replace the word, or
- Drag the I-beam pointer over a range of characters to select them and then type to replace the selection.

Deleting

You can delete a file by dragging it into the Trash icon on the desktop. If you delete a file by mistake, you can open the Trash icon and drag the file out of the Trash back onto the desktop. If you empty the Trash (or if the System empties the Trash) before retrieving the deleted file, you must use a file recovery utility (such as Norton Utilities or Symantec Utilities) to recover the file—and even then it might not be recoverable.

B

Using Fonts with Aldus FreeHand

What Are Fonts?

In traditional terminology, a *font* is a complete set of characters in the same size, weight, and style or typeface. A typeface is the collective name for all the different fonts of the same style. For example, Helvetica is a typeface, and Helvetica Bold 12-point is a font. With the advent of scalable font technologies such as PostScript, the terms font and typeface have become interchangeable, much to the annoyance of purists. In this discussion, however, we will follow Macintosh usage rather than the traditional terminology.

Bitmap and Outline Fonts

The Macintosh uses two basic kinds of fonts. Bitmap fonts, commonly used on the Macintosh as screen fonts, are pixel-by-pixel representations of each character. Because they are pixel-by-pixel representations, each size requires a different representation. If you use a bitmap font, and specify a size for which no bitmap font is available, the Macintosh will scale an existing size, but the results might not look good, appearing jagged both on the screen and in the printed output. Macintosh bitmap fonts are generally limited to the resolution of the Macintosh screen, 72 dots per inch, so their printed appearance is noticeably jagged. Some non-PostScript printers produce acceptable printed output by looking for a bitmap font that is three or four times the size of the one being requested, depending on the resolution of the printer, and scaling it down to produce output at the resolution of the printer, but large size bitmap fonts take up a great deal of disk space, and you need two sizes of each bitmap font, one for screen display and a larger size for printing. On the Macintosh, the more common printer fonts are outline fonts.

Outline fonts, also known as printer fonts, contain a mathematical description of the shape of each character that can be scaled to any size. Outline fonts are also resolution-independent, that is, they will print at the maximum resolution of which the output device is capable. Two different outline font technologies are now available for the Macintosh, PostScript (developed by Adobe Systems), and Apple's new TrueType technology. You can use either or both of these technologies, but FreeHand, as a PostScript-based application, offers more capabilities with PostScript fonts than it does with most TrueType fonts.

PostScript Fonts

PostScript fonts have two components: bitmap screen font files, and PostScript outline files. The bitmap screen fonts are used to display type on the screen, and to identify the PostScript outline that will be used for printing. The bitmap screen fonts are stored in suitcase files, and the PostScript outlines are stored in separate files for each style and weight in a font family. For example, the outline fonts for the basic Helvetica family are named Helve, HelveBol, HelveBolObl, and HelveObl, corresponding to the screen fonts Helvetica, Helvetica Bold, Helvetica Bold Oblique, and Helvetica Oblique, respectively.

To make full use of these fonts, you must install both the bitmap screen font and the PostScript outline font. PostScript fonts for the Macintosh are available from many different vendors, including Adobe Systems, Agfa-Compugraphic, Monotype, BitStream, and ATF-Kingsley. When you buy a font from any of these vendors, they supply a suitcase file containing bitmap screen fonts, and the corresponding PostScript outline file(s).

INSTALLING POSTSCRIPT FONTS UNDER SYSTEM 6.0.X

Installing PostScript fonts under System 6.0.x takes two steps. You use the Font/DA Mover utility supplied by Apple to open the suitcase file containing the bitmap fonts and to install the bitmap fonts in your current System file. Then you place the PostScript outline files in the root level of the current System Folder. You can do this by simply dragging them into the System Folder in the Finder. To remove fonts, you reverse the procedure. Use the Font/DA Mover to open the current System file and remove the bitmap fonts, then drag the PostScript outlines out of the System Folder.

You must install at least one bitmap font to use the corresponding outline font. The bitmap font can be any size, but small point sizes take up less disk space than do larger ones. You can install bitmap fonts for additional point sizes to improve the appearance of type on the screen, but these will have no effect on the appearance of the printed artwork. If disk space is not a consideration, you may want to install bitmap fonts for all the point sizes you regularly use.

INSTALLING POSTSCRIPT FONTS UNDER SYSTEM 7.0

The procedure for installing PostScript fonts under System 7.0 is similar to that for System 6.0.x, but the Font/DA Mover is no longer required. You can install and remove fonts directly from the Finder. Under System 7.0, you can double-click a font suitcase to open a window that displays the individual bitmap fonts it contains. To install these, you drag the font files into the System file. If you drag them onto the System Folder icon, a message box appears telling you that bitmap fonts must be installed in the System file, and asking you if you want to do so. If you click OK, the bitmap fonts will be installed automatically in the System file.

The PostScript outline font files must be placed in the Extensions Folder inside the System Folder. Again, if you simply drag them onto the System Folder icon, a message box appears telling you that these fonts must be installed in the Extensions Folder, and asking you if you want to do so. If you click OK, the outline fonts will be installed automatically in the Extensions Folder.

To remove fonts, double-click the System file icon to open a window displaying the fonts that are installed, then drag the fonts you want to remove out of the System file window. Similarly, double-click the

Extensions Folder to open it, then drag the outline fonts you want to remove out of the Extensions Folder.

FONT UTILITIES

Adobe Type Manager 2.0 is a software utility published by Adobe Systems that uses installed PostScript outline fonts to display type accurately on the screen at any size. It also lets you print PostScript fonts accurately at maximum resolution on non-PostScript printers. This eliminates the need for multiple sizes of bitmap fonts. You must, however, install at least one size of bitmap font for each outline font you want to use. To use Adobe Type Manager 2.0 with System 7.0, the PostScript outline fonts must be placed in the root level of the System Folder, rather than in the Extensions Folder. Adobe Type Manager 2.0.2, the earliest version that is fully System 7.0-compatible, works properly when the PostScript outline fonts are installed in the Extensions Folder.

Suitcase II is a utility published by Fifth Generation Systems that allows you to keep your fonts anywhere on any mounted hard disk. You can activate and deactivate fonts via the Suitcase desk accessory, which appears in the Apple menu. The only constraint with Suitcase is that, for outline fonts to be available for printing or for use by Adobe Type Manager, they must be in the same folder as a bitmap font that is currently active.

TrueType Fonts

TrueType is Apple's new outline font technology. It provides functionality similar to the combination of PostScript fonts and Adobe Type Manager for both screen display and printing. FreeHand is fully compatible with TrueType fonts, but some of the special effects that are available with PostScript fonts cannot be obtained with most TrueType fonts. For example, FreeHand cannot convert TrueType fonts to editable paths, nor can it create filled and stroked type, inline type, or other special type effects using TrueType. An exception to this rule is the case of TrueType fonts created using Altsys' Metamorphosis Professional, for which the special effects are available. However, most commercially-available TrueType fonts cannot use FreeHand's special effects. For this reason, we recommend using PostScript fonts with FreeHand whenever possible. You can mix TrueType and PostScript fonts in a single document, and print

TrueType fonts on a PostScript printer. However, TrueType fonts take longer to print and require more printer memory on a PostScript printer than do their PostScript equivalents.

INSTALLING TRUETYPE FONTS UNDER SYSTEM 6.0.7

You install TrueType fonts the same way you install bitmap fonts, using the Font/DA Mover to open the font suitcase and install the font in the current System file. Some, but not all, TrueType fonts include bitmap fonts. You can install these if you wish, for faster screen display, but unlike PostScript fonts, TrueType fonts do not require an equivalent bitmap. To use TrueType fonts, you must use System 6.0.7 and Font/DA Mover 4.1 or later, and you must place the TrueType INIT file in the root level of your current System Folder.

INSTALLING TRUETYPE FONTS UNDER SYSTEM 7.0

To install TrueType fonts under System 7.0, you use the Finder. Double-click the font suitcase to open it, then drag the fonts you want to install into the System file. If you drag them onto the System Folder icon, a message box appears telling you that fonts must be installed in the System file, and asking you if you want to do so. If you click OK, the TrueType fonts will be installed automatically in the System file.

Printing Issues

FreeHand identifies fonts by name rather than ID number, so font conflicts are rarely a problem. However, kerning and character metrics information for a PostScript font is kept in the corresponding bitmap suitcase file. If you send a document to a service bureau for printing, their fonts may have different kerning or character spacing built in.

The best way around this is to always include the fonts used along with your document. You need only include the bitmap font, since PostScript fonts have unique names.

An alternative strategy is to use the Convert to paths command in the Type menu to convert the type in your document to paths. This strategy works best with small amounts of type. If you convert large amounts of type to paths, the document becomes very large and printing times are increased considerably.

C

Time and Space: The New Frontier

The old adage "bigger is better" can be reversed to "better is bigger" when applied to computer programs. Early versions of Aldus FreeHand fit easily on an 800K floppy disk—version 3.0 comes on several disks and compiles into a 1.3 MB file. Early versions ran on any Macintosh with 512K of memory—the latest version runs better with 1.5 MB of RAM or more. Many of us have expanded our computer systems to more than 2 MB of RAM to run full-featured applications like FreeHand more efficiently, but we still run into the limits of disk space, memory space, screen redraw time, and printing time when working with large, complicated illustrations.

Here are a few suggestions for overcoming these limitations. Most of these concepts are covered elsewhere in this book—in Tips or scattered throughout the command descriptions in Chapter 14. We collect them here for easy reference.

To Decrease Screen Redraw Time...

The screen image is recreated every time you open an existing illustration file, scroll on the page, change the magnification of the page, close certain dialog boxes or windows that cover the artwork, or change large portions of the artwork in a single step. If you find that you are waiting what seems like a long time for the screen to redraw, or if you are planning a change to the artwork that will result in a long wait for the screen to refresh, try one or more of these solutions *before* you make the next change:

- Turn off all of the Performance/display options and increase the point size for on-screen Greek (i.e., grayed) type in the Preferences dialog box. These options are specifically designed to let you specify fewer display options (such as not displaying high-resolution TIFF images on-screen) in order to speed screen redrawing.
- Work in keyline view. Choosing Preview from the View menu (⌘K) toggles between Preview and keyline view. You can change between these views as often as you like while working. Also, if you save the file in keyline view, it will open a lot faster the next time.
- Put imported TIFF images, clipping paths (i.e., objects with other objects pasted inside), and other complex elements on layers of their own and make these layers invisible until you need them.
- Use the Group command to group portions of the artwork that contain a lot of separate related objects. Grouped elements can be selected and moved a lot faster than ungrouped elements. Bear in mind that all elements in a group move to the current active layer, so the stacking order of the elements in the group may be affected.
- Use the Macintosh Control Panel (under the Apple menu) to turn color off or reduce the number of colors displayed on your monitor. For example, a screen that took 20 seconds to display in 256 colors required only 17 seconds to display in 256 shades of gray. Display time can be further shortened by choosing fewer colors or shades of gray.
- Before starting FreeHand under MultiFinder or System 7.0, select the FreeHand program icon on the Macintosh desktop and use the Get Info command from the File menu (⌘I) to increase the memory allocation for FreeHand.

To Decrease Printing Time...

Illustrations that take a long time to print can be handled by planning to print the files during lunch breaks, during meetings, or at the end of the day. Unfortunately, these solutions are not always practical when you have deadlines to meet or when you share the printer with others who might want to print their own files while you are at lunch. Here are some suggestions for decreasing the time it takes to print your artwork:

- Set the page size close to the size of the artwork. Do not create small illustrations surrounded by white space in a page size that happens to match the paper size in your printer. The amount of printer RAM required in printing a page is directly related to the size of the page specified in the Document setup dialog box. In one test, a simple 4-inch by 4-inch image required 14 seconds to print on a Linotronic 300 when letter-size paper was specified, but only 8 seconds when a 4-inch by 4-inch page size was specified.
- Use composite paths rather than clipping paths to "mask" parts of the artwork whenever possible. See Chapters 4 and 6 for examples of these two techniques.
- Use duplicated objects rather than tiled fills. Tiled fills take longer to print, and very complex tiled fills might not print at all.
- Use blends rather than graduated or radial fills. This will speed printing time, but increase the file size.
- If your printer allows different printing resolutions, or if you have a choice of printers with different printing resolutions, choose a lower printing resolution when printing drafts. You can do this through the Print command in FreeHand, in the Print options dialog box (see Chapter 14).
- Decrease the screen ruling setting in the Print options dialog box.
- Use the Element info command to change the flatness setting of selected elements in your artwork, or modify the *UserPrep* file to change the flatness for an entire illustration. FreeHand constructs curves by linking anchor points with a series of very short straight line segments—though the resulting curves appear smooth to the naked eye. The flatness setting determines the maximum distance, in device pixels, of any point on a rendered curve from the corresponding point on the true curve. In simpler terms, a low flatness setting will yield smoother curves than a high flatness setting (see Chapter 14 for an illustration). The normal default is zero, but you can increase this to 5 in most cases without introducing any differences that would be apparent to the human eye.

TIP
Increasing the flatness settings for long paths can also eliminate *limitcheck* errors in printing.

To Minimize Memory Requirements...

Some of the suggestions in "To Decrease Screen Redraw Time" will also reduce the amount of memory required by FreeHand—such as turning off all of the Performance/display options and increasing the point size for on-screen Greek type, turning color off, and turning Preview off. Here are some other ways to reduce the amount of memory required by FreeHand:

- You can decrease the amount of memory allocated to the program under MultiFinder or System 7.0 through the Get Info command in the Finder's File menu, but this can slow the speed of some operations and might prevent you from opening large files. Do not use an allocation of less than 1500K.
- Decrease the number of undos allowed. Choose the Preferences command and click the More button in the dialog box to get the More preferences dialog box.

To Minimize File Size...

Many of the problems you may have with screen redraw time, printing time, and memory limitations are caused by large files. You do not want to limit your creativity or restrict your artwork simply to save time and space, but here are some suggestions for minimizing file size:

- Draw efficiently. This means drawing curved paths with as few anchor points as possible. See Chapters 3 and 12 for tips on placing anchor points efficiently.
- Use graduated and radial fills instead of blends where possible. (This will decrease the file size but is likely to increase printing time.) Otherwise, in blending use as few blends as necessary to get the best effect. See Chapter 6 for suggestions and examples.
- If you have imported TIFF files that you have used as guides in tracing your artwork, and the TIFF image is not part of the final printed artwork, delete the TIFF image after the tracing is complete rather than keeping it in the file on an invisible or background layer.

- If you plan to use an imported TIFF image as part of the final, printed artwork, set the resolution of the TIFF to 150 dots per inch (or less) and scale it to the desired size *before* you import it into FreeHand—either by scanning it at the desired resolution and size or by using a program that lets you manipulate TIFF images.
- If the artwork is very large or complicated or includes TIFF images, plan on printing the final directly from FreeHand rather than exporting it as an EPS (Encapsulated PostScript) file. EPS files are always larger than the source artwork in FreeHand, sometimes dramatically so. This is particularly true when the FreeHand document contains imported artwork such as TIFF, PICT, or bitmap images.

D

Glossary

actual size A view of a page on the screen, scaled to approximately the same size it will print, depending on the characteristics of your screen display.

additive primary colors Red, green, and blue. The three colors used to create all other colors when direct, or transmitted light is used (television, for instance).

alignment How type lines up. FreeHand gives you four choices: align left (flush left, ragged right); align center (ragged left, ragged right); align right (ragged left, flush right); and justify (flush to the edges of the text block on left and right).

anchor point The point on a line segment that determines where the segment starts or ends. Anchor points are invisible when any segment of the path they form is selected. Anchor points that end curve segments have direction levers and handles associated with them.

auto trace To trace around the shapes or lines of an object on the screen automatically.

baseline A horizontal line that coincides with the bottom of each character in a font, excluding descenders (tails on letters like "p").

benday An old printing term for screen tints. Taken from the name of a company that used to produce screens for the printing industry.

bevel join A squared off corner that is created when the notch that is formed when two lines meet is filled with a triangle. Compare *miter join* and *round join*.

Bezier curve A curve, named after Pierre Bezier, that is defined mathematically by four control points. These control points are the four direction points at the ends of the two direction lines that are tangent to each curve. All curves in FreeHand are Bezier curves. See *curve*.

bitmap An electronically-displayed graphic image made up of a matrix of dots. TIFF images and MacPaint graphics are bitmaps.

blend To create a series of successive shapes or shadings between two selected paths.

blueline A prepress proofing material, used to proof black-and-white art before printing.

butt cap A square line cap that is perpendicular to the end of a line. It is called a butt cap because the cap butts up against the end of the line. Compare *round cap* and *projecting cap*.

cap See *line cap*.

click To press and then immediately release the mouse button.

clipping path A mask as defined by pasting objects inside another object or composite path. See also *composite path*.

closed path A path with no endpoints. A loop. Compare with *open path*.

coated stock Paper that has a light clay or plastic coating. A glossy or slick paper is coated. Often, the color you want depends on the type of stock on which you are printing.

coincident Occupying the same position. In a straight line, an anchor point and its two direction points are coincident.

collinear Occurring along the same straight line. The anchor point and two direction points of a curve point are collinear.

color keys A color overlay proofing system produced by the 3M Company. (See *overlay proofs*.)

color separations In offset printing, separate plates used to lay different colors of ink on a page printed in multiple colors, to reproduce the proportional amount of cyan, magenta, yellow, and black in the original. FreeHand prints color separations of documents created in color.

comp A graphic arts term for comprehensive drafts. In FreeHand, a paper proof printed on a color printer before you print the final negatives is the equivalent of a comp.

composite path A single path created by joining two closed paths, thus creating an object with a window or hole through which other objects—on lower layers—can be seen. For example, if you draw two concentric circles and join them, they become a composite path and the smaller circle becomes a window like a hole in a donut.

condensed type A narrow typeface having proportionally less character width than a normal face of the same size. Although you can achieve this effect by graphically scaling characters from the normal font, usually condensed characters are individually designed as a separate font. Condensed typefaces are used where large amounts of copy must fit into a relatively small space (tabular composition being the most common area of usage). See also *kerning*.

constrain To restrict drawing, moving, or transforming to an angle you specify.

continuous tone image A photographic image which contains gradient tones from black to white. When you scan an image, it is converted from a continuous tone image to a halftone.

corner point An anchor point in which the anchor point and its two direction points are not positioned on a straight line. Corner points are used to join two segments traveling in different directions. Compare with *curve point*.

corner radius The radius of the circle used to form rounded corners in a rectangle.

corner point An anchor point connecting two segments in which the anchor point and its two direction points are located on the same straight line.

cromalin An integral proofing system produced by DuPont. (See *integral proof*.)

crop marks Lines printed on a page to indicate where the page will be trimmed when the final document is printed and bound. FreeHand prints these marks if the bounding box is smaller than the paper size.

current attributes The fill, stroke, and type attributes that are in effect when you create a path or specify type. The current attributes appear in the Fill and line dialog box when no objects are selected.

cursor key distance The distance that selected objects move each time that you press a cursor (arrow) key.

curve A smooth trajectory defined by two anchor points and two direction points. The anchor points define where the curve starts and ends. The direction points determine the shape of the curve.

custom color An ink color that you assign to objects in your drawing. With custom color, you produce one negative for each color used in the artwork. Compare with *process color*.

cyan The subtractive primary color that appears blue-green and absorbs red light. Used as one ink in four-color printing. Also known as process blue.

CMYK Shorthand notation for cyan, magenta, yellow, and black.

dash pattern The pattern of lines and gaps between lines that make up a dashed line. You create a dash pattern by specifying the length, in points, of each dash and of each gap between the dashes.

default The initial setting of a value or option. Used to describe the value or mode that FreeHand will use in processing information when no other value or mode is specified. A preset response to a question or prompt. Default settings can be changed.

dialog box A window or full-screen display in response to a command that calls for setting options.

digitizer See *scanner*.

direction line or lever The straight line connecting an anchor point and its direction point. A curve touches the direction line at the anchor point.

direction point or handle A point that defines the direction from which a curve enters the curve's anchor points. The position of a curve's two direction points determines the curve's shape.

dots See *halftone dots* and *pixel*.

drag To hold down the mouse button while you move the pointer.

dylux A brand name for blueline proofing material.

emulsion The photosensitive layer on a piece of film or paper.

Encapsulated PostScript (EPS) format A file format that describes a document written in the PostScript language and that contains all of the code necessary to print the file.

endpoint An anchor point at the beginning or end of an open path.

fill To paint an area enclosed by a path with a gray shade or color.

film Photosensitive material, generally on a transparent base, which receives character images, and may be chemically processed to expose those images. In phototypesetting, any photosensitive material, transparent or not, may be called film.

flatness The maximum distance, in device pixels, of any point on a rendered curve from the corresponding point on the true curve.

folio Page number.

font One complete set of characters in the same face, style, and size, including all of the letters of the alphabet, punctuation, and symbols. For example 12-point Times Roman is a different font from 12-point Times Italic, 14-point Times Roman, or 12-point Helvetica. Screen fonts (bitmapped fonts used to display text accurately on the screen) can differ slightly from the printer fonts (outline fonts used to describe fonts to the laser printer) because of the difference in resolution between screens and printers.

ghosting The shift in ink density that occurs when large, solid areas interfere with one another. Also, a procedure in which two images are combined together electronically. The images are given specific weight in relation to each other to create the effect.

grid The underlying design plan for a page. In FreeHand, the grid can be composed of a series of non-printing horizontal and vertical guides that intersect to form a "grid" of dots that can be displayed on the screen.

group To combine two or more objects so that they act as a single object. You can manipulate groups just as you do individual objects.

hairline The thinnest rule possible—generally 0.25 point.

halftone An image composed of dots of different sizes. Using a scanner, you can convert continuous tone images, like photographs, into halftones.

halftone dots Dots as they appear on the printed page. The size of the halftone dots depends on the screen ruling used.

insertion point A blinking vertical line that indicates where characters you type will appear.

integral proof A color proofing system that bonds all four process colors to a single sheet.

interpreter Software built into PostScript-compatible printers and typesetters that converts PostScript commands into a form the printer can use to draw an image.

join (noun) See *line join*.

join (verb) To connect the endpoints of an open path, or to join two paths into a composite path. When you join two overlapping endpoints of one path, FreeHand closes the path by making them one point. When you join the overlapping endpoints of two open paths, FreeHand combines them into one longer path. When you join two closed paths, FreeHand creates a composite path. (See *composite path*.)

kerning The amount of space, in points, that is added or taken away from between a pair of characters in a type block.

knockout A generic term for a positive or overlay that "knocks out" part of an image from another image. The most obvious example of this is white type on a black background. The white type is knocked out of the background.

landscape A printing orientation in which the "up" direction is along the short side of the page. Compare *portrait*.

layer To place objects in layers that are in front of one another. See also *stacking order*.

leading The amount of vertical spacing, in points, between every line of type in a type block.

line The straight line between two anchor points. In a line, each anchor point and its corresponding direction point occupy the same location.

line cap A cap is placed at the end of a solid line or segments of a dashed line. FreeHand provides three kinds of line caps: butt, round, and projecting.

line join The style of connector used when FreeHand strokes a path. The choice of joins becomes important when stroking paths that contain corners. FreeHand provides three kinds of joins: miter, round, and bevel.

lines per inch (lpi) See *screen ruling*.

line weight The weight or thickness of a line, expressed in points.

magenta The subtractive primary color that appears blue-red and absorbs green light. Used as one ink in four-color printing. Also known as process red.

marquee A dashed rectangular region created by dragging the pointer to select objects.

mechanical Traditionally, the final pages or boards with pasted-up galleys of type and line art, sometimes with acetate or tissue overlays for color separations and notes to the offset printer.

mechanical separations Color separations made based on black-and-white art.

memory A hardware component of a computer system that can store information for later retrieval. The area inside the computer where information is stored temporarily while you are working (also called RAM or random access memory). The amount of memory a computer has directly affects its speed and the size of the documents you can create.

menu A list of choices presented in either a drop-down or pop-up window, from which you can select an action.

miter join A corner created by extending the edges of two converging lines until they meet. Compare *bevel join* and *round join*.

miter limit The ratio that determines the angle at which FreeHand switches from a mitered (pointed) line join to a beveled (squared off) line join. The miter limit is equal to the maximum ratio of the diagonal line through a line to the width of the lines producing the join. The smaller the miter limit, the less sharp the angle at which FreeHand switches from a mitered to a beveled line join.

moiré pattern A grid pattern (usually undesirable) that can result when two or more screen tints are overlaid incorrectly. (See also *rosette*.)

negative A reverse image of a page, produced photographically on a clear sheet of film as an intermediate step in preparing plates from camera-ready mechanicals for offset printing.

object An anchor point, segment, path, or type block, or a group of anchor points, segments, paths, and type blocks.

offset To move the image away from the right edge of the film or paper on which it is printing.

offset printing A type of printing that uses an intermediate step to transfer a printed image from the plate to the paper. The type of printing done using a printing press to reproduce many copies of the original that is printed out on a laser printer. The press lays ink on a page based on the raised image on a plate that is created by photographing the camera-ready masters.

open path A path with two endpoints, that is, a path that has a beginning and an end. Compare with *closed path*.

orientation The page position: portrait or landscape.

overlay A transparent acetate or tissue covering over a printed page, where color indications and other instructions to the offset printer are written. Also, an overhead transparency that is intended to be projected on top of another projection.

overlay proofs A color proofing system that uses transparent overlays for each of the four process colors.

overprint To specify that a colored object show through another colored object that overlaps it. Normally, the object underneath is hidden by the object in front.

paint To fill a region defined by a path with a gray shade or color, or draw a line that is centered on its path.

Pantone Matching System (PMS) A popular system for choosing colors, based on ink mixes.

path One or more connected segments. You can fill a path or you can draw a line that is centered on the path.

pattern One or more objects that has been defined as a tiled fill pattern.

phototypesetter A device that sets type photographically, using a photochemical process and special film as output.

pica A pica equals 12 points, or one-sixth of an inch.

pixel Short for picture element. A point on the graphics screen; the visual representation of a bit on the screen (white if the bit is 0, black if it is 1). A single dot on the Macintosh display. A template is a collection of pixels.

PICT format A format used to store MacDraw documents.

place To import a TIFF image, paint-type bitmap, PICT format, or an EPS format file into a FreeHand document.

point Unit of measure, used in FreeHand for specifying type and line attributes. There are approximately 72 points in an inch.

point of origin A fixed spot that you specify in your artwork from which a transformation begins.

portrait A printing orientation in which the "up" direction is along the long side of the page.

PostScript A computer language invented by Adobe Systems that is used to define the appearance of type and images on the printed page. When you save a FreeHand document, you are actually saving a PostScript program.

PPD file PostScript Printer Description file. The document used by the FreeHand program to set the default information for the type of printer you are using.

preset attributes The paint, stroke, and type attributes that are in effect if you have not specified any other attributes. Default attributes.

Preview The view of your FreeHand artwork that is displayed on your screen as a bitmap and approximates the printed output. Opposite of keyline view.

primary colors The elemental colors of either pigments or light. Red, green, and blue are additive primaries. White light is produced when red, green, and blue lights are added together. Cyan, magenta, and yellow are subtractive primaries. The inks used to print three-color process or four-color process with black.

process color One of the four colors—cyan, magenta, yellow, and black—blended to produce colors in the four-color process. With process color, you produce a maximum of four negatives, regardless of the number of colors used in your artwork. Compare with *custom color*.

process separations Four-color separations made from color artwork.

progressive colors The four process colors plus white and the various combinations of cyan, magenta, and yellow. The Colors option in the Preferences dialog box allows you to adjust the appearance of the progressive colors on your computer display.

progressive color bar A bar displaying all the possible combinations of cyan, magenta, and yellow. Progressive color bars are printed on each sheet of a process color printing job to ensure proper ink coverage and color. The bar is usually trimmed off before the job is shipped. Sometimes the progressive color bar will also include black and screen tints of the combinations.

projecting cap A square line cap placed at the end of a solid or dashed line. The cap is perpendicular to the end of the line and extends one-half of a line width beyond the line's endpoint. Compare *butt cap* and *line cap*.

QuickDraw A graphics language built into the read-only memory (ROM) of the Macintosh.

reflect To create a mirror image of an object.

reflected light See *subtractive primary colors*.

registration The accuracy with which images are combined or positioned, particularly in reference to multicolored printing where each color must be precisely aligned for the accurate reproduction of the original.

registration mark One of a number of small reference patterns placed on separations printed by FreeHand to aid in the registration process.

resolution The number of dots per inch displayed on a screen or printer. The Macintosh screen has a resolution of 72 dots per inch. The Apple LaserWriter has a resolution of 300 dots per inch. The resolution of PostScript language imagesetting devices (LaserWriter Plus, Linotronic 300, and so on) is measured in pixels per inch. (See *pixel*.)

RGB Shorthand notation for red, green, and blue. (See *additive primary colors*.)

rosette The circular dot pattern that occurs when screen tints are overlaid correctly.

rotate To revolve an object about a given point.

round cap A semi-circular line cap placed at the end of a solid or dashed line. The diameter of the cap is equal to the width of the line. Compare *butt cap* and *line cap*.

round join A corner created when two lines are connected with a circular arc whose diameter is equal to the width of the line. Compare *bevel join* and *miter join*.

scale To change the size of an object either vertically, horizontally, or both.

scanned image The image that results when a photograph, illustration, or other flat art is converted into a bitmap. Most scanning applications let you save scanned images in MacPaint, TIFF, PICT, or EPS format.

scanner An electronic device that converts a photo, illustration, or other flat art into a bitmap. A video camera is a scanner that converts three-dimensional objects into bitmaps.

screen ruling The number of lines per inch in a screen tint or halftone.

screen tint A screened percentage of a solid color.

segment A line curve that is defined by an anchor point and its direction point.

select To define an object to be acted upon by the next command or mouse operation. You must select an object before you can change or edit it in any way. You generally select an object by selecting the Pointer tool and then clicking on the object with the pointer or dragging the selection marquee around it.

selection marquee A dashed rectangular region used to select objects.

skew To slant an object vertically, horizontally, or along an arbitrary line.

spacing The amount of space, in points, that is added or removed between every pair of characters in a type block. Spacing affects the amount of white space in a type block.

spec sheet A mock-up, or copy of the drawing showing the various color values.

spot color See *custom color*.

spread A negative image that has been fattened to create trap.

stacking order The sequence in which the objects in a document are layered. Objects are stacked from back to front, meaning that in a number of layered objects the frontmost object will obscure all or part of the objects that lie behind it.

stripper The person who takes the negatives and "strips" them in the proper position so they will run correctly on the press. The stripper is also usually the person who cuts the color-separation masks when mechanical separations are made.

stroke To draw a line that is centered on its path.

subtractive primary colors Cyan, yellow, and magenta. The three colors used to create all other colors when reflected light is used (for instance, in printed material).

tangent Touching a line or curve at only one point. The direction line is tangent to the curve at the anchor point.

tangent line See *direction line*.

template A document set up with text and graphic elements that will be included routinely in a series of documents based on the boilerplate without the need to recreate the repeated elements each time.

tile (page) To divide FreeHand's drawing area into blocks to fit the paper size of the printer.

tile (pattern) To create a repeat pattern that fills a closed path.

tint A percentage of one of the process or custom colors.

toggle A command that lets you switch between two settings. The Rulers command is an example of a toggle.

Toolbox The set of tools displayed to the left of the drawing area when a document is open.

transmitted light See *additive primary colors*.

transverse Rotation of the page on the film or paper on which it is printing. Currently, this term is applicable only to Linotronic imagesetting machines.

trap Overlap needed to ensure that a slight misalignment or movement of the separations will not affect the final appearance of the job.

uncoated stock Paper that is not coated. Uncoated paper is usually less smooth and absorbs ink more readily.

ungroup To separate groups into individual objects or into subgroups.

x-axis The horizontal reference line to which objects are constrained.

y-axis The vertical reference line to which objects are constrained.

yellow The subtractive primary color that appears yellow and absorbs blue light. Used as one ink in four-color printing.

zoom To magnify or reduce your view of the current document.

Index

A

About FreeHand command, 28, 399
active layer, 324, 381
adding points, 349
   corner point, 354
   curve point, 353
adjusting color monitors, 416
Adobe Illustrator 1.1 format, 15
Align command, 41
Align to grid, 240
alignment, 233-253
alignment aids, 9
Alignment command, 217, 221, 233, 240, 465
   text, 215, 490
Alignment dialog box, 42, 240
Alignment (Type menu), 490
anchor points, 4, 321, 337
   number of, 345
   selecting, 322
anchor points—see also points
angle, 316
   of movement, 315, 325
   of rotation, 315, 357
   of reflection, 359
Apple menu, 398
applying colors, 375
applying styles, 387
arrow keys, 325
arrows, 82-83, 101-103
Attributes menu, 32, 492
auto leading for type, 479
Auto tiling option, 420
Automatic curvature option, 453

B

background color, 27
Background layer, 229, 253, 258, 279, 291, 380
banding, 289
bar charts, 108
based-on styles, 389
Baseline shift command (Type menu), 488
Basic fill options, 494
Basic line options, 499
basic shape tools, 24, 317, 333-336
Bezier curves, 4, 336-337
bitmapped fonts, 13
bitmapped versions of line art, 286
Bleed area, 405, 413
Blend command, 161, 243, 251, 291, 468
Blend dialog box, 455
blending colors, 468
blending for spot color separation, 188-193, 283
blending shapes, 468
blending to create new colors or grays, 190
blends, 7
   optimal, 182-187
   recalculating, 455
boilerplate document, 228
bring forward, 260
Bring forward command, 449
Bring to front command, 449
"bump" rule, 346
business development map, 306

C

calligraphic lines, 90-95
carriage return, 48, 329
cartography, 297-306
case studies, 275-306
changing defaults, 417
character width, 331
charting programs, 106
charts, 106-117
circles, 334
Clear command, 433
clipping paths, 194, 276
   creating, 434
   moving contents of, 439
   removing contents from, 433
Clone command, 76, 438
close an open path, 351
Close box, 23, 312
Close command, 409
closed paths, 6, 99-139, 337
closing a path, 344
closing an open path, 99
coils, 142
color, 8
Color editing, 374
Color editing pop-up menu, 44
color library, 176-181, 377
color reference sheet, 173
color separations, 267
   printing, 421, 424
color templates, 172, 373
color TIFF images, 365
Colors command, 506
Colors dialog box, 376
Colors palette, 11, 23, 26, 167, 312, 371, 373-379
   rearranging colors, 379
   showing or hiding, 441
colors
   changing default, 376
   copying, 174
   defining, 506
   display, 193, 374
   editing, 506
   PANTONE, 507

columns and rows of text, 218
comic strip, 286
commercial art, 275-296
composite path, 6, 70-71
composite paths, 7, 118, 194, 276
   as masks, 120
   creating, 473
compound arrows, 82-83
compound dashed lines, 78-81
compound lines, 75-82
connect the dots, 339
connector points, 337-338, 349
Connector tool, 24, 317, 336, 355
Constrain command, 233, 470
constrain movement, 325
Control Panel, 402
Convert to paths command, 230, 278, 330, 489
converting a curve point to a connector point, 343
converting a point, 343
Copy command, 431
copying a color, 377
copying a style in the palette, 390
copying and pasting into other applications, 431
copying styles from one illustration to another, 390
corner point, 62, 64
corner point handles, 348
corner points, 337-338, 349
corner radius, 335, 454
Corner tool, 24, 317, 336, 354
creating a new color, 377
creating styles, 388
Crop marks, printing, 423
cubes, 144-150, 245
Cursor key distance option, 417
curve, 4
curve depth, 342
curve direction, 341
curve handles—see direction handles,
curve levers, 342
curve points, 57, 62, 337-338, 349

Curve tool, 24, 317, 336, 353-354
curves, 57-97
curving parallel lines, 88
Custom fill options, 170, 499
custom grids, 242-247
Custom line options, 80–81, 503
Cut command, 431
Cut contents, 433
cylinders, 154

D

Dash pop-up menu, 74
dashed lines, 72-81, 501
　as grid elements, 85
　as text background, 84
Dawson, Henk, 289-293
default color, 376
default Layers palette, 380
delete a point, 349
depth of curve, 342
deselecting, 45, 324
dialog boxes, 394
direction handles, 4, 57, 67, 337, 341–343
direction of curve, 341
disk space, 12
Display curve levers, 342, 415
displayed colors, 374
dividing equally, 250
Document setup command, 411
Document setup dialog box, 20, 238, 327, 412
document window, 22, 27
DOS, 15
dotted lines, 72-81
　as design elements, 85
drop shadow, 156-158
Duplicate command, 38, 436

E

edit box, 21

Edit menu, 29, 428
edit text, 50
editing a path, 347
editing an existing color, 377
editing portions of text, 331
editing styles, 391
Effect submenu (Type menu), 481
Element info command, 327, 350, 451
　via Pointer tool, 327
Element menu, 30, 240, 448
elements, aligning, 465
elements, locking and unlocking, 463
Ellipse dialog box, 327, 334
Ellipse tool, 24, 317, 333-336
ellipses, using dotted lines, 84-85
endpoints, 337, 342
EPS (Encapsulated PostScript), 14
equal segments, 250
equipment requirements, 12
Equitz, Susan, 276
Eureka Cartography, 304
Even/odd fill option, 451
Export command, 426
export FreeHand documents, 15
exporting artwork, 426

F

File menu, 29, 404
Fill and line command, 168, 493
Fill and stroke command, 227, 330, 482
fill color, 375
Fill indicator, 43–44, 374
fill patterns, 6, 165-210, 494–497
　applying, 167-169
　basic, 494
　custom, 499
　graduated, 495
　overprinting, 495
　patterned, 496
　PostScript, 497

tiled, 200-210, 497
film recorders, 13
film, printing, 424
Fit on paper option, 423
flatness, 335
Flatness option, 452
flower petals, 134, 159
Font submenu, 477
fonts, 13
   choosing, 477
foreground layer, 380
formatting text, 330
four-color process, 8
freeform drawing tools, 24, 59, 317, 336-355
FreeHand capabilities, 4
Freehand dialog box, 339
Freehand tool, 24, 317, 336, 338-340

G
grabber hand, 318
Graduated fill option, 182, 495
graduated fills, 6, 182, 289
grayscale images, 279, 365
grayscale images, modifying, 459
Greek type below option, 415
grid, 9, 61, 233, 238, 279, 445
   custom, 242-247
   dimensions, 238
   invisible in reduced views, 239
Grid command, 238, 445
Group command, 463
Group dialog box, 327
Group transforms as unit (option), 455
grouped objects, 321
   stacking order in, 464
   subselecting, 463
Grubb and Ellis Company, 306
guides, 9, 233, 235
Guides command, 446
   creating, 445
   locking, 446

guides layer, 380

H
Halftone screen command, 503
handles, 36, 57, 67–68, 321, 341
   from a corner point, 67, 348
handles—see also direction handles,
hard disk, 12
height, 315–316
Help button, 28
Help command, 28, 400
"hidden" notes, 228
highlighting, 161, 197, 289
highways on a map, 88
holes in solid objects, 118
horizontal location, 315
Horizontal scaling command (Type menu), 488

I
I-beam pointer, 47
IBM PC, 15
Illustration page, 23, 312
Image dialog box, 328, 459
imagesetters, 13
importing artwork, 425
importing charts, 106
importing scanned images, 14
importing text, 225
including TIFF images in exported artwork, 427
Info bar, showing or hiding, 441
information bar, 9, 23, 24, 233, 311-316, 325
inline type, 277
Inline type effect, 483
installing FreeHand, 17
Interactive Design, Seattle, 286
interlocking objects, 151

J

jigsaw puzzle pieces, 138
Join elements command, 71, 99, 118, 471
joining open paths, 352, 473
joining text to a path, 220-224, 474

K

K2 Skis, 283
kerning, 316, 333
keyboard shortcuts, 333, 336, 372
keyline mode, 45, 443
Knife tool, 24, 317, 336, 351–353

L

Laney, John, 286
Layer dialog box, 383
layering spot color separations, 267
layers, 255-272
Layers palette, 11, 229, 253, 255, 265, 269, 312, 324, 371, 379-384
  benefits, 257
  default, 380
  showing or hiding, 441
layers
  adding and editing, 383
  moving, 382
  printing, 423
  removing, 384
  simplifying, 257
  visible or invisible, 382
leading, 316, 331
Leading command, 479
length of the curve levers, 343
letter spacing, 316, 327, 331
library, 378
limitcheck errors, 452
line art from a halftone photograph, 366
line breaks, 328, 331

line cap options, 500
Line indicator, 44, 374
line join options, 500
line miter limit options, 500
Line pattern dialog box, 74
line spacing, 327, 331
Line tool, 24, 59, 317, 333-336
line weights, 6
Line/fill pop-up menu, 44, 374
lines, 57-97
  arrowhead options, 501
  basic, 499
  custom, 503
  dashed, 501
  hand-drawn look, 90-95
  of dots, 73
  of squares, 73
  overlapping, 75-82
  patterned, 502
  PostScript, 502
Lock command, 462
Lock guides command, 446

M

MacPaint, 14
MacTech Journal, 286
magic stretch feature, 326–327
magnification, 367
Magnification submenu, 442
magnifying glass, 367
Magnifying tool, 24, 52, 317, 367-369
  temporarily activate, 318
Manual tiling option, 420
map work, 138
maps, 297-306
masking, 120–121, 194, 434
  to change fills, 196
  to create highlights, 197
masking—see also clipping path, composite path
Master Juggler, 14
Mate Punch and Die Company, 294

measurements, entering, 397, 407, 414
measuring, 251
  with a point, 241
memory, 12–13
Menu bar, 23, 312
menus, 28-33
METRO, 302
Metropolitan Transportation Commission, 299
Microsoft Excel, 106
moiré patterns, 326
monitor, color, 374
Monitors, Control Panel, 403
Move command, 241, 263, 438
Move dialog box, 241
moving elements by a specified distance, 439
moving elements from one layer to another, 382
moving layers, 382
moving objects with Pointer tool, 324
moving the page view, 318
MTC, 299
Multilayer, 324, 381
Municipality of Seattle, 302
Murata Wiedemann NC, 294

N
New command, 20, 404
non-breaking space, 222, 328
non-printing elements, 258
Number of undo's option, 416

O
Oakland, 306
off-center radial fills, 198
one-point perspective, 242
open path, 6
open a closed path, 351

Open command, 15, 407
open path, 57, 337, 345
opening a new file, 19
organization charts, 114
Orientation, 405, 412
overhead transparency, 271
overlapping lines, 75-82
Overprint ink option, 424
Overprint option (fills), 495
Overprint option (lines), 501
overprinting lines, 501
overprinting text in color separations, 227

P
packaging design, 148
page layout, 246
page layout applications, 15
Page Setup command, 418
Page size, 405, 412
page spread, 294
PageMaker, 15
palettes, 9, 371-391
  displaying, 26
palettes—see also Colors palette, Layers palette, Styles palette,
Paper size option, 422
parallel lines, 88
Paste command, 432
Paste inside command, 434
Pasteboard, 23, 312
pasting artwork into other applications, 431
Path dialog box, 327, 351
Path/point dialog box, 350
paths, 4, 57-97, 337
  closed, 99-139
  splitting, 352, 475
pattern fills, 7
Patterned fill options, 496
Patterned line options, 502
patterns, 165-210

Pen tool, 24, 60-71, 317, 336, 340-352
Performance/display options, 415
perspective, 148, 242
photographs, 306
PICT, 14
pie charts, 110
Place command, 15, 104, 106, 425
Point submenu, 461
point type, changing, 343, 349
Pointer tool, 24, 37, 317, 319-328, 347
   temporarily activate, 40, 318, 320
Points command, 350
points (anchor)
   changing from one type to another, 461
   number of, 339, 365
   removing, 462
   three types, 337-338
polygons, 122
pop-up menus, 395
PostScript, 3, 8, 337
PostScript fills, 497
PostScript fonts, 13
PostScript line options, 502
PostScript—see also EPS,
"power-duplicating" elements, 437
Preferences command, 235, 414
Preferences dialog box, 342, 414
Preview command, 443
Preview mode, 45, 443
Print command, 53, 419
Print dialog box, 53
Print this ink option, 424
printer, 13
printer resolution, 327
printer type, choosing, 422
Printing a composite proof, 421
Printing tile options, 420
printing time, 258
process color, 8
puzzle pieces, 138

Q
quadrille rules, 96
Quark Express, 15
Quit command, 53, 428

R
radial fills, 198
   off-center, 198, 292
radial symmetry, 134-137
radio button, 21
railway lines, 75
RAM—see memory,
rearranging overlapping objects, 260
Rectangle dialog box, 327, 334
Rectangle tool, 24, 34-36, 317, 333-336
rectangles, using dashed lines, 84-85
Redo command, 430
Reducing tool, 367
Reflect dialog box, 102, 359
Reflecting tool, 24, 102, 132, 224, 317, 355, 358-360
   reflecting by a specified amount, 359
   reflecting visually on the screen, 358
registration marks, 285
   printing, 423
Remove fill command, 505
Remove line command, 506
removing colors from the palette, 379
resolution, 8
resolutions, grays and tints, 374
retract a handle, 350
Revert command, 411
ribbon effect, 86
road map, 304
roads, 75
Rotate dialog box, 39, 97, 357
Rotating tool, 24, 39, 97, 134, 136, 317, 355, 356-357

rotating by a specified amount, 357
rotating visually on the screen, 356
Rounded-rectangle tool, 24, 317, 333-336
roundness, 335
rulers, 9, 233, 235
Rulers command, 25, 444
rulers moving the zero point, 444
rulers, displaying, 444

S

San Francisco Bay Area, 298, 304
San Francisco Business Times, 306
Save as command, 409
Save command, 46, 52, 409
Save document as dialog box, 46
Scale dialog box, 361
scale type proportionally, 331
scaling, 315
   by a specified percentage, 361
   text, 327
   visually on the screen, 360
   with Pointer tool, 325
Scaling tool, 24, 317, 355, 360-361
scanned images, 14
scanned line art, 279
scanned photo, 291
scanner, 13
screen angle, 504
screen angles, global, 425
screen redraw time, 258
screen ruling, 422, 504
screen type, 503
Scroll bar, 23, 312, 312
Seattle street map, 302
segments, 337
Select all command, 436
select and edit lines, 76
Select library color(s) dialog box, 378
selected text, 321, 330

selecting
   active layer, 381
   anchor points, 322
   multiple objects, 322
   objects below other objects, 320
   objects on different layers, 324
   one object, 320
   one object that is part of a group, 321
   text, 330, 332
   tools, 317
selection marquee, 322
selection methods, 323
Send backward command, 260, 450
Send to back command, 260, 450
Set note command, 505
shading effects, 198
shadow, 156-158
shapes, 99-139
shared borders, 138
Size box, 23, 312
size of the text, 331
Size submenu (Type menu), 478
Skew dialog box, 363
skewing, 315
   by a specified amount, 363
   visually on the screen, 362
Skewing tool, 24, 317, 355, 362-364
Snap to grid, 238
Snap to grid command, 448
Snap to guides, 9, 235
Snap to guides command, 447
Snap to point command, 447
Snap-to distance option, 417
Snap-to grid spacing, 406, 413
solid leading for type, 479
space between lines, 331
space between the letters, 333
space, non-breaking, 222, 328
spacing, 233-253
   between characters in a text block, 316
   between lines, 316
   between words, 316

Spacing command (Type menu), 487
spacing guides, 252
Split element command, 475
splitting a path, 352
splitting text from a path, 475
spot color, 8
spot color separations, 283
spot colors, 267
   blending, 188-193, 283
Spread size option, 422
springs, 142
squared rules, 96
squares, 334
stacking sequence, 380
stars, 124-131
starting FreeHand, 18–19
stipple effect, 94
straight line segments, 57
style reference sheet, 171
style system, 385
Styles command, 510
Styles dialog box, 389
Styles palette, 11, 169, 171, 300, 304, 312, 371, 384-391
   advantages, 385
   defining styles, 510
   removing styles, 391
   showing or hiding, 442
submenus, 23
   choosing commands from, 394
Suitcase II, 14
symbol fonts, 83
symbols, 224
symbols in the information bar, 315
symmetrical objects, 101-103, 132, 357
symmetry, radial, 134-137

T

tabular text, 218
tangent, 341
target printer, 327

Target printer resolution, 406, 413
TechArt, San Francisco, 278
technical illustrations, 294
template document, 247
template system, 246
template, color, 373
text, 7, 211-231, 227
   alignment, 215-219
   along a curved path, 220-224, 456, 458, 474
      alignment, 456
      orientation, 456
      show path option, 458
   converted to a composite path, 230
   editing, 212-214
   entry, 212-213
   formatting, 212-214
   from another application, 225
   handles, 331
   in columns, 218
   joined to an ellipse, 278
      alignment, 458
      orientation, 458
      show path option, 458
   selecting, 49, 213, 330, 332
   size, 331
   text block size, 331
   text boxes, 20
   wrap, 328
Text dialog box, 47, 212, 327, 328
text shapes as clipping paths, 231
Text tool, 24, 47, 212, 317, 328-333
three-dimensional effects, 141-163
three-dimensional objects, 244
three-dimensional perspectives, 148
three-dimensional representations of buildings, 306
TIFF image, 8, 276, 302, 365
Tilde key, 345
tiled designs, 7
Tiled fill option, 497
tiled fill patterns, 200-210, 276
Tiling illustrations, 420
tints, defining, 509

Title bar, 23, 312
Toolbox, 23, 24, 311-313, 317-369
   showing or hiding, 441
Trace dialog box, 365
tracing imported graphics, 104
Tracing tool, 24, 70–71, 104, 279, 317, 364-367
Transfer function option, 423
Transform again command, 439
transformation tools, 24, 317, 355-364
transparencies, 271
TrueType, 13
tutorial, 18
two-point perspective, 242
Type effects, 481
type leading, 479
Type menu, 32, 476
type size, 478
Type specifications dialog box, 49
type specifications, layers, 269
Type specs command, 49, 486
Type style command, 480
type
   alignment, 490
   converting to paths, 489
   horizontal scaling, 488
   spacing, 487
   subscript, 488
   superscript, 488
type—see also text
typographic controls, 7

U
U.S. News and World Report, 279
Undo command, 429
   operations that cannot be undone, 430
   setting number of undo's, 416
Ungroup command, 464
unit of measure, 25, 406, 413
Unlimited Downloadable Fonts in a Document option, 418

Unlock command, 463

V
vanishing points, 245
version, 19, 28
version 3.0, features of FreeHand, 11
versions of artwork, 259
video card, 13
View menu, 30, 440
visible grid, 96, 238
   hiding and showing, 446
   spacing, 406, 413
visible layer, 324
VM_error message, 419

W
watercolor effect, 93
width, 315–316
   character, 331
Windows, 15
Windows command, 312, 317, 372
Windows submenu, 440
wine label, 276
wireframe view—see keyline,
word space, 316
word spacing, 331

Z
Zapf Dingbats, 83, 224
zero point, 25
Zoom box, 23, 312
Zoom text effect, 485